"For anyone who has ever dreamed of getting off the mortgage rat race and creating not just a house, but a cozy nest that fits—this is the book! Every page is an inspiration, filled with real-life stories and the author's philosophy and lessons on creating better, more affordable, sustainable, and very personalized housing."

—Janet Luhrs, author of *The Simple Living Guide*, *Simple Loving*, and publisher of *Simple Living*

"*Little House on a Small Planet* is revolutionary—in a gentle, soulful way. . . . Read it and learn how to get back to what life is really all about."

—Carol Venolia, architect, columnist, *Natural Home Magazine*, and author of *Natural Remodeling for the Not-So-Green House*

"*Little House on a Small Planet* is the emergency user's guide needed by humanity at this moment of global environmental crisis."

—Gregory Paul Johnson, President of the Small House Society

Simple Homes, Cozy Retreats, and Energy Efficient Possibilities

LITTLE HOUSE ON A SMALL PLANET

By Shay Salomon

Photographs by Nigel Valdez

The Lyons Press
Guilford, Connecticut
An imprint of The Globe Pequot Press

The Lyons Press is an imprint of The Globe Pequot Press

10 9 8 7 6 5 4 3

Printed in the United States of America

Designed by LeAnna Weller Smith

Floor plans by Chris Armstrong on pages 15, 30, 53, 79, 86, 87, 90, 101, 109, 111, 129, 180, 181, 183, 187, 210, 217, 236, 248

Unless otherwise specified, all photographs by Nigel Valdez. Additional photography: Sarah Patterson, pages 12 and 13; Avi Friedman, page 47; Shay Salomon, pages 48 (both), 50, 52 (bottom), 68, 70, 71, 81, 83, 105, 139, 160, 176, 178, and 237; Donald MacDonald, page 72; Ross Chapin, page 190; Helen Walters, page 197; Suzanne Lichau, page 203 (right, top); Nathan Welton, page 223.

ISBN 10: 1-59228-868-5
ISBN 13: 978-1-59228-868-7

Library of Congress Cataloging-in-Publication Data is available on file.

DEDICATION

For Jean and Bob, Chris and Lil
And to the beloved memory of
Polly Strand (1932–2003)
Jane Jacobs (1916–2006)

Someone who goes with half a loaf of bread
to a small place that fits like a nest around him
someone who wants no more,
who's not himself longed for by anyone else.
He is a letter to everyone. You open it.
It says, "Live!"

—RUMI

contents

Acknowledgments

The author and photographer of this book have never had an original thought. All the ideas in this book were taken from others, pasted together from our shared thought space and from the stories and advice of the people we visited and corresponded with. Their names are in the book. Many of them also read and reviewed parts of the book. This book is the manifestation of their generosity.

There were also many people who are not named in the book who helped us. Due to a limited space and memory lapses we aren't able to remember them all here. A short list includes: Patricia Rosas, Germaine Shames, Edward Matthews, Jim Schley, Esther Bloomingfeld, Nina Schmidt, Paul Moore, Missi Rust, Alan Weisman, Buddy Williams, the Wallace Family, Sandra Lubarsky, Diba Siddiqi, Catherine Wanek, Dan Chiras, Bill and Athena Steen, Mark Piepkorn, Gayle Borst, Guy Moussalli, Kate Randall, Kay Sather, Michael G. Smith, Stacey Tarquinio, David Corker, Karen Smith, Thomas H. Greco, Margie Glover, Bob Banner, Jeanne Leimkuhler, Ann Edminster, Robin Edwards, Gregory Johnson, Claire Scheuren, Josefina Cardenas, Kim Young, Jack Challem, Robert Andrews, Christopher Daniels, Peter Harnik, John DeGraaf, Antonio Cafiero, Marc Seidman, Elaine Romero, Dorothy and Al Andersen, Grace Lee Boggs, Susan Modisett, David Eisenberg, Lindsay Vurek, Sarah Britton, Janette Rhee, Roberta Brandes Gratz, Jess Wilson, Benjamin Jervey, Nalini Visvanathan, Shanna Leonard, Jean Saliman, Robert C. Leonard, Jean-Louis Bourgeois, Eleanor Nemirow, Marty and Connie Remaly, David Keith, Julie Leonard, Teresa and Carolena Quiroga, and Aaron Leonard.

We received research assistance from a number of public libraries, the US Environmental Protection Agency, The US Census Bureau, the National Association of Homebuilders, and the Canadian Mortgage Corporation. We appreciate the support provided by the Mesa Refuge, Lama Foundation, Arcosanti, the Small House Society, *The Last Straw Journal, Environmental Building News* and the Simplicity Forum. This book would not have been possible without a grant provided by the Graham Foundation for Advanced Studies in the Fine Arts, nor without the help and forbearance of editors Ann Treistman, Carol Venolia, Jane Crosen and Holly Rubino.

A chunk of tree was cut to make the book you are holding. We've tried our best to make the ideas worth the paper they are printed on.

Foreword

Growing up in the 1950s was no picnic. Actually, I hated it—the racism, the sexism, the anti-intellectualism.... Yet one particular, warm memory lingers.

I'm at home, in Fort Worth, Texas. I'm lying in my bedroom, down a short hallway from the kitchen. The door is ajar, and intense conversation and laughter flow in, along with the smell of fresh coffee percolating. Around our yellow Formica table, my parents and their friends are hashing out what matters most to them—how to racially integrate the church they as laypeople were helping to found, whether to sponsor a Hungarian refugee family after the Soviet crackdown, and what stands they should take on nuclear armament. I can't follow most of their chatter. All I know is that they are doing what grown-ups do: They are talking about the "big, important things," and that's what I want to do when I grow up.

Now, over fifty years later, as I read Shay Salomon's moving book, I realize that my powerful childhood experience was possible because of something I'd never before credited: the scale of our modest, wood home. If my family had lived in one of the new "ranch houses" just beginning to be built on the outskirts of town, I would not have heard the "hum from the kitchen," a memory that has shaped me over a lifetime.

Today Americans assume living in a bigger personal space to be evidence of progress, but I know in my bones that growing up sharing with my family our one bathroom, one TV, and one car nurtured a sense of belonging that is my strength today.

Shay's empowering book helps me to make another connection as well.

To explain, I'll back up again, though not quite so far: In my mid-twenties I was shaken to discover that I was part of a global food system that transforms abundance into scarcity. Poor people overseas were starving and malnourished, yet the world was producing plenty of grain for everyone to be fed. What, I wondered, was going on?

As our harvests rose, poor people abroad had no money to buy it, so North American farmers were feeding the grain to animals, in feedlots. Animals, especially cattle, are inefficient. It takes a lot of grain—literally—to grow a steer. In fact, if we were to eat directly the 16 pounds of grain that it takes to produce a pound of meat, we would have eight times as much protein available to us.

And feedlots come with other problems: disease, overuse of antibiotics, groundwater contamination, cruelty to animals.... In a world where millions suffer from hunger, such practices make no sense at all.

So, imagine my sense of excitement when as a young woman I realized I could choose something else. I didn't have to remain a victim of a scarcity-making system. I didn't have to expose myself and farm workers to pesticides. I could choose a diet that was best for the Earth and at the same time best for my body. What could be better?

What could be more satisfying than realizing that my daily food choices—my most intimate tie to the nurturing Earth—could, instead of reinforcing waste and pollution, be sending out ripples of sanity and health?

What if my choices about my personal dwelling space could likewise send out ripples of sanity and health? Isn't this just what Shay is telling me? Just as hunger isn't caused by scarcity of food, homelessness and our "housing crisis" aren't caused by a lack of houses.

The Union of Concerned Scientists ranks housing third among destructive human enterprises, just after transportation and agriculture. But our housing need not be a destructive. Again, we can choose! We can choose human scale, enhancing our connection with those we love. We can choose eco-scale, reducing our demand for the kind of energy that is disrupting life now and for future generations. And we can choose econo-scale, freeing up our time, directing it away from our mortgage and toward our dreams.

I've come to believe that to pull back from planetary eco-cide, and from the accompanying misery of isolation and meaninglessness, requires of us precisely the rethinking to which this book calls us. To revitalize ourselves, our communities, our homes, and our planet is not a question of sacrifice. It's a question of listening within ourselves to discover what *really* makes us happy. It's about finding our power.

FRANCES MOORE LAPPÉ
MAY 2006

Introduction

How much space does it take to be happy? Most of us have noticed the dramatic increase in new-house size, and some of us have asked that question. Working in construction, I watched people's dream houses balloon into unmanageable giants. I saw the effect on homeowners, the psychological, social, and financial toll, and I looked for new options that could lead them to a simpler, happier home.

Construction has some alarming effects on the environment. Forty percent of all the raw materials humans consume, we use in construction. Most of the trees we cut down become buildings. Half of the copper we mine becomes wire and pipe inside these buildings. Building an average house adds seven tons of waste to the landfill.[1] It's estimated that humans, using machines, now move more materials than rivers do.[2] New-house construction is arguably the single greatest threat to endangered species: even in areas where human population is on the decline, animals and plants are more threatened each day, due to the construction of new houses.[3] Might our homes feel more comfortable if they weren't also destructive?

Working as a natural builder, I tried to ease the destruction of construction by using nontoxic, natural materials, and by designing homes in alignment with the sun's path, the prevailing winds, and other natural factors. Throughout North America building has been influenced by "green" thinking, and houses have improved, but despite major advances in insulation and design, the typical house built today requires almost as much energy to heat and cool as one built in 1960.[4] Why? Because it's bigger. House size and location are the greatest determinants of a home's effect on the environment. The challenge to builders is to construct a single-family house as efficient as a New York City apartment, which, on the average, uses a fraction of the energy of a typical detached house.

"Most of us have noticed the trend: new subdivisions filled with McMansions pumped up on steroids, neighbors who demolished their cottage and replaced it with a mini-castle, the friend of a friend's childless brother who just added on a third bedroom. Maybe you've heard the story of a couple who "lost" their toddler in their new, huge house. Many of us know someone who has suffered the consequences of an inflated mortgage, an overwhelming construction project, or a house simply too large to keep clean. Will our dream home always be a celebration of excess, and a drain on our lives? Is it, as one of our former presidents said of the American way of life, 'not up for negotiation'?"

All over North America, people are taking up this challenge, and they are bucking the trend. They see that excessive housing has not led to excessive happiness. They build, remodel, redecorate, or just rethink their needs, prudently and calmly, constructing a joyful, sane life around themselves. The following pages report on the designs and patterns they've come up with, and the values they share. The fourteen principles of the book are a condensation of a few hundred people's experiences, and offer the foundations of a simpler and happier home.

This is not the first time in history that people have seriously rethought their built environment. Archaeology shows us a variety of sudden and drastic changes in ancient people's lifestyles. Near the end of their empire, the Romans attempted to preserve their last forests through what we'd now call "conservation easements" and solar building codes. Their situation had some parallels to ours: it was common for wealthy Romans to own huge villas, heated by *hypocausts*, furnaces that burned as much as two cords of wood in a day. By 100 A.D., wood had to be imported from the Caucasus, more than 1,000 miles away.[5]

Our situation is a result of decisions that our nation has made. Modern North Americans decided early on to occupy land in a way that encouraged further subdivision, and instead of preserving and separating vast commons from private, concentrated settlements, as some societies have chosen, we created a pattern we now call "sprawl." We debated, and then in most cases chose the single-family estate over the more compact, ideal city model. We created tax and lending institutions to promote our choice. Our collective national "dream" has materialized in the form of perfectly spaced, heavily gabled, tiny mansions that spring up overnight, covering up the sloppy diversity of farms and wildlands.

How did the "American Dream" become a dream about a big house? Some say that "bigger is better" is simply in our nature. Indeed, men lie about their height, and women pump up their breasts and we drive big cars down big streets. But there has also been a parallel trend, of Quakers and Shakers, and modest, happy Lutherans in semi-fictional towns. North Americans have a long history of frugality.

Some say we like big because we are a nation of immigrants, and any immigrant feels homeless, and tries to compensate for that feeling by overbuilding. Indeed, when my grandmother looked at new subdivisions, she didn't see what her grandchildren saw—the destruction of the view and wildlife habitat—but instead she saw a miracle, that thousands of families could live in freedom and luxury, next to each other, as equals, so different from the muddy, freezing village her parents described in their tales of the old country. New subdivisions embodied for her the promise of America. Why wouldn't we want this for everyone? Our suburban homes seem to express the Jeffersonian idea of a nation of small, equal landowners.

This notion that connects single-family homes with equality and democracy is related to the original definition of *husband*, which once meant *house bound*—that is, a man who lived and worked in his own home, neither serf nor servant to a lord, but also not a lord over another. In other words, middle class. His female counterpart was the housewife.[6] If building single-family homes could create a solid middle class, who wouldn't want them? It would even make sense for a democratic nation to support their construction through tax laws.

I understand the desire to build houses. During a brief stint as a social worker, I became certain that if the women I counseled just had their own homes, they'd be able to work out their other problems easily. It's a simple, straightforward solution, and I wanted to be part of it. So I returned to the kind of construction labor work I'd done before college.

Fairly quickly I was attracted to solar architecture, or sustainable design, and I learned about adobe, and then straw-bale construction. There's a deep pleasure in watching an edifice rise from the ground. Construction allows interaction with the rough material world—something I'd missed in the office. Many people crave this interaction so much that they dedicate weekends to it, either working on our own homes, or volunteering. I understand the attraction of building.

But there were two problems that began to nag me. One was that most of the jobs available involved building second homes, or large houses for couples, often at the end of a long road, freshly bulldozed in the wilderness I thought I wanted to protect. Have you seen a forest right after it's been plowed? The birdsong is eerie.

The January 1999 issue of *Environmental Building News* caught my eye. One graph[7] showed the incredible rise in house-to-person ratio. Another table[8] showed that house size affects energy consumption more than insulation does. Now, as builder Jug Tarr, told me, "it doesn't take a PhD in physics to see that energy cost is a direct correlation of cubic feet," but somehow this graph, and Alex Wilson's simple statement, "It is easier to reduce the embodied energy of a house by making the house smaller than by searching for low-embodied energy materials," allowed me to begin to move in another direction.

I looked for other research. I saw data about the shrinking size of households, and how it contributes to higher energy demand. The most compelling argument I read was in *Nature* in 2003. Jianguo Liu, a biologist from the University of Michigan, and three fellow scientists studied seventy-six "hotspots" around the world—places where species are rapidly becoming extinct—and linked their doom to the adoption of the suburban pattern. He writes, "Even when population size declined, the number of households increased substantially." Our modern, separated lifestyle added 155 million households in hotspot countries between 1985 and 2000. In China, for instance, although population is declining, the beloved panda has less and less space, because Chinese houses are growing larger.

I also visited older houses. In Bokrijk, Belgium, I saw houses with 6-foot ceilings, and imagined that, packed with people and a few farm animals, they must not have used much heating fuel. I learned that historically in Japan rooms were measured in tatami mats, which are about 3 feet by 6 feet, so a four-and-a-half-tatami room measured about 9 feet by 9 feet, or 81 square feet. Four tatami also meant the room had space to host four visitors overnight, since each tatami can host one sleeper.

I read more local history. The stories are complex, and some of the theories are contradictory, but most historians cite a few things that have contributed to the jump in house size. One is simply that our raw resources permitted the change: North American land was vast, and there was a national desire to claim it through physical occupation. Technological innovations sped things up, notably the chainsaw and bulldozer, to clear the land, and later such inventions as balloon framing (a technique which allows builders to construct upper stories without heavy, long pieces of wood), premixed concrete, gypsum board, and the screw.

The trolley car and automobile also receive much credit for allowing us to spread out and then commute to work, which allowed the separation of spheres—home life from work life—in the nineteenth and early twentieth centuries. This separation came with theoretical backing. In 1841 Catharine Beecher published *Treatise on Domestic Economy, For the Use of Young Ladies at Home and at School*, a popular textbook that linked the home with piety and purity, and promoted the separation of female (suburban, home) from male (business, urban) life, and the separation of mothers from grandmothers. Reprinted dozens of times over thirty years, it was one of the most popular textbooks of that time. Hers wasn't the only voice: in 1880 Charlotte Perkins Gilman denounced suburban private dwelling as "lace-curtain prisons" for women,"[9] and other North Americans were busy promoting "ideal cities" where tasks were highly specialized—hotels offered year-round inhabitants of all ages three meals a day and laundry service—so that each person could develop his or her own potential, freed from domestic labor. But the Catharine Beecher model won out.

The Levitt brothers are credited with the invention of the tract home. On Long Island in 1947, the brothers turned 4,000 acres of potato farms 25 miles east of Manhattan into 17,400 750-square-foot (plus unfinished attic) detached single-family residences on 6,000-square-foot lots. Houses were sold complete with a washing machine, an option on a television, and a covenant that maintained racial segregation. This pattern inspired millions of houses. But potentially more important was William Levitt's work, with other developers and bankers, during World War II, to create the Veteran Administration mortgage program and later the Federal Housing Agency, which has steadily promoted the single-family home by backing bank mortgage financing.

The theory behind the FHA is that houses are good, and that everyone benefits when this economic engine is stimulated. After World War I, surviving soldiers returned home to a depressed economy, a housing shortage, and populist social movements that worried some parts of the U.S. government. Developers proposed the FHA as a solution to many problems: In 1948 William J. Levitt was quoted as saying, "No man who owns his own house and lot can be a communist. He has too much to do."[10] The Canadian Mortgage Housing Corporation was founded later, and made a cornerstone of its mission the creation of affordable housing. It has acted more conservatively, insisting on higher down payments and lower interest rates (see Chapter 4). Still, the Canadian and U.S. patterns are very similar.

Of all the research, the most compelling information I saw was about vacancy rates. In 2005, after hurricane Katrina, I read a newspaper story about a family that offered their huge second home to a refugee family. Another story said that refugees in Houston were greeted with a 14 percent vacancy rate in that city[11] (Chapter 6). I turned to the trusty U.S. Census, which reported in 2000 that 10.4 million units of housing were vacant. In comparison, about 250,000 people slept in homeless shelters. So there are about forty-five vacant homes per shelter occupant! If we assume each unit is 1,100 square feet, or half the size of the average new house built in 2000, it sounds like there's over 45 square feet of vacant house per every single U.S. resident. It's not that much, but it's over twice the size of a tatami mat. If we created a huge national time-share, we could travel anywhere in the U.S., any of us, and still have a place to lay our heads at night. How is it that we have a housing crisis? Maybe a homing crisis, or a sharing crisis, but this isn't a *housing* crisis.

What does the future hold? As this goes to press, it seems possible that some changes are in store. Fannie Mae, the U.S. federal mortgage broker, is about to be fined for falsifying its accounting so that executives could claim bonuses. Warren Buffett has divested from the real estate market; executives at the Toll Brothers, one of the largest builders of luxury homes, have sold off their shares, indicating they aren't so sure their stocks will be rising soon.[12] Houses for sale in my town are staying on the market much longer, and sellers are starting to drop their prices a bit. As noted in Chapter 10, some cities are placing caps on house size. Les Walker, author of the classic *Tiny Houses*, says there's more interest for his book now than when it was published twenty years ago. Almost everyone is talking about simplifying their life. And someone has taken to torching new luxury subdivisions.[13]

In 1975 the humorist Andy Rooney, who quipped that the addition was America's great contribution to the history of architecture, said he knew folks who had hired a contractor to subtract part of their house. He predicted a major trend toward house subtraction. It's hard to predict what happens. But what we do know is that we're safe from a lack of housing. We have plenty of it. If we went back to 1955 housing patterns (350 square feet per person), we wouldn't have to build another thing until our population doubled again.

Now, that doesn't mean a lack of work for builders. Our houses are undermaintained, and some weren't built well to start with. The FHA and CHMC could decide to fund retrofits on existing houses for solar and wind energy, and to create apartments from our too-large houses. Tenants-in-common could receive easy financing. There's plenty of work if we can figure out how to finance it.

The question really lies with banks. Banks hold an enormous amount of national debt, in the form of mortgages. If these houses drop in value, what will happen? Do banks really want to hold and maintain all those buildings? And how will we free up our money to use it for retrofits? As David Eisenberg says, "Having no money in the economy is like arriving at a construction site and finding the tools and materials are there: the workers are there, but we've run out of inches, so we don't build."

In the meantime, while we figure out an economic distribution system that works for everyone, there are things people in the small-house movement are doing to make their own lives, and their local communities, better. This book tells their story.

Eight years ago I began collecting floor plans and photographs of people who live in much less space, to show them to clients who came to me for carpentry work or building consultation, and also to include in building classes I taught. I had noticed something from the classes: People were very interested in the mechanics, the physical reality of building, how things fit together, and what's inside them. But they were equally interested in the bigger picture. They wanted to know how things were financed, how people got along during the build, how people felt about the process. They wanted to know personal details.

Home tours are a good example of this hunger for details. Homeowners who put their house on tour are sometimes shocked to find visitors peeking in their fridge. I doubt this happens because the visitors are hungry. We are just so curious about each other's lives. It's from these details, like the contents of the vegetable drawer, that we build a story we can learn from.

These stories include details. I collected them for a few years, and five years ago was joined by Nigel Valdez, who took photographs. As we traveled across the country interviewing and photographing people and houses for *Little House*, we began to understand the breadth and depth of the small-house movement. Over the past few years, we traveled to about a hundred locations in twenty-four states and four Canadian provinces. Pockets of people all over the North American continent are realizing the benefits of scaling down. They are designing a new dream, one that reunites extended families, makes space for friends, and emphasizes home life over home maintenance. They are taking advantage of new technologies—the laptop and flat screen, to name two—that miniaturize offices. As the price of construction materials and gasoline rises, they are making secure homes for themselves. They invite you to join them.

How to Use This Book

This book is divided into three parts. The first is especially for people who are considering building new. The second is about existing structures, remodeling, and how people have rearranged themselves socially to better use space that's already built. The last section is the big picture of the larger, inner and outer forces that shape our homes.

QUESTIONS YOU MIGHT ASK:

[Q] Are these people real?

[A] All of these stories come from interviews with real people, mostly in person, but also over the phone, or very rarely, by correspondence. Some people have chosen to identify themselves just with a first name, and a few have chosen pseudonyms.

[Q] Who is "we"?

[A] "We" generally refers to the photographer and author, since we traveled and worked on most of this together. Occasionally "we" means North Americans or the human species in general.

[Q] Where is North America?

[A] North America extends at least to Chiapas, Mexico, and on some maps to Panama. However, in this book North America means Canada and the United States. Generally speaking, these two countries have very similar settlement patterns, house designs, and energy use. As noted in Chapter 4, financially there are some significant differences—Canadians have more equity in their houses, and they pay a lower price for housing, compared to their salary. Also, Canadians are concentrated in three urban areas that have good public transportation. Still, the similarities are strong, and several of the stories in the book are Canadian. If you find the word "American," it probably means United Statesers, but since that isn't a word, I couldn't use it.

[Q] Did you follow your own advice?

[A] Some wise person said, "People write about what they need to learn about." Indeed, we learned. Both Nigel and I had lived in little spaces, sharing houses, and living overseas in small apartments and shacks, and camping for months at a time in the forest. I have also built a few tiny houses for others. Ironically, in the course of this book, I acquired an 1,100-square-foot house, on a semi-suburban street, which I inhabited alone for about five months. Initially, the empty space seemed freeing and the solitude enriching, but eventually, the costs outweighed the benefits. There were two rooms I really only entered to clean, so I've moved into about a third of the house, and share the rest with another person and a massage studio.

YOUR 900-LINE FOR HOUSE LUST

For many years I've been part of a network of women who refer construction work to each other. For a number of years, when we were organized and ambitious, we hosted classes and kept a phone line dedicated to the group. Almost daily we'd receive a call from someone who wanted to share her (or sometimes his) house dream with us. Sometimes it was about new construction, or sometimes a remodeling project. It was elaborated with great detail and imagination. It was pleasant to talk.

These calls took a lot of our time. And they suggested an ethical dilemma. We couldn't pay ourselves to chat on the phone. We would only profit if the fantasy panned out as paid work. But we knew that often our callers couldn't afford, financially or otherwise, the cost of construction. It was likely that in many cases, the best thing for the caller to do was something quite different than what they were calling about.

We often joked that we needed a pay-to-talk 900 line. That way, we'd have no incentive to encourage people to embark on misguided projects. And we wouldn't be rushed on the phone. We could listen deeply to people and maybe help them figure out if their needs could be better satisfied by a much smaller change in their home, or something completely different—a picnic in the park, a vacation, or, in some cases, couples counseling.

We hope you will consider this book your 900 line when you indulge in house lust. You may look through it and decide that building or remodeling is still what you need to do, and it can help you do that. But it can also help you realize that just a small change, or a subtle, less tangible one, may be plenty.

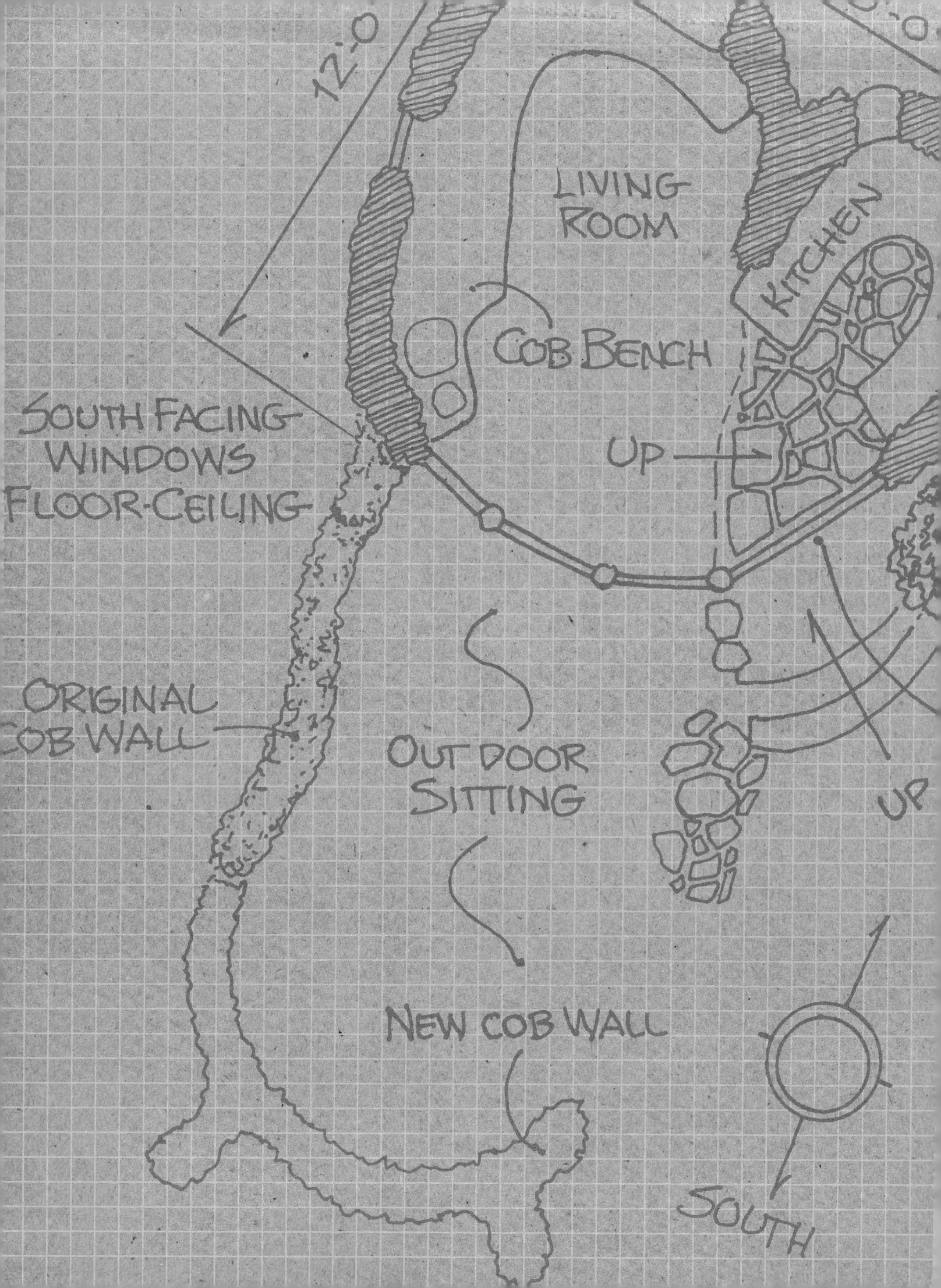
12'-0"
LIVING ROOM
KITCHEN
COB BENCH
SOUTH FACING WINDOWS FLOOR-CEILING
UP
ORIGINAL COB WALL
OUT DOOR SITTING
UP
NEW COB WALL
SOUTH

PART ONE

re•duce

determining need and designing new homes

SUBDIVISIONS THAT FEATURE FEW VARIATIONS ON FLOOR PLAN AND FAÇADE AREN'T JUST AN EXPRESSION OF A LACK OF IMAGINATION.

1
Quit Jonesing

Money don't make you happy and money don't make you not happy. —BOB MARLEY

WHY THE BIG HOUSES? Why so many additions? Why the round-the-clock home-improvement shows? If you've been alive in the last few decades, you've probably noticed the jump in house size, and house luxury. As we traveled around the country, we asked people why. The second most common reply was, "Because we can. The banks are funding it and new technology is allowing it," a topic further addressed in Chapter 4. The most common, and often most emphatic, reply was, "Everyone wants to 'keep up with the Joneses.'" Is it really that simple? If we want a swimming pool, a new kitchen, or a vacation home, is our desire just coming from wanting what others have? Are our neighbors really that important?

Maybe more to the point is this question: how do huge houses, houses much larger than yours, make you feel? What thoughts pop into your mind when you see a new subdivision of minimansions, or a cottage torn down and replaced with a modern castle? Do you feel envy and admiration? Surprise? Anger? Confusion and disgust?

If you don't feel anything, you're in a tiny minority: psychological and social research shows that essentially every normal person cares about others, both about what they do and think, and about their status relative to ours. Houses are graphic proof of our social status. When we watched people's faces as they answered our question, "Why the big houses?" we saw plenty of emotion: rolled eyes, pursed lips, clenched jaws, nodding heads....

If you're thinking about scaling down, you might want to consider your emotions and your motivations first. The exercise in this chapter (see "The Meaning of Home") is one way to get started.

How Did the Joneses Get Here?

THE HOME SOCIAL CLUB

For a small minority of North Americans—those who build cardboard huts, camp in the woods, or sleep in their cars—"home" is primarily a shelter from the elements. But for everyone else, houses are an expression of status, and neighborhoods are a social club. As we return home each day we pass by our neighbors' façades, finally

The plane takes off, and soon I'm watching my hometown spread out below me from a thousand feet above the runway. A few small dots between the riverbed and the few skyscrapers are the oldest houses, small farmer's houses, hand built at least three generations ago. Next, spreading out unevenly in every direction, are the bungalow rows of the 1940s and '50s, followed by the '60s and '70s ranch homes of my childhood. Is it just because I was a child that those small houses seemed bigger then? No, the tract-home spreads of the '80s and '90s really do dwarf them. The newest mansions on the foothills are such giants the plane seems to dip toward them, then sails to the outer limits where villages of big roofs with no space between them reverse the bungalow-to-yard proportions of the 1940s.

reaching our own place, our worldly face set in its row of contemporaries. Most of us live near neighbors who aren't too different socially from ourselves.

Neighborhood conformity provides a kind of security. People who want to sell their house at a profit know that neighborhood ranking is worth more than home improvement, and they know that signs of "lower class" activity on their street will drop their price. Home buyers accept codes, covenants, and restrictions to ensure that everyone will stay at a similar level—at least on the façade. We don't just want to keep up with the Joneses; we want the Joneses to keep up with everyone else.

New 500-home subdivisions that feature less than half a dozen variations on floor plan and façade aren't just an expression of a lack of imagination. Tract housing is a less-expensive way to build, but tract homes also sell because many residents enjoy the sameness, as a shelter from greater social competitions outside the neighborhood. One of the first residents of Levittown, the first major tract subdivision in North America said of her neighbors, "Our lives are held closely together because most of us are within the same age bracket, in similar income groups, live in almost identical houses, and have common problems."[1] Many small-house dwellers agree. Some have chosen to live together in communities where there's a cap on maximum house size, in an apartment building, or in historical neighborhoods where the lot size won't allow mansionization, so they know they won't be small relative to their close neighbors.

A HOUSE OF RELATIVITY

House size has crept upward in batches. Furniture and appliances have slowly grown larger, to fill our megahomes. Because we judge everything in relative terms, and because the new McMansions usually sit next to each other, or on a lot far away from other houses, the tremendous increase in house size has been a bit hidden from perception. But replace a single 1920s bungalow in an established neighborhood with a minipalace, and suddenly shocked neighbors organize and enact new zoning laws prohibiting "Monster Homes."[2] The Joneses should keep up, but we hate it when they go overboard.

An architect sold a lot in his own neighborhood to a colleague, another architect who also had an interest in ecology and preservation. The neighborhood was shocked to see the newcomer build a house that towered over the others, three times the size of the next largest house, intended for use by himself and his wife. When confronted bluntly with the neighbors' feelings, he appeared to have no regrets, and no apology, no understanding of why such a tall, wide house seemed out of place to the rest of the neighborhood.

There are two possible explanations: Either the newcomer was so deeply embarrassed, and had so much energy and resources invested in his project, that he could not allow himself to recognize his huge mistake (most humans are familiar with that situation). Or perhaps he had absolutely no sense of scale, which places him in a miniscule minority of people. A minority of people who dwell happily in tiny houses near other, larger houses seem to have this condition: they don't seem to notice that they are a tiny fish in a big pond, and truly don't seem to be affected by the difference.

But most people, including most small-house dwellers, do notice. They have found that if you don't live near other small houses, you can tweak your sense of relative size by expanding your world, and comparing your house to places beyond your neighborhood.

If you leave the United States and Canada, you'll find that most of the world has houses a fraction the size of ours. Or don't leave; just take a trip across town. It is likely that someone not too far away from you lives simpler, cheaper, and smaller. Many of the people profiled in this book volunteer in literacy programs, in hospitals, or with the homeless, giving them a fresh perspective on their own living situation, something more moderate to compare themselves to.

Choose a New Jones

Some small-home dwellers compare themselves to themselves: a variety of traditions have a story of a family or individual displeased with the small size of their house. They are advised by the local sage/priest/rabbi/oracle/guru/medicinewoman to bring a goat/cow/gnu/elephant/ ox into their home for a few weeks. When it leaves, they find their house magically has expanded. Modern small housers mimic this by taking a vacation on a sailboat or in a monastic cell, or by inviting a dozen friends to spend a week in their home.

Others stay right at home, and study history or anthropology, and compare themselves to our ancestors, or to people in faraway places. Understanding the normal scale of human existence tends to make most North Americans aware of our good fortune, at least in the material realm.

One reason we desire so much to "keep up" is our deep cultural belief that we are all born equal and treated fairly, and that people "get what they deserve." Equality has been a central ideal to North Americans for a few hundred years. We who hang onto our belief despite the evidence before our eyes experience cognitive dissonance: we find ourselves disbelieving what we see, and try through mental acrobatics to make reality match our preconceptions. Extended periods of cognitive dissonance can lead to disorientation and depression.

People who read history and anthropology are more likely to understand that although there have been times in human history when the trend was toward increasing fairness and sharing, this is not one of them. They are aware that one's social and economic status has at least as much to do with one's parents as one's own efforts. They know that most people who purchase expensive houses have inherited or gifted money, and that some millionaires live in modest homes while other people with no savings at all live in palaces built of credit cards.[3]

FIND NEW FRIENDS

But most of us care less about abstractions, theories, statistics, and faraway tribes than we do about our friends, colleagues, and extended family. Since 1992, Cecile Andrews (see Chapter 10) has brought people together in simplicity "study circles," where people share stories and advice about how to reduce their consumption and live more simply. Currently there are similar groups all over the country, run by a variety of churches and other groups. Some people who make a decision to scale down find these groups essential, and those who don't usually have carefully built their own network of friendships through other means.

The Joneses we choose as our friends frame our perspective. Once upon a time we had just a small village to compare ourselves to. Now we watch television and movies, and our needs multiply. Air conditioning, a second car, three clocks—luxuries of the past have become today's "needs." Our houses bulge with our new possessions. Polls show that most Americans believe we must earn about twice the median income to be solidly middle class—that is, we believe that what we earn, on average, is just not enough.[4]

Where does this idea come from? Which can you recall better: your neighbor's living room, or the studio set of a television show you like? Television is one reason why, says economist Juliet Schor, our "needs" have increased so rapidly: "We now compare ourselves to the super-rich." Bill Gates has become Mr. Jones. John D. Rockefeller owned a bigger share of America than Bill Gates does now,[5] but prior to television we didn't spend much time knowing details of the homes of the rich and famous. Currently, viewers can "visit" a different multimillionaire's 10,000-square-foot mansion each week via cable TV. There are plenty to visit, as it appears that almost anyone who can afford it has one. The main effect of a 10 million dollar house on most of us is to make a $300,000 house seem quite modest.

"I was surprised to learn that my house qualifies as 'small' but then everyone's in this neighborhood is about the same size. Around here, affording even this is so very difficult. I feel a little uncomfortable to hear living in a perfectly good-sized house being discussed as if it were something almost heroic. What are we coming to, I wonder?

"Not keeping up with the Joneses is not a constant struggle. It doesn't take a lot of discipline. I think that once you start it's actually easy and fulfilling, not grim at all.

"For example: My messy, sometimes barren and weed-filled vegetable garden in lieu of a front yard has taught me that there are no Joneses. My neighbors like it and are encouraging. Strangers stop to discuss what I'm growing. People with gorgeous but traditional yards talk with me about their vegetable experiences and tell me that I've inspired them to put in fruit trees or strawberries. Neighborhood kids gather to play in the mud and I've never felt like anyone gave a thought to a negative impact on property values, though it certainly is a hell of a mess most of the time." —Rita Schmidt

CLOSE YOUR EYES

Most people we visited accept the fact that we are all affected by advertising. They take steps to limit their exposure. Some throw out their television. Some move to the countryside. Some avoid what Chris Patterson (see profile) calls "house porn" by unsubscribing to most magazines. Some develop a habit of "talking back" to billboards and screens, and teach their children to do the same. (It looks silly, but it works for them.)

THE JOY OF NONCONFORMITY

Closing your eyes, resisting and not-doing works for a while, but eventually you might find that if you're grimly swimming against the tide, you'll run out of energy. But if you're hilarious, happy, or at least having a moderately pleasant time swimming, you might keep it up forever.

Some people quit Jonesing by evicting the imaginary Joneses

from their minds, and meeting their real neighbors, instead.

What If You *Are* the Joneses?

MAKE PEACE WITH YOUR FAMILY

Some people cite family pressure to own too much house. Parents offer to cosign a mortgage, but only for a big house. Relatives refuse to visit, "Because we'd just be in the way in your little house," and inheritances of antique furniture provoke descendants to build museums to store all the stuff—when all they dreamed of was a little shack.

Others have discovered that addressing old issues head on, and resolving old disagreements, eliminated their need to comply with family expectations.

Shelly's parents were dismayed when their debutante daughter moved out West and built her own tiny house at the end of a long, dirt road. "It's not the life they imagined for me, so at first it was rough between us," she says, but by showing them how many things she appreciates about her background, like family recipes and stories, and "by building a little extra just to fit in just a few pieces of the inherited furniture, even though it's out of place here," they've maintained some common ground. "It's worth it," says Shelly.

QUALITY, NOT QUANTITY

And what if a huge home is required for your occupation?

A former building supply company executive acknowledged that his family of four didn't really need the seven bedrooms and five living rooms in their house, but it was occasionally part of his job to entertain clients and partners. "To make the sale I had to show *them our success," he said. "The fact that we were overextended financially burdened us, maybe even harmed my health, but the clients couldn't* see *that."*

Some small-housers, including people who believe their livelihood requires them to display their wealth, build a precious, tiny jewel. This is the method used by Polly Strand (see profile), who built a home a sixth to a tenth the size of her neighbors, but spent freely on bath fixtures, lighting, and bamboo floors. It's Sarah Susanka's plea in her book, *The Not-So-Big House*: if you have the spare change to build 5,000 square feet, cut your size in half, and spend your savings on an architect, skilled craftspeople, and high-priced materials, and show off the gorgeous results.

Meanwhile, other business people see their wealth as capital, to be invested in productive enterprises, research, and development, not in their homes. At the top of their game, they have nothing to prove.

Jirka Risavy, founder of the most successful office supply company in the world, lives in a four-room, woodstove-heated cabin in the woods. He wonders, "Why, just because people have a lot of money, do they need to spend it?[6]

Forget the Joneses?

But what about the rest of us, who aren't at the top, who aren't rich or even famous? Can we jump out of the game too?

Try it. Tell yourself you don't care that the person you trained now makes almost twice your salary. Push your thoughts away when you find yourself staring at your neighbor's new guesthouse. And when your cousin marries the nicest, smartest, best-looking human in town, remember the tenth commandment and feel nothing but sympathetic happiness.

We know that envy and comparison will bring us unhappiness. There will always be someone richer, funnier, or faster than we are, so "Give up that race. You're fine just as you are," insists the little voice our parents tried to install in our subconscious. "Comparing yourself to others is both odious and odorous,"[7] reports a famous newspaper in one essay. Meanwhile, on the next page, other articles inform us in detail of the age, income, and appliances of current celebrities. If comparison brings us no pleasure, why do we do it? How can we stop?

The bad news is that we probably can't stop. It appears to be hard-wired. Psychological and anthropological research point to the extreme importance we place on "relative status." Research has found that you are about as likely to stop comparing yourself to others as you are to reach enlightenment in this lifetime.

HOMO ECONOMICUS OR *HOMO SOCIALUS*?

Would you like five dollars? No strings attached. Right now. Five bucks. Well, the answer is: It depends. You'll probably first want to know how much everyone else is getting.

A much-repeated economic research experiment, called the "Ultimatum Game," went like this: researchers gave one person in a pair a sum of money, and asked that person to offer the second person part of it. If the "acceptor" accepted the portion, both parties could keep their money. If not, both parties received nothing. The offerer had only one chance to offer. Over 80 percent of the time, the first party offered an even 50 percent. Rare was the acceptor who would take less than 40 percent of the total.

This research showed that it's not in our nature to tolerate inequity, and, unless we're starving, we'd usually rather get nothing than let someone else get a lot more.

These studies challenged orthodox economic theory, which holds that individuals, a.k.a. "*Homo economicus*," act "rationally," always trying to increase their absolute wealth. Study after study shows that people care more about their relative wealth than their absolute wealth. Would you prefer to live in a $200,000 house or a $300,000 house? There again, it all depends on who your Joneses are. If the $300,000 house is surrounded by $2,000,000 houses, you will likely prefer the $200,000 house when you find out it is surrounded by houses similar in price.

Sue Fry watched for fourteen years as the farms all around her in rural Connecticut were sold off and converted into subdivisions. Eventually, everything adjacent to her own farm was eaten up. "When my neighbors started complaining that we still had horses, we knew it was time to move," she says. Although houses sold easily all around them, their four-bedroom, two-and-a-half-bath, 3,400-square-foot-plus-full-basement Colonial farmhouse stayed on the market for many months. Their real estate agent explained, "No one wants to live in the smallest house on the block."

Orthodox economic theory tells us we are "irrational" to prize relative over absolute wealth. Money buys us goods, goods make us happy, and, like the word implies, the more goods the better, regardless of what our neighbors have. Are we irrational?

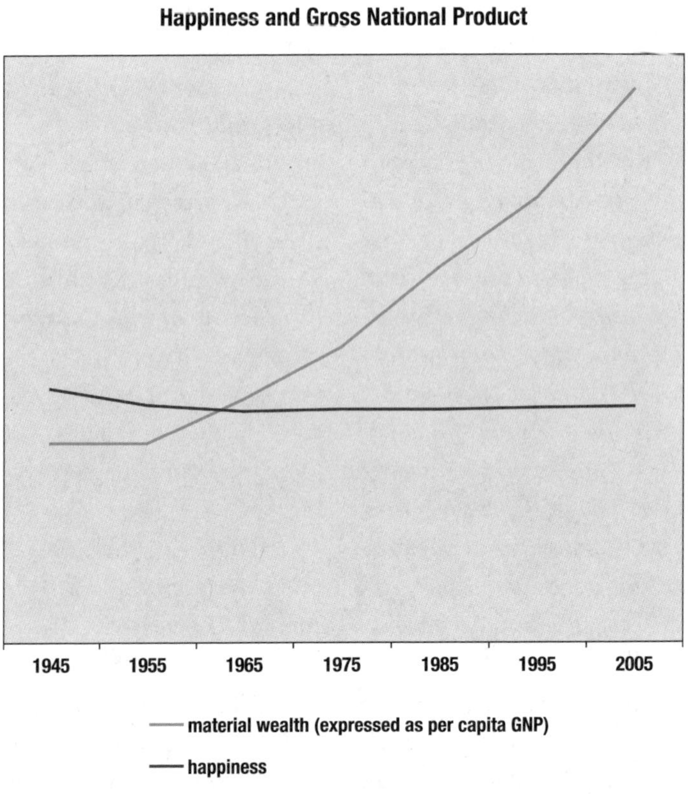

GRAPH 1.1 HAPPINESS HAS BEEN STUDIED BY THOUSANDS OF RESEARCHERS FOR THE PAST SIXTY YEARS IN A FAIRLY STANDARDIZED WAY. ONCE BASIC NEEDS ARE MET, THE AVERAGE LEVEL OF HAPPINESS DOES NOT INCREASE AS OVERALL CONSUMPTION INCREASES.

Maybe we are irrational. However, it turns out that "the more goods, the better" is just not true. Once basic needs are met, increases in absolute wealth don't make us happier. However, research has also shown repeatedly that the *relatively* rich, all over the world, and regardless of their *absolute* wealth, tend to report higher levels of happiness than their relatively poor neighbors and fellow citizens. Are we irrational, then, to care so much about the Joneses?[8]

Of course not. In extreme situations, such as famine, it matters extremely who is relatively richer: that's who gets to eat.[9] In our more moderate situation, if you believe there is a finite supply of resources, electricity for example, you might be concerned to find out that the rich *are* different. They use more resources. For example, the wealthiest section of the population uses 80 percent more electricity to cool their homes than the poorest.

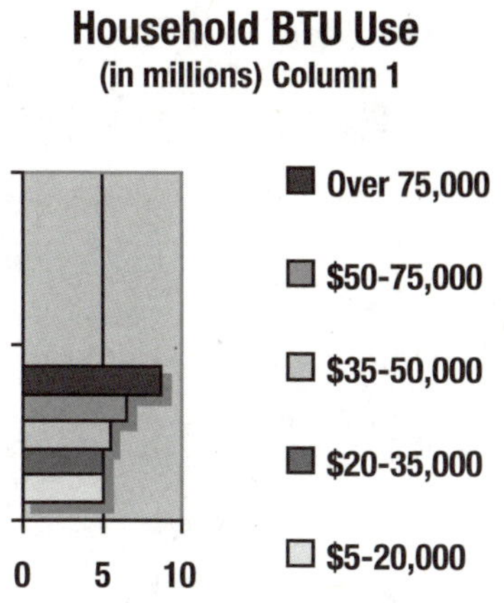

GRAPH 1.2 SOURCE: RESIDENTIAL ENERGY CONSUMPTION SURVEY/HOUSE COOLING DATA, CONGRESSIONAL SURVEY 1997. IN OTHER STUDIES, EVEN AFTER DATA WAS CONTROLLED FOR NUMBER OF RESIDENTS, AS HOUSEHOLD INCOME INCREASES, SO DOES BTU USE. RESEARCHERS THEORIZE THE PRIMARY REASON IS THAT HOUSE SIZE INCREASES WITH INCOME, AND HOUSING DENSITY DECREASES. AND LARGE, DETACHED HOUSES ARE MORE EXPENSIVE TO HEAT AND COOL.[11]

THE PROPER SCHOOLS

Even in luxurious places, minor differences in status matter: the wealthier diner gets the nicer table; better-dressed students get more attention from teachers, and fancier neighborhoods often have schools with higher test scores. Numerous families report the reason they bought a too-big house was because it was in a neighborhood with good schools.[10]

The growing gap in school quality is a serious problem for a number of reasons. Many smallhousers address this by using the extra time they receive (by having a lower mortgage and less house to maintain) to support their children directly. One father said, "I'd rather have time to know my kids well enough to be sure they're doing well in a mediocre school, then send them to a great school but have to work so much to send them there that I have no idea who and how they are." Many homeschool, or volunteer in their children's classes, or travel or farm in the summers with their children (more on this in Chapter 11). They know they've taken a step down in status, but they compensate by providing other "luxuries" for their kids.

MIND THE GAP

A twenty-five-year study (called the Whitehall studies) surveyed 17,000 British civil servants who all had access to advanced education, health care, and good nutrition. The researchers controlled the data to weed out the effect of smoking and genetic problems. They discovered something odd: the single most reliable determinant of age at death and general health throughout life was ranking in the civil servant hierarchy. That is, any boss was likely to be healthier and live longer than those under him. They even found a correlation between having a larger house and having good health.[12] Could living in a small house shorten your life?

Later analysis of the Whitehall studies suggested that people who have control over their own lives, who juggle their own schedules, and can rest before they get sick, are healthier and live longer. In most jobs, those higher up on the ladder have more autonomy. Making a living from your own business, early retirement, working only part-time or seasonally, or finding a job with flexible hours are other ways people gain autonomy over their lives.

Other studies, of apes and of college age males, have found that leaders have a heightened seratonin level. Low seratonin levels are associated with depression. When researchers manipulated the group so that the leader lost status, his seratonin level dropped.[13] If you associate large house size with leadership, will a smaller house depress you?

FRIENDS IN COMMON

Most of the people interviewed in this book love their hobbies. They

Madeleine, a psychotherapist explains, "The simplest task, simple successful interaction with the material world, lifts one out of depression," so she figures out what her most difficult clients know how to do—such as how to shine a shoe or bake a pie—and starts from there, slowly drawing them out of their condition, not by talking about the task, but by doing it.

Her methods were inspired by the way of life she adopted in the Gandhian community where she lived in France. "Each family or person lived in an apartment, cut out of a giant, domed, sixteenth-century stone sheep barn. We provided for much of our own needs by farming, cooking, weaving. Our sense of self came from developing our spiritual and material abilities, not through our possessions, which were minimal."

dance, sing in choirs, paint, garden, camp, rock climb, sail, and travel. They throw parties. Living smaller frees up their time and money to pursue fun. Luckily, having good friends is a proven mood elevator.[14] And friends are often central to their lives.

In our own lives, we know widening social gaps harm us. If your best friend becomes a corporate executive while you choose a more modestly remunerated profession, even if your interests remain the same, the income gap between you can hurt the friendship. What if your house size doesn't keep up with your friends? Sarah Patterson (see profile) screens new acquaintances by announcing right away that she lives in a small house. If it isn't an issue for them, then it won't be for her.

Aristotle wrote, "Friendship is Equality,"[15] and commented that friendship is rooted in having things in common, both metaphorically, and literally. On the domestic scale he saw the possession of common goods as a source of the bond between spouses. On the larger scale, a sense of friendship within a nation, or between all members of our species, is enhanced when we hold "things" in common: air, water, land, as well as institutions, customs, and agreements that mediate our actions. When our physical world is diced up and owned by individuals and private organizations, our common sense is diminished. We share less, and feel less immediately friendly. With this in mind, many small-house dwellers make friends by working toward common goals.

Taking the Lead

FIGHT FOR A CAUSE

The "Ultimatum Game" proved what we already know: most of us care deeply about fairness. Currently products are sold by appealing to this sense of ours: "Be fair to yourself. Others have it. You *deserve* it too." This style of advertising has great success with most of us. Some people express their fairness cravings by working for causes that promote equality. As one hospital union member put it, "I deserve to get more when we all get more. It's no fun alone." (More on this in Chapter 13.)

DEVELOP SKILLS

People who use their own hands to build their home take more pleasure and pride in the process than they do in the possession of a certain quantity of house. People with a large variety of distinct skills often feel more secure in themselves and less in need of material possessions.

House building and maintenance skills in particular tend to lessen the desire to possess too much house, because they inspire respect for the tremendous amount of energy that goes into building a house. Curiously, the act of, say, planting a garden or building a bunk bed, creates in many people a sense of home security that buying or building more house does not.

REMEMBER THE MONK

Researchers in one of the serotonin studies mentioned earlier found that a Tibetan monk was consistently and well-above-average happy, despite the various pranks the researchers played on him. Even if you can't achieve total enlightenment in this life, dedication to a spiritual practice, a special connection to nature, or a faithful relationship with God, often creates a happiness less dependent on possession. Many of the people in this book rate that connection as the source of their contentment. Is it more house that you need, or something much better, something you don't need to buy?

Whatever appeals to you, you'll find, if you choose to live smaller, your scaling down is best if it's also a ratcheting up, because, as David Omick and Pearl Mast say, in Chapter 13, "Reductionism itself is no code to live by." It's a path to that something better.[16]

EXERCISE: THE MEANING OF HOME

For her profound book, *House as a Mirror of Self* (Conari Press, 1995), architecture professor Clare Cooper Marcus, over a period of twenty-five years, interviewed sixty people regarding their emotional relationship with their home. The book offers a variety of exercises to help readers understand how physical aspects of their house can represent aspects of their psyche, and the stories they tell about their home can open the door to self-knowledge. The interviews were themselves a kind of exercise, based on Jungian psychology and Gestalt therapy. Conduct your own interview, by yourself, or with a good, impartial friend:

1. Sit with a large pad of paper and colored pencils or crayons and plenty of time, and draw a picture of your feelings about home. Draw carelessly, and without regard for art, and avoid criticizing the drawing. This is an opportunity to focus on your feelings, and watch what appears.
2. When you've finished drawing, sit quietly for a few minutes, then look at what you've drawn, and describe it in words.
3. Place the drawing on a chair 4 feet away from you and speak to it as if it were your house, starting with the words "House (or apartment, etc.), the way I feel about you is..."
4. When you've finished speaking, switch places with your drawing, and speak back to yourself, as if you were your house, expressing its feelings and thoughts.

You'll probably be surprised at what you learn.

SARAH AND CHRIS PATTERSON

NICK, RYAN, AND CATIE

Built early 1950s

AREA:
970 sq. ft., plus 375-sq.-ft. finished basement

INTENDED NUMBER OF OCCUPANTS:
5

PURCHASE PRICE (2000):
$220,000

UTILITY COSTS (2005, MONTHLY):
electric, $121; water, $30; gas, $40; heating oil, $101

LOCATION:
Ridgefield, Connecticut

ABOVE: **THE PATTERSON'S HOUSE OUTSIDE**

The Pattersons live in the smallest house on

the block, near the bad side of town. Well, okay, there are two other houses about as small as theirs, but those houses only have single people in them. And, with one of the lowest crime rates in the country, there is no bad side of Ridgefield. But honestly, most of their neighbors have houses about twice the size of theirs, and two blocks away are houses four or five times as large. With a kitchen smaller than many Ridgefield foyers, how do the Pattersons possibly manage? Sarah answers,

"That's the question I imagine people have in their heads when they come to visit. Sometimes my house is smaller than their pool house. It's the only time I wonder whether we don't have enough. When I meet people, I head off any discussion by trying to fit into the conversation, 'I live in a really small house,' so that's cleared up right away. When they visit, they see we live just fine. It's a terrific house. When I was in college, I house-sat for the people who lived here then, and I loved this house—it always made me feel like baking a cake.

"I've heard that in most marriages it will happen that one spouse has climbed up in a tree and the other has to talk them down. Every once in a while I go up the "Why didn't we buy the bigger house?!" tree, and Chris comes and talks me down: "Remember how much we like our neighbors? Isn't the location great? Would you like to be in debt? What about our view of the lake—don't you like that?" Then he plays the song 'Little Bitty' and the kids dance around to it."[17]

In 2005 in Ridgefield the average house sold for over a million dollars, or about nine times the local median household income of $116,000. So even though the Pattersons are not poor in any sense of the word—Chris earns more than the median income—if they had to move there now, they couldn't currently afford to buy a house in their hometown. People who are from the area, like the Pattersons, are relatively lucky, because "wherever you bought, before prices jumped, at least you can stay there." Newcomers must arrive with significant savings or inheritance, or they will find it absurdly high-priced and have to rent, or live somewhere else. "Except for the people from New Canaan," says Sarah; "it's even more expensive there. They say, 'Oh it's so reasonable in Ridgefield!'" Many workers commute into the town daily from other towns, and many workers from Ridgefield commute daily to Manhattan, especially Wall Street, for work.

It wasn't always like this. From the 1880s until the 1930s there were huge mansion estates, for families with names like "Rockwell," "Lynch," and "Morgan," and many smaller houses for the people who served them. The 1950s brought the era of corporate headquarters—IBM and Pepsi-Cola, and a middle class.

"The lake is really what makes the house. Seeing ducks and beavers, and being able to go right outside and skate or fish for bass or pike, right in our backyard, makes the space seems huge. Size is completely relative. I think about New York City and I imagine living in an apartment this big there—and then I add the lake. We're in a beautiful spot." —Chris Patterson

Chris Patterson's dad was a policeman, and his mom was a secretary. "But cops can't afford to live in Ridgefield now," says Chris. Most newcomers are employed in finance, in banking or the stock market.

The Pattersons' house is a simple rectangle, originally built as a four-season lake retreat cottage. The front door is on the wide side, close to one end, and opens to a 24-by-16-foot great room, with a

THE KITCHEN ISLAND

"I admit, we have worried about the children growing up as the 'small house' family. Even though they are still very young, we hear kids say things like, 'My daddy has a new Ferrari.' No parents want their kids to hurt from peer pressure. It's human nature to want to fit in. But the fact is our kids are healthy, and athletic, and they do well in school. They are all very honest, good children. The boys have become friends, sharing a room—being together is really a gift we've given them. We don't think that they'll regret our house size because it's meant that their mother doesn't have to go away and work, and their dad can stay in a job where he doesn't have to travel much—he even coaches little league. He's been here for everything. Many men in our town travel for weeks at a time, on business, or they work every night until ten. We keep reminding ourselves that we're lucky." —Sarah Patterson

36-by-54-inch dining table on one end, which is currently primarily used for homework and crafts. Near the door, each family member has a basket, for hats and gloves, and coats are stored on high hooks on the door for the parents and low hooks on the wall for the kids.

The 10-by-11-foot kitchen is in the center, and it features Sarah's favorite element, "The secret to the little house that could": a large, tall island with six stools around it, perfect for cooking, hosting guests for coffee, surfing the Internet, and also where the family gathers twice a day to share meals. "The kitchen is fine as it is; it could even be a bit smaller," says Sarah. Beyond the dining area is a living room, with a hearth raised 1 foot off the ground, which means that people can sit right next to the fire. A huge bay window is directly opposite the front door, and next to sliding glass doors that look out on a 26-acre lake.

The eastern half of the house is divided into bedrooms, one 10 by 12 feet for the boys, an 8 by-10-foot bedroom for their daughter, and for the parents a roomy 13 by 11 feet. The closets are tiny, sized for the storage needs of families vacationing fifty years ago, and so Chris uses the parents' closet while Sarah shares with her tiny daughter. Downstairs half of the basement contains the washing machine and furnace; the other half is finished as a playroom, with space for a large television and a home office for Sarah. "But I really don't go down there. It's easier to stay up in the kitchen. But the playroom is great for the kids."

Is there anything they would change in their house? Chris wishes he had an extra half bath—"You can't really read in there with three kids in the house!"—and Sarah thinks she would like a storage bench for shoes at the entrance, or better yet a mudroom, but even though she reads glossy house magazines ("Chris calls them porn for housewives"), she continually reassesses whether her wants are real or just "Jonesing."

The Oakland Hills, uphill from University of California,

Berkeley and overlooking San Francisco Bay, were rolling grasslands a hundred years ago. The first neighborhood development plan, drawn in the 1920s, was based on principles developed by a neighborhood committee, and explained in Charles Keeler's 1904 book, *The Simple Home*. By 1950, the grasslands had been replaced by handsome, Arts and Crafts–style homes with large yards backed up against a recently planted forest of eucalyptus, bay, and pine trees.

Today, the area is packed with what architects' portfolios refer to as "skyline castles," "minicastles," or, more plainly, "insurance settlement homes." One giant house is built in the form of a saxophone. Another, three-million-dollar house made *Forbes* magazine's list of "Best Houses in the Best Places." This latest neighborhood change took less than five years. The cause: a massive forest fire.

In October 1991, the fifth year of drought, "a single ember," the fire commission later reported, blew into a tree. "The tree exploded into flames, and the resulting fire was quickly out of control," eventually killing twenty-five people and destroying over 3,000 homes. The Oakland Fire Department called the disaster the worst since 1906, and "far beyond the experience of any living American firefighter."

Cars, computers, heirlooms, photographs—everything burned. "Artists lost their life's work. A man died trying to save his home," reports Kathy Whealdon, an Oakland Hills resident whose 1920s 1,000-square-foot cottage was spared. "We weren't allowed to return to the area for days, so we didn't know which homes had been lost. The fire department had a video they were showing over and over in the basement of someone's house. There was a line of people that wrapped around the block, waiting to see this video, which would either show their house destroyed or left standing. It was an emotional scene.

POLLY STRAND
Garage built 1986, cottage completed 1994

AREA:
Cottage 610 sq. ft., plus 400-sq.-ft. garage below

INTENDED NUMBER OF OCCUPANTS:
1–2

COST, LAND AND UNFINISHED GARAGE:
$285,000

ADDITIONAL CONSTRUCTION COSTS:
$150,000

UTILITY COSTS (MONTHLY):
$4 electric, $20 gas (winter only)

LOCATION:
Oakland, California

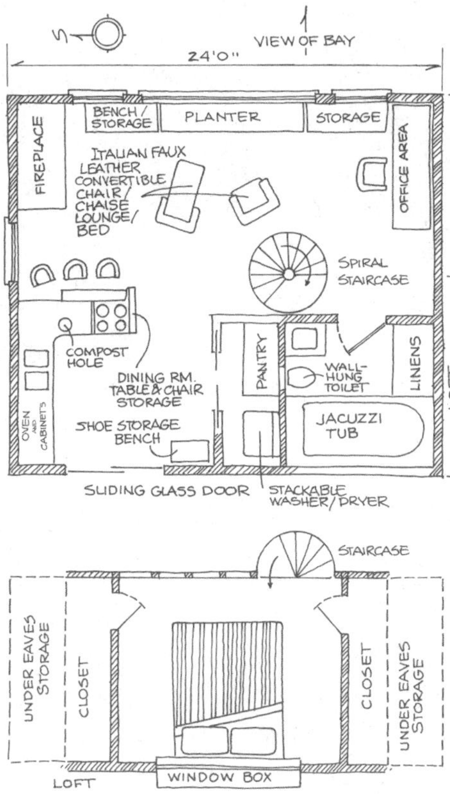

ABOVE LEFT: **POLLY'S HOUSE IS A SIXTH TO A TENTH THE SIZE OF HER NEIGHBORS' HOUSES.** ABOVE: **POLLY'S FLOOR PLAN**

POLLY'S HOUSE INSIDE

"Many people divorced. If you were married, after the fire all visible signs of it were gone. Maybe before you made peace with your situation, but now you let go," says Whealdon. Many moved away. Paul Otterson, now a travel advisor, took his first international trip soon after losing his home. "I found myself wonderfully freed of both materials and responsibilities." Those who remained hunkered down to rebuild.

"With the fires still raging you could already hear people talking about insurance settlements, calling their agents," recalls Polly Strand, a resident who eventually built a new home in her old neighborhood. "It's a very professional, high-class neighborhood. People weren't going to be cheated."

One woman had her cottage meticulously reconstructed, but most of the cute bungalows were replaced with houses two to five times their size. "People were shocked, scared, and vulnerable. What they were told to build, they built," says Whealdon. As big as they could, and as close to the lot line as allowed.

Polly Strand was different. When she and her partner were burned out of their 1940s "ranch," first they moved away to the countryside. They soon found themselves commuting back to Oakland too much. They decided to return to their old neighborhood, and found the perfect place on a lot where the main house had been lost to the fire, but a small, unfinished guesthouse, built on top of a garage, remained. Polly redesigned and built the interior, and now lives in a 610-square-foot "jewel box" overlooking an 8,000-square-foot yard. Polly told me that in the whole area, her house is unique.

[Q] Why did everyone else build so big?

[A] They were keeping up with the Joneses, I guess. Everyone has a marble kitchen, a marble bath. Everyone has an industrial refrigerator and a restaurant-size stove and a master bedroom that's as large as most people's houses.

Some of the new houses were spec houses, and I guess they felt like once you establish a whole building, it's not that much more expensive to add on another 1,000 or 2,000 square feet.

[Q] What was your design process?

[A] I had been partner in a jewelry business, with stores in shopping malls. I designed and built thirty-three stores, so I knew something about materials and layout. We'd go into the malls when they were still under construction. They give you a dirt floor and a space, and you are responsible for everything in between the walls.

I design quickly and intuitively. When I designed stores, I first worked in stores so I could learn. I paid attention to how people moved around the store, and what they needed. I did the same for myself here. I had an unfinished space, and I designed what I needed inside it in a matter of hours. But I'd practiced for this all my life.

[Q] What are your suggestions for others?

[A] Make an inventory of all your belongings. Decide what you really must have, and what it takes for you to function every day. Then build around that. Find space for each thing, each activity, but don't build space for activities you really don't do.

Originally I planned my house for two people. I designed two desk spaces, but the stairway was too close, so it didn't fit in.

[Q] But now you live alone?

[A] After twenty-three years of living together, we find we get along better if we each have our own place. He's a collector, so he has mountains of stuff: books and papers, mostly. I prefer to keep my own house. He has a huge office totally filled with things.

[Q] Would you have built anything differently?

[A] I would have had the stairway go down into the garage, and used that space better, but although I walk to town, zoning in this area requires that I maintain a two-car garage.

I wouldn't have had an oven. I don't bake. Why do I need an oven? I was told I needed an oven. I might have put a drain in the kitchen floor. I would have made the house smaller, but the basic structure already existed. This is pretty comfortable.

The best part is the deer, which come to graze. They used to be all over the neighborhood, before the fire, but now that everyone covered their lots in house, they don't have many yards to go to.

[Q] That's amazing to have deer in your backyard, with a view of the city lights from your bed and dense housing packed all around you.

[A] I am planning to divide the lot so that the deer have one half and I have the other. I will put a fence up, halfway up, so they have access on both sides. There are gophers in my garden. People say, "Kill the gophers!" I refuse. I put prickly things, raspberry bushes around my plants, so the deer don't eat them.

When I die, someone may decide to build on it. Then the deer won't come and graze anymore.

A HOLE IN THE COUNTER OPENS TO A COMPOST BIN.

On the day I visited Polly, she had just returned from a visit to Burger King, where she and others had, after many demonstrations, convinced the company to require their chicken suppliers to place only seven instead of eleven chickens in each 4-square-foot cage. "Humans take up more and more of the world," Polly notes, "and we cram animals into smaller and smaller spaces." Polly's full-time passion is to change human attitudes so that animals are safer.

When her children and grandchildren come to visit, a dining table emerges from underneath the kitchen counter, and her Italian suede (synthetic, not leather of course) living room chairs fold out into beds. When Polly doesn't have visitors, she eats at her kitchen counter. The Italian swivel stools are specially designed not to scratch the floor.

Metal drying racks above the kitchen sink double as shelves, so when Polly washes she doesn't have to dry nor move her dishes twice. A hole in the Corian countertop makes it easy to collect compost, and her electric stove can be cleaned in "a single swoosh." Underneath the counter she stores a small electric piano on a sliding shelf.

The bathroom features a space-saving wall-hung toilet (the tank is inside the wall, leaving only the throne exposed) and a tiny whirlpool jet bath. Her mezzanine bedroom has closets built into the roof "attic" space, and drawers underneath the futon frame.

Polly designed the house to stay immaculate and bright: cabinets and drawers organize and hide her books, television, office equipment, and "zillions of

ABOVE, LEFT AND RIGHT: **A PLACE FOR EACH THING** BELOW, LEFT AND RIGHT: **CABINET DOORS HIDE "ZILLIONS OF PAPERS AND WIRES."**

papers and wires." A fastidious homemaker, she hung the venetian blinds upside down so no messy string hangs out. Four 10-foot, operable skylights and a bank of windows overlooking the bay shed an even light on the laminated bamboo floor. Polly notices a single, short hair fallen on the shiny floor, and stoops to pick it up.

[Q] What do your neighbors think? Do they worry about you lowering property values?

[A] This gives them a little green space to look at. Everyone has told me they could live in a smaller place, and they wonder why they have such a large house. People have said to me, "You know what?

We live in two rooms. We don't need all the space we have."

Luckily, we aren't a subdivision, so we don't have neighborhood covenants that could have forced me to build more. Those places want to keep up a certain image, "Stop the invasion of the smallies!"

Some houses here are 6,000 square feet. That house over there, it's over 3,500 square feet. It cost $1.3 million. They built up to the lot line, on all the buildable space. They have a three-year-old child who has no place outside to play, so they built retaining walls, to make a flat area. It cost $100,000 for those walls, for a 5-foot-wide yard.

[Q] Couldn't they cut off some off the house?

[A] They didn't think of that.

[Q] Did you stay within budget for this project?

[A] Well, I had the insurance check, and then we sold the Mendocino house at a profit. I went from a 3,000-square-foot house down to a 610-square-foot house. Finances weren't a problem. When you're building with economic restraints, it's totally different. That Duravit wall-hung toilet was very expensive. On a budget, you don't buy a toilet like that—unless you eliminate something else!

[Q] Do you have financial advice for people starting out?

[A] Watch out for the title company. The first time we sold our house, we had a $500 problem with the title company. I took them to small claims court and we won.

You know, I'm sixty-nine, so obviously that makes a difference. Throughout my life, my real estate appreciated considerably. People in my economic strata who accumulated wealth that way didn't do anything to create that wealth. We just happened to buy a house at the right time, in the right place. That's not going to happen again. For people who are scraping to buy a house, this system is cruel.

A VISITOR RESTS PEACEFULLY IN PATRICIA KERN'S GUEST HOUSE

2
Choose What You Need

If we could just have the kitchen and a bedroom, that would be all that we'd need.—JULIA CHILD

THE THINGS YOU REALLY NEED—air, food, sleep, sunlight, laughter—you can't carry, at least not in any significant quantity, and you can't store them long in a house. But there are tools that help you find your way to these things. Your job is to figure out which of your possessions and other attachments help you, and which you just trip over as you try to get home.

Choosing what you need requires whittling away the excess to discover your own essence. What is your essence? "Hoarders" are people who compulsively keep everything they've ever owned. They see their possessions, including their house, as an essential part of themselves. They aren't completely mistaken. What's a painter without paint, or a nurse without a patient? A hoarder *needs* his hoard to be a hoarder. Who do you want to be? And what do you need to have, or not have, so you can be that?

Build as Big as You Can?

The standard advice has been: "Build (or buy) as much house as the mortgage company will allow. You will end up using it all, and besides, once you get started, a little bit more doesn't cost much." You may have been told about the economy of scale: a larger house is a better deal, per square foot.

Most people find that stuff does indeed expand to fill the space provided. Do you want to encourage this tendency with the stuff in your house? Extra space will cost you in several ways: money and time to decorate, clean, and maintain; energy to heat and cool all that space; and outdoor space (the more you put under roof, the less you'll have outside). There's also the house law of diminishing returns: the difference between having one bathroom or none is enormous, but between two and three may be negligible.

Small-house dwellers are revising the conventional wisdom, and say instead, "Build just what you'll use. Avoid excess." They find that their stuff does better with *less* space, because it requires them to keep only what they appreciate and have time to maintain, and

Chris's parents were moving out of the house he'd grown up in, downsizing to something half as big. He drove across the country to help and was offered a share of the furniture. Chris, who had spent the last fifteen years never owning more than he could fit in his car, found himself driving a moving van back to his small apartment, which he then furnished with two dressers, a dining table, end tables, mirrors, and chairs. At first, the furniture, which was mostly at shoulder height, since he still preferred to sit on the floor to read, eat, and entertain guests, comforted him. It recalled memories he wanted to reconsider. After four months, I found him one day dismantling the table, and fitting as much as he could into a closet. He wanted the emptiness again. In a year he had sold the furniture, quit his job, and moved back to his hometown. Listening to the furniture, he learned he craved his family and wanted more than anything to be near his father.

allows them to give up any excess that distracts them from their happiness. By eliminating the excess, they have energy and resources left over to enjoy and maintain what they've chosen to keep.

To figure out what your excess is, examine your present house. Most people start by examining their storage areas, which are taking up an increasing percentage of under-roof, air-conditioned space.

WHAT'S IN YOUR CLOSETS?

If the façade of a house represents your ego, your closets, garage, basement and attic hide your subconscious. Study them. When will you learn tennis? Will you go back to your life as a potter? Storing some things may cost more, in rent or in worry, than letting them go, and buying a replacement again later, if you ever need it again. Cutting out some options may free up energy to spend on your current priorities. Saying "no" to some of your dreams may help you sleep better at night. This won't be your last chance to have lots of stuff: more opportunities will present themselves in the future, if your hands are free to accept them.

What about that mohair coat? Do you keep it for its sentimental value? Would taking a picture of it, or writing a paragraph in your journal be just as good? Try that. Or do as Brigitte (see Chapter 11) did when she melted an old family ring into something she could use. Barb and Tom Demith, estate sale coordinators in Chicago Heights, advise, "If one of our nieces admires something in my house, I say 'Take it!' Don't wait for the lawyers to disburse your estate!"

Or maybe you just need to keep some things: Great-grandmother's writing desk holds a story a photograph won't tell: the skilled hands that made it, the storekeeper who displayed it, the decades of correspondence that flowed from it. Things hold history. Some peoples believe their ancestors dissolve into things after death (not an unscientific theory), and so each thing must be touched and spoken about with respect. Those who believe each and every thing has a soul, a history, and a community don't acquire things without carefully considering them first. For them possession becomes a relationship, a state of mutual caring. Deep materialism helps some of us realize the weight proper possession requires.

CHERISH THE GIFT

It isn't particularly noble to move items from a dusty attic to a landfill across town. "I never get *rid* of things," Larry Chase explains (see Chapter 11). "Anything I have, I ask myself, 'Could someone else use this better?' Even if I give my stuff to someone anonymous, via Goodwill, I see it as a gift to someone else, and I imagine how much happiness it could bring them."

It doesn't help anyone much if you simply send your things to the landfill, and start overaccumulating again. Better then just to leave them in your yard, where you can watch the pile grow, until you find yourself "shopping" at your own home yard sale. Or consider going to the source to stop the flow.

STOP THE FLOW AT YOUR DOORSTEP

Be like the woman who sorts her mail at the garbage can: don't let advertising into your home. Over $1,500 was spent on each American last year, trying to convince us of this and that. It works. Women buy wrinkle creams and men buy penis "supplements," and it can even trick you into buying a very nice couch. Avoid it. Beware of home magazines. Small-home dwellers prefer to create their own dreams.

CHOOSE HOW MUCH, AND THAT'S ALL

One small-house strategy is to choose an amount of space for storage, and simply not allow more. Like a well-packed suitcase you may find your things will shrink and pack down to fit in very little space, and anything else, it turns out you just don't need. Karin and Kushi live with their two children in a 800-square-foot condominium, as part of a cohousing community.

ESTATE SALE COORDINATORS BARB AND TOM DEMITH AND THEIR COLLECTION, WHICH THEY STORE ON OPEN SHELVES TO DECORATE THEIR HOME

"Each household (regardless of size) gets the same amount of community storage space (approximately 4 feet by 4 feet by 10 feet). Kushi and I use this space for essentials like our backpacking, camping, and sports equipment, coolers, etc.

"Inside our house, our personal belongings are pretty limited. We regularly give away our excess things, which are mostly things that people have given us; every three to four months or so I load up clothes, books, toys, other items that are not being used and take them to thrift stores or non-profits. We no longer have the boxes of old schoolbooks, tapes, records, etc. that we first had when we moved in here." —Karin

THE LONG-TERM STORAGE COMMITMENT

The pull is great: over a billion square feet of personal, away-from-home storage space is now rented in the U.S., much of it heated and cooled. Interestingly called *self*-storage, this "industry" has increased forty-fold since 1960, making it larger than the music business, and economically more profitable than the movies. It fills a space about the size of 300 huge office towers, or about 100,000 city pocket parks.[1] And much placed in long-term storage is never valued again (unless it's old files subpoenaed for court). So which do you prefer: another hundred square feet of concrete for your stuff, or trees? Storage, or music?

Sometimes we save something just because it was once expensive, and we think that day may come again, so we insist on its value by saving it, even though "objectively" we have no use for it.

Economist Juliet Schor explains "the Diderot effect": Diderot received a lovely silk dressing gown as a gift, which he enjoyed until he saw how shabby it made everything else in his room look.[2] Ask yourself, does your item peacefully fulfill a pleasant desire, or does it promote the tendency to grasp at wealth? Some small-house enthusiasts turn cleaning house into a spiritual practice that reminds them to trust that they will always have enough. They free their objects, and in turn are freed. Others turn it into a game.[3]

"Every year when I can't shelve a new book or close a drawer, I am inspired to get rid of one hundred things. It's a nice round number, and a manageable task. I number a sheet of paper from one to a hundred and begin to scout for items I can do without."

—Joyce Marques Carey

Giving away a few pieces of furniture or old clothes is just a game compared to the task that most people face at some point late in life: leaving a home they love and that holds dear memories for them. In less-mobile societies some people live their whole life in a single house, born into it while their grandparents still live there, then passing away while their grandchildren sleep in another room. Some North American families live this way, but most end up with empty bedrooms and too much yard.

In 1954, Christina Jones and her family were the second family to move into the new tree-lined subdivision of Plano, Texas. Each street was connected to a long park with winding pedestrian paths, and each new home had its own yard and driveway and at least three bedrooms—luxurious and perfectly suited to her young dreams. Forty years later, her sons had each moved to Houston or Austin, and she stayed home alone, despite her sons' invitations to move closer. She knew she had too much space but couldn't find the courage to leave the decades of memories and the things most familiar to her. In 2005, reading a newspaper article about the inability of most families to afford homes near good schools, she finally found a compelling reason to move forward: "I realized a young family could really benefit from my

Cheryl grew up sad in a one-bedroom apartment, the only child of an alcoholic mother. She insisted on large dwellings for her first twelve years of adult life, but then a brush with death and thus a spiritual awakening led her to a Christian community where she was given a tiny (10-by-6-foot) trailer to sleep in. The first weeks were a claustrophobic nightmare, and she dreamed of escaping her cell. She had no trouble getting to early-morning prayers. With time and prayer she became comfortable in the trailer (which had windows that looked out on velvety fields she finally noticed). Now she happily shares a small apartment with her own teenage daughter.

home, especially if I gave them a good deal on the price. Why not give someone young the same chance we were given?"

THE TRIP

Almost every small-home dweller traces her ability to live small to a trip. A year in a Parisian apartment or on mission in Bolivia, or two months hiking the Appalachian Trail: everyone has a memory of an adventure that involved very little stuff, a small place, good company, and fun.

As a young man, Lucas gave up his apartment and left with a tightly stuffed backpack to spend six months in India. Within a few weeks the backpack felt large, and he scaled down, giving away his third, and then second pairs of shoes, exchanging the backpack for two smaller bags, eventually giving away two-thirds of the clothes and even the tourist guide he had brought. "By the end of the trip even my money began to feel like a burden. Maybe I was going nuts, but the friends I made and the sights I saw made my possessions seem useless. As I gave things away I felt lighter and lighter, more filled with faith that I'd find what I needed on my path. Now I keep hoping to find that light feeling back home."

Small-house dwellers often strive to re-create in their homes the happiness they felt on a trip.

Conversely, if your memories include an unhappy childhood or marriage in a very small place (like Cheryl, left), you'll need to do something to change your mental association.

WHERE DO YOU REALLY LIVE?

This exercise has been suggested by a number of teachers and designers in the Natural Building Movement.[4] Because they understand the material world to be precious, and they often build by hand, without machinery, they tend to make every house space efficient, to minimize waste and overwork.

1. Make a list of activities that you do at home and things that you need in your house. Be as detailed as possible. Fold up your list and stow it away.
2. Over a period of one to two weeks, keep a log of where you go in your house, and what you do there. You might post paper at doorways, and accurately record exactly where you go and how long you spend there, or just take notes from memory, once a day. In larger rooms, be specific about which part of the room you used.
3. Look around your house for spaces that you never inhabit. Imagine what would change if that space magically, poof, disappeared.
4. Make another list of "activities and needs," without reviewing the first list. If you have patience, make a new list once a week for a few weeks.
5. Uncover your first list and compare it with later ones. You may be surprised.

PRACTICE YOUR DREAM

M. Tournon, of La Maison Ecologique in Grenoble, France, reports: "Parisians dream of the country, so they build a big house out here, which they inhabit for one year, rarely emerging to enjoy the country they say they came for. In two years, the house is on the market, and they are back in Paris." How often have we chased and caught a dream, only to realize it's not what we expected?

Maybe you dream of a room where you can throw large dinner parties, yet you've never thrown a dinner party. Don't wait for the room: try it now. Henry David Thoreau fit twenty people in his cabin; surely you can fit six in your apartment. Trying it out will give you some taste of whether you enjoy it, or whether you might only want to do it twice a year, in summer, outside. Maybe what you need is a porch, at an eighth the price.

A new house is probably not going to drastically change the way you live, so plan it around your actual activities. Otherwise, you'll end up with a pretty park bench in your garden that no one sits on, a delightful guest room that no one sleeps in, and other expensive reminders of a dream you didn't realize.

Sometimes older people easily trim down their possessions and design a small house. Maybe they've been through something like this before, and they can imagine clearly the life ahead of them.

Suzanne and Jan planned their house by arranging a bed, and some other prized possessions, as well as themselves, on a concrete driveway. They encircled the arrangement with an extension cord, creating an irregular oval that was the floor plan of their home. Later, on their building site, they re-created the pattern with another cord.

Younger people, especially if they are expecting to raise a family they don't yet have, can't imagine what's ahead. Have you ever known a pregnant woman who, six months into it, suddenly decides she needs to remodel her kitchen? The baby books advise against adding new stresses, the husband is confused, and here comes the plumber, ready to tear out the sink.

One imagines that in traditional societies the lack of resources and wisdom of the elders prevail over such madness, but in our world, couples are on their own. An unimaginable change rolls towards them whimpering "need need need" from someplace deep, and the mortgage payment is extended an extra decade. Hannah and Kiko (see profile in Chapter 8) tried a different tactic: they had the baby first, then slowly figured out what in fact needed to change in their house. They spent almost nothing on the changes.

A HOME TO FIT YOUR LIFE

To plan new construction, make a list of your activities. Then, on blank paper, draw circles, and place those activities within the circles. If one activity can take place in exactly the same place and same time as another, you'll put them both in one circle. If some activities should or can be near another, you'll put those circles near each other. If some activities can share a space, or part of a space, at different times, overlapping the circles will show this. As you make more drawings of circles, a shape, or a floor plan will emerge. As you study the circles you'll see where a door fits well, and where the bathroom shouldn't be. You may find that everything can basically fit in a single circle. Consider doing the same activity, as Suzanne and Jan did, not on paper, but in real space and time, on a flat surface.

TRIMMING THE EXCESS

Once you have reduced your extra storage needs, and figured out your actual activities, here are a few specific areas to reconsider:

Garages. Garages (Old French for "storage") are reverting to their etymological roots. Except in the coldest climates, and even in snowy Québec, unless there's a special neighborhood code enforcing their use, most people don't store their cars in them. And most nonmechanics, once they've gotten rid of their excess, don't need such a large shed anymore. So what's left?

For starters, don't build one. Garages account for over 15 percent of the size of the average new house.[5] They're considered ugly, earning many tract homes the name "snout house" for the image they evoke on the façade. Although they are less finished than the rest of the house, they still have a foundation, a roof, and walls, and some garages are heated, cooled and insulated, which makes them almost as costly per square foot as a bedroom. Instead, wouldn't a larger porch be nice? If you have a garage, or are required to build one, imagine how it might be converted into something else—a guesthouse, storefront, or office—and plan for that eventuality. More and more municipalities, realizing the benefits of "infill," are permitting such conversions.

The Basement. Some people swear that a house without a basement is a shack, and will never be properly heated. Basements, if they are daylighted, can provide some of the benefits of earth-bermed building, and can increase the living space without widening the façade: architect Rick McDermott daylighted a below-ground space by taking out a section of the ground floor, creating a tall slice of vertical space so the ground floor could share its natural light with the basement. Before you build one ask yourself first, what will you do in your basement? If you can't imagine living there, question whether you need one more place to store things.

Ductwork. Ductwork, metal tubes and canals that force heated, cooled, or filtered air to different parts of the house, may be necessary in a large building, but small, well-planned houses are often better off without them. Ducts seem to allow us to share heating or cooling, and still close doors and isolate ourselves acoustically from each other, but sometimes they conduct sound quite well. To live in a ductless house, ask yourself why you want to close a door, and when. If you are able to leave doors partially open, or place transom windows above them, air should move well through your small house. You might add ceiling fans, placed to force hot air down in winter and up towards high windows in summer, and move air around corners and through the house. If you keep in mind the simple fact that heat rises and moves away from its source, toward the cold, you can place heating elements in a way that maximizes their efficiency. Or, better yet, insulate and orient your home towards the winter sun, but shaded in summer, so that you need little or no mechanical heating and cooling. The best thing about no ducts is not having to clean them.

Appliances. Large and small appliances account for as much as 10 percent of the increase in house size since 1948, and, depending on the climate, about half of the energy use. Some appliances are easy to cut out: the pasta machine, the unused waffle iron. Serious small-home dwellers take a hard look at the largest home-energy hog: the beloved fridge.

Most North American homes contain refrigerators almost twice

IF YOU HAVE A GARAGE, OR ARE REQUIRED TO BUILD ONE, IMAGINE HOW IT MIGHT BE CONVERTED TO SOMETHING ELSE.

A house at the base of the Rocky Mountains has a tiny, super insulated (R-40) pantry on its north side, which has vents that open at night and close during the day (nighttime temperatures there are 25–40 degrees Fahrenheit cooler than daytime temperatures). Four to seven months of the year items can be kept frozen in the pantry. About six weeks a year (July–August) the pantry warms up to over 55 degrees, and the family is restricted to fresh produce from the garden.

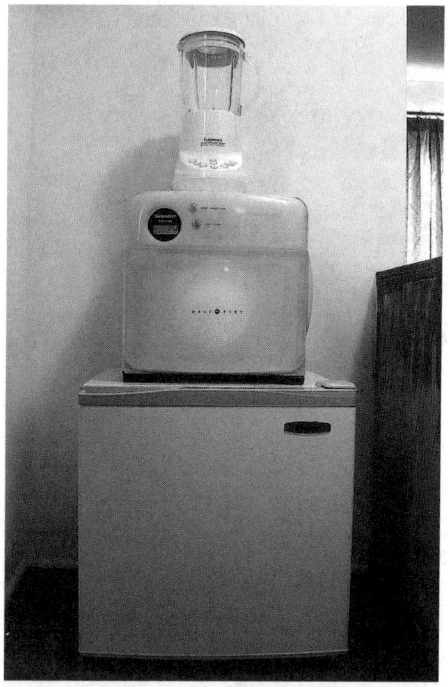

THE FRIDGE IS THE LARGEST SPACE AND ENERGY HOG IN THE KITCHEN. TAKE OUT THE ROTTING VEGGIES AND THE OLD CONDIMENTS, AND YOU MAY ONLY NEED A FRIDGE A THIRD THE SIZE.

the size of their European counterparts. A typical refrigerator built in the 1990s uses as much energy as leaving six small television sets on for 10-12 hours a day.[6] Newer models are increasingly efficient, but efficient at what? Look inside your fridge. If it is like most refrigerators in our area, over half of its 18 cubic feet are empty or filled with old "C&C" (condiments and compost). Refrigerators vary substantially in their efficiency. If you are purchasing new, consider a European-sized model that can fit under a counter. Consider not using the fridge in winter (although your house will no longer benefit from the heat the fridge constantly produces) but storing things outside (perhaps via a small opening in your kitchen wall); and if you live in a mild or warm climate where you prefer not to heat up your house, consider moving the fridge itself outside to a shady location. The most efficient option is to share a single fridge or freezer with neighbors, since one full-sized fridge typically uses less energy than two half-sized models. Your magnet collection and children's drawings can move to the side of a file cabinet or sheet metal mounted to a wall for that purpose.

Foods that were developed for storage, and can be kept for a month or longer at 55 degrees Fahrenheit, include hard cheeses, sauerkraut, miso, root vegetables, and pickled items. Soft cheeses, live cultured yogurt, tofu floated in water, unwashed eggs from local chickens, open jars of jam, and many green vegetables wrapped in damp towels, or suspended in water will last a week or more,[7] and breadboxes were designed to store bread.

The water heater is another space thief. In warm climates, some people simply move it outside. Solar water heaters save space because they rest on the roof, or outside, but most solar water heaters use a backup system as well. Some people turn their woodstove into a water heater by running water pipes along the firebox. Another international standard, the "demand" or "tankless" water heater, saves space and energy because it doesn't store any hot water but produces it as needed. This system has the advantage of providing an endless (as long as the water and fuel supplies last) quantity of hot water.

Bathrooms. How many bathrooms do you need, and what function should they serve? How does one couple need two or three bathrooms? Deborah Brady (see Chapter 7) asks, "Have our bathrooms become libraries, or sewing rooms? What are people doing in there that they need three?" Those who need them believe that conflicts about schedule (rushed morning showers) and cleaning make multiple bathrooms a marriage-saver.

As most Americans don't get dirty everyday, our bathrooms are not primarily used for cleaning the body, but instead take the place of morning exercises ("The shower wakes me up.") and are used for dressing, styling hair, and applying makeup. It is one of the few places that offer mothers time alone. We have no boudoir. That's why we use so many "bath" rooms.

How does everyone else in the world get along? In places where most bodies actually get dirty during the workday, people bathe at the end of the day, which is easier to stagger, and keeps beds cleaner. In most temperate climates, office workers don't shower daily. Houses sometimes have sinks in the bedrooms. And bathrooms don't include that embarrassingly unpronounceable item, the toilet.

Why are our toilets in the bathroom? I have wondered while waiting for someone to finish her shower. Is it because otherwise we'd be too shy to ask where it is? Let's call it a W.C. (water closet), or a powder room, or a loo, then, and put it in a separate room. That will add maybe 2 square feet of interior wall, and 10 square feet of floor space, and an extra door or two, but can save you from "needing" a second bathroom. You can now put a drain in the bathroom floor, and tile the whole room if you'd like to be able to clean it more easily. A shower room can easily be as small as 4 by 4 feet, if the room is all shower, all tiled, with no space nor need for a curtain. If you protest this change because you want to be able to hop undressed from the shower to the toilet, first I must let you know that urinating into your shower drain is harmless (unless you're very sick, your urine is practically sterile).[8] Or maybe you plan to hurry from the toilet to the shower: consider a toilet-top bidet, as is common in Japan, and now available in North America, or a pitcher of water next to the toilet, as is common all over Asia. Now if you still insist on a connection between the toilet and bath, let's put a pocket door between the two rooms. (See color section.)

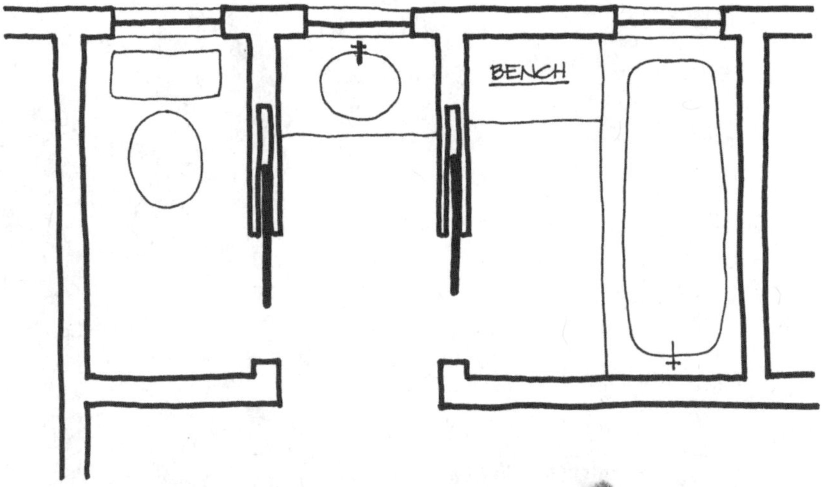

SEPARATE THE TOILET FROM THE BATH, AND DOUBLE THE USEFULNESS OF A BATHROOM. (ILLUSTRATION BY CAROL VENOLIA, ARCHITECT)

Sheila needed pleasure and relaxation more than she needed a guesthouse, so she made a single promise about the guesthouse she would build in her backyard: she'd only work on it when she could enjoy the work, when she was inspired by creativity, and not motivated by a deadline. It took her years to finish, but she stuck to her plan. Finally she stood inside and had only happy memories as she looked at each bit of her peaceful creation, covered in elaborate mosaics, hand-refinished antique cabinets, and earthen plasters made from the mud outside the door, luxuries she could afford because she had the time and a small enough space to build it herself.

THE LUXURY OF SMALL

Now that we've gotten the toilet out, and can build just one bathroom, maybe you'll spend your savings on beautiful mosaic tile work, a clawfoot tub, or an exterior door that leads to a small, sunny porch where you can dry off.

Or choose another some other fantasy to indulge. The luxury of a small house is that it leaves savings for quality, and the time to enjoy it. Since you are creating a home tailored to your being, now that you've eliminated the unnecessary, you can discover what you want around you that will mirror your soul. And if your house is very small, you are more likely to create it or remodel it yourself, with your own hands, so you'll be living with a reminder of days of self-love poured into your house.

Small-house dwellers have realized that their material needs are not separate from their social and spiritual needs. They build a happy life by making sure that the fulfillment of each kind of need supports other aspects of their being. Through conversation, prayer, journaling, meditation, reading, and other practices they survey themselves, asking questions until they've discovered how to find and fulfill the need buried below the need. Eventually, their home and their inner clarity begin to reflect each other.

PATRICIA KERNS
Main house built 1997
Guesthouse built 2000
Office built 2001
Shower house 2002

AREA:
Main house 190 sq. ft.
Guesthouse 120 sq. ft.
Office 150 sq. ft.
Shower house 60 sq. ft.

INTENDED NUMBER OF OCCUPANTS:
1–2

COST, LAND AND CONSTRUCTION:
Under $40,000

UTILITY COSTS (MONTHLY):
$10 gas, solar electric

LOCATION:
South Texas

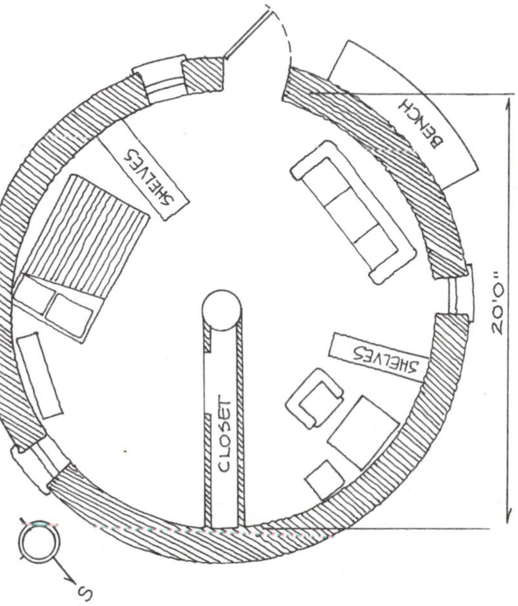

ABOVE: **PATRICIA'S FLOOR PLAN**
ABOVE RIGHT: **PATRICIA AT HOME**

The southwestern edge of Texas is as wide and

open as our Texan friends insisted it would be. As we drove through, my mind imagined how a person could dream of filling up the space with human endeavors, to soften the sun's glare and break up the unfenced waves of desert soil and tiny wildflowers. Such an attempt would be foolish: the area's precious feature is its emptiness. To fill it would diminish this great something to nothing.

Despite the open vistas and clear air, Patricia Kern's settlement appeared to jump up suddenly when we were less than a quarter mile away. We saw the guesthouse first, an adobe dome a few shades paler than the ground that it rises from. Beyond and below it, in a small, flat depression, was Patricia's open-air kitchen, shade structures, and her small round, straw-bale casita.

Patricia told her story. After almost twenty years of working in the corporate world, Patricia did what she'd dreamed of for years: she left her job, sold her house and her stuff, and moved far away. She asked herself if she'd gone crazy. As a middle-aged attorney "whose only experience with a hammer was to hang diplomas," how could she believe she could build her own house? Not hire someone to build it, but build it herself with her own hands. "I tried to get the idea out of my head," she recalls, but as she learned more, attending a workshop and volunteering at several building sites, she decided it was possible, but only if the house were very small. To make it small, she'd have to reduce her needs. She writes:

"I got some excellent advice at one of the building workshops I attended: record the amount of time spent in every area of my home for a week. I was living in an 1,100-square-foot home when I conducted this experiment. I was amazed to find that there were two rooms in my house where I rarely set foot. I realized that the primary purpose of those two rooms was to store furniture, which I had only bought so those two rooms wouldn't be so empty. This was a happy realization since all I had to do to cut my space needs in half was sell furniture!"[9]

So she held a big garage sale, gave away what was left, packed everything she wanted into a 10-by-6-foot trailer, and headed for Texas. "I'd never felt so free in my life," she recalls. By spending her first several months camping she learned more about minimalism, so that when she moved onto her newly purchased land she was ready to simplify further. She realized, for instance, that she preferred to have her kitchen and bathroom outside her home, and ten years later is still glad she made that decision.

In a few months she had a foundation and walls up. As the wind whipped around her tiny structure, even though she had no roof, she felt secure, and lucky. "I had learned to live with so little during my journey here that every addition now seems like an unaccountable luxury." The rest of the house took less than a year to finish, which is as fast as many people build larger structures, but she used almost no hired labor.

The straw-bale walls circle a central cob post, and sixteen 4-by-4-inch beams radiate out from the center to form the roof, which is covered in corrugated steel panels, enclosed with radiant barrier reflective heat wrap and further insulated with 10 inches of blown cellulose. Cloth attached to the beams forms the ceiling. A closet and two sets of shelves divide the space, acting as partial walls that point toward the center. The floor is made of cedar strips that radiate from the center. The house is used primarily for sleeping, for office work (her computer is powered by a photovoltaic system), and for catching rainwater. Since attaching gutters and connecting cisterns to her roof, she is able to catch all the water she needs.

Windows are minimal: three 1-by-2-foot openings are sufficient, since she's outside much of the day. Their size is reminiscent of houses in older desert cultures, which conserve coolness by having few or no windows. As temperatures rise to 115 degrees Fahrenheit, the inside temperature, unassisted by any mechanical device, stays below 85 degrees.

THE GUEST HOUSE IS LESS HUMBLE THAN THE MAIN CASITA.

A few years after she built her straw-bale house, Patricia tapped ancient Nubian knowledge[10] to build a second structure. With the help of Simone Swan and Jesusita Jimenez, and a workshop full of volunteers, she created a 10-by-10-foot square-walled adobe room with a domed roof. Plastered with lime outside and smooth earth inside, the space is sunlit with solid-glass "skylights" set in between the bricks of the dome, and a single, south-facing door that admits a bright column of light when open. The only furniture in the room is a large bed, covered with a thick, white comforter. The room has perfect acoustics, Patricia discovered, playing guitar in this lovely, inverted cup of a house. As is traditional in North African and Arabian culture, this beautiful work of art, less humble than the main casita, is the guesthouse.

Unable to find a good place to store the bricks left over from the dome construction, Patricia asked them to build the walls of a shower house, which she roofed with a reciprocating frame, a kind of hexagonal roof that requires no center post. A year later, in 2001, friends taught a course in cob building at her house, and built an office for her in the process. She wasn't immediately sure what she'd do with her office, but she was happy to have it.

Before the end of the year a giant national disaster prompted vast changes that specifically affected her new hometown. Previously people in Big Bend—whose town name refers to a curve in the Rio Grande—crossed the river to visit and shop in their Mexican sister city of Ojinaga, Chihuahua, and vice versa, with no visa nor passport. In the fall of 2001 border policy changed, creating a new division, separating friends and families. Patricia opened an immigration law practice, for people whose children or parents or spouses were left, paperless, on the other side of the border. "Now that I have taken care of my own needs," she says, "I have the freedom to pursue the dreams and gifts that come my way. If I were still tied down with my old house, my too-many things, and my mortgage, I'd never have this luxury."

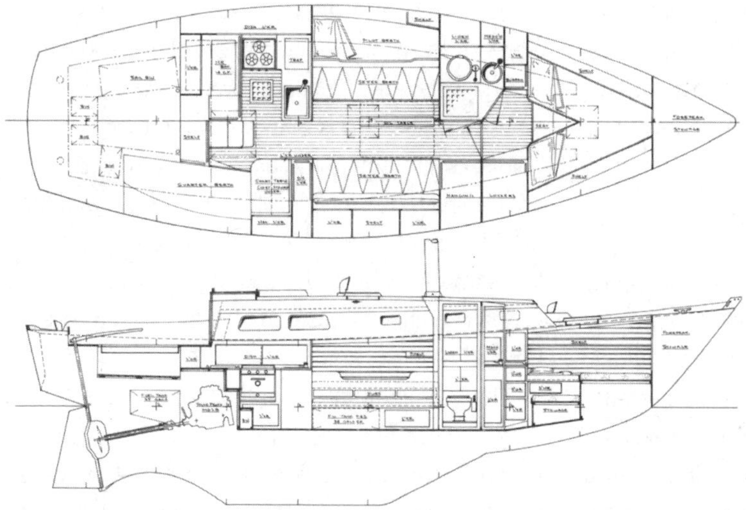

LYNN BASKIND AND JACK BRITTON
Three different boats,
built 1976, 1974, and 1983

AREA:
95–130 irregular sq. ft. of living space (boats' overall length ranged from 30–41 ft.)

INTENDED NUMBER OF OCCUPANTS:
2

PURCHASE PRICE:
$23,000 on average

DOCKING FEES:
$0

UTILITY COSTS (MONTHLY):
Solar electric free, $4 propane

ADDITIONAL (MONTHLY) COST:
$7 fuel for dinghy and for boat engine

LOCATION:
Various Caribbean islands

ABOVE: BLUEBONNET FLOOR PLAN

On January 1, 1992 Lynn Baskind and Jack Britton

stood on the dock at Seabrook Shipyard facing the Gulf of Mexico. Lynn threw her last pair of pantyhose into the water. Jack threw a big wad of keys. "We wanted to do something to mark the occasion," says Lynn. The next day they set sail on a voyage of indeterminate length, with all their possessions packed into their 30-foot fiberglass sailboat.

Lynn's path to the boat began in 1980 in Friendswood, Texas, as she stood with her children in the attic of their 3,000-square-foot house, and watched the floodwaters rise beneath them. The family lost most of their possessions, including yearbooks, baby clothes, and the only portrait ever taken of Lynn's grandfather. "I learned about what matters." One thing that did survive was Lynn's collection of a hundred dolls, which she'd begun at birth, and kept inside a china cabinet. The cabinet spent the flood rested on its back, on top of the dining room table, floating with the waters.

Lynn then spent six years developing a local chamber of commerce that lobbied for floodgates to prevent future flooding. In 1987 Lynn and her husband divorced. Lynn let her ex-husband keep their large house, and moved with her college-bound son to a town house half the size. Two years later, she stood on the dock, about to move into 95 square feet of living space.

"From a selfish standpoint, I'd say the flood that Lynn endured was the best thing that ever happened to me," says Jack. Because of that flood, Lynn had very little to get rid of, no old school books, no antique clothes. She just had the doll collection, which she took care of without any tears, giving a few dolls to her niece and the rest to charity. The flood gave her the idea that "If my stuff isn't making my life better, why do I have it?" Ultimately, the flood made her available to sail with Jack.

"All my life I'd lived in houses. Then I met a sailor, and I thought, 'He's probably right,'" Lynn explains. "I didn't spend my life dreaming about sailing, but of the few books I have from childhood, *The Wind in the Willows* is one, and the page I dog-eared was the one with the Water Rat saying, "Believe me, my young friend, there is nothing—absolutely nothing—half so much worth doing as simply messing about in boats.'"

Lynn prepared for her new life by giving away her clothes to charity, and all her kitchenware, except her gumbo pot, to her newlywed son. Jack prepared by reading every book he could find on saving money, including books by Annie Hill, a British woman who sailed with her husband and without an engine on a junk they built from plywood, living on the interest of a £20,000 note she'd left in a British account. "All these books boil down to the same message: 'Resist the urge to buy.' Once you learn how to do it, it becomes second nature." Jack and Lynn put nothing into storage, and they made a pact about pets, that if either started to crave one, "Well, we'd just pet each other."

Jack's life had taken a path parallel to Lynn's. In 1981 he was a licensed, trained, and degreed builder, and fast on his way to becoming the top roofing contractor in South Texas. Jack was driving to a job one morning when a fellow driver ran a stop sign. Five people died in the chain reaction, and Jack spent two years on crutches. He had to sell his house and his business, "which changed my life and my income completely, and led also to my divorce...and started my path toward scaling down. It seems like most people need to have it forced on them before they will change."

Now Jack and Lynn stood by the ocean, catastrophes and divorces behind them, ready to travel. Earlier that week they had unloaded all their possessions into a giant mound on the dock, one so large they couldn't see the boat past it. Jack looked at the mound and said, "It's too much." Lynn, eyeing the boxes of tools and spare parts that made up most of the cargo, replied, "Most of it's yours." Annoyed, Jack decided it was the right time to run an errand, fetching a replacement for the missing toilet seat that Lynn said she couldn't live without. While he was gone, Lynn and her friend fit every single thing into the boat, removing packaging, compacting, and logging it all in a notebook, alphabetically, since finding it again would be a chore. Lynn learned every detail of all available storage—"I could store thirty-six little tomato sauce cans in each of the galley drawers"—and she learned about a new way to measure her possessions: the waterline.

The waterline of a boat shows how deep the boat floats in water, and is marked by a change in paint color—in their case the boat's bottom was black, above which was a wide white bootstripe with blue topsides above. If no black was visible, the boat was too heavy. If the white stripe was not visible, they were in deep trouble. "We started off that day overloaded," Lynn recalls.

The pair spent fourteen years at sea. Because they preferred to moor (anchor away from shore), they paid no marina fees, and no utility fees. Because there is only one pumping station for small boats in the entire Caribbean, sewage was pumped into the ocean, ideally a few miles from the coast. They grew accustomed to their small quarters, and when they went into port and saw lawn mowers and vacuum cleaners for sale, they enjoyed reminding each other how much "we sure don't need any of that anymore."

"In a house, there's the dining room, and the office, and there's a place you sit to sew and a place to read. In the boat we have all those places, but they are the same place," Lynn explains. "We also have the deck. That outside area is what made our home spacious. The ocean is never small."

"It's hard to even talk about square footage," explains Ted Brewer, who designed their last boat, "because the walls aren't straight, and as you descend, the space narrows. That's why boats have pedestal chairs—there's no room for four legs." Berths are generally slipped in parallel to the centerline, so a body can sleep level as the boat lists side to side. The kitchen is a tight U-shaped "galley" at one side, and the "head" (toilet) is on another side, traditionally toward the "head" (the bow). After that, every nook and cranny is filled with storage, which is typically outfitted with "fiddles" (a lip across the outside of a table or shelf, or a front panel/bar across the front of a bookshelf) to hold objects in place, and locker doors latch closed. Jack discovered on the boat that if you don't put things back in their place—and every single thing has a place—they suddenly come flying at you, or fall off the deck. And even tools, the only thing Jack admits he hoards, are only worth their weight if no other tool can perform their function.

When Jack and Lynn had guests, they'd take them to haul water first, in five-gallon jugs, so they could feel the weight and know what a two-gallon sweet-water shower means. They washed dishes with a spray bottle, and brushed their teeth with saltwater. But they didn't host many guests; most of their friends opted to stay in hotels and visit them during the day. "I guess most people can't adapt to this life. A few did and really took home a good memory," says Jack, but most friends wouldn't trade comfort for adventure. In fact, Jack has noticed that he and old sailors can swap tales all night, while nonsailors "glaze over, eyes rolled back in their heads, once the stories come out. But for us, these stories are what we have."

In the first years, if a storm came and Lynn felt unprepared, she'd suddenly miss the comforts of home, but once she acquired a single-sideband radio that connected her to the Herb Hilgenberg world weather forecast, she stopped missing home and wanted fewer and fewer things. On the dock near her she saw some people follow a different pattern from hers:

“In the marina there's a kind of camaraderie and the same types you see in a neighborhood: Some people are always getting a bigger boat, but rarely sail. They soon end up moving back to a house. Other people keep their boat beautifully varnished and shiny, while people like us made sure our boat was mechanically sound, rather than making cosmetic changes, because we sailed often. For some of our 'Joneses' our first boat was the one that made theirs look good. Or, if they kind of thought they had too much, we were their guilty conscience.

People who get boats larger than they can manage don't understand the cost of maintenance. For some people it's status. The racing boats are long—60–80 feet—for speed, but some people want a racing-style boat even though they never race.

"Then there's the subset of folk heroes, men and women who are revered. They have very small boats. They've had the philosophical and physical stamina to go around the world, say, in a 28-foot, sometimes a 22-foot boat—like a Bristol Channel Cutter.

"When we got our 41-footer, I had a hard time hauling the mainsail up by myself. On the 30-footer it was no problem. As I was moving that sail, I realized that if something happened to Jack, I'd be in trouble. We needed a smaller boat. We went from a 41-foot boat to the 37-foot *Bluebonnet*—really 35 feet in terms of functional living space because the boat has a 3-foot bowsprit. Coming onto the dock we looked like clowns coming out of a clown car, because our boat was small, and we are big—almost 400 pounds between the two of us. But it was roomy down below. Very good design.”

In 2003 Jack and Lynn came home to be closer to their mothers. They bought a 1973 vintage Airstream trailer, and sold their boat. They liked the instant community Airstream owners form, similar to the one they found on the marina.

Curiously, although Lynn now works as a real estate agent, and Jack fixes up run-down houses and sells them at a profit, they don't live in a house. Instead, they buy a house and park the Airstream in the back, which is good for tax purposes, and means that they don't have to endure the chaos of remodeling. "When we sell a house, we move the trailer, and our lifestyle doesn't change," says Lynn. The trailer also means that Lynn cannot inherit her mother's furniture.

“My mother spent her life at home and kept beautiful furniture, which she inherited from her mother. She was a curator of museum-quality furniture. I was the only girl with all brothers, and I refuse to become the next family archivist. There's guilt about selling it, but we can't get the grandchildren to take it. My father's mother was different. She was a lawyer. She used furniture, but she wasn't interested in it.”

After life on the boat, any house over a thousand square feet seems huge to Jack and Lynn. Jack's own sister "just bought 3,000 square feet and seventeen acres twelve miles from a loaf of bread. She says herself they don't know why—it's just two of them." He wonders if such purchases stem from a lack of imagination. When people talk to him about their dream of sailing, he advises them, "Imagination is all you need. We weren't anything special. We just had imagination.

AN ALCOVE SET INSIDE A THICK WALL, LOOKING OUT ON A WIDER SPACE

3

Build a Glove, Not a Warehouse

Reply of Senses to Intellect: Miserable mind, you get your evidence from us, and do you try to overthrow us? —DEMOCRITUS OF ABDÊRA

A WEDDING DRESS OR TUXEDO IS A PLEASURE FOR AN EVENING, but few of us want to live in a costume. So why are so many new houses filled with gimmicks such as whirlpools, and multiple fireplaces, that don't fit the actual activities of their owners?

Most designs are drawn from the head, and not from the body. The head schemes for status or intrigue, or conformity. It plans a house that fits into a neighborhood, a dream of a distant place, or is made to hold already-bought furniture. The body has no choice, and is dragged along by the head.

Conventionally, interior decorators are restricted by earlier decisions made by an architect. The architect works within the confines of the urban planning and zoning department, and the developer. The urban planner may answer to politicians, who, in places where construction is a major industry, are often indebted to the developer. The developer is also indebted, to the bank. The bank says your home is an investment, not a location. The bank makes rules—"2,500 square feet minimum," "three bathrooms minimum"—for their investment. Your house may have been defined by an outside rule before your own dream was born. Do you want to live in a house designed by a bank? Or would you rather reverse this process? Consider designing or remodeling your home from the inside out.

Hear, Taste, Smell, Touch

Reenter your body and use every hole in your head to notice what you do during the day. Watch where your body tries to lead you. Contrary to Puritan fears, your body probably doesn't beg to indulge in crime or even excess.[1] You may notice that you are drawn to light, warmth, or something soft. Probably you will find that there are parts of your house that are used only by dust mites—below the bed, above the fridge, the corners. Notice what pleases or intrigues you, and dream of new functions for ignored spaces.

You might notice that there are just two or three places at home where you spend all your time. Where do you like to be? Do

In a Palestinian village I visited a four-generation family who shared a central, busy living room. The stone house was built against a hill, and in one wall of the living room a small cave had been carved out, into the hill, at waist height, 4 feet high and about the width of a king-sized bed. The great-grandmother spent the night and most of the day inside this nook. She participated in the conversation and watched as the children played, and as the adults made business deals, and processed the harvest. When she wanted to rest, she rolled back away from the room, out of sight, into the cave.

In a California bookstore there's a narrow stairway leading up to a cubby-loft, with a door too small to allow adults passage. Pillows and a tiny window, and picture books, fill the space. Its coziness has an appropriate quieting effect on the children who visit it while their parents shop.

On a mesa in New Mexico, Carole Crews built an adobe dome, a single round room for herself and her daughters. She added a small, square kitchen to one end. They all slept together in the dome at first; then, when she added a bedroom for herself, she did just that: she built a room just large enough for a bed, with storage underneath, two windows to the outside, built-in bookcases, and a small shelf for candles. Carole remembers, "At first, as I was building, I made the bed just long enough for me—about five and a half feet. Then I thought, 'You never know,' so I added on an extra foot of length."

you follow the sun's path? Do you stay late in bed in the morning? Do you read in the bath? Where do you like to eat? Where do your friends congregate? Where do your children play? Develop your own design sensibility by becoming sensitive to how your body and spirit resonate in the spaces you experience.

THINK 3D AND 4D

Get beyond two dimensions. No set of floor plans, drawing, model, or book (including this one) is going to significantly improve your ability to understand space and plan accordingly. Ideas on paper or miniature models can help us plan, but don't let them limit you to just one of your many fine senses. Often floor plans are drawn far from the building site, sometimes by people who never see the finished structure. They take a bird's-eye view, and reduce your home to a few thin sheets of paper. You can do better. You have what it takes to design well.

Go out and start noticing the space around you, both as it exists at a given moment, and over time. Wide awake, notice every space inside a space—the hallways, the front stoop, the corners, the distance between chairs, and the space above a shelf. Notice how the light moves, over the course of a day, and a year. Where does the sun warm you in winter, and where does it bake you in summer? What blocks sunlight from your house? Notice how spaces change in the course of a day, and a year. Imagine yourself as a young child (on your knees) or an elderly grandparent (in a wheelchair) inside the space.

When you've come back from your research in the world, to find out what other people find pleasing in their small homes, read on.

DETAIL AND PATTERN

Below are some of the details and design patterns that we noticed in the small homes we visited, as well as some of the home dwellers' thoughts about why those details and designs work so well. Note that these aren't guidelines; you will have to choose those for yourself. These are ideas. And in some cases, what one home dweller insists makes his home work so well is almost opposite to a design another person loves. You'll have to go figure for yourself.

Alcoves. Almost everyone has a use for an alcove, and its cousin, the small loft. A bay window seat for reading, a sleeping nook for a child or guest, a desk set into a thick wall or between closets, all provide space that in some ways is better than a full room.

Alcoves make any house spacious—that is, filled with spaces—without increasing its footprint.

Levels. Varying the level, both in floors and ceilings, allows activities and view to be separated vertically and reduces the need for horizontal space. Lofts that have a desk, a couch, or storage beneath them are a dramatic example, and even a 4-inch step down, or a ceiling raised 8 inches, can give the feeling of "separate activity" without building another wall.

Ceiling shape and height. High ceilings are one way to add space without much construction expense, if the wall material is not expensive. Since heat rises away from the people below, high ceilings aid cooling, and hamper heating. One current fashion in new developments is a high, "cathedral" ceiling under a thin roof, which reduces the potential for insulation, increases heating costs, and eliminates attic storage. A room that is much taller than it is wide has an unsettling effect on some people.

Almost everyone likes a domed or gently vaulted ceiling. In new construction, one way to achieve this is to use a naturally curved pole as a ridge beam, and let the rafters run long (since the distance from ridge to wall will now vary), trimming them before roofing. Some people dislike a high-pitched, "apex" ceiling that comes to a high point in the center; others dislike a ceiling that slopes in one direction like a shed. Almost no one likes a concave ceiling, although fabric billowing down from the ceiling like a tent can be pleasant. Ianto Evans (see profile, this chapter) insists, "The eye, from the center of the room, registers a flat ceiling as concave, since the center seems closer than the sides, and the inhabitant feels pressed down upon," but most people tolerate or even like flat ceilings.

VARYING THE LEVEL, BOTH IN FLOORS AND CEILINGS, ALLOWS ACTIVITIES AND VIEW TO BE SEPARATED VERTICALLY AND REDUCES THE NEED FOR HORIZONTAL SPACE.

A CLOTH "DOOR" ELIMINATES THE NEED FOR SWING SPACE.

Some decorate very low flat ceilings with reed matting, or fabric, to make the thought of brushing against them more pleasant. This is also a simple way to hide added insulation and soundproofing materials to any ceiling.

Floor life. Some North American small-home dwellers imitate Asian cultures, drop their lifestyle a few feet to the floor, and eat, play, sleep, and relax on carpets or mats. They cite "good exercise for the knees," "easier for children," "good for posture because it's simple to lie down or shift positions," and "the ceiling feels so high now" as reasons. Indeed, if you live closer to your floor, your ceiling and windows will seem higher. Radiant floor heating (heated water run through pipes in or under the floor), can make floor life cozy in winter. Or you can raise a floor in one room a few feet, leaving enormous space for storage—or heating—underneath, and use the room without furniture, and always seated. If you install Japanese *tatami* (padded rice straw mats), a soft and comfortable flooring, and keep your shoes off in that certain room, you'll create a very restful, playful space.

Doors. Exterior doors that swing out conserve indoor space and are especially suited to mild climates, since they are more difficult to weatherproof. Inside, pocket and other sliding doors and curtains make space available that would otherwise be used for the swing of the door. Interior "pocket" doors may slip into an adjacent wall, fold up like an accordion, or may be a simple curtain or heavier "blanket door," which requires no swing space, and can insulate fairly well if velcro strips or hooks are mounted around the door frame so the fabric seals the space.

Doors should be placed carefully, since the foot traffic they bring can create a "hall" that cuts down a small space unintentionally, and doors allow heat out in winter; some small housers insist that any house that needs more than one door is already too big. Extra exterior doors make it easier for the house to grow later, and best of all, they entice dwellers to enjoy the big world outside. Sliding glass patio doors, French doors, and Dutch doors in particular can make a room feel like a porch, increasing the connection to the outdoors, but minimizing the storage space on the wall.

Windows. Orienting windows toward a vast view, or even a moderate, walled garden, balances the snugness of a small space. Glazing that descends to floor level brings the outdoors in, and makes it possible for a small child to play outside and still keep an eye on a parent working indoors. Windows indoors, glazed or unglazed, widen space as they connect it. An outdoor window that looks through an indoor opening to a window on the opposite wall can have a magical effect, sometimes evoking the possibility of traveling through the looking glass to something new. Clerestories, "dormers" and operable skylights a.k.a. "roof windows," expand the space without expanding the footprint, and offer a summertime hot air vent.

High windows allow privacy, admit light without much heat, and leave space on the wall below them for shelves or furniture. Small bathrooms and kitchens sometimes have a full wall of glass blocks. Resist the urge to live in a fishbowl, and keep an area free from the glare of sunlight, maybe placing just one tiny "Zen" window aimed specifically at a small view you'd like to see often.

Wheelchair accessibility. Dimensioning for wheelchair access, which might involve just widening a few passageways, is cited by a few small-home dwellers as a reason their home "doesn't feel the least bit cramped." Excellent small homes are planned for the inevitable day when someone will want to bring a wheelchair through their doors.

Wall texture. What is beautiful in a church or tavern (e.g., rough-cut, unsanded posts, or sharp rocks) can be painful in a small house. If your walls aren't covered in shelves or other furniture, they should be finished with something durable and pleasant to touch. In a cold climate, the best wall materials either store heat (e.g., an earthen plaster that gains heat from a southern window) or don't feel cold to the touch (e.g., a woven wall hanging).

Wall color. People believe that light colors make a small space seem bigger. It's probably more complex than that. Painting adjoining walls two different, contrasting colors can have the effect of "loosening the corners," which may appear spacious. Continuing a wall or floor finish through two spaces, especially to the outside (for example, a stone floor that continues under a glass door outside to a landing), suggests that the living space goes on indefinitely, melding into nature.

Wainscoting (two contrasting wall colors or finishes, one above

OUTDOOR STORAGE IS AS SIMPLE AS A BENCH NEAR THE DOOR.

SIT WITH YOUR FRIENDS COMFORTABLY, AND SEE HOW MUCH SPACE YOU LIKE TO HAVE BETWEEN YOU. THIS NOOK HAS A 6-FOOT DIAMETER.

the other) can make a room seem taller, and allows you to treat the lower, touched portion with a durable washable finish. But first ask yourself, why are you trying to make a room seem taller or wider? Is its size not right?

THICK WALLS ALLOW FOR A "COOL BOX" INSIDE THEM.

Choose colors you like, and love your home.

Wall thickness. Thick walls provide the possibility to live literally inside them. Alcoves, niches, and storage areas can be carved into a thick wall, and will hold dishes, benches, and shrines. Even a standard 2-by-6-inch wood-framed wall can be made to hold books. Thin walls, framed, or, more simply, screens used to partition areas maximize floor space. Furniture can be placed to create separate rooms, eliminating the need for walls at all.

Kitchen. The kitchen may be where the guests congregate, but if you actually cook, consider designing it as super-efficient work space. Expensive cabinetry, especially if it's deep (with items hidden behind others), is not as effective as shelves, hooks, pegboards, and crocks. As Julia Child said, "Tools should be out where you can see them." Why move them twice—from dish drainer to drawer? Build shelves that are dish drainers, and cut that work, and space, in half.

Plan your kitchen like you plan the whole house. Arrange the things you use every day around you, and imagine how you could best use them. Sitting or standing? Alone or with a partner or two? With visitors at a table near you, at a bar, or kept at a distance, in a separate room? Will the kitchen also be a hallway, that can be crossed to reach another area or will it be an "end-space" kitchen, used only for cooking, with no passage, a place of focus, and not of multitasking.

Determine how much counter space you really need, and consider an old-fashioned pull-out cutting board. Will you store all your food within easy reach, or away in a pantry? The "three-step" kitchen, where no cooking action takes more than three steps, is a common goal. Consider also the two-step, one-step, and no-step, pivot kitchen. Consider whether the steps you take should be up a stool to high storage, in cabinets, or hung from baskets, as Laurel does in her kitchen (see Chapter 11). Why do people like their very small kitchens? "Nothing is far from the stove," "No room to be messy," and "I like to cook alone. It's my time to be focused."

Indianapolis socialites Shannon and Michael Brown-Callahan weren't sure how their new house, which has no single large room, would work for parties. The small rooms turned out to have the effect of drawing people together. To their surprise, the most popular spot is the loft above the living room. The ceiling height allows only sitting and lounging, and guests like to crowd together to enjoy the close company.

Storage. Efficient interior storage complements the design. Closets maximize corner space that would otherwise be wasted, and storage is nestled under beds, floors, alcoves, eaves, and coffee tables. Storage hangs from the ceiling, or emerges magically from inside a wall, or it might be exposed: a pegboard with hooks or a dozen Shaker dowels on the wall. A simple shelf all around and a foot below the ceiling provides long-term book storage, and may make the ceiling appear higher, or slightly domed. Look around any room, and you may notice spaces that could be

SHANNON AND MICHAEL'S SMALL ROOMS HAVE THE EFFECT OF DRAWING PEOPLE TOGETHER.

LINDA SMILEY BUILDS A MODEL USING COB, A MIXTURE OF EARTH AND STRAW THAT IS USUALLY HAND-SCULPTED.

enhanced by shelves. Ideally, some of your storage space will be outside, where you won't need to spend resources heating and cooling it.

Have you heard that stuff expands to fill the space provided? The reverse is also true: stuff can contract once space is limited. Some small-house dwellers simply decide how much storage for various types of items they will have, and then pare down until it fits. It's amazing how much can fit in a closet once it's reorganized.

Genkan. It may seem absurd in a tiny space to find a place for an entrance hall, but most small-home dwellers (perhaps because they want a clean house without cleaning) have a place, either just inside or just outside the front door, for hanging coats, removing shoes, and resting groceries. Something as simple as a hat rack, or a bench with shoe storage inside can create a tiny bridge between in and out, one that catches mud from shoes, and holds objects that are ready to move on to another location.

Built-in and movable furniture. The jury is still out on built-in versus movable furniture. The built-ins argue that once the optimum space for an object has been found, there's no need to move it. The movables say, "Everything changes."

It seems wise to have some movable furniture—at least chairs—for company. But if you can find a way to make a corner of a room useful, consider making it permanent. If you do it right, built-in cabinetry will be easier to clean than something movable. Before you build it in, make sure it will be easy to clean, and comfortable. Plenty of built-in benches are lonely and unused. Experiment with temporary setups to find out what works best in the space before committing to a permanent built-in.

Some small dwellings change significantly with the seasons. The movables in particular want a house that changes over time. They store and display decoration seasonally: a vase for flowers in summer replaced by a marble carving in winter. Holidays are an event, requiring complete—but temporary and inexpensive—redecoration. This movement inside the house provokes a sense of widening space.

Woodstoves and fireplaces. Stoves and fireplaces are tricky in a small space. You may prevent small children from burning themselves by welding a guard around a woodstove. An otherwise useless corner might be the best place for a fireplace even if it's against an exterior wall (and thus heats outside air). One solution is to feed the stove outside and let the back of the stove and the flue run through the house. Another is to coat the whole stove and its flue in cob, and turn it into a heated bench.

Fireplaces and woodstoves are typically kept away from bedrooms; otherwise, you may breathe in particles, get ash in your bed, and compete for oxygen whenever the fire is burning. An exception is when the flue of the stove is run under the bed, through a high-mass material such as cob or stone, so that the sleeper can benefit from the warmth.

Living room. A 15-by-16-foot living room (240 square feet) is not considered large, but consider this: "The upper range for full casual voice is about 8 feet. A person with 20/20 vision can see details of facial expression up to 12 feet. People 8 to 9 feet apart can pass an object if they both stretch."[2] (Maybe this is why groups of more than seven or eight seem large to many people. If seven people of moderate girth sit in a circle, with about 2 feet between each person, the diameter of the circle will be about 9 feet.) So why are the walls in new living rooms 15 feet apart? Sit with your friends comfortably, and see how much space you like to have between you.

Open plan or separate rooms? Open floor plans that minimize division are currently popular, but consider your actual life before you accept one. Do you live with a light sleeper? Does someone in your family enjoy music that no one else does? Visit some older bungalows that have several small rooms before you decide.

Since needs and residents change over time, some houses, including the Grow Home (profiled in this chapter), are designed so that most or all interior walls can be moved without affecting the roof. In any structure a minimum of walls that are load-bearing makes it easier to remove walls, reshaping rooms to fit the current reality.

THE WHOLE

House shape. Round houses are best for people who don't want (much) divided space. Nonrectangular buildings are best made from nonstraight material (stone, adobe, or cob, or even straw-bale or logs). Cob advocates, who hand-sculpt their homes, fitting the walls to their body and activities as they build, say that cob is the most likely material to create a body-shaped building.

If you build near existing homes, you will probably build straight, or basically straight, walls with right angles. And if you use milled lumber and/or industrial building materials (tin roofing, plywood, drywall), you'll certainly want to build a box, or some variation of a box.

Boxes work fine for most people. A square box has a smaller perimeter than a rectangular box with the same floor space, and therefore may reduce heating costs. A long, skinny box with windows oriented south (in the northern hemisphere) allows light and solar gain into most rooms. An L-, U-, or doughnut-shaped box, or a collection of small structures, creates protected outdoor areas.

Models, made to scale, out of mud or cardboard, or whatever best mimics the building materials you plan to use, can be easier to understand than drawings, and may help you see pitfalls in your plan sooner.

Setting. If you are building on a street where the houses are giant, you may feel strange to have a dwarfed façade. One architect solved this by building a tall, wide façade on a house that was actually quite shallow. Conversely, if you are building in an old neighborhood of bungalows, building two stories may make your neighbors hostile. In the forest, you might build tall, as you search for light and solar gain. On a prairie you might bury your house in a hillside, and maintain the flow of scenery.

The setting is crucial to any successful home. Siting the house is normally an irrevocable decision, so take time before you break ground to pick the optimum setting. Remind yourself of the proverb, attributed to the Chinese, "When a man finishes his house, he dies." Take your time getting started.

Slow down. Camp, in a tent or a trailer, at the site where you intend to build. Or rent in the area and meet your neighbors before you move in. In an urban setting, even a few nights will help you understand what the neighborhood patterns are. Ideally, you will rent or camp for a full year or more. Direct experience with the changing seasons and sun's trajectory will make it easy to build a home that is well oriented. You will know where the sun sets in December, and in June, where the coldest winds blow, and where the ground seasonally softens from an underground spring. The camping year will help you understand your real needs.[3]

The Boyer-Young family camped for a few months on land they owned in coastal Maine, where they intended to build a summer home. They fell in love with the land that first summer. The children spent all day outdoors. The family grew to understand that sewer lines, a septic tank, and the foundation itself would inevitably destroy a part of nature they had grown to cherish. They resolved to always tent, instead.

LA CHANCE-VEZINA FAMILIES
Built 1997

AREA:
2,880 sq. ft., spread between two houses

INTENDED NUMBER OF OCCUPANTS:
8–9

COST:
$152,000 (Canadian dollars) for two houses

UTILITY COSTS (MONTHLY):
$80 per house;
plus $120 for heating in winter

LOCATION:
Montréal, Québec

Currently, "architect-designed" is synonymous

with "don't ask how much it cost." Can architecture be used to design better houses for average people? Yes, insisted Professor Avi Friedman and his colleague, Witold Rybczynski, and they marshaled the resources of McGill University architecture school to produce an adaptable, affordable model house.

Students and professors surveyed prospective buyers to find out what they wanted, and what they would be willing to give up. They looked at historical and international examples of popular models, and they studied the construction industry to find out what keeps housing costs high, and what builders needed to make their product affordable.

The result was the "Grow Home," a row house that derives its low cost mainly from three areas. Its narrow façade allows three homes to be built on a single conventional (60-by-100-foot) urban lot, which reduces land costs, and all service (sewer, electric, water, etc.) costs, while shrinking but not sacrificing the beloved backyard. Its dimensions

ABOVE: **AVI FRIEDMAN AND WITOLD RYBCZYNSKI AND THE PROTOTYPE GROW HOME**

ABOVE LEFT: **GEOFFREY BARDEN AND FRED MOREAU SEE THE UNFINISHED INTERIORS OF THE GROW HOME AS A BLANK CANVAS.** ABOVE RIGHT: **A KIND OF BED NOOK**

are based on standard, easily available sizes, so builders cut and waste less material. And its basic duplicability makes it easy for contractors to predict their labor costs and needs, resulting in fewer headaches for everyone involved.

The most popular aspect of the Grow Home is price. At about $45 per square foot in 2002, most Grow Homes are sold prior to construction, which is a comfort to builders, who conceivably could charge more, but prefer the quick sales.

The Grow Home was not designed primarily with energy efficiency in mind, but is economical to heat because it shares walls and is multistoried. If oriented properly and insulated as recommended by the McGill plan, it tends to need about 35 percent less heating than a typical Montréal home. It fits easily into small inner-city lots, making Grow Home dwellers more likely to walk or use public transportation.

Home dwellers like the house because, since its load-bearing walls are exclusively on the perimeter, they have freedom to design and change their floor plan, placing interior walls where and when they see fit. Normally, the house is sold partially unfinished, and the occupants add interior walls, and finish second floors, attics, and/or basements as they like, as finances allow.

The typical Grow Home buyer is a young couple. They may choose to build or install the kitchen cabinetry themselves, at considerable savings. They start by living on one floor, and leave the second floor empty and unheated, until they have a child old enough to require a second bedroom. At that point they can divide the second floor into two or three rooms. Later they may finish the attic into teenager territory, or, in old age, retire to the basement apartment and rent out the rest of the house for income. The house through its life continues to develop inside, without adding on.

Grow Home dwellers such as Jacques and Carole Fournier take advantage of the Grow Home's flexibility to turn one floor into a home office (more on the Fourniers in Chapter 7). And some, such as Geoffrey Barden and Fred Moreau, two Parisians who celebrated the millennium by moving to

KEEPING THE LOAD-BEARING WALLS ON THE PERIMETER MEANS THAT INTERIOR WALLS CAN BE MOVED TO ACCOMMODATE DIFFERENT NEEDS OVER TIME. THE GRANDPARENTS GAVE THEIR THIRD FLOOR AND MOST OF THEIR BASEMENT TO THEIR CHILDREN. EACH UNIT IS 16 X 40 ON THE GROUND FLOOR.

Montréal, see the unfinished interiors as a kind of blank canvas for imagination.

M. Moreau, a fourth-generation painter who specializes in reproductions of masterpieces, explains, "There's something inside me that pushes me, compels me to create a sense of Louis XIV wherever I go. Now, we don't have the money to buy a castle, but this works just fine." The couple bought the house unfinished, then splurged on wooden molding, oak floors stained a majestic mahogany, and a four-post bed enclosed in a velvet curtain. The walls are graced with murals: a garden scene in the bathroom, a life-sized portrait of the king himself on the stairs. They are pleased that their house happens to be located on Rue Versailles, near the antique shops.

Grow Home owners Nicole Vezina and Rabéa Khemece, who have been friends for twenty years, didn't really want to leave their government-sponsored cooperative apartment complex where they were neighbors. "Decisions there were made democratically. If we needed to fix the roof, for example, we would vote to raise the rent. It wasn't one landlord's decision. We all knew why," Rabéa explains. They both appreciated the clustered apartments that allowed a giant open green space where their families could find a corner to picnic, far away from anyone else.

But when her fourth daughter turned two, Nicole and her family wanted a third bedroom, which was something the apartment complex could not offer. They looked for similar opportunities for

THREE GENERATIONS OF THE LA CHANCE-VEZINA FAMILY AND RABÉA KHEMECE.

neighborliness and sharing. The Sable Grow Home development, at the east end of the Montréal metro line suited them well. So well, in fact, that Nicole and her husband and four daughters joined forces with Nicole's parents to buy two adjacent Grow Homes. The Khemece family chose a third one, across the street.

The entire first floor of each home is common area: a large living room and a kitchen with a table large enough for children to spread out homework. "It is important that the entire common family area be close together," says Nicole, a professor of ergonomics at the University of Québec. "The kitchen is distinct from the living/dining room, but close enough so that a parent can cook"—Nicole was grilling fillet of sole as she spoke—"and still know what is going on in the living room" (which on this particular day included a showing of a hundred pounds of quartz the children had recently gathered on a hike). The long, outside walls of the duplex feature narrow, tall bay windows that are glazed and framed out from the wall at an angle that allows a glimpse of the street and not of the neighbors.

In Nicole's house, the kitchen's back wall is mainly glass and looks out on the joined backyards, green in summer and large enough for a small, above-ground swimming pool. In winter they flood their yard with a garden hose, the water freezes, and the children skate on the lawn.

The second floor holds two bedrooms, one for the parents, and another shared by the youngest daughters, stuffed with art projects and toys and equipped with a triplex bunk bed for Rabéa's daughter when she visits. The large bathroom offers the Grow Home standard, a separate shower and bath.

The third floor of Nicole's house is twice the size of the second floor, because it includes the top floor of her mother's house. Nicole's mother explains, "I was one of eleven children. I would feel strange having empty rooms in my house." So she gave her third floor to her daughter. The Vezina–La Chance family punched a door through the 16-inch concrete firewall, and closed off the staircase on the Vezina grandparents' side. Now the two older girls share a giant bedroom and each has a her own large bay window. The third floor also holds Nicole's home office, which is slowly being taken over by Nicole's eldest daughter, a prolific painter, whose bright creations cover every square inch of floor and wall space on that floor.

The house was designed without a mudroom. Like most Québécois, even in snowy winter, the family parks on the street. By cutting a human-sized door into the garage door they created a winter entrance where they can leave their shoes and coats before climbing the interior stairs to the first floor. The rest of the precious basement garage space is used for guests, laundry, watching television, and storage. The La Chance family punched another door through the 16 inches of concrete firewall and has taken over about three-quarters of both houses' basements. The children use this "secret" underground passageway to escape to their grandparents' house, for overeating and other forms of special attention.

Avi Friedman and his students continue charting the evolution of their design. The newest model, called the "Next Home," makes it easier to expand horizontally as well as internally, allowing home buyers to buy floors and rooms of a multifamily building, combining them into the home they presently need. Later, they may rent or sell to neighbors portions of their house as their needs change. In 1990 the first Grow Home was built. Today there are over 10,000 in Canada.

"How large is this house?!

How many SQUARE feet?!" Ianto's voice trembles in mock disbelief as he repeats my question, and then continues, "What do you guess?" People guess 300, 500 square feet, but how are you going to measure? From where are you going to measure? The inside of the walls? The outside? This isn't a box, so you can't measure it as a box."

"Well, if you superimposed circles on it...," I start to interject. "There isn't a Cartesian form in it," he insists. "You see, this is the whole issue of Natural Building: the old rules don't count, the numbers don't count. It all has to do with feelings, attitude, spirit. Things that you can't quantify." He pauses for breath, and finally gives in: "We tried to fit this building in on less than 130 round feet."

In 1989 Ianto Evans and Linda Smiley began living in their first "cob cottage." In 1993, they joined Michael Smith to found the Cob Cottage Company. That same year, Ianto and Linda began work on their current residence, the "Heart House," a small cottage that contains spaces for cooking, dining, "desking," sleeping, and entertaining a few guests, arranged in a heart-shaped floor plan. This surprising structure is much more spacious than measuring tapes would lead one to believe. Maybe that's because it is literally spacious: a tiny home filled with many little spaces.

LINDA SMILEY AND IANTO EVANS
Built 1993–95

AREA:
130 "round" sq. ft. downstairs; 50 sq. ft. upstairs

INTENDED NUMBER OF OCCUPANTS:
2 adults

COST:
$500 construction materials, trade for land rent

UTILITY COSTS (MONTHLY):
Less than $20; about 1 cord of wood per year for heating

LOCATION:
Oregon

ABOVE: THE HEART HOUSE KITCHEN IS DESIGNED SO THE COOK NEVER NEEDS TO DO MORE THAN TURN.

THE KITCHEN FORMS ONE HALF OF THE HEART SHAPE, WHILE THE SNUG CREATES THE OTHER HALF.

When Ianto first began designing cob cottages, he thought he had become a brilliant designer. Then he saw that everyone else who was designing with cob had equally brilliant designs. He's decided now that it is the medium itself that leads the builder to good design, because it's free-form, wet, and is slowly hand-sculpted as the builder works. "You could do it with any material, but cob begs to become a house that fits like a glove, not like a box." That's his first principle of small-house design: "Build gloves, not boxes. Wrap the space around the actions of your body, rather than building a neutral space and trying to fill it." Each space in this tiny house fits the body. Nothing is wasted. The kitchen, designed so the cook never needs to do more than turn, is a good example.

THE FLUE OF THE WOODSTOVE RUNS INSIDE THE COB BENCH.

A house that fits like a glove has no rectilinear spaces, and thus no square feet. "I'm fascinated by the psychology of round feet. I'm not sure why, but it appears round feet are about twice the size of square feet," Ianto claims. This is the second principle: "The bottom line is, curved walls make buildings seem bigger: sine curves, spirals, platoids. The trick is to turn off your conscious mind and let your intuition take over, even as you lay the foundation."

Ianto's third principle is contrary to some modern architectural teaching: To use a small space well, divide it up. Use half walls, a change in flooring; use edges and shelves, things that divide without closing off. Linda points out in their house: "You enter under a high ceiling, but then step down into a low sitting area here, or climb the ladder to sleep or write—two separate activities which themselves are at two different levels. Just having this tiny partition which separates the kitchen from the telephone, for instance, makes all the difference."

Linda calls each of these spaces an *embracing space*. "In the kitchen we embrace kitchen activities.

The kitchen forms one half of the heart shape, while the 'snug' (their name for the curved sitting area) creates the other half of the heart. It embraces us. The same form is echoed upstairs. That way we live in a nest, a soft container."

Because the house is so intimate and close, they used soft finishes. A rough plaster can be beautiful in a large public space, but here everything you touch is smooth: no rough 6-by-6 beams, nothing sharp to bump into. Everything is rounded and soft. Ianto prefers low ceilings in a small space, and short doors, saying, "As you come into a small space you register it in proportion to what you just went through. The shorter you can make the door, the bigger the space seems, because you squeeze through, like coming out of the neck of a bottle." He adds, "The largest U.S. door manufacturer is based in Portland. They just made it illegal to install public doors shorter than 6 feet 8 inches. We purposely cut ours down." Ianto adds, "Never put two doors into a small house. It changes a 'being-in' space into a 'going-through' space, which will never be a peaceful place to rest."

One special feature is the cool box, set into the wall of the kitchen. It uses the cool air of the Oregon night, and the cold stored in the thermal mass of the walls, to keep yogurt, cheese, and leftovers moderately cool. A simple screen on the exterior keeps the animals out. Thick cob walls lend themselves to shelves, nooks, and generous window seats.

Builders of small, wood-heated homes run into the problem of how to place the stove so that people won't bump into it. The Heart House solves this problem by having a down-draft "rocket stove," made of two steel barrels—one for the firebox and one for the heat exchanger—buried along with its long flue, in the built-in cob bench. A fire is built in the firebox, the exhaust gases recombust in the second chamber, and then the exhaust passes through the flue in the cob bench, leaving all its warmth in the house before it exits. The exhaust coming out of the chimney is almost cool; the heat stays inside the house. The stove heats the house so efficiently, they haven't made any effort to cover their windows properly. "With a small space, you can get away with a lot less efficiency," says Linda.

Windows are plentiful, and the south wall is mainly glass. "Light is important here in Oregon," Linda explains. "Without this glass it would feel very enclosed and small. We are always able to see the outdoor room, so the courtyard becomes part of the house. We watch the outside, see the rain, or a snake that passes by. The scene is always interesting, changing. And we watch it from our snug, little house."

EPILOGUE:

Linda and Ianto lived primarily in the Heart House for about ten years, and then in 2005 moved to a nearby area where their colleagues and students have begun constructing a small village of tiny cob cottages.

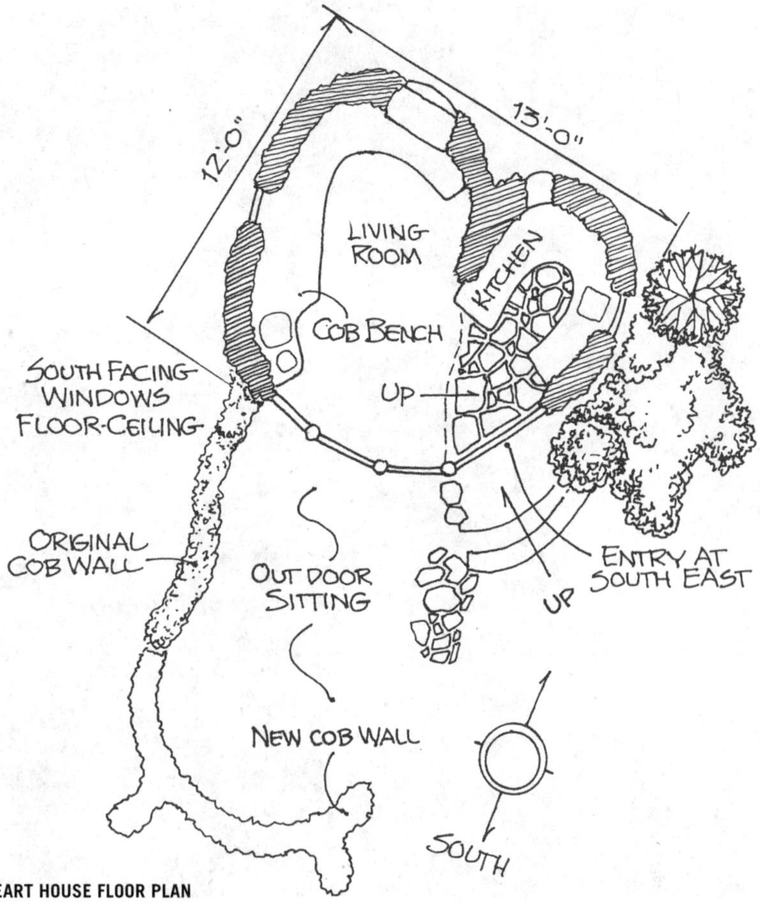

HEART HOUSE FLOOR PLAN

KIRSTEN JACOBSEN PLASTERING HER EARTHSHIP

4
Pay Off Your Debts

Let us clarify the difference between money and wealth.—HAZEL HENDERSON

IMAGINE COMING HOME TO A PLACE THAT'S REALLY YOURS. A place you can stay for as long as you want. You can relax. There is no possibility it will be taken from you. You really do own it.

Can such a place exist? No location is guaranteed, but as long as you own a mortgaged house, one thing's for sure: what you own is the mortgage, not the house. That is, you own the right to inhabit, maintain, and pay taxes on what is fundamentally bank property, while paying a monthly sum close to or exceeding the rental value, for fifteen or twenty-five or sometimes even forty years. Mortgages are so consistently accepted as unavoidable that most of us, if we are lucky enough to qualify for one, confuse having a mortgage with owning a house.

A surprisingly large number of small-house dwellers, of all ages, have chosen another path. Many of them pay no mortgage on their home, and the amount they spend on housing is very low. Why are houses so expensive? And how have a small but steady number of families and individuals bucked the trend, turning their mortgage from a "death note" into a memory?

THE DEATH NOTE

"Mortgage" (from Old French, "mort" and "gage") literally translates as "death pledge," so perhaps it makes sense that many of us pay it for so long. In the past, human lenders sometimes placed a clause on a mortgage, that if the lender died, the mortgage would be forgiven. Modern banks, alas, don't die, but are instead sold, so a bank-held mortgage is never suddenly forgiven.

Sixty years ago, a large majority of homeowners owned their house free and clear. In 1929, six months before the famous stock market crash, *Better Homes and Gardens* advised readers not to take out more than a five-year mortgage, warning them of "rascals who like to sell people houses they can't afford, then deprive them of them when they can't meet the payments."[1]

Today, a minority of North Americans own their house outright,[2] most because they have worked a whole lifetime, or have inherited their house or other wealth that enabled them to buy.

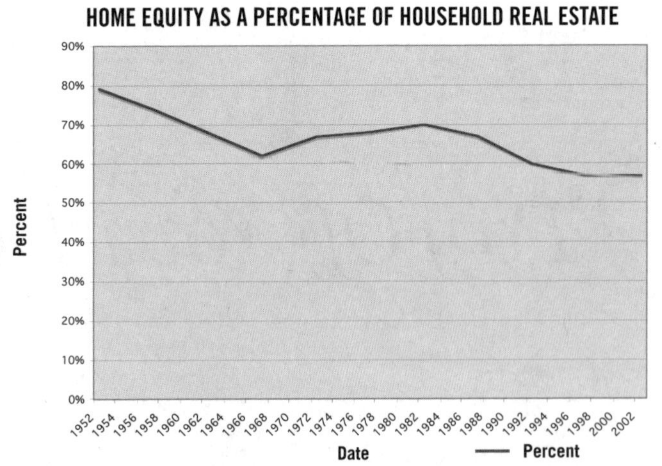

Source: Calculations based on data from the Board of Governors of the Federal Reserve System, Release Z. 1 Flow of Funds Statistics of the United States, Washington, D.C.: BOG.

CURRENTLY, HOMEOWNERS IN THE UNITED STATES OWE MORE AND OWN LESS OF THEIR HOUSE.[3]

LOAN AMOUNT	INTEREST RATE	TERM (YEARS)	TOTAL PAID
100,000	5%	15yrs	142,342
	10%	15yrs	193,430
	5%	25yrs	175,377
	10%	25yrs	272,610
200,000	5%	15yrs	284,686
	10%	15yrs	386,858
	5%	25yrs	350,754
	10%	25yrs	545,220

A MORTGAGE, DEPENDING ON THE TERM, DOUBLES OR TRIPLES THE COST OF THE HOUSE. THE LONG-TERM SAVINGS IS SIGNIFICANT IF YOU PREPAY A PROPORTION.[4]

Eighty years ago, it was common for families, especially in small towns, where most people lived, to build their own homes, spending their own savings to pay cash for materials and using volunteer labor. Others saved up until they could buy, free and clear.

As urban America grew home ownership dropped: in 1940 only 44% of homes were owner occupied. Since the creation of government-insured mortgage financing that number has grown: up to 62% in 1960 and to 66% in 2000. But under 30% of U.S. homeowners currently own their house outright, and of the 70% that have mortgages, 23% have more than one mortgage on that house. The percentage of house that homeowners hold—that is, the equity they have, compared to the appraised value of their home—has gone down from 80% in 1952 to about 56% currently, even as appraised value goes up.[5]

The median price of a new house—adjusted for inflation—is almost 4 times what it was in 1940.[6] Houses are so expensive now that almost no one expects to own one without taking less than a twenty-year mortgage. And that mortgage means that buyers typically pay two to three times the stated cost of the house: If you buy a $200,000 house, and invest $20,000 as a down payment, at 8.5% interest you'll pay about $250,000 in interest, or $450,000 total, before you own the house outright, twenty-five years later.

Better Homes and Gardens, in 1929, suggested that the "extreme limit" of expenditure on mortgages should be one-third of household income, and one-fifth or one-forth was suggested. They calculated their figures based on a single salary. Currently, even two-income households commonly pay over half their income toward their mortgage.

Why Do Houses Cost So Much?

One reason is that houses have become big and fancy. Sixty years ago, closets had just recently become a standard feature in new homes, but now people expect, or at least accept, multiple bathrooms, bedroom suites, built-in appliances, and more. Most builders complain that a primary reason for high house prices is government regulations. A variety of studies[7] show that codes, zoning, licensing, and insurance costs do impact housing prices. One consolation is that in places with high regulation, wages tend to be higher, but not usually high enough to compensate for the higher housing cost. Chapter 10 discusses ways to mitigate the effect of codes and zoning locally.

Other primary reasons for the high cost of housing are rising construction material and labor costs, land costs, and bank interest. Let's look at interest first, since its impact is staggering.

REASON #1: INTEREST

Here's a reason the rich get richer and the poor get poorer: *bank interest.*

Interest is the "rent" the bank or lender charges us to use our national currency. Most of us charge "rent" on our working hours—that's our income. The difference between our rent and the banks' rent is that your work hours are restricted by your humanity. Money never gets sick or tired, nor dies, so it can earn interest as long as interest is an acceptable social reality.

Plato, the Magna Carta, and even Adam Smith (who developed the philosophy of free-trade capitalism) warned of the negative effect interest has on human economies, yet the lending of money and the charging of interest continues to multiply and mutate. Albert Einstein was amazed to discover how compound interest works, and is said to have called it "the eighth wonder of the world," or "the greatest invention of the twentieth century," although it arguably dates back more than two thousand years.[8]

Compound interest is an exponential celebration of interest. It is charged by calculating interest at regular intervals before the loan is paid off, adding that interest to the loan, and then charging interest on the new sum.

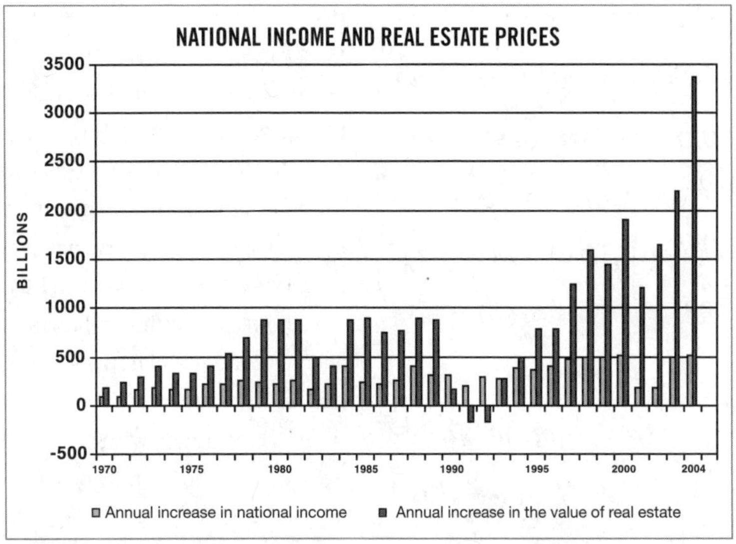

THE VALUE PLACED ON REAL ESTATE HAS OUTPACED U.S. NATIONAL INCOME[9]

Home mortgages are considered an example of simple interest; because borrowers usually pay the full interest each month, no interest is charged on the interest. However, since a mortgage term lasts for so very long, and the amount of money is so very high, the effect is similar to that of compound interest: modern borrowers pay two to three times as much interest to the lender than they owe in original debt.

The Bible and the Koran specifically limit this kind of human interaction. The Koran forbids all interest, and the Bible is typically interpreted to allow no more than 2% annually, and to require no loan to last past the next "sabbatical year" a celebration that happens each seven years, when loans are forgiven and fields are left fallow.

What we call the "business cycle"—the rise and fall of the economy— in a sense forces a kind of sabbatical on us eventually: once too many high-interest loans are in the economy, and everyone is spending their money paying back their debt, too little money is left for other economic activities, and the economy shrinks. If the

When Teresa Quiroga was twenty-one she worked as a waitress. Every morning a customer came in for breakfast, and every morning he left her one quarter as a tip. One morning he told her, "I'm not going to tip you a quarter today. I'm going to give you something much more valuable." And she sat down and he explained compound interest. "If it weren't for him," she says, twenty years later, "I wouldn't be about to burn my mortgage in four years, after a ten-year term.

Gita Mehta reports that in one Indian village, Farmer Minu had borrowed 500 rupees (US$4) to buy food and was still working off his debt after 17 years. Farmer Nanda had borrowed 100 rupees and had labored without wages for 12 years. Farmer Sukha had worked 10 years to pay off a loan of 20 rupees to buy a wooden box.[10]

economy contracts enough, and many people become unable to pay their mortgage, banks may offer interest-only loans. That is, they allow the homeowners to stay in the house if they pay interest on the loan, without gaining equity, and not getting any closer, month by month, to owning the house. It's a bit like renting. The bank does this because, if the market is slow, they don't want your house—it's too much trouble to maintain and manage a rental. The bank only wants your economic "rent."

Or the bank may foreclose on the mortgage, taking all the equity their borrower has built up. And, of course they take the house, as well. It's a winning situation for banks.

Polly Strand says in Chapter 1, "It's a cruel system." It can get worse: A number of people are taking out interest-only loans, because they can't afford to pay a normal mortgage. This sort of mortgage option can only make sense if you assume that home prices will rise so much in the near future that you will be able to sell at an enormous profit. It's a risky proposition, since markets both rise and fall. If you are buying a house to live in, and not as a speculative financial investment, it makes no sense.

You may end up with "negative equity:" your house may be worth less than the loan that bought it. And it can get worse still. In Japan, banks offer 100-year mortgages, which children—or possibly grandchildren—inherit.

Beat the Bank

Many people think they have few other options than to borrow from a bank to buy a house. The simplest thing is to be born rich. But if you didn't have that foresight, there are a few ways that you can reduce or avoid bank interest.

Be poor. If you never qualify for a loan, you'll never pay interest. Yet some very income-poor people in the small-house movement manage to own their own house. Because they were never eligible for loans, they were motivated to find ways (most typically by building their own house) to get around a bank-loaned house. Additionally, there are a few local programs that offer no-interest loans to very low-income families. Clearly, there's far more demand for these programs than there is supply, but it may be surprisingly worthwhile to contact your local governments and nonprofit foundations.

Borrow from mom. The bank rate that savers receive is lower than the rate borrowers pay. Sellers therefore may be willing to "carry the loan" (charge the buyer monthly, instead of one lump sum), and sometimes charge a rate lower than the bank. Some friends or relatives are willing to make low- or no- interest loans, in exchange for feeling like they are helping someone they love realize a dream.

In 1958 when Derald and Margie were told by the United States Air Force that they would be stationed in Shreveport, Louisiana, they were also warned that there would be no houses to rent there, so they'd better come prepared with a down payment. With just six months' notice, they surprised themselves, saving and scraping together to buy a house there. Seven years later, with twenty-one years to go on the mortgage, they were relocated again, and they debated whether to sell or rent out the house.

As a child, Derald was part of a prosperous farm family in Nebraska. They owned many acres, a beautiful farmhouse, had modern farm equipment, had lovely furniture. During the seven years of drought in the dust bowl times of the 1920s they resorted to borrowing money from the bank. Year after year brought more debt and eventually the bank repossessd their beloved farm. The once wealthy family found themselves penniless and on the street, and Derald vowed never to go into debt again. Having watched his family lose their farm, Derald felt that keeping this Shreveport house restored in him a sense of security.

In 1974 Derald and Margie sold the house in Louisiana and carried the loan, charging the buyers less than they would have paid a bank. Amazed at the profit that they made by carrying the loan, they looked for other places to invest their growing nest egg. In 2002, wary of the stock market, and discouraged by the low interest rates offered by banks, they instead hired an accountant to create a family trust and offered to assume the mortgage of each of their five children, at the lowest federal rate available, reducing the rate when it falls, but keeping it low when it rises—the opposite of what a bank would do.

Terry, their fifth child, says, "What I like about this is the safety net: in the long run, none of my sisters or brothers will lose their home, and the grandchildren won't have to go through what their grandfather did. A lot of middle-class people find that the retired generation, if they are healthy, are considerably wealthier than their children, so this is a safe way to enrich the whole family, and then share the wealth inside the family." Their low mortgage rate also allowed Terry and her husband David the luxury of reconsidering their work hours: when their son was diagnosed with cancer, Terry left her job and David stepped down to thirty hours a week. "We live frugally, but we are time rich. The fact that our family of five can survive on essentially one three-quarters job is very lucky right now."

The five children grew up wary of debt and don't carry a credit card balance. "I've seen my friends become slaves to their credit card payment and pay more than I do for similar things through the trap of interest. Our family has understood interest from both sides," Terry says.

Of course, this option only works for those lucky enough to have relatives or friends with significant savings.

Look to religion. Religions throughout the ages (Hinduism, Judaism, Christianity, Buddhism, and Islam) theologically forbade excessive interest rates. Banks following Shari'a (Islamic rules) in various parts of the world, including North America, offer loans without interest, sometimes using a partnership program where the bank shares in equity until the loan is paid in full. Habitat for Humanity, a Christian housing mission, is the only significant U.S. homebuilder that finances all its projects without charging interest. They do require future homeowners to help Habitat build houses. Neither Habitat nor the Islamic banks in North America require that the borrower be of a religious background.

In Sweden, JAK—*Jord, Arbete och Kapital*[11] is one of several secular savings-and-loan programs in which individuals accrue points by saving money over time, and then eventually are allowed to withdraw their savings and borrow additionally, at no interest, similar to one of the schemes that Islamic banks often offer.

Start a savings group. Not to be confused with pyramid schemes, savings groups create a savings pool that is used by each member in turn. Asian-American and other immigrant groups, as well as some women's small-business groups, use this strategy. Obviously, there must be a high degree of trust among members, and it works more easily for small sums of capital, but if each member is building a tiny structure at minimal costs, or if it will be possible to get more conventional financing once the building shell is finished, this system can work.

Some local groups have institutionalized this system a bit. They find a local bank or credit union to hold deposits, and create their own committee to manage the fund. Group members make deposits into the bank, and the committee determines who may borrow. The bank endures no risk, and the depositors know that the money they put in the bank is going to fund activities right in their community. The SHARE microcredit program in Massachussets is a long-time example of this, and although they typically make business loans, a similar system could be used for mortgages as well.

Live in town, and build green. The average annual cost of owning a vehicle is over $5,000. Not having a vehicle, or not having two, frees up income to pay for a house. Lower utility costs do the same. A few large cities have programs that offer special mortgage rates for people who live near public transit, and/or superinsulate and solar-design their houses.[12]

Pay off more quickly. By prepaying just $500 per year on a 9-percent, $100,000 loan, you'll save about $45,000 on a thirty-year mortgage[13]

Jonathan and Pam Allan of Rochester, Minnesota, decided to look for a house that "we could afford even if we lost our jobs and ended up flipping burgers." In 1992, with $13,000 saved for a down payment, they searched for a "smallish" house, rejected several as too pricey, and finally bargained down the owner of a 1,600-square-foot house to $68,800. As the real estate agent went through the paperwork, noting their combined salary of $47,000 and their nearly 20-percent down payment, she exclaimed, "Do you realize how much house I could have sold you?" "Do you know how much house we didn't want?" replied Jonathan.

They started with an 8.5-percent, fifteen-year loan and made extra payments for two years, then refinanced at 7 percent when interest rates went down in 1994. "But we put everything back into the mortgage, and kept with our double payments," says Jonathan, "even though Pam was in graduate school for most of the time and not earning much more than her tuition." In April 1997 they burned their mortgage, having paid a total of $55,000 in principal and $15,889.60 in interest. Prepaying saved them $14,979.90 in unpaid interest.

If you take out a mortgage, make sure there is no penalty for early repayment, that prepayments will apply to the principal and not (just) to the interest, and that there will be no charge for "reamortization" if you pay part of the loan back early. Some lenders are happy to have you pay back early. Choose one who is.

Paying off early is a strategy for people who really want to live in their home. Other people speculate on houses, and figure that the interest rate on a mortgage is lower than the interest on another kind of loan, so they use equity in their house to finance other endeavors, and own less and less of their house.

Scrimp and plan. If you move every few years, it may be tempting to take out the equity from a house you sell and use it on something else. But if instead you carefully reinvest it in your next house like Georgette Thompson (see right), you may eventually own a house, free and clear, even if you recently moved in.

Get paid to live. Some people abandon the idea of owning a house, and rely on the excess of vacation homes, living for years caretaking others' houses, often being paid to be there. Coupled with a regular job, this option can be far more lucrative than investing in a mortgage. Internet services match caretakers with owners.

Dream. A few of us seem to rely on angels, found in the form of other people.

Lisa loved a certain neighborhood. Almost nothing was ever for sale or even for rent there. She walked through the neighborhood slowly on her way to work each day. The neighbors started recognizing her. An elderly lady invited her in for tea, and there began a long friendship, which involved Lisa moving in for very low rent. Fifteen years later, the widow, who had no living children, willed the house to Lisa. Lisa, who's an artist, says that like most things in her life, she had dreamed of this house before she entered it, and

"Say my investments earn 7 percent, and my mortgage is at 5.5 percent. It may still make sense to pay off my mortgage, first of all because the investments are not a sure thing, whereas the mortgage is, and second because the peace of mind of having your mortgage paid off is worth at least 1.5 percent to most people. Maintaining a mortgage and investing elsewhere is best for people who have no emotional attachment to their house."

—Lu Bauer, an accountant and financial advisor in Maine, questions the wisdom of maintaining a mortgage with a low interest rate, and investing savings elsewhere at a higher rate.

Georgette Thornton didn't use a magic formula to retire her mortgage, and herself, early. At her first job she simply learned to live within her $8 per hour paycheck, and throughout her career with each promotion and increase in income, she never increased her "standard of living," and instead invested the difference in savings, in her education, or in her house. She has always maintained the same daily spending habits as she had when she had made $8 per hour, and with meticulous attention to detail–she knows down to the cent how much she spent on each house, its maintenance and mortgage.

She bought her first house, in a "cookie-cutter subdivision," in Orlando, Florida in 1989. She paid "$75,300." Several months later she was promoted in her job, and she invested the difference in her salary into additional payments towards her mortgage principal. Six years later, she sold the house for $80,000, extracting $32,000 worth of equity from the sale, which she immediately invested in a bank savings account. She continued this pattern even as she put herself through graduate school. In her fourth house, and in less than fourteen years of home ownership, and without any family financial support, Georgette burned her mortgage. It was a good thing: two years later, her job as an administrator was "downsized" out of existence, but because she owned her house she was able to retire to part-time work, at the age of 55. She now volunteers her time teaching recently released inmates, and others, how to create savings, even if they earn barely over minimum wage.

had dreamed of Ana, her adopted grandmother, as well.

Even if you're prone to miracles, it will benefit you to understand, eyes wide open, how money, interest, and budgeting work.

Factor in the Cost of Land

The price tag on American land has increased infinitely in the last 500 years. In 1500, land was priceless, subject to the indigenous belief that a location—the sky, the sea, the land—is limitless and as such cannot be owned or sold. The native, local people paid an enormous price when they were dispossessed of their homeland. During westward expansion, immigrant individuals, businesses, and government agencies surveyed, divided, and claimed every valley, plain, and mountaintop. Those who were harmed by the rising cost of land in the East were advised to move west.

In recent generations, the last free acres of the U.S. and Canada became priced and owned, and even large parts of Native American reservations that once resisted have been surveyed. Most nonpublic land is currently owned, directly or through mortgages, by banks, individual speculators, and investment groups. In the U.S. less than 5 percent of the population owns about 95 percent of nonpublic land. In 2002, major banks began an

Go into your home-building adventure with your eyes open and your safety will be infinitely greater

attempt to convince Congress to reclassify land as a financial instrument, equal to stocks and bonds.[14] Over the last several hundred years, land has shifted from being a location to be used for production and enjoyment, to a being a possession worthy of counting, an object of speculation.

We all must be somewhere, so land is, like food and fuel, a commodity that is always in demand. We tell each other, "They aren't making any more," and agree that it's always smart to buy land. In the last generation it has become particularly difficult to sleep anywhere that isn't rented or privately owned. Towns and cities that once allowed people to sleep in parks, or at the edge of town under bridges, and in fields, have passed ordinances that essentially forbid lying down in public, creating a growing class of sleepless poor. Meanwhile, cities that relied on undeveloped but private land for recreation are either scrambling to create open space or accepting that their city will be a chain of subdivisions, with few or no places for people to share common ground.

Land is expensive because it benefits the majority of nonfarming landowners, who see land as a financial investment, to continually raise the price. Governments that rely on property taxes, or on selling public land, are happy to see rising land prices. But people who use land as a place to live, or grow a crop, locate an industry, or provide a service are harmed by the rising price of land, since taxes rise with price, and rising land prices tend to encourage general prices for food, merchandise, and labor to rise as well.

Land is also made expensive by our greed, which is fueled by our fear of scarcity. Land is only a little like food, which has both a natural and social consumption limit. The Roman *vomitoria* and bulimia are now seen as a sickness. Almost no one wants an endless, excessive supply of food. Diet choices among the affluent are said to encourage malnutrition in the rest of the world. But the way that land greed creates land scarcity is more obvious.

Land in North America is not treated like water or fuel, which most governments recognize as so basic to human and economic life that they are either publicly owned or subsidized. Instead, land is more like diamonds: a precious commodity, a sign of wealth, and therefore achievement. Just as we "can't be too thin or too rich," we can't own "too much land." Unlike owning too many shoes, having too many love affairs, or eating too much cake, there is no social stigma about being "land fat."

The price of land is strongly influenced by local factors: a company moves in or out; a toxic dump site is rediscovered; the local government announces plans to build a new park; a wave of artists move into a neighborhood and make it chic. Understanding localized land price variations is a way that some people minimize their land costs, and others make a killing.

MAKING OUR LAND (A LITTLE MORE) FREE

Sell high; buy low. This is a common way that small-home dwellers live mortgage free. They use the difference between local conditions to become full homeowners: typically they sell their larger house in a high-price area and move to a smaller house in a low-price area—sometimes just across town—and use the equity they gained to buy free and clear. Or they save money while working in a big city, then buy land in a remote area, and scrape together a new home, never taking a loan. Coastal Californians move inland. Inland Californians move to Oregon. Urban Oregonians move to rural Oregon. Rural Oregonians move to New Mexico.

New Mexicans move to Mexico. The U.S. Census Bureau's 2003 American Community Survey showed that a majority of people (excluding college students) had lived in their current residence fewer than eight years. There's a cheaper place for almost anyone to live, and some people keep moving until they are mortgage free.

Other ways that people lower their land price include:

Band together in a group. Land is usually less expensive per acre when you buy in bulk. Sometimes the group subdivides their land into small homesteads, or they focus housing in one area and maintain the greater area in common. Zoning ordinances may or may not allow this kind of clustering.

Build on someone else's property. Follow the example of Henry David Thoreau: In both rural and suburban areas there are people who see the benefits of having others live close to them, and are willing to let someone build an additional dwelling, and give them a long-term or even perpetual lease, in exchange for a small rent or another form of help. The American Farmland Trust is one organization that preserves small farms by matching young farmers with old farmers, and the American Association of Retired Persons encourages older people to partner with young people to build guesthouses in their too-large backyards (see Chapter 10, "accessory dwelling units").

Share land with a wealthy "silent" partner. Occasionally people have wealthy friends who, for reasons of friendship or tax advantage, are willing to finance all or part of the acquisition of a property, even though they will almost never be there. This is particularly common with cooperative associations and schools.

Lowering Construction Costs

Rising construction costs have driven up prices too. In the late 1940s it was expected that the industrialization of housing production would lower housing costs soon after the war, and it did. Gypsum board, ready-mix concrete, asphalt shingles, factory roof trusses, linoleum floor tiles, fiberglass insulation, prehung doors and windows, particle board, and aluminum siding are a few of the innovations that transferred production from the high-wage construction site, to the factory. On-site labor now accounts for 15 percent of the cost of a house, down from 30 percent in 1949.

Savings from these innovations didn't lower sales prices in the long run; the savings have been spent instead on increasing house size and costly financing. RVs and double-wide mobile homes currently offer the best per-square-foot price on the market, and modular homes, more popular in Scandinavia and Japan, are starting to appear in the North American market. It's difficult to lower construction costs— the forests have fewer and fewer trees to give, and the fuel that burns cement is climbing in price—but there are a few ways to try.[15]

MAKING EVERY SQUARE FOOT COUNT

Once you've thought out your needs and realized they are quite a bit less than you first assumed, and begun to sketch floor plans, do this exercise: look for a hundred square feet on your floor plan that you could possibly eliminate. Can't find any? Listen to this.

If you are spending $70 per square foot of construction, eliminating 100 square feet will save you, over the course of twenty-five years:

$7,000	construction
$12,000	mortgage interest (assuming 8%)
$400	maintenance (paint every 5 years)
$400	cleaning costs (1 hr/month, at $10/hr plus supplies)
$200	insurance cost
$3,000	heating/cooling (conventional, moderately insulated house)

These figures may not seem like much, but if you drop your twenty-five-year $100,000 mortgage to $93,000 (by eliminating $7,000 in construction costs) and prepay $160 each year (the cost of those last four items, divided by twenty-five years) instead, you will burn your mortgage about two years early and save over $20,000—enough to send a child to college for a semester or three, or enough to take a long and luxurious vacation to celebrate the end of your mortgage.

THE ECOLOGICAL DEBT

Some people don't just want to know the material cost of their house; they want to know the

Elise decided that eight four-year-old trees were worth one eighty-year-old tree. Then a forester told her that she'd be lucky if one in four of her trees lived to reach eighty. She calculated she'd need thirty-two trees per hundred square feet of house. Where to plant them all? He also told her planting those trees was not going to bring back the complex forest they had come from. Used wood in any quantity was not available in her area, so she decided to buy only wood certified as from a "well-managed forest" by the Forest Stewardship Council. That almost doubled her wood costs.

Had her builder been willing, she could have switched from the 2-by-8-inch rafters and ceiling joists to a truss system which usually reduces wood use by 18 percent. She could have switched to 24" on center framing. She looked for 2 by 3s to substitute for 2 by 4s in the interior, but realized she'd have to mill them herself. She thought long and hard, stared at some trees, and realized the simplest thing was to significantly reduce her house size.

One late evening she trimmed her 1,000-square-foot plan down to 480 square feet plus an outdoor storage shed. The lumber costs shrunk by about half, since although the perimeter didn't shrink in half, the shorter boards to span her roof cost less than half. She's planted eighty trees (not as many as what she figures she ought to), and she's yet to miss the 510 square feet of her first plan.

environmental cost. The intricate web of life makes this impossible to figure out completely: every nail, every sheet of glass comes from a system more complex than our little minds can imagine. But we do know that the creation of each ton of Portland concrete releases a ton of CO_2 into the atmosphere. The creation of a gallon of latex paint leaves a quarter cup of petroleum residue, and it takes an Oregon fir sixty years to produce 120 board feet of lumber.[16]

What's the ecological cost of these items? And how can you repay the debt? You could be like Elise Gamez (see left), who promised to plant a tree for every one that went into her house. But what age tree?

CABINETRY, PLUMBING

Not all square feet are created alike. A 100-square-foot closet costs less than a 60-square-foot bathroom. Kitchen cabinetry often costs more than the walls of the whole house. And if you dream of hardwood, the environmental cost is that much higher. One method used around the world is to build multifamily dwellings as shells, allowing the families to customize the interiors inexpensively, over time. You can see the principle at work in the Grow Home (see Chapter 3), and you can benefit from the concept by finishing a bare minimum of your kitchen, and furnishing it either with inexpensive manufactured cabinets—perhaps steel cabinets from a demolition yard—or (temporarily or not) with shelves and hanging racks.

If you can't shake the idea that you'll need a second or third toilet or bathroom, consider running just the plumbing to a room that you initially use as storage. If after some years you still feel the need, you can add the expensive fixtures and tile, and won't have had to increase the mortgage. Carole Fournier and her family (see Chapter 7) did that, and have yet to upgrade theirs, but if they ever divide their house into tiny apartments it will come in handy.

DO IT YOURSELF

Labor costs are high. Owner building is sometimes the most significant way you can reduce new-construction costs. The first rule of owner building is always to remember there's a reason it's called *skilled* labor. It will take you two or four times longer, and you may not do it as well.

Owner building is particularly suited to people who are handy; whose wages from their usual work are average or low; who have time, and no debt; who are patient and like to learn new things; and who know how to live on very little (owner building is not free: someone has to feed you). Owner building makes it feasible to build a house only a multimillionaire could buy: owner-builders will lovingly arrange a rock foundation, or learn an ancient plaster technique that no sane professional would waste time on. And owner-builders can reduce their environmental cost by choosing methods that are more brute labor–intensive (such as adobe, straw bale, and cob) but with a lower embodied energy.

The second rule of owner building is that going fast will usually heighten the cost. To speed things up, you will need to use more finished, higher-cost materials, and hire some labor. Go too fast, and you might find yourself paying hospital bills. On the other hand, going too slow can end up in divorce. Another underlying rule is, if you're not (both) going to enjoy the process of building your own home, don't do it. There are other ways to save money, and better reasons to end a marriage. Make sure you'll (both) enjoy it by volunteering at a Habitat for Humanity site or a friend's project for a dozen weekends first.

Donna Leach made a brilliant decision when she decided to build a home in many ways identical to the one Carolyn Roberts, across the valley from her, had built. Both women did much of the labor themselves, and oversaw all of it, so Donna was able to call her new friend for advice as she built, and suffered fewer surprises than most owner-builders. If you copy a home, choose one in your climate, and preferably very close by, and note the orientation.

One super-low-cost strategy is this: Build a storage structure. Slowly collect materials from dumpsters and demolition sites; you can find or buy very cheaply everything from windows to sinks to roof trusses. Design a small building around the materials you have. Or build one room, and live in it until you have saved up enough to build a second. Another way to reduce expenses is to copy a building you like: the plans will cost less, and if you share contractors, the contractor may charge you less, and by minimizing uncertainty you will probably lower your labor costs all around (see above).

Many a precious home has been built by novice hands that feel the delicacy of life on Earth, and take the time to notice the grain of each board, or each layer of old paint that comes off, when sanding an old window frame. Robert and Jacinte, Kirsten (see profiles this chapter), and others in this book enjoyed the process. If it's a joy for you to build, consider that path.[17]

Worth the Investment?

THE LONG VIEW

Experts disagree as to whether new construction or energy and materials spent on long-term maintenance and operation contribute more significantly to our environment's decline. Depending on how long a house stands before it is demolished, long-term heating and cooling costs may matter more. The simple, solar decision to have the largest windows face the equator (for warmth in winter), and to insulate the roof and walls (R-30 or better), will save plenty in the long run. If you save $100 per month and heat or cool seven months of the year, after five years a $3,500 investment in insulation will have already paid for itself. A solar water heater generally pays for itself in five years. It's beyond the scope of this book to explain the details of solar design and intelligent retrofitting. It is an

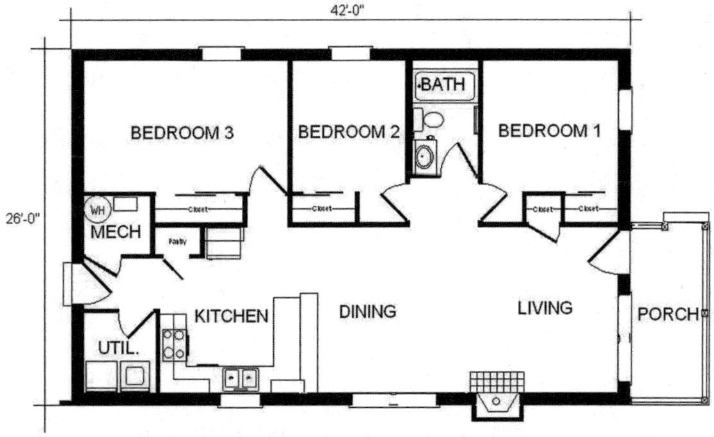

"IF YOU WANT TO DO A FAVOR FOR A LOW-INCOME FAMILY, DON'T BUILD THEM A HOUSE THAT COSTS A BUNDLE TO HEAT AND COOL," SAYS BARBARA MILLER OF THE NATIONAL AFFORDABLE HOUSING NETWORK (NAHN), BASED IN BUTTE, MONTANA WHICH HAS DESIGNED AND BUILT, IN PARTNERSHIP WITH THE LOCAL HABITAT AFFILIATE, HOUSES WITH R-60 INSULATION, THAT USE WELL UNDER HALF THE ENERGY OF COMPARABLY SIZED HOUSES.

AFTER STUDYING ENERGY MARKETS FOR A FEW DECADES, NAHN CURRENTLY RECOMMENDS INSTALLING ONLY ELECTRIC APPLIANCES, FOR HEATING, COOLING AND COOKING, FOR THREE REASONS: (1) FOR AN EXTRA $10,000 UP FRONT INVESTMENT, THE HOUSE CAN RUN ON SOLAR PHOTOVOLTAICS OR WINDPOWER AND (2) GAS APPLIANCES TEND TO BE MORE EXPENSIVE, PLUS RUNNING TWO SEPARATE ENERGY SYSTEMS COSTS MORE THAN RUNNING JUST ONE, AND (3) ELECTRIC POWER CAN BE GENERATED FROM A VARIETY OF SOURCES, ALLOWING MORE COMPETITIVE PRICING. IN 2006 NATURAL GAS JUMPED SUDDENLY IN PRICE.THE NAHN OFFERS A VARIETY OF PLANS FOR HOUSES THAT USE LESS THAN $500 IN UTILITIES ANNUALLY.

essential to your finances that you inform yourself of these issues. Before you buy a house, ask to see a year's worth of utility bills.[18]

MULTIPLY BY DIVIDING

Since most existing houses are too large for their occupants, some people make their homes pay for themselves by using part of the house as an apartment, an office, or a daycare center. As you look at houses, find out whether an exterior door can be added to a room and whether neighbors or code officials would protest the additional traffic that could come from a home business. You'll find more on that in Chapters 6 and 7.

BUILDING TO LIVE VS. BUILDING TO SELL

Some say, "We don't need this (second bathroom, jacuzzi, etc.), but if we don't have them, and we have to move, we'll never find a buyer." But selling a house is like finding a mate: you don't need the whole world to approve of your house. You just need one buyer. Owner-builders who try something new have been surprised to find how many special buyers—people to whom they would love to pass their home on—do exist. In fact, smaller houses are desirable enough that they tend to sell at a higher price per square foot.

DO YOU LIVE IN A BANK?

Some people count their home as their financial security. They assume they will be able to sell their house at a profit, and that the larger their house the greater the profit. They have total faith that the market will rise, and reward their investment.

One factor that encourages people in the U.S. to see a mortgaged house as a wise investment is the Internal Revenue Service's deduction for interest paid on mortgages. (Canada doesn't offer a deduction.)[19] But depending on your tax bracket, and the cost of your house, it may not be worthwile.

Travis Thrower, Jr., a tax advisor in Denver, Colorado, remembers the local real estate busts of the 1970s and '80s. He notes that the market doesn't always rise, and real estate doesn't necessarily give a greater return than treasury bonds or mutual funds. "If rent exceeds mortgage payments, it may make sense to buy, especially for people who like home maintenance work. But if you are going to hire the maintenance work out, you'll be surprised at what you spend." Well aware of the income tax advantage of buying, he still rents. "Renting offers me both freedom to move whenever I want, and financial security, because I know much more predictably what my investments will give me."

Speculative decisions turn your house into a bank, and won't be useful unless you sell your home in your lifetime. But what if it turns out that with time, you have grown accustomed to your friends and activities near you, and you never want to leave? You'll have an oversized house to maintain, and no profit to spend. Maybe at the moment that you want to sell, the market will suddenly be at a fifteen-year low. Imagine the anxiety. As a billboard in San Francisco reads, "'My house is worth a million dollars' is not a retirement plan."

You will probably be safer to consider your house as your home, with the minimum that you need, and invest your surplus in treasury bonds, mutual funds, or even gold ingots. Property values in much of the country, over the long term, have not always kept pace with inflation.[20] Once you have your home paid off, the market can fluctuate, and you will float.

"If a family buys a house for $300,000 with a down payment of $30,000 and a mortgage of $270,000, spends little on maintenance, and sells it ten years later for $300,000, will they come out ahead, considering the tax deduction?" Answer: It depends. We would have to say, "Ahead compared to what?" If they would have rented a similar house instead, then we would compare the amount of rent they would have paid to a landlord with the amount of interest they would have paid to the bank (less the reduction in tax due to the tax deduction).

"Either way, for most middle-income families, that housing expense takes a very large chunk out of family income. Hence, most such people are counting on the house appreciating to justify their "investment." While that has worked lately, it is a risky strategy. House prices do fall, as well as rise. The better question to ask is why is the family spending so much for housing in the first place? What might their other options be?"

—Judith Robinson, economist, Castleton State University

SOCIAL SECURITY

Some small-home dwellers minimize their reliance on financial security and invest instead in social capital:

Ettiene Bruwer, a white South African, built a small house twice the size of an average black South African's home, but small compared to the other houses in the white neighborhood where he lives. He devotes himself to his friendships, and plans to share more and more of his house as his children leave home. He takes care of others and expects them to take care of him in the future. "I invest in social capital. My retirement policy is developing my relationship ability. To care for and be cared for by a familiar is why we are human," he explains.

Talking about Money

The *Better Homes and Gardens* article notes, "It is painful to have to put down such figures." Does your mind go blank when you see numbers? Do rocks drop in your stomach when you talk about money? If so, it might be hard to read this chapter. So skip it, go on to another part of the book. Later, come back to this chapter and be easy on yourself. Read a little, slowly, until you understand it. It's a pity when good-hearted people end up tricked or in debt because they didn't have the training or emotional strength to understand finances.

KIRSTEN JACOBSEN
Built 1999–2005

AREA:
130 sq. ft. 1999, 1,100 sq. ft. 2006

INTENDED NUMBER OF OCCUPANTS:
initially, 1

COST OF ORIGINAL HOUSE:
$5,000 for land, plus $5,000 materials and hired labor

COST OF EXPANSION:
$50,000 (bank loan)

UTILITY COSTS (MONTHLY):
$0/month

LOCATION:
Taos, New Mexico

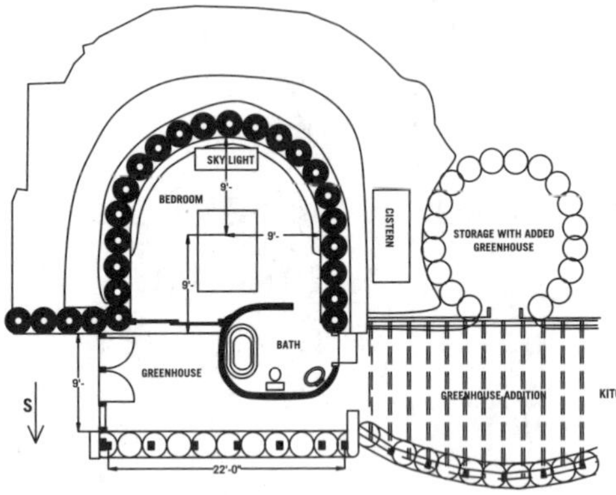

ABOVE: **KIRSTEN'S EARTHSHIP**
ABOVE RIGHT: **INSIDE AN EARTHSHIP**

Highway drivers in northern New Mexico may

occasionally notice in the far distance windows peeping out of hillsides. These are "Earthships," stationary homes built semi-submerged in the earth, and ideally containing systems within them—water catchment, solar electricity, solar heating, a composting sewer, a garden—that make them self-sufficient "pods" on a sea of high desert, independent of the electric grid, municipal water lines, and other attachments of civilization. Since 1989 over two thousand have been built, most of them in the southwestern United States. At least a few dozen have burrowed into beaches and mountains as far away as Mexico, Belgium, and Japan.

One architectural critique of Earthships is that they are composed entirely of two elements, a large cave and a small greenhouse. Depending on your perspective, Earthships offer either the best of both worlds, or two distinct structures, neither of which is ideal for human habitation. But it's hard to complain that Earthships ruin the view, as most of them are modestly hidden under a ripple of hill.

Kirsten Jacobsen's Earthship started out as a 12-foot-diameter circle. Its roof is a ferro-cement "double dome" made in place on a form of rebar and stucco netting. The floor is a cement slab. The walls, which must be strong enough to retain the earth behind them, are made of used car tires, which Kirsten sledgehammered full of soil from the site. "Kips," she says, is the word engineers use for 1,000 pounds when smaller measurements become insignificant. Kirsten moved tons of kips to build her little house.

Kirsten first learned of Earthships in the summer of 1994 when she traveled from San Francisco to Taos to be a college intern. She intended to spend a month, but she never returned. "My parents loved that," she frowns. By the time she started her own building in 1999 she was an experienced tire pounder. Her goal was to complete her home for less than $1,000 in materials and labor, and to be mortgage free before she turned thirty. I first interviewed her in 1999.

[Q] Why are you doing this?

[A] **KRISTEN:** When I was a kid we lived in a residential subdivision. You could see that the houses were crappy. You could see big power lines and power plants. I had a sense that this just isn't right.

Before I even heard of recycling, my mother wouldn't buy plastic tubs of margarine or plastic jugs of milk. She'd reuse everything. It was embarrassing. We had paper lunch bags, and she'd make us bring them home, all crumpled, but they would still be used the next day. I was raised not to be wasteful, at least not in that way.

Living in an Earthship, even if you lie around all day reading, at least you aren't burning coal for your electricity, and you are conserving water, water that you caught off your own roof. You can do nothing, and not be a drain on the environment.

Most of all I see this as a chance to have time and money to do other things with my life, to travel, to write, to perform. This is an investment in myself. It's going to cost less to build this than I would have spent in rent in just one year. So if I can live with a dirt floor for a little while, then I have something that's never going to be worth less than I put into it. Coming from the San Francisco Bay Area, I don't know anyone my own age that can afford to own their home. What a profound thing, in a way, to make a space for yourself in the world.

[Q] What's the hardest part?

[A] Sometimes it's hard for people after they have achieved a certain degree of comfort: they're warm, they're dry, they have a place for their stuff. It's hard to keep on going. This happens, of course with the largest houses most of all, after they are partially finished. It's a huge commitment.

The physical exertion can be draining, especially if you are working by yourself and don't see much progress. That's why I am psyched about this project—it's so small. Some people laugh and say, "My cistern is bigger than your entire house," and I reply, "Let's see who can finish more quickly."

If you have a crew you are paying for, that's one thing, but if you have your own job and work on your house during the time you should be resting, that's brutal.

[Q] You said yesterday you have some fear about moving into such a small place.

[A] It's going to take preparation and planning. I need to have a bed. I need a place to write. I need a place for guests. It's going to really make me evaluate what I do need to be comfortable in this space. I hope I don't spend all this time planning and building and then when I move in flip out with claustrophobia. I don't think that will happen. This isn't exactly my dream house, but it's a big step.

[Q] Any suggestions to other people?

[A] Do it. Trust yourself, especially women. Even if they have construction experience, women get all kinds of guys saying, "What you really need to do here is blah blah blah." Listen to yourself. Women can be great homebuilders. So much of it is planning, making a shopping list—you're a homemaker making a home. Measure it like any recipe, measuring wood, or cement. Do it just right.

In June of 2000, Kirsten spent her first night in her home. She emailed me, "It was a starry, starry night."

In July 2001 I visited her again. Her house was habitable, but not finished to the level she had intended. She told me, "Falling in love is what has been the biggest obstacle for me. Both summers, I fell in love. When your lover has a beautiful house in Taos, where is the motivation to finish?" But now she was back home on the mesa, at work on her little house, finishing plastering the inside.

Meanwhile, the 600-acre Earthship community where she lives had been ordered by local authorities to cease construction. Since Earthships need no water, sewer, gas, and electrical service, and since Mike Reynolds, the architect who started the community in 1994, had government support for his project, and a waiver to develop the community without a typical subdivision permit, no one had applied for building permits. But the laws changed in 1996, and in 1997 the county suddenly came down hard on the project: in addition to variance permits for their nonuse of water and electricity, they were required to pay for an archaeological study to determine if any ruins had been disturbed. Their previous agreement to cluster homes closely and preserve and share the open space was disallowed, and they were forced to divide the land into three-acre lots, and build roads wide enough for a fire truck to pass to each lot.

[Q] Was the county trying to set a precedent?

[A] We fought the subdivision for two years. We even had the endorsement of the governor. We spent days going to meetings. The people at the county level, their job is to be on our case. We are such a small company that we couldn't afford to fight them anymore. The county commissioner in charge of our case now is a solar architect. This allows us to move forward, at least.

Every winter you see people in Taos struggling to keep warm, chopping wood, or paying for propane, and it's hard to think that the county permit board would resist a solution. Here we are,

OUTSIDE THE ENTRANCE TO AN EARTHSHIP

ANOTHER VIEW OF AN ENTRANCE TO AN EARTHSHIP

offering a solution and we aren't asking for any state money, no tax credits, nothing.

We need a contest to think of the next word that will describe what we are doing, because the words get weakened. Ford Motor recycles a little of the steel in their trucks, so they are called "green." Someone puts two southern windows on a house and a few halogen lights inside, and they get a "sustainability" rating. The power structure commodifies whatever popular movement is going on and figures out how to make a profit off it—natural food, tattoos or solar buildings, or whatever. But this kind of building is uncommodifiable. People sometimes ask, "But what if we run out of tires?" First I have to ask, is that a serious question? There are 2.5 billion tires stockpiled in the U.S. alone. If it happens, we will be able to stop.

Our community will be a jewel on the landscape in twenty-five years, when Kmart is half a mile away. It will be an oasis. The land is being destroyed all around us, but we'll be here, because we don't need to go anywhere. We have it all here.

In the fall of 2005 I called Kirsten. The dispute with the county had been resolved, and Mike Reynolds had been invited to join the county's permit and zoning board. Kirsten was on her way to apply for a mortgage. Her house had expanded to a little over 1,000 square feet, including a bedroom, bathroom, electrical storage space, water heater, and garden planters. To finish the last 500 square feet, she wanted to hire a crew. The market had risen so that the bank assessed Kirsten's projected house, once it will be finished, at $200,000. Her loan is for $50,000. The monthly payments are less than she'd have to pay for rent in town.

DONALD MACDONALD

LOCATION:
San Francisco, California

ABOVE: **MOBILE HOME**

Even developers can take a quality-instead-of-quantity

approach to their financial security.

San Francisco architect Donald MacDonald, builder of bridges, apartment buildings, and custom homes, financed and built over 300 small (less than 900 square feet) single-family dwellings in the Bay Area, making home ownership possible for 300 families who had no other chance to buy a house. His uncommonly fair formula for success: 20 percent is plenty of profit. Never take more.

Mr. MacDonald's small houses are designed around families' expressed, essential needs, and the funding available. The mortgage payment, he says, should be equal to what the family previously paid in rent. "I went into a crummy neighborhood in San Francisco and asked, what do you pay for rent here? The going rate was $800. We designed houses they could buy for $800 a month. They are nice houses."

He first tried to work with nonprofit organizations. "Those guys trained in the 1960's, they say everyone should have big spaces. They said my design is too small. I said, 'Look at what people are renting.' Nobody would do it, so I financed it myself," he remembers.

His small houses typically sold for $50,000 below market value. I asked him, "Is this an act of charity?" and he insisted no, it just makes good business sense. He further explained that at this rate, his market is endless.

"Look at it this way: there's a market that nobody serves, nobody. It's a huge market in the city. If you can sell for fifty grand under anybody else, and still make a 20 percent profit, you can build forever. Sneak in and make a fortune. The market never ends if you stay in your niche."

He's taught young architects his thrifty method, but they won't stick to it. They switch to a more complex design, and add expensive materials. "One guy I trained, he said, 'Look, Mack, why not put better materials in the design?' I said, 'It will cost more.' He said 'The market will take it.' He did it, he changed the design, and the market took it for a while, but when the market crashed, he had overbuilt. He lost his shirt; I kept on building. People think the market only rises. It's not true."

The first houses now have more then doubled in price since he sold them (from $140,000 in 1988 to $300,000 in 2002), but because they are small they are affordable relative to their surroundings. (The Victorians down the street quadrupled in price.)

Mr. MacDonald gained fame in 1989 for his "city sleepers," an $800 8-by-4-by-4-foot plywood unit, with room for a bed, some storage, and a window. He stationed them in a parking lot below a freeway, and they were promptly occupied by "roofless" men. With positive media coverage, and popular support, the city allowed these tiny homes to stay for a few months, but soon enough, the Department of Transportation, concerned with "liability," sued to have them removed.

"They weren't concerned with their liability when these men slept outside on the asphalt," Mr. MacDonald notes. "The average homeless person dies after five years. Many of these people, all they want is to be safe, and left alone. Is that too much? I want every American to have their own space. There are people sleeping out in the rain."

JACINTE WIKOW AND ROBERT DUBOIS
Built 2004–2005

AREA:
1,215 plus an unfinished basement

INTENDED NUMBER OF OCCUPANTS:
2-5

COSTS:
Land: $48,885
Foundation, services, and shell: $96,900
Finishing costs: $38,128

UTILITY COSTS (MONTHLY):
Electric: $150/month (all included).
Water: free

LOCATION:
Eastern Canada

Soon after Jacinte and Robert were engaged, Robert proposed they buy a house. Jacinte replied, "Well, maybe, but it can't cost more each month than paying rent, and we have to be able to afford it on just one of our salaries, just in case...."

Their friends were buying houses in new subdivisions, so they made the rounds viewing new models too. They noticed they were drawn to the smallest houses in the new developments. "We saw a lot of what we didn't want. I don't understand why anyone needs two living rooms, or why a child needs room for a queen-sized bed," says Jacinte.

The couple was leery of taking out more than a 20-year mortgage, but with house prices so high, they decided that the only way to reduce their cost substantially would be to do much of the work themselves. So they looked for months, until they found a reasonably-priced lot near public transportation. The Canadian government allows people to cash in their RAP (Régime d'Accession à la Propriété –similar to an IRA in the U.S.), to use as a tax-free down payment, so Robert cashed his in. Jacinte took out her savings, and they combined these two sources with a small interest-free loan from a relative and paid cash for the land. Next, they moved in with Robert's mother, who charged them no rent, so their entire paychecks could go towards construction.

Perhaps due to the long winters, Canada has advanced various ways of prefabricating walls and other parts of houses, so they can be quickly erected outside. Prefab was the best choice for a couple who had never built before. Jacinte and Robert chose a two-story design from the company Maison LaPrise. They received prenumbered parts that form a giant jigsaw puzzle, fitting neatly together because the wood is thoroughly dried in a warehouse beforehand. The exterior walls are R-25 structural insulated panels (SIPS) and built to comply with "NovoClimat" standards, which costs more up front, but ensure that the house will have low electric and heating bills.

"It's brought us much closer as a couple. When it's 3 o'clock in the morning, and you've got to finish closing the walls before the next morning, after having spent four days and nights on a wild sprint, and then you screw something up, it tests your patience. Now we know we can go through anything. It will take so much to break our spirit. Since having built the house, we hardly ever argue anymore. We know each other much better and we have respect for each other. I suggest it to anyone who has the courage." —Jacinte Wikow

At the end of 2004 the couple negotiated a 25-year $115,000 bank mortgage, including a clause that allows them to pay it off early, and by making weekly instead of monthly payments they will retire their debt in 19 years. In February, the contractor and his crew broke ground. At the end of March, the foundation, exterior walls, and roof were up and the service lines were in. It was time for Jacinte and Robert to take over. From March through December they spent all of their vacation days, every weekend and essentially every evening hanging drywall and exterior siding, blowing cellulose into the attic, building cabinets and hanging doors, painting, tiling, installing fixtures. They hired an electrician to complete the wiring.

“Since so many people have helped, there’s a little piece of every family member in the house. The walls were closed by our friend Maria, and Robert’s mom, and uncle. My dad framed all the windows. My brother did the tile work. Robert’s brother was there with us on that crazy night we worked around the clock, and he helped with the vinyl. My uncle did the masonry. My mom used the saw (she did—that was a surprise) to cut the 2 by 4s and she helped put up the aluminum that insulates the walls. Our house is the smallest among all our friends, but we love it. Our appreciation for every corner of it has grown over the months we spent toiling over its every nail and screw.” —Jacinte Wikow

Suddenly there was a surprise: the contractor had neglected to charge them $8,000, for city hook-ups to services. Determined not to return to the bank to extend their mortgage, the couple used their savings, and Jacinte found a bit of contract work in addition to her regular job, which covered the extra cost. “We spent absolutely nothing during that time, except on the house. Who has time to go see a movie or shop if you’re building every day? It makes you frugal.”

They were also frugal in their design: the two children’s rooms are 100 square feet each. Their own bedroom is 195 sq. feet, including a walk-in closet and alcove. They will wait to build a garage or workshop, if they have the resources and desire in the future.

Two zoning regulations increased their costs by about $4,000: they were required to have a façade covered at least 50 percent in a brick veneer and at least 25 feet wide, 1 foot wider than their house plan called for. (They solved this by building the façade out 6 inches on each side.)

One reason they kept their house small is because they prefer to do their own housework: “It keeps us fit.” Robert’s a mechanical engineer, but the couple started out with very few manual skills. Now they’ll be able to repair their own house.

Thanks to good solar orientation and high insulation, they can turn the heat off in April and don’t turn it on until November, even though outside temperatures can drop to around freezing even in May and October. Their heating bill is about what it was in their conventionally-insulated apartment, which was half the size. They chose appliances that are energy-efficient, and that are expected to last at least two decades.

The discrepancy between the figures above and the financed amount comes from “move-in” costs, which many people include in the mortgage, but they have been paying out of pocket as they furnish their house. The $735 per month that they pay is a little higher than their previous rent, but rents are rising, and in this house they have space for kids.

GO OUTSIDE.

5
Go Outside

A growing body of evidence has indicated that the air within homes and other buildings can be more seriously polluted than the outdoor air in even the largest and most industrialized cities.—UNITED STATES ENVIRONMENTAL PROTECTION AGENCY

GO OUTSIDE. I MEAN IT. RIGHT NOW.

Bundle up or strip down, grab a hat, or find a flashlight. Do what you need to, and go outside. What do you find there? Light. If it's daytime, you'll be drenched in "full-spectrum light," the ubiquitous, sunny substance that, amazingly, manages to be sold by mail order ("The HappyEyes™ Floor Lamp brings the benefits of natural daylight indoors...$129 Made in Taiwan"). Why is that floor lamp so popular?

The Big World Outside

OUR FRIEND, THE SUN

For over 99 percent of our existence, our species spent most of its time outside. Today, North Americans spend about 90 percent of our time indoors. We are designed to live in sync with the sun, and we know we're missing something.[1] The sun gives us vitamin D, and cheers us up. Its warm light allows us to see clearly the colors in a painting, the details in a flower. Ultraviolet light, especially UVB rays, which is minimized or blocked by window glass, seems to be an immune system booster, possibly protecting against Hodgkin's disease and some forms of cancer.[2] So bask in that sun, and feel it protect you.

What about skin cancer? There are gaps in the ozone layer, so maybe you're afraid of the sun. Robin Harris, a researcher at the University of Arizona Cancer Center, wants you to know that, of course, going out uncovered (no hat, bare arms, no shade) during the most UV-intense hours (10 AM–3 PM in most areas) will increase your chances of all kinds of skin cancer. "But sitting indoors fearing the sun is not going to help, either," she says, adding, "Inactive, indoor people are at a higher risk of skin cancer." Scientists are trying to figure out why skin cancer is so much more prevalent among the highest-paid workers. It may be because upper-class people are likely to be low in the pigment hormone melatonin (a.k.a. "white"), but it also appears that working inside all day heightens the chance of skin cancer, especially if you "balance" it with sudden week-long sunburns at a tropical beach in February. So cover up, but do go outside.

FREEZING?

Maybe it's snowing outside. Maybe the wind chill factor has driven the reported temperature

Kathy and John Early realized a dream when they completed their cabin high in the woods, lovingly finishing the interior all by themselves. But before they finished the work they began to notice that their two youngest boys almost always had a cold or headache. It took about a year for them to link the fresh lacquer, plywood, and particle board in their home, coupled with brand-new carpeting in the school their sons attended, to what was eventually diagnosed as "environmental illness."

down to far below zero. Maybe it's dangerously cold. Should you run back in?

Even cold-climate small-house dwellers report that living outside is central to their life. If their warm season is short, or if sunny days are rare, they want to maximize their ability to enjoy good weather. In rainy but otherwise mild climates, rain structures, varying from sturdy steel roofs, to glass-covered walkways, to simple blue tarps allow residents to work through a drizzle. An unheated sunroom can moderate the temperature of the house it adjoins, as well as giving people a place to be in between the realms of "in" and "out." Going outside can help a body adjust to the change in seasons, and moderate the perceived need for heating inside.

OUR FRIEND, THE MOON

Maybe it's night where you are right now. The stars might be obscured by all the "Happy Lamps," but at least you'll see the moon, that small core of cooled lava with a pale gray surface that swells 4 inches every twenty-six days. It bathes you in cool light. Sailors know the power of the moon. Some people once thought that direct moonlight can make you crazy, but more now believe that sleeping in the moonbeam's path will stabilize a woman's menstrual cycle. Others claim that sleeping with the moon and rising with the sun boosts immunity.[3] Some farmers say the moon influences fluid flow in plants, and plant when the moon is near full and waxing, and cut trees and harvest seed when the moon is thin and waning.

AIR INSIDE AND OUT

Feel the cool evening air. If you are sensitive to pollen, night is a good time to be outside. Most pollen counts begin to rise midmorning, or early afternoon, peaking a few hours later and dropping off around 8 PM.[4] On the other hand, if you are like most allergy sufferers,[5] you are at least as allergic to things inside the house (dust mites, mold, and pets) as outside. Pollution aggravates allergies, but as auto makers (upset that their product is so heavily regulated) like to point out: indoor air, all over the country, tends to be about three to twelve times more polluted than outside air.[6] Outdoors is the air purifier we all rely upon.

Paint, caulk, carpet, telephone wire, linoleum tile, chlorinated water, cleaning products, plastic shopping bags, nail polish, and human-made methane are a few of the many items that cause your house to exhale polluted air. Buildings with very poor indoor air quality were once said to suffer from "tight building syndrome," because the problem was first noticed in sealed buildings where operable windows had been eliminated (an attempt at energy efficiency). The problem is now called "sick building syndrome," because it's linked with several severe diseases.

TURNING INDOOR AIR INTO OUTDOOR AIR

Non- and low-toxic alternative finishes and materials, which pollute less or not at all, are available.[7] They are one of the "luxuries" you will want to afford. Source reduction is by far the most effective way to reduce indoor air pollution. Otherwise, ventilation is key.

Large buildings make it necessary to rely on forced-air systems, which ultimately need filters, since the ducts themselves become habitat for dust mites and mold. The small house has this advantage: windows can be sufficient. Four square feet of window for every hundred square feet of floor,[8] assuming casement windows (because they open wider), should suffice. In a warm climate, consider one small operable skylight, or better yet, a clerestory. Opened at night, this "roof window" can exchange all the air in a small house in a few hours. Some thoughtful warm-climate designers put low windows on the windward walls and high windows leeward, so hot air will be encouraged to speed on its path up and out, through the high windows. Single-hung windows, which are modern imitations of the traditional double-hung windows, have only one operable sash, and don't ventilate as well as windows that open top and bottom, encouraging the natural tendency of air to circulate.

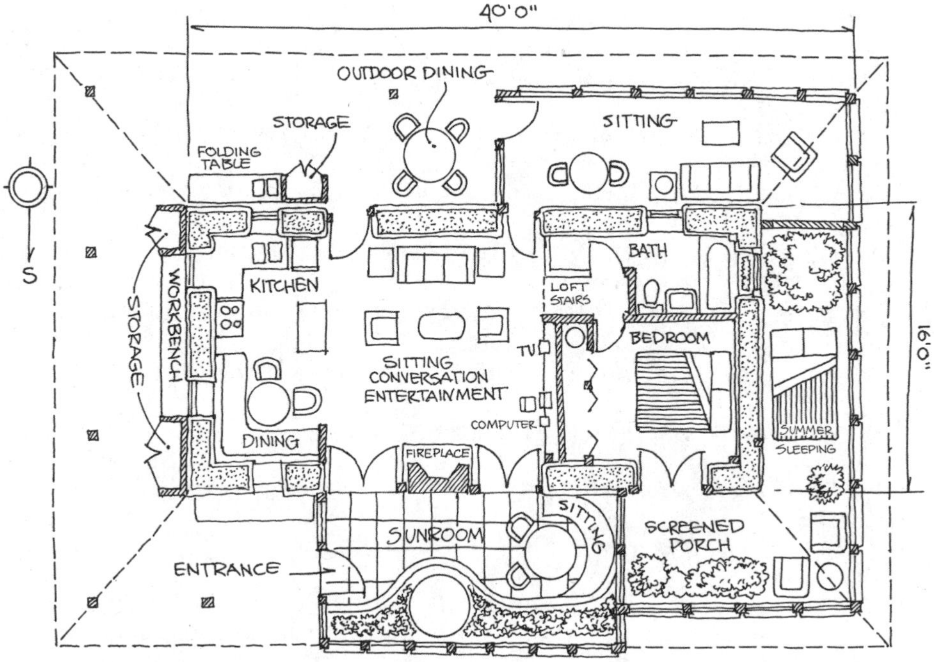

CAROLYN ROBERT'S HOUSE INCLUDES A WRAPAROUND PORCH THAT MORE THAN DOUBLES THE LIVING SPACE OF THIS 720 INDOOR SQUARE FOOT HOUSEPLAN. CATHEDRAL CEILINGS AND A SLEEPING LOFT MAXIMIZE INDOOR SPACE. THE PORCH CREATES A MIDDLE ZONE BETWEEN INSIDE AND OUT, WITH A GLAZED SOLAR SUNROOM ON THE SOUTH SIDE, AND A SCREENED PORCH WRAPPING AROUND THE SOUTHEAST TO THE NORTHEAST CORNERS, ALLOWING BUG-FREE OUTDOOR SUMMER SLEEPING. ARCHITECT WAYNE BINGHAM, WHO DESIGNED THE PLAN AND HAS A WRAPAROUND PORCH ON HIS OWN HOUSE, ADDS, "A SCREENED PORCH ALLOWS DOORS TO BE LEFT WIDE OPEN, ALLOWING MAXIMUM AIR CIRCULATION, WITHOUT THE ADDITION OF SCREEN DOORS." THE PORCH ALSO PROTECTS EXTERIOR FINISHES, MINIMIZING MAINTENANCE AND MAKING NATURAL PAINT AND PLASTER OPTIONS MORE FEASIBLE.[9]

Traditionally, in very cold climates, people moved into small quarters during winter, shutting off a part of their home. A smaller space is heated more easily, but ventilation is essential to maintain air quality. A Swedish experiment showed that human and animal bodies ("three-dog night"), plus electrical appliances, could produce sufficient heat for a super-insulated small home, but the house was too sealed, so the air inside was unhealthy. As Michel Bergeron, a designer and builder in Montréal who doesn't worry if some of his window sashes let in a little air, says, "When we work so hard to make our buildings tight, we end up having to use air filters, at an extra cost in every way."

THE PORCH

Porches on farmhouses were essential for food processing, entertaining guests during harvest, and summer sleeping. Front porches in neighborhoods used to serve as telephones and TV sets: they announced to neighbors you are available to chat, and livened up the street life for those out on an evening stroll. Porticoes, balconies, terraces, and verandahs were signs of a complete house. Some people credit the arrival of air conditioning with the decline of neighborhood cohesion, especially in the South.

Porches on small houses provide extra storage, party, and summer guest space. Some are designed and built to convert easily into four-season space, if necessary, at some point in the future. They filter or block sun, and rain and they can be shallow on the south side of the house, to allow in warm winter sun but block summer heat. They protect finishes, making it possible for the owner to choose natural, inexpensive, nontoxic plasters or wood finishes that otherwise would be hard to maintain. Screened porches provide mosquito-free outdoor relaxation.

Excellent outdoor space, even when architect-designed and contractor-built, is typically one-third to one-tenth the cost of indoor space. "But unfortunately, the outdoor space comes last," landscape architect Irene Ogata explains,

The feast of the tabernacles, called Succot *in Hebrew, is a biblical holiday that requires families to build a small shack outside, one with a roof flimsy enough to let in the rain and the starlight. They inhabit the shack, at least to eat meals, for a week in autumn. Shauna and Rivka bought a kit they saw on the Internet and set it up in their backyard, decorating it with grasses and cornstalks and flowers. "It became the most beautiful room of our house. We've ended up leaving it up most of the year; we enjoy it so much. Is that in the spirit of the holiday?"*

"literally—it's built when everything else is finished, and after the finances have been depleted." For this reason, some landscape architects complain that their profession is relegated to providing the "parsley on the pig," when, as the two profiles in this chapter show, in many locations, it makes more sense to treat the outdoor space as the main course.

A ROOM WITH A VIEW TO THE SKY

Owner-builders are less likely to forget the value of the outdoors when they make the building site itself livable, first with a shady place to eat, then an outdoor toilet, kitchen, and shower. More than one owner-builder has discovered that after the outdoor structures and the "guest" house were built, and the garden planted, there was no longer any need for the main house.

What these owner-builders discover is the efficiency of moving activities outside, at least for part of the year. Outdoor kitchens remove a source of heat from the house, and help remind people how much they enjoy barbecuing, solar cooking, and eating outside.

Ideally, outdoor kitchens are located near the indoor kitchen (maybe on the opposite wall, with plumbing running through to a second sink), and they include an animal-proof box or cabinet to

SHAUNA AND RIVKA MORGAN-SHERMAN IN THEIR BACKYARD

store food. In fantasy, they are self-cleaning, since birds come to eat the crumbs, but some people throw a cover over the stove and counter to keep leaves and dirt from accumulating when it's not in use. Some people move their stove in and out with the seasons; others leave their large oven/stove in one place (inside in cold climates, outside in warm) and use a smaller countertop or camping stove in the other area. In some climates it's practical to have *only* an outdoor kitchen. Or consider trying it for just a week.

MICHAEL G. SMITH AND KRISTEN GARDNER SLEEP OUTSIDE AT EMERALD EARTH SANCTUARY.

SLEEP UNDER THE STARS

Did you ever camp out in your backyard as a kid? Some couples reverse this play by leaving the kids in the house, and making a romantic getaway somewhere in the yard. Others sleep outside so they can sleep—one man turned his bed in every direction, read a book on feng shui, tried sleeping in the living room, and nothing worked, until he simply set a pad on the outside ground. Here again, you don't need much of a structure to try it: a tarp to spread over your bed while you're gone is enough. Over time you might find yourself adding mosquito netting, a rain-proof bookcase . . . .

If streetlights flood your yard (front, side, or back), they are probably pointed incorrectly, and a call to the road department or your city council member might improve them. If your neighbors' lights flood your yard, talk to them nicely before you check into whether an ordinance in your area bans strong porch lights. Noise (e.g., your neighbor's air conditioner), unfortunately, is both harder to control and less legislated.[10]

BATHE IN THE SUN

Outdoor bathhouses can be as simple as a bucket hooked to a tree and a pallet on the ground or as elaborate as a wood-fired hot tub next to a sauna. It can be easier to build a solar-heated shower outside than to try to retrofit an existing house, because you don't have to make it mesh with the existing water heating system. Or, you can run extra piping from a shower located inside an exterior wall, and build its outdoor twin next to it. It's easy to use gray water from an outdoor shower on your garden. You can collect the shower water in a basin and with a hose or bucket spread it over your garden, right after your shower, leaving no standing water for mosquitoes, or plant very water-loving plants around the shower, and use gravel and trenches to spread the water out. Almost all commercial, and most homemade soaps and detergents will eventually salt up the soil

As fall begins, start each day early by standing unclothed outside first for just fifteen seconds, gradually increasing each day until you stand for three or four minutes. Notice the cold, and remember that it won't harm you, that your body is fine and strong. Feel the cold on your skin, and imagine it as a friend. The rest of the day, you will feel warm and comfortable.

and kill most plants. Consider giving yourself a real mud, sand, ash, or oatmeal bath, or look for safer, nitrogen-based, commercial alternatives.[11]

An outdoor bathing area allows sun to shine on the bather but is normally (and sometimes legally) hidden from public view. Some people find that a few minutes of sunlight on their whole body clears up rashes. I found that an outdoor shower was the perfect place to do an exercise recommended by Wataru Ohashi (a Zen shiatsu teacher) to improve poor circulation, and lower heating bills (see above).

It worked for me.

SHIT IN THE WOODS

Some small-house dwellers want to use a compost toilet but they want to save on space indoors. They fear that the small space might be contaminated by the smell, if they do it "wrong" (which is hard to do, but not impossible). Or they live in a one-bathroom house and are reluctant to replace the flush toilet with a composting one. So they build an outhouse.

Architectural designer Richard G. Brittain and his wife Wendy D. Brittain have spent more than twenty years slowly and lovingly renovating, repairing and maintaining a complex of three apartments where they live with their tenants. The oldest deed to the property dates back to 1870, and the rooms are arranged around a courtyard that is planted with flowers and trees. To reach the bathroom, residents cross this courtyard, which is the equivalent of a long, open, sweet-smelling hallway. They could have modernized by installing bathrooms in each unit, but, Richard says, "We like the idea that regardless of the weather conditions, we'll walk outside, and enjoy the stars and the flowers and maintain a healthy relationship with the outdoors."

THICK WALLS THAT ABSORB HEAT EXTEND THE GROWING SEASON.

THE PATIO PLAN

Many traditional Chinese, Korean, Middle Eastern, Mediterranean, and Latin American houses consist of rooms wrapped around a courtyard that provides protection from the wind and street traffic, and light in every room. The outdoor space is a natural gathering place, and those inside the rooms communicate easily with the activity in the patio. Thick walls that absorb heat, such as those that surrounded the *giardino secreto* (secret garden) of the Italian Renaissance, extend the growing season. A small pond reflects light and moderates both winter and summer temperatures, and a *chiminea* or small firepit can warm the area in fall or spring.

If you are adding a small "granny" flat, garden shed, or an outdoor room to your home, consider placing it in a way that creates a patio between it and the existing house. Place it to shade something you want shaded, or block a view that you'd rather not see. If you are building new, planning several tiny structures can be rewarding, especially if you are building them yourself: you can complete one fully before you go on to the next, and use the knowledge you gained on the first for the second. Since long, thicker-dimensioned lumber is more expensive, and harder to find used, a few smaller structures can be less expensive than one large one since you can use shorter, thinner joists and beams to span the roof.

A collection of small buildings works particularly well in a warm or mild climate. The walls between the structures can create storage, garden, and private spaces. In cold climates some people prefer this plan if they tend to have many visitors in summer, but just want to heat one small structure in winter.

If there's a view you like to watch, but an unwelcome wind always comes from that direction (e.g., a northern ocean beach), a wall of thick, tempered glass on the windy side of your patio can create a calm suntrap that extends the beach barbecue season.

In humid climates where wind is welcome, consider the traditional Japanese *engawa* design: a wide corridor of two parallel, movable, sliding walls and a wooden plank floor that wraps around two or more sides of the house. The house expands in summer, with both sets of rice paper or glass walls slid open, or stowed away, and contracts in winter, the corridor serving mainly as a cold air break or giant storm window for the rest of the house.

A FORMER BEDROOM IS NOW A PORCH.

OUTDOORS, UP HIGH

It's hard to recommend building a flat roof, since they often leak, but if you have one already, climb a ladder and see what you find. You may have just found an ideal summer sleeping area, or a private meditation space. One small house in a warm climate has a flat roof, with a gabled porch roof

The Hunters, of Toronto, Ontario, purchased a house with a balcony that had been converted into a bedroom. After using it while their children were young as extra bedroom space, they finally decided to simply remove it. The whole second floor, previously darkened by the enclosure, brightened up. "In our climate, the summers are precious. We want to have every opportunity to be outside while it lasts," Mrs. Hunter explains.

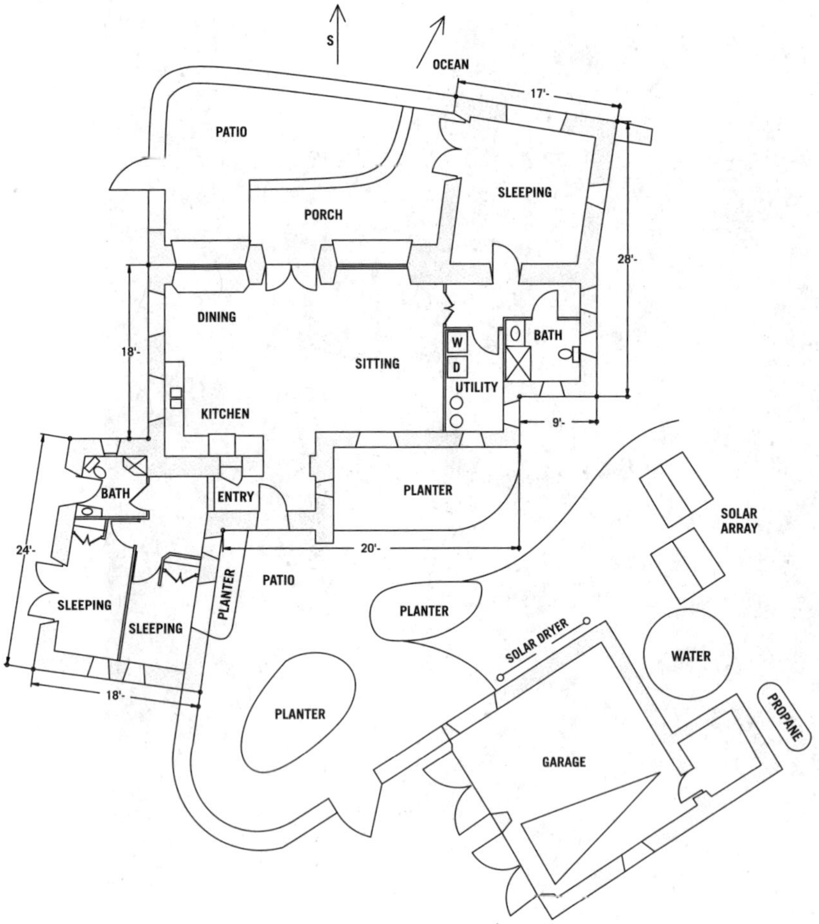

PACIFIC WINGS

THIS 1300 SQ FT OCEANSIDE HOUSE SPREADS ITS WINGS TOWARDS THE PACIFIC OCEAN. THE LAYOUT MAXIMIZES VIEW, AND SOUTHERN EXPOSURE, AND SHELTERS THE OCEANSIDE PORCH FROM THE NORTHWESTERLY WINDS. ARCHITECT ROBERT MEHL CAMPED OUT ON THE SITE SO HE COULD THOROUGHLY UNDERSTAND THE WIND AND SUN PATTERNS, AND THE VIEW, BEFORE HE SITED THE BUILDING.

INSIDE, BEDROOMS ARE MINIMAL, TO ENCOURAGE SOCIAL INTERACTION AND OUTSIDE ACTIVITY. THE PATIO IS SURFACED IN CHUNKS OF CONCRETE, SALVAGED FROM THE FLOOR OF A FORMER LOCAL DAIRY, AND ORIGINALLY CAST WITH A BRUSHED, ROUGH-FACED PATTERN TO PREVENT THE COWS FROM SLIPPING. "SITTING ON THE PATIO, YOU MAY FIND THE IDEA OF MILK AND COOKIES PERMEATES YOUR THOUGHTS," SMILES BUILDER KIT BOISE-COSSART.

THE WALLS OF THE HOUSE ARE MADE OF SALVAGED CONCRETE FROM OLD SIDEWALKS, WHICH CONTAIN NO REBAR AND THEREFORE CAN BE CUT INTO FAIRLY UNIFORM "BRICKS." DESPITE LIMITED SOUTHERN EXPOSURE, THE GARDEN BEDS ON THE NORTHEAST SIDE ARE PRODUCTIVE, DUE IN PART TO THE MICROCLIMATE CREATED BY THE LONG PATIO WALL.

high above it, adding both shading for the whole house, and a giant upstairs sleeping porch. Other houses have a porch roof built flat, but with plenty of easy drainage (like a very high deck) and placed near a large upstairs window so it can be reached from inside, via the window, serving as a balcony. Or you might have an upstairs bedroom that would rather be a balcony.

A tree house may better suit your need to get up high. A tiny platform balanced in an old tree makes the best gazebo; live leaves cast green shade in summer, and bare branches allow winter sunlight. You can design a house around the existing trees, or if there are none, plant a young tree or vines near a very simple, "temporary" *ramada*, early on in construction. Some existing homes have shade trees in a perfect spot, but the house needs one more exterior door, or a better path, to entice people to the tree.

DOWN TO EARTH

The least costly form of outdoor space is the earth itself. In some places the fashion is to brick or

Adrienne, after a life spent entertaining her husband's clients and cleaning up after children, dreamed of a retirement of no cleaning, all gardening. She spent several years designing her house, and by the end the house plan had shrunk to a quarter size, and the garden had quadrupled. Previously she had imagined hiring someone else to clean once a week, but after moving in she realized she could clean such a small house in a few hours. Instead she hired a gardener. Her investment now pays off in fresh food and flowers. "What would you rather pay someone to do?" she asks, "vainly try to stem that tide of entropy, dirt, or make flowers from the dirt?"

AN OUTDOOR ROOM

pave the entire nongarden space. Especially if you have young children, consider leaving an area free, as mud pit, sand pile, or wild land: continual contact with the bacteria and other life in mud is thought to be the reason farmers' children have much stronger immune systems.[12] A garden isn't a farm, but it can provide a lot of dirt. And a lawn, though maybe criticized for the pesticides sometimes sprayed on it, or for its thirst for water, can make sense if it's small: Laurel Robertson and Charles Gibson (See Chapter 11) have "A lawn sized to our house, about 6 feet square, that is big enough to sit, lie, and picnic on without consuming much water, time, or fertilizer."

On any bit of earth where you plan to live, the choice is the same: Roofed, or open to the sky? Closed, or open to the wind? Choose more of one, and have less of the other.

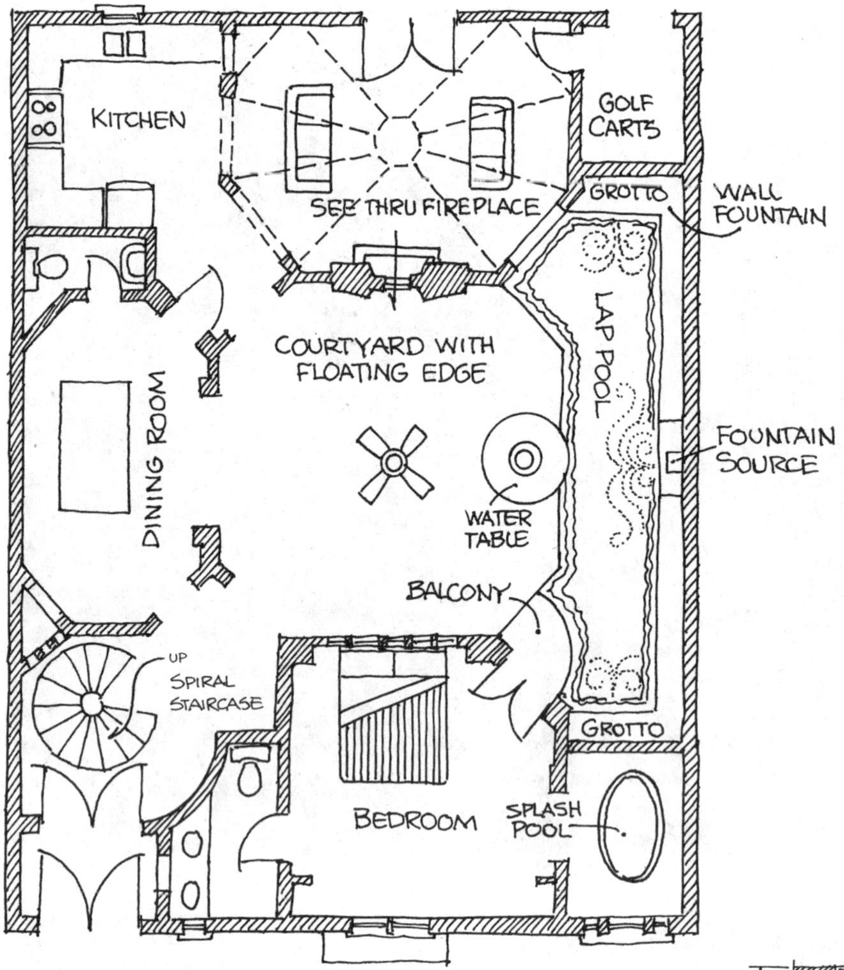

CASA SENSUALA BY MELANIE TAYLOR
ARCHITECT MELANIE TAYLOR DESIGNED THIS HOUSE FOR AN URBAN SETTING IN MEXICO. THE HOUSE WRAPS AROUND THE LOT LINE, CONSERVING A CENTRAL OUTDOOR CORE THAT FEATURES A SWIMMING POOL, A FLOATING DINING TABLE IN THE POOL, AND AN OPERABLE SUNSCREEN THAT COVERS THE COURTYARD. EVERY ROOM OPENS TO THE COURTYARD.

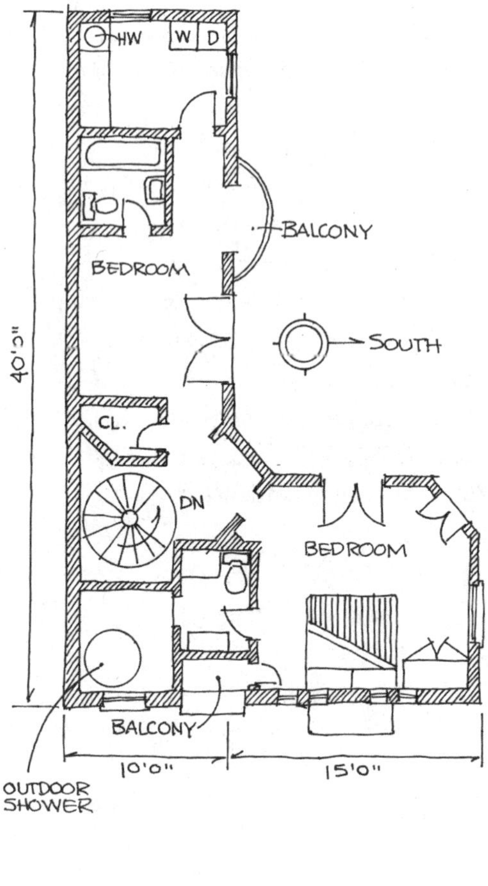

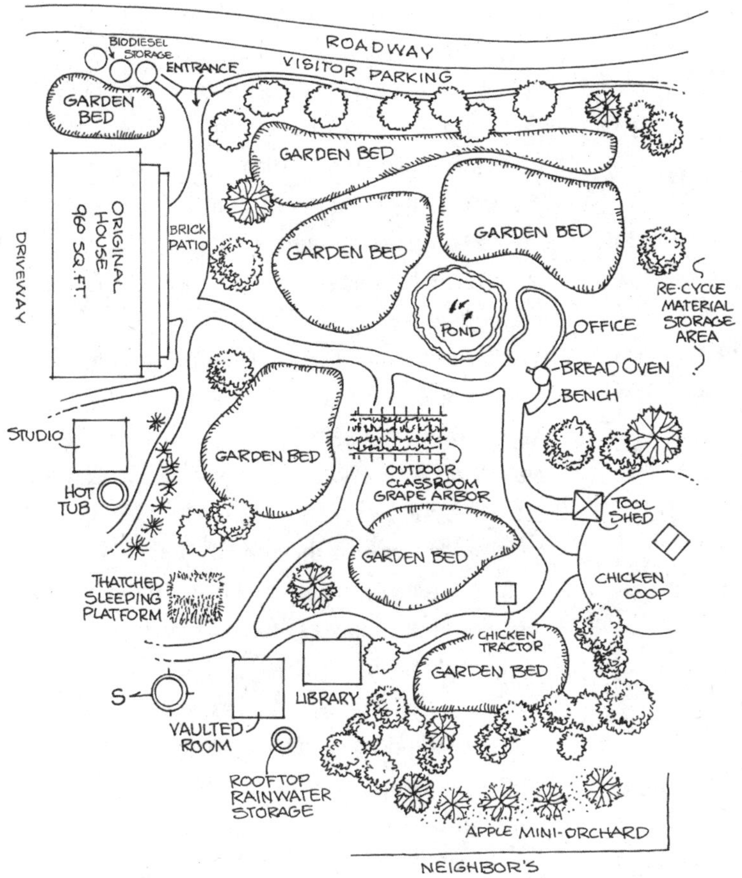

PENNY LIVINGSTON AND JAMES STARK
Main house built 1950s
Outbuildings built late 1990s

AREA:
Main house: 1,200 sq. ft.
Outbuildings: 380 sq. ft.

INTENDED NUMBER OF OCCUPANTS:
2-4

PURCHASE PRICE (1988)
Undisclosed

UTILITY COSTS:
Undisclosed

LOCATION:
Point Reyes, California

The Permaculture Institute of Northern California,

is home of Penny Livingston and James Stark, and is a collection of gardens, ponds, trees and small buildings, on a one-acre lot in Point Reyes, California. Tucked into a conventional suburban neighborhood, PINC presents a physical example of a garden-based, locally-reliant lifestyle. "The suburbs are here to stay," says James. "The question is 'how can we turn them into paradise?'"

The PINC gardens don't serve as "landscaping" for the building. On the contrary, the gardens are the centerpiece, and the buildings seem more like garden follies. The ground is soft with leaves and wood chips. We walk past a dozen oval garden beds filled with common vegetables — greens, legumes, tomatoes, cucumbers, onions— and less common ones like perrenial nastursiums, amarynth, and jerusalem artichokes. A small orchard of apple trees is on one end of the property, watched over by the neighbor's minimansion. The garden has a dozen varieties of fruit trees, including Asian pears, woven into a living fence. We pass and ripe pears thud to the ground. Chickens cluck at us from their location in a huge, handwoven inverted basket made of branches from the orchard. This mobile "chicken tractor" allows them to "plow" sections of the

ABOVE LEFT: FLOOR PLAN ABOVE: THE PINC OFFICE CAME OUT OF THE DUCK POND.

"One definition of permaculture is simply applying what you observe to what you do. To garden, you need to be outside, observing, learning, all day long. Listen to the birds. They are farming this place too, and they teach us. If you only go out for a short time each day, the birds have a certain song, "She's coming! She's coming," a danger song, but if you stay out all day, they share their whole vocabulary with you. You become part of their world."

—Penny Livingston

garden without running free and destroying new sprouts.

When Penny first arrived, in 1987, she started with hard ground covered in grasses and thistle. "We never plowed the ground. We mulched it up instead." says Penny, The 150 "round" foot cob/light clay office building literally came out of the ground: Penny was looking for a place to put the earth she removed after digging a deep duck pond. "We made the pond deep, so the koi could escape from predatory birds," and ended up with a huge pile of earth, which became the walls of the office. With six arched, bay windows and French doors on the south side, this curvaceous structure provides ample, airy space for two people to work comfortably, as well as plenty of bookshelves and file cabinets. An attached cob bench/oven area outside is a good place to meet clients or read. The roof of the building is guttered to feed water to the pond it came from.

In the center of the garden is a "classroom" for visiting students, a large grape arbor with a flagstone floor. PINC schedules classes to correspond with the seven months of the year that rain is unlikely. Sitting there one wonders why anyone teaches gardening or agriculture from a closed, air-conditioned building.

Inside the main house, the couple clay-plastered the conventional gypsum interior walls, adding curves and color that blend with the small outbuildings and

AN OFFICE IN THE GARDEN

PENNY HERDING DUCKS

the vitality of the garden. "We avoid creating dead zones," says James. "For us, a dining room is a dead zone, so we don't have one—the table in the kitchen seats eight. We've tried to fill our home with life, minimizing dead corners and empty space."

A small vaulted straw bale structure roofed in corrugated steel serves as a massage studio, or an extra bedroom. With the aid of architects Bob Theis and Dan Smith, and a group of volunteers, the building went up in a weekend workshop, plus "a gazillion hours," of finish work. Skylights were formed by leaving spaces between bales, and substituting clear fiberglass for steel roofing over those spaces, so the room is evenly daylit inside. Next door is a 120 sq. ft. library. A square building with a large south window, its roof is made simply of curved glulam beams, sheathed in steel. Tucked into rich vegetation is a Balinese bamboo sleeping platform, that allows the couple to spend their nights outside as well.

Penny says she prefers to have a few smaller buildings rather than one large house because it lends itself to a village feeling, and offers the possibility of "getting away," by retreating to a small outbuilding right at home.

"Smaller buildings are more conducive to experimentation. This whole project is an experiment, a process. We apply consistent principles, but we try all kinds of things, some of which work, and some which fail, but since everything we try is small, it's just a small failure. If it works, we let it grow larger. If you come back in a few years, everything will have changed."

—James Stark

LYNN AND MARLEY PORTER
BRANDON GRIFFITH
Built 1999–2001

AREA:
1,100 square feet indoors, within a 5,000-sq.-ft. lot outdoors

INTENDED NUMBER OF OCCUPANTS:
About 3

COST:
Land: $250/month
Construction Tree house: $18,000
Studio, $35,000
Bathroom/wine deck $25,000
Master bedroom $55,000
K-L-D (most work owner done) $65,000

UTILITY COSTS (MONTHLY):
$25(winter)
$75 (summer) electric and propane

LOCATION:
Austin, Texas

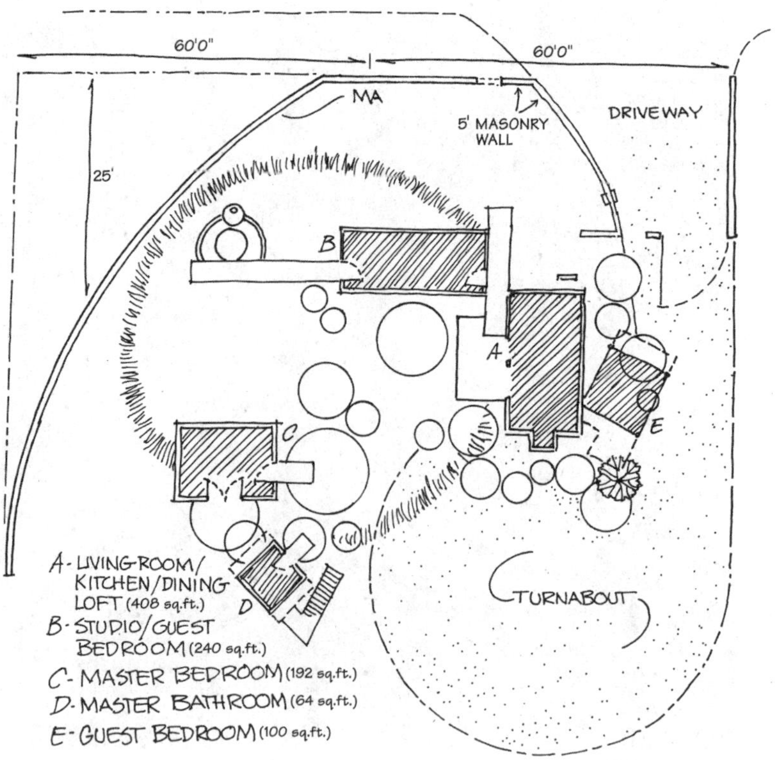

ABOVE : **FLOOR PLAN**

Above the huge boulder that forms the north wall

of Marley Porter's architectural office lies a flat bit of land, about 50 by 100 feet, and owned by but inaccessible to Marley's neighbor, a convenience store. Before Marley acquired the office, it had been a bikers' bar, and the land up above was a beer garden that patrons reached by ascending a narrow slope. Knowing that the convenience store couldn't use the lot, Marley offered the owner $250 a month to lease it, and she accepted. Knowing that the lot would never be considered suitable for permanent habitation, he and his wife Lynn decided to build a number of moveable "storage" structures, and nestle them into the land and trees that were already there.

Their house consists of five tiny houses. Each "pod" is built on a steel skid using 12" junior beams, 2 by 10 joists, and 24"-on-center balloon framing. To discourage waste, the division between rough and finish framing is minimal: for example the studs double as door frames and as the window mullions for the clerestories in the master bedroom, and the roof is designed with a slope and length so that a 4 by 8 foot sheet of plywood sheathing fits perfectly, with no need to cut. Cedar rough texture siding covers 1" by 2" cedar battens. The walls are insulated with sprayed cellulose at R-19. The roofs are a tight sandwich, of sheathing—typically scrap 2 by 4s perpendicular to the rafters, covered with R-9 rigid polystyrene insulation and topped with corrugated steel.

The kitchen-dining-living-room, is called the "hearth room," and at 408 square feet it is the largest single structure. With a fireplace, a ¾ bathroom, a television, and upholstered furniture, it is a comfortable place for the family to gather inside. Upstairs a loft holds Lynn's sewing room. The structure is covered with a "butterfly roof," which Marley describes as "a marriage of wind and water." The opposite of a standard, gable roof, the wings of the "butterfly" come together near the center of the structure, where a sturdy galvanized steel gutter gathers water from the roof and doubles as a ridge beam (one might say "valley beam") to carry the weight of the roof rafters, which are exposed to the interior.

North of and perpendicular to the hearth room a guest room/studio, that will give Lynn a place of her own for creative work, is under construction. East of and slightly above the hearth room Brandon's room rests 10 feet above the ground on steel pipe columns, and embraced by an oak tree. A wire mesh aviary filled with doves and more exotic birds hangs between the steel columns. The 10 by 10 foot tree house has glass double doors, and two square 1-foot windows for ventilation, as well as a ribbon of translucent green corrugated roofing around the top of the wall that casts a colored tint on the room. Brandon, a teenager who likes to sequester himself for hours in his room, says it's a perfect size for him, and that the only downside is that he wasn't allowed to chose his own colors for the walls and door; they are light brown and yellow.

The tree house is oriented so its front door cannot be seen from the master bedroom's front door, across the central patio. "Brandon is trustworthy," the couple explains. Marley believes their bedroom, called "the red room," is the best example of a sound "feng shui" design he has ever built. The red room is sized like the golden rectangle, in both height, and width. The head of the bed is towards the east. A clerestory window encircles the entire space, but on the north side rises higher—starting at 8 feet and going to 12, with a 6 foot overhang, while on the south it bows to the southern sun, rising to only 10 feet and with just a 2 foot overhang. This butterfly roof is off center by a third, so the gutter

THE SENSE FROM INSIDE THE DEEP TUB IS OF EXPANSION.

LYNN, IN THE AVIARY, UNDER THE TREEHOUSE

that bonds and carries its two "wings" doesn't appear to divide the bed, but is off to one side of it. The clerestory light bounces off the "valley beam," in a pattern that "locks the couple in bed together, " according to Marley, "but if you sleep there alone you'll crave company all night."

Next door, the main bathhouse has space both indoors and out for bathing. The walls lean slightly out, so the sense from inside the deep tub is of expansion and a wide view. Outside, the showerhead leans with the wall to cover the showerer. A staircase winds up to one, final glass step ("It requires a small leap of faith to cross that threshold," says Marley) to the roof-level "wine deck," which itself is one-third glass, allowing visual communication between everything above and below. "If you stand on the wine deck, and imagine the traffic noise is ocean waves, you transport yourself into nature, and far away from central Austin," says Lynn.

But by far the dominant aspect of the house is nothing indoors, but the sequence of outdoor space created by the placement of the pods, and the natural features of the land. Lynn used these natural features to create a meditation circle in one private edge of the lot. She imagined it would be 13 feet in diameter, and when she found the right place, and measured, she saw that a tree, its huge roots, already created a 13-foot diameter circle, with a boulder at its center. She drystacked rocks to form a low wall, filling in the circle where the roots didn't reach, and a long, low curved bench emerged. "I am happiest outside," says Lynn. "I spend most of my day out. The best thing about our house is that it forces me to go outside; I can't forget that it's there." The only thing she might add is a covered walkway between buildings, for rainy days.

Marley explains how his new home has influenced and been influenced by his architectural practice: "1+1=3. Two structures, plus the space between them. The space in between is creative. If you get all your ducks in a row, you'll have problems. Our pods are locked together in a hierarchy of spaces. We used existing decks from the beer garden, and built others. Each pod is private. It's a choice to come out and go to a common space, and when we make that choice we come together under the sky.

"Especially when each unit is mobile, like these, it's all a process. It's you, and you rearrange it. It's not 'Marley Porter, Architect.' You, the occupant, can take architecture as your second skin, and mold it until it fits you, and fits the space."

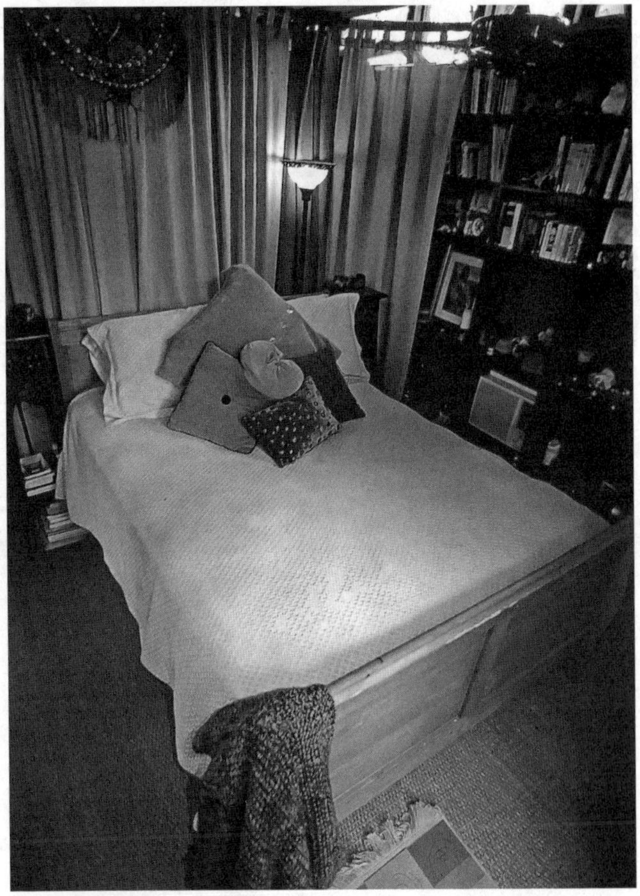

MARLEY AND LYNN'S BEDROOM

EPILOGUE:

Marley and Lynn bought land in town outside of Austin, and planned to move their new home there. A moving company jacked up the pods, bolted them to axles, and squeezed them out the narrow passage to the road. The couple were then informed by the town that local zoning would not permit their pods. The pods spent two years on the side of a highway as the couple tried to convince the town council to allow a variance. Finally, in 2006, they negotiated instead to move them to Lake Travis, where they were slightly remodeled—in one case bending a wall to fit around a tree—and are now used as bedrooms in a bed and breakfast. A steady stream of visitors enjoys them.

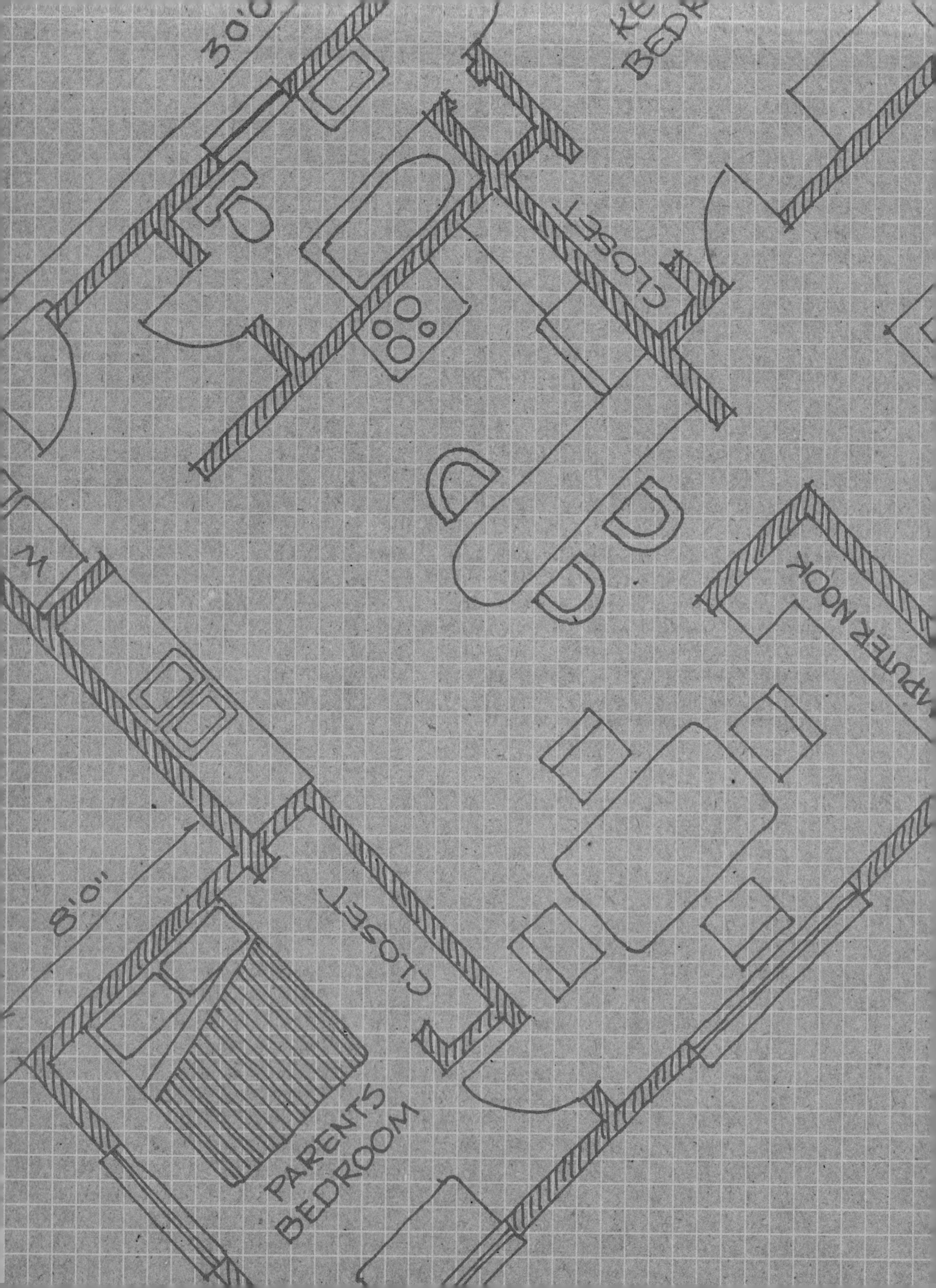
CLOSET
CLOSET
8'0"
PARENTS BEDROOM

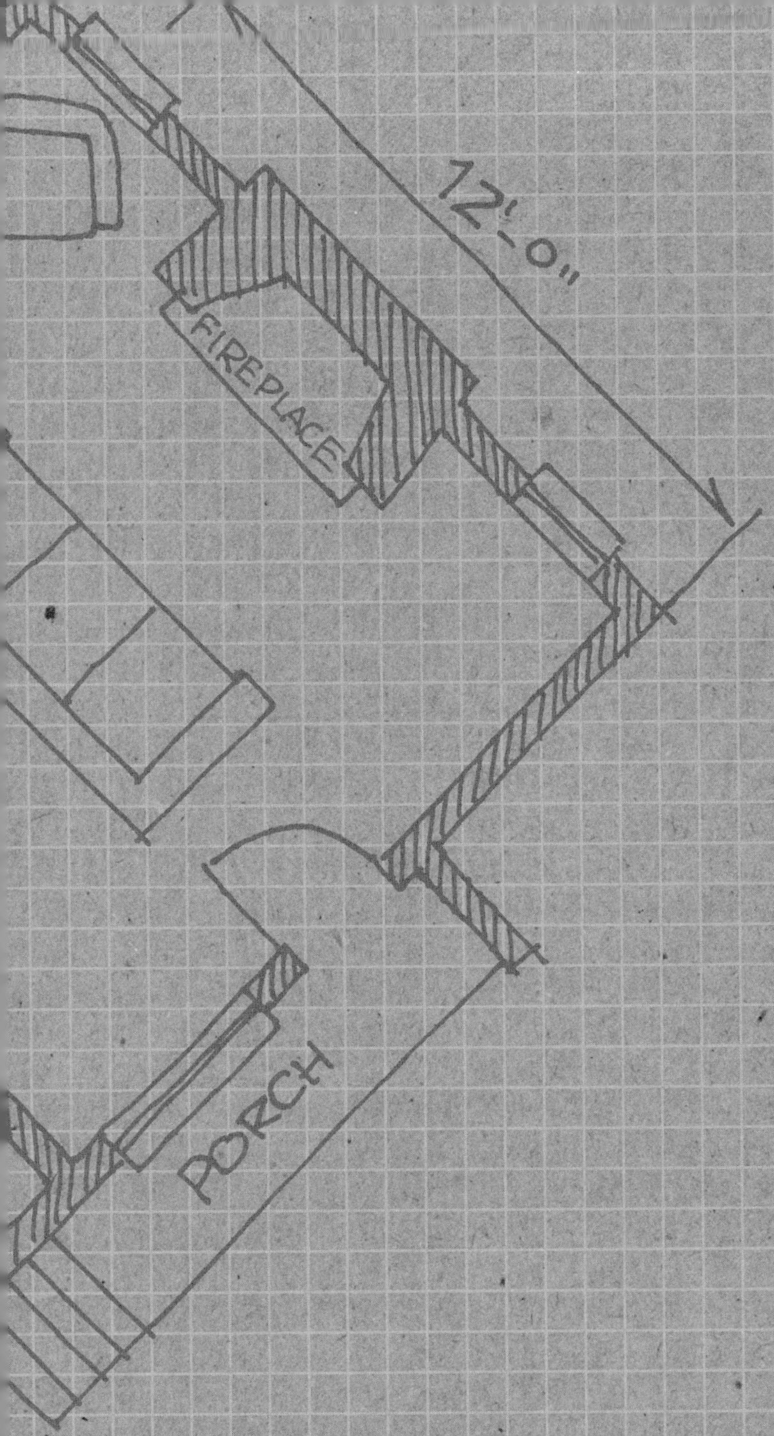

PART TWO

re•think

remodeling existing housing and living better right where you are

SCRAP 2 BY 4S STACKED LIKE BRICKS FORM THE WALL OF THIS TURRET IN ANNIE ZELLAR'S HOUSE.

6

Make Friends with the Past

The walls of my house are without memories, or secrets, or laughter. Not enough of life has been breathed into them—their warmth is artificial; too few hands have turned the window latches, too few feet have trod the thresholds. The boards of the floor, self-conscious as youth or falsely proud as the newly rich, have not yet unlimbered enough to utter a single cordial creak. In time they will, but not for me. —BERYL MARKHAM

IMAGINE A CRACK IN THE PLASTER OF YOUR WALL. Imagine the paint is a little dingy. Or maybe you don't have to imagine, and you can just look at them. What is the most environmental, economical solution to your problem?

Usually, it's doing nothing, and learning to accept things as they are.

If the crack indicates a serious leak in your roof, or a shift in the foundation, then eventually you'll want to attend to the root of the problem. Or if the paint is so old it's filled with lead, you might want to seal it, to protect yourself. In general, maintaining the basic elements of a house so it lasts without major renovation will save everyone energy in the long run.

But there's a thick gray line that runs between what's "basic" and what's an aesthetic (some will say "neurotic") choice in maintaining your home. Painting over dingy walls, no matter how "natural" or "green" or "low-VOC" the paint is, never uses less energy, nor creates less waste than doing nothing. And building on an addition, no matter how "eco," will always use more resources than simply not building one. Learning to accept the physical environment as it really is, can have a profoundly liberating effect on your life.

The small-house movement isn't just about building small. It's about environmental balance and social harmony. Sometimes "building small" won't help us reach our goals, because sometimes *building* is the last thing we need to be doing. How can we gracefully accept the gifts that already exist around us, as they are? How can we better use all the thousands of old, abandoned structures in our communities, and what can we learn from the history that surrounds them?

Why *Not* Build
THE OLD GREEN

A typical new house sends three to five tons of waste to the landfill. It adds 30 tons of carbon dioxide to the atmosphere—about the equivalent of driving the family

On a quiet street in small, affluent city, a "green" building company worked to tear down a 1940s cottage. They destroyed the roof, which had been renovated just two years prior, gutted the house completely, and dug up even the foundation. They left a few walls so they could access tax benefits intended for renovations but not new construction. Neighbors noticed that the materials used—plywood, concrete, Tyvek—were standard for all houses. In less than a year the cottage was replaced by a new two-story house, twice the size, and built close to the lot line.

"It's not that it isn't a pretty house," said one passerby, "it just looks funny because it's totally out of sync with the street. It isn't built to scale." His companion agreed. "I live down the street in a small, old 'reused' house. I haven't sent any of it to the landfill, and it hardly costs me anything to heat and cool. My yard is filled with a giant, productive organic garden. Why is this new house called 'green' and mine isn't?"

Good question.

car around the world six times—and takes down three-quarters of an acre of forest in the process. Add to that the environmental cost of transporting and dumping the old house, and you begin to see the environmental cost of "neighborhood improvement." *Not* building is an easy, green choice, as is renovation: a typical renovation adds 1–2 tons of carbon dioxide to the atmosphere, or the equivalent of driving from Montreal to San Diego and, perhaps, back.[1] So why is there an epidemic of "tear-downs"— demolishing old houses and replacing them with new ones—in some parts of the continent?

To laypeople it seems obvious that improving an existing house should be simpler than building new, but in fact maintaining, or carefully renovating an old building takes more skilled, educated, and cautious labor, and labor is the greatest cost in building. Renovations require more imagination and planning because there are many more constraints to keep in mind. Just as it takes more time, care, and money to repair an old television than to buy a new one, caring about and for old buildings typically has a lower profit margin.

Some builders justify tear-downs by saying, "Those old buildings weren't worth a thing—poorly insulated, badly designed, they wasted more energy than my new building will save." But Department of Energy statistics show something different: houses built between 1940 and 1997 use fairly similar amounts of energy, on average varying less than 10 percent.[2]

In the 1950s buildings were beginning to benefit from innovations in insulation and glazing, and household energy. Their efficiency peaked in the 1970s, but average house size and number of appliances contained within them continued to increase. Today's new houses approach or surpass the energy use of homes built in the 1940s. Meanwhile, old homes benefit immensely from the installation of new insulation, window coverings, and weather-stripping.

CONSTRUCTING MARITAL HARMONY

Now let's add up also the social cost of building. M. Tournon, an eco-building materials supplier, sums up many builders' observations of homeowners: "An excellent marriage can stand one year of construction. Much more than that, there's one more giant house, empty, with a 'for sale' sign on it." Construction projects disrupt almost every aspect of home life, and the decisions and negotiations required make even the mellowest families emotional (see right).

Some couples have a different experience: the project brings their family together, and is a basically pleasant adventure. Such families usually already have some construction skills and a history of working together, or they are the type of people who would still be happy with each other after a year living on a tiny sailboat, or camping in a Red Cross tent after a natural disaster. They don't look to the house to create their home. If they choose to build, it's because they enjoy building, and not because they think it will improve their family life. Many of them pare down their goals to more modest projects.

Ana Ribas-Scott never wanted to learn how to drive and her husband Alan wanted to learn how to stop driving, so they looked for a house near public transportation, and ended up with a 870-square-foot 1904 Queen Anne cottage in an old part of town, walking, biking, and bus distance from everything.

When they started planning for their children, they reconsidered whether their house was large enough. They didn't want to steal space from their much-beloved garden. After long discussions and imaginative drawings by Alan, who is an architect, they realized that all they needed was a half bath, a larger closet, and a few more square feet of floor space added to their bedroom to feel that their house was suitable for a family. Over a period of fifteen years they made the renovations, carefully reusing whatever they dismantled, and never needed to make a trip to the dump.

When Jason and Michael moved in together they made a long list of what they wanted to do to their new house. Soon almost every weekend was spent driving back and forth to the hardware store, scraping old paint, laying new floors. Their "to do" list was growing as quickly as their "done" list, and in less than six weeks they each separately questioned the original decision to buy a house, but masked their doubts and continued working. A few weeks later, their quiet bickering erupted into their first all-out, noisy fight, complete with broken tiles.

"So we went to a counselor," says Jason, "and we found out that we both desperately wanted our relationship to be picture perfect. We both care so much about what we imagine other people are thinking that we kept on working, even when we hated it, because the perfect house seemed necessary to the perfect relationship. We forgot that our real friends don't care what our house looks like—well, we were so busy, we forgot we had friends at all!"

After a long weekend of counselor-prescribed getaway, they returned to a house that suddenly didn't seem so much in need of change. "Now when one of us has a new decorating idea," says Michael, "the other asks, "Would you rather do that, or a weekend at a B&B?"

Alan and Ana love their old house and enjoy imagining the families that had lived there before them. Judging from the highly embellished trim and other fine details of the house, they imagine their predecessors had chosen the house with joy, not out of any dire necessity.

HOW DID 5.3 PEOPLE MANAGE TO LIVE IN 1,000 SQUARE FEET?

Thousands of bungalows were built between 1920 and 1960s that were smaller than 1,000 square feet and intended for families

Since 1969, Deanne Bednar has watched a number of giant new mansions and some smaller, but not so small, additions pop up around the small lake in Michigan where she lives. We left her house by paddling across the lake near sunset, headed toward the only leafy, natural area left on the shore. The trees and bushes turned out to be the garden of the oldest, and smallest, house on the lake, currently the house of Louie Lawton and Bessie Weatherspoon. These two sisters have known the 1,100-square-foot house since 1926 when their family bought it from Mr. Walter Flanders' farm manager.

Walter Flanders, according to the sisters, was the unrecognized genius behind the Ford Motor Company. He was an intelligent, wise, and compassionate man, as evidenced by the trim in their house. "What kind of man would have put up that kind of trim for his farm manager?" asked Bessie. "And the doors—he used the same door stock for his house as for this one!"

Louie and Bessie maintained their house and its polished trim beautifully, and without any need for modernization. The kitchen is one of the larger rooms. The stove, long sink, cabinets, and counters covered all four walls, and the center is filled with a large, square table. This kitchen, so different from modern kitchens with their open, narrow counters, is intended for days of food processing and long conversations around the table, such as the one Bessie and Louie treated us to, detailing the history of Mr. Walter Flanders.

with at least two children and often an extra relative. People interviewed for this book, who grew up in such houses, explained that they didn't think of their houses as small: "Our expectations were different. When you don't expect to have a whole lot of personal space or luxurious items, well, you have what you have, quite happily." They added specific details: "People had fewer clothes. They had clothes for dirty work or play, and clean, "Sunday" clothes kept separately, so they didn't wear out and didn't need to be washed as often. We didn't need large closets." "Most people didn't shower daily, and if they did it was brief and didn't tie up the bathroom. Women had dressing tables in the bedroom where they applied makeup and brushed their hair. Some houses had sinks in the bedroom as well." "Children played outside in all kinds of weather. Everyone spent more time outdoors."

Old houses also benefit from design details that maximize space. When you visit old houses, notice the kitchen in particular. A pull-out chopping board is common. Some kitchens have narrow vertical drawers that hold cans or jars, like a mini-pantry. "Lazy Susans," composed of round, revolving platforms in a corner cabinet, make good use of the corner. Shallow closets to store brooms and mops sometimes include a built-in dustbin in the floor. Cabinets typically rise up to the ceiling, requiring a stepladder to reach them, and making full use of vertical space. Perhaps there's a tiny door in the floor that opens to a miniature root cellar. The oldest houses may have very wide sinks that double as a giant counter and can turn a tiny kitchen into a food-processing center.

In other parts of the house you may find bay windows, window seats, and desk alcoves, telephone niches, and cabinets behind the stairs or built into corners, the walls, or even the ceiling. There may be a screened-in sleeping porch or a Dutch door, windows with real shutters, or a grate outside the front door to catch the mud from your shoes. Many older houses benefit from skilled, patient craftwork, and solid materials that have withstood use over time. Some are beautifully decorated, with hardwood floors, carefully tiled kitchens, and molding no one can afford today.

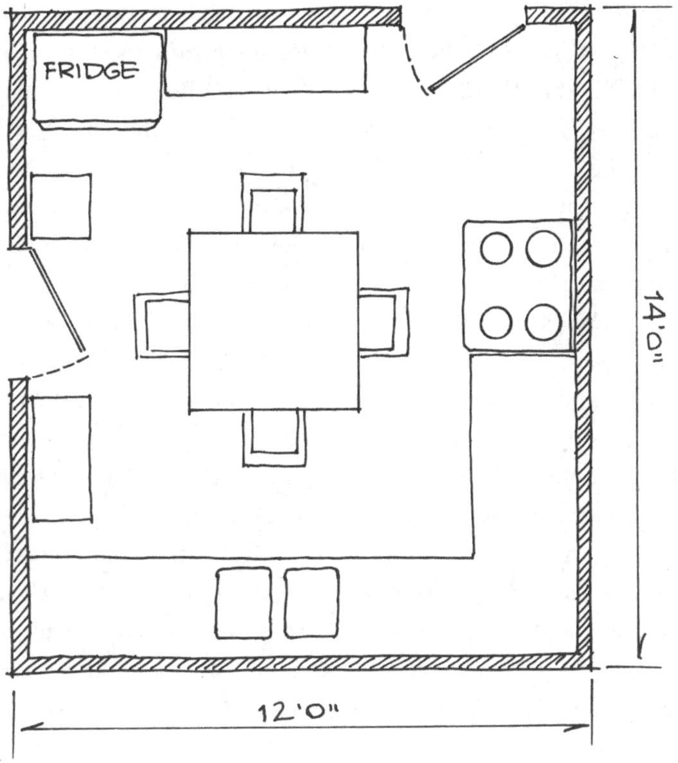

LOUIE AND BESSIE'S KITCHEN IS INTENDED FOR FOOD PROCESSING AND LONG CONVERSATIONS.

OLD CHARM

What is the extra quality that some people find in old houses? Estate sale coordinator Barb Demith calls the photos sometimes found in old furniture, "instant relatives." Her expression conveys the sense that people get from furniture that has been touched by others for decades or centuries. Sure, *my* grandfather didn't use this dresser, but someone's ancestor did, and here we are, both pulling the same drawer, just a century apart. When meaning and emotions are imbued in the furniture and decorations of a house, people find they need less space to feel richly at home.

THE COMFORT OF TRADITIONAL HOVELS

Many people are nostalgic for houses they have never even visited. People dream of everything from big farmhouses, mudded huts, and igloos to Mediterranean domes, log cabins, and thatched cottages. Some people are cheered up by just the curve of a particular old trim, or a picket fence. Builders try to accommodate some of these feelings in new construction. They add fake shutters and vigas, brick façades, and unnecessarily high pitched gable roofs. They adhere earthen plaster to industrial wallboard and artificial rock around fake fireplaces. Architectural historian Dolores Hayden writes, "Americans still crave aesthetic and emotional gratification from single-family dwellings that no architect or builder can possibly provide."[3] Do we fool ourselves when we imagine that old houses can give our lives more meaning, a sense of history or community?

Clearly, remodeling an old house is not going to create the "good old days" of happy families, apple pies, and endless summers. That feeling comes from, well, happy families, apples pies...and lively neighborhoods. When real estate agents say "location, location, location" is what sells a house, they mean that the greatest asset a house can have is the community around it—proximity to schools, parks, grocery stores, cafés, and other life supports. Really nice old molding and antique furniture won't create the dense networks of service and friendship that most people crave.

The Old Neighborhood

DE-GENTE-FICATION

Chapter 9 discusses in more detail how to build vital community around your home life, but there's one community issue many small-home dwellers face that applies specifically to old houses: gentrification. Also known as *de-gente-fication*, and closely related to *urban renewal*, a.k.a. *urban removal*, gentrification occurs when people of privilege move in waves into working-class neighborhoods. The upgrades they make in their buildings and demand from local governments increase the sales price of houses in the area. Property taxes and rents rise so much that older residents can no longer afford to stay in their homes. Other old residents are tempted by the higher prices their house can now fetch, and sell, reasoning that they don't really like their new neighbors anyway. Often the first wave of gentrification consists of artists, students, and world travelers who are attracted by the "culture" of the area. Later, like Brad and Rodd, they watch that culture disappear as the privileged move in.

Psychiatrist Mindy Thompson Fullilove, in her book *Root Shock*,[4] describes the psychic and social toll of the huge federal urban renewal program of the 1960s and '70s on the neighborhoods it destroyed. Urban renewal was justified in part by the theory that poverty can be "cured" by moving poor people away from each other. Programs that encourage gentrification don't acknowledge what Dr. Fullilove calls the "emotional ecosystems" that grow only when people spend many generations in the same place. Many upper-class people haven't cared to understand that vital, intact, working-class neighborhoods (an increasingly rare species) efficiently provide for free a great number of informal services that charitable and government agencies have not been able to match. This pattern, of course, is not unique to North America, nor to any specific time. The

Brad and Rodd Lancaster, two white brothers, purchased an empty 748-square-foot adobe house in an historically African-American neighborhood. For eleven years they worked steadily and generously, both to create an oasis of self-sufficiency on their urban homestead, and to improve the neighborhood. They planted street trees, coordinated an after-school youth program, started a community garden, strengthened the neighborhood association, and convinced the city to improve the bicycle and pedestrian routes in the area. They were very successful, and ended up with an award-winning garden and a solar house that catches and conserves its own water and electricity, with no need to exploit any person or thing.[5]

Eventually, however, their girlfriends doubted that all four of them, with future children, could live together happily in 748 square feet, so they started looking for land or a house nearby. But thanks to the neighborhood improvements, a general rise in prices, and a new city government program designed to encourage affluent homeowners to move to the area, house prices had risen 400 percent since they moved in. They no longer could afford to buy a house in their beloved neighborhood. One of them is now moving away.

famous boulevards of Paris are said to have once been villages that protested their empavement.[6]

Community land trusts such as the one in Durham, North Carolina, offer one way to preserve the human culture that has thrived in old neighborhoods. A neighborhood-based board acquires houses and holds the land equity beneath them. They sell the houses to families, with the restriction that the houses may only be resold for a low price, affordable to other, similar families.

EMPTY HOUSES

In many of the states and provinces we visited, and particularly in the Midwest, we discovered whole towns where many to nearly all houses were empty. These houses are available without displacing anyone. Many of them are beautifully built, with hardwood floors and delicate kitchen tiles.

It's hard to know exactly how many empty houses there are. A Department of Energy researcher explained to me that government statistics are better at tracking inhabited houses. But the census placed the figure, in the United States, in 2000, at about 10.5 million housing units (including apartments, counting duplexes as two, and so forth). For comparison: less than a quarter million people lived in homeless shelters in 2000.[7]

Why are there so many empty houses? A post office worker in Luray, Kansas, explained the situation there. Her family's 3,500-acre farm is now considered "smallish." Sixty years ago, most farms were less than a tenth the size, but now payments on farm machinery, insurance, and various chemical supplements are so high that conventional farmers can't afford to run a small farm, and must run a large farm, or none at all. Also, many farmers' children prefer city life. In the past two generations, most families have sold their land to a neighbor and moved away, causing a ripple in the economy. They took with them students (so the schools shrunk, and many closed), customers (stores went out of business), and patients (so doctors moved away and clinics closed). The eventual result is ghostlike towns where retired farmers who can't afford to move away worry because the nearest nurse is eighty miles down the highway.

Other towns and some city neighborhoods are empty because a factory closed down, a train stopped passing through, or a mine ran out, and each town has experienced the domino effect of all the supporting services fading away as well. Some small towns have converted successfully from industry or farming to retirement and tourism, but in places where the weather is better for farming than for relaxing, it's hard to attract retirees. Some towns survive by attracting artists.

Mri Pilar worked as an educational filmmaker in New York City during the 1980s. She woke up one day to discover she had become a painter. "It came out of nowhere. I didn't ask for it. Suddenly all I wanted to do was paint," she says. The 1990s found her in Lawrence, Kansas, supporting herself by selling fine art through a gallery. "But once you start selling, the gallery wants you to stay in the same style. There's no freedom in that."

In December 2001 Pilar and her friend took a trip to Lucas,

Founded in 1987, the Durham, North Carolina, Community Land Trust has acquired one hundred homes and two office buildings on the west side of town, near Duke University. When they started, the neighborhood was overlooked and run down, with many houses held by absentee landlords. Neighbors created the land trust and started renovating. In part due to their efforts, the neighborhood is now fashionable, and prices have skyrocketed. "We weren't able to eliminate gentrification," says board president and land trust homeowner L. D. Burris, "but at least the 100 properties we have are still affordable to normal families."[8]

MRI PILAR

Kansas (population 436), to visit the Garden of Eden, a 100-year-old homemade, front-yard exhibit of larger-than-life statues that depict Genesis. Around the corner was the Florence Deeble House, that features a garden decorated with pointillist bas-relief made from colored concrete and marbles, resembling picture postcards. But the garden was grown over and the house boarded up. "I knew right then that I would turn this house into the Garden of Isis. It came like a flash, no shilly-shallying about it," recounts Pilar.

So in January of 2002 she drove back to Lucas to meet the board of directors of the Grassroots Arts Collective, which owned the property. "I told them that I was an alien, that I would be covering the house in motherboards, and that I needed at least nine years to turn it into the Garden of Isis. The board replied, 'How can we help you?'"

Pilar's timing was serendipitous. In August 2002 Lucas was slated to become the smallest town ever to host a traveling Smithsonian exhibit. The theme of the exhibition was what, in 1950, people predicted would happen in the future. Lucas welcomed Pilar's contribution to the Alien theme.

From January until August Pilar built wall sculptures out of all kinds of plastic and metal trash, including computer motherboards. In August she covered the walls of the house in Mylar foil insulation, and began attaching her sculptures. "All this stuff is toxic in the landfill, but on the wall it's beautiful."

"My heavens!" is the most common expression uttered upon entry. Every surface is covered with familiar objects, transformed into unfamiliar, new images. Old Barbie dolls have become "Re-barbs" and Ken resembles the Virgin of Guadalupe. Everything is framed and decorated with colorful computer innards. By 2005, even the bedroom had become "part of the environment," and Pilar began sleeping on a trundle bed in the kitchen.

"The creative potential of a location depends on the cost per square foot of space," Pilar *believes. "In New York there's actually less space for art because rent is too expensive to afford to take chances. Art requires chance." She encourages all artists to find an empty town where they can be free. "There are thousands of them in this galaxy alone," she reminds us.*

Secondhand Houses

MOVE A HOUSE

Tearing down intact houses has become so common in affluent neighborhoods that some people purchase them, usually for the cost of moving them (it's cheaper than demolition for the seller), and set them up elsewhere. Emily Hunter (see profile, page 115) got her house that way, and the Island Housing Trust of Martha's Vineyard has acquired five such homes in the last two years.

A law in several of the townships on Martha's Vineyard requires that before a house is torn down it must be advertised so that someone can offer to take it away. The IHT Director Phillipe Jordi says his group gets an offer of a house about once a week, which is more than they can handle. With 15,000 houses on the island, and 15,000 residents, the islanders theoretically have a house per person. In fact, 70 percent of the homes are owned by out-of-towners, and local people have a difficult time finding a place to live.

Street trees on Martha's Vineyard are protected by local laws, so the roads are heavily canopied. When a house is offered, the first step is to determine how much it will cost to move. It can easily cost $40,000. Phillipe explains how:

"We cut the roof off, and then sometimes cut the house into two pieces, or cut off a part that sticks out. It takes a crew that really knows how to do this. They use a lot of tarps. They mostly use chain saws to cut the house where it's attached. They place steel girders under the house, then drive trucks that have a very special kind of wheel base that can pivot on a dime, that pick up the

A GUESTHOUSE MADE BY CONNIE AND MARTY REMALY FROM ALUMINUM CANS

Middlebury College demolished their seven-story science building. Humans and robots dismantled it piece by piece, recycling 97 percent of the building, including 48 tons of wood, 547 tons of steel and iron, 76 tons of limestone, and 650 tons of leftover concrete. Deconstruction created jobs and added no net financial cost. It's estimated that normally over 70 percent of these materials would have been sent to the dump instead.

Until the 1970s, Midwestern farmers normally stored dried corn-on-the-cob in mesh storage silos, under sturdy metal roofs. Nick Durrie, with his friends Erik Viik and Meredeith Jabis, converted a 6-meter-diameter corncrib into a tiny cottage. They lined the mesh walls with straw bales, plastered them with earth, and framed a sleeping loft inside. Nick estimates that there are 100,000 "corncribs" in the Midwestern U.S.[9]

girders. The low gear ratio is necessary: they travel at two to three miles an hour the whole way. It takes a series of teams: an arborist who trims or pulls back the trees before we pass; some guys with a 'bobcat' pulling mailboxes out and putting them back in; cops to redirect traffic. They are supposed to move the telephone lines before we pass, for free, but sometimes we don't have time to wait, so we do it ourselves. We have used a crane to put a roof back on at its destination. Once a house fell off. We just lost it. We got it all on video, though.

"It's not an easy task for a do-it-yourselfer. An amateur bought a house and moved it, but didn't tarp it well, and all the drywall got soaked in the rain so the interior walls were destroyed.

"When Catherine Graham (the Washington Post *owner) passed away, her son Bill didn't want anything to do with his mother's huge mansion. It's a giant estate—100 acres maybe—and he kept other smaller houses on it, I guess. He hired South Mountain Company to deconstruct it. They dismantled the whole thing, down to the ground, left only the two chimneys. The company's Christmas card will feature the company posed around the chimneys. The local companies just don't have enough space to store all the stuff we are getting. Soon we'll start exporting these used materials off the island."*

Norma Miranda and her husband Juan Saenz began with a 1970s Airstream, which they parked on a lot they bought near Norma's birthplace. With savings and their own labor, they built a tiny brick kitchen and pantry that opened to the trailer. Six years later they took out a low-interest loan of $40,000, moved the trailer to the other end of the lot, and added on two bedrooms and a living room.

THE HERMIT CRAB HOME

Other people look for existing structures not necessarily built for human habitation, and turn them into a home. Since industrialization, a variety of giant abandoned objects have become available. During the housing shortage after World War II, people lined up to acquire old railroad cars, which they trucked to various locations and turned into homes. Hermit crab types today have turned grain silos, water tanks, abandoned mines, giant culverts, school buses, whiskey vats, unseaworthy boats, and empty airplanes into homes.

There's also a large stock of used trailers, mobile homes, and recreational vehicles. Thought by some to be the true American vernacular, because they represent flexibility and mobility, they can be renovated into a permanent home in a variety of ways.

Because mobile homes depreciate in value quickly, they can sometimes be acquired for the price of moving them. Although they may be difficult to repair and sometimes include toxic materials, they provide an instant kitchen core that can be built around. Older trailers can be less toxic—they have had time to offgas—and Airstream trailers are famous for being quite healthy.

SALVAGE THE PAST

Perhaps you've acquired a house that is truly uninhabitable, and will require much more work to rehabilitate than to build new. There is a middle ground between renovating the building and sending it to the local dump. You can deconstruct it. Formerly called "demolition and salvage," the new, postmodern name indicates an exceptional commitment on the part of certain companies to reuse materials from old buildings. This commitment ranges from just saving the most expensive and durable parts for resale at a salvage yard, to using over 90 percent of the materials from the old building, on the same site, in the new building. The ability to completely "deconstruct" a building is limited by the fact that some materials are essentially impossible to reuse or even recycle. On some deconstruction sites, materials with no imagined future use are hidden inside the building, so at least they don't contribute to the flow of waste.

Dan Phillips and his company "Phoenix Commotion" in Huntsville, Texas employs people willing to work at a minimum wage, carefully dismantling the precious homes of his town, then converting them into "new" houses that are affordable to people on low incomes, and cost no more monthly than what they paid in rent. Annie Zellar bought Dan's first completed house. The floor came out of "Mrs. Martin's house, which is funny because I visited her house as a child, and thought that it was haunted, and now here's her floor, in my home," says Annie.

Small-house builders who carefully dismantle a part of a home or an outbuilding often gain respect for those who built it. Some have reported finding notes written a hundred years ago, inside beams or doorjambs, and they are intrigued by the old hardware they discover. By acting kindly toward whatever they are removing, their construction process maintains a positive feeling, and they imagine themselves as a part of a long process of growth, change, and creation.

What deconstruction typically requires is more time. Once we've reduced our needs, our debts, and our cravings, many of us find that we suddenly have more time, and that time was in fact what we craved most. Time not to do more, but to undo more, by not building, or by unbuilding, very carefully.[10]

MICHAEL HARRIS AND DEBBIE HART-HARRIS AND KEVYN
Built 1920

AREA:
890 sq. ft., plus a 200-sq.-ft. detached storage/garage

INTENDED NUMBER OF OCCUPANTS:
3–7

UTILITY COSTS (MONTHLY):
$50–100

LOCATION:
Eureka, California

ABOVE: A PULL-OUT CHOPPING BOARD IN DEBBIE AND MIKE'S KITCHEN

Eureka, California, is a treasure trove of three-

and four-story Victorian homes, well built between the gold rush and the Depression, and left intact because economic success continues to mostly ignore the town. The strip malls that mark most of North America are largely absent, the old buildings still maintained and used.

In 1973 the federal government briefly considered siting the route of a new freeway smack through the downtown. Protesters invited the national director of historic preservation to visit Eureka. Surprised and delighted at what he saw, he dispatched a team of researchers to survey and classify 10,000 "significant" houses, and so convinced the authorities to build no freeway. Driving north on Highway 101, motorists still must stop at half a dozen traffic lights in Eureka as they pass a few gorgeously detailed façades.

Folks escaping the high-cost, overbuilt environment of Los Angeles and the San Francisco Bay Area are delighted by the age and size of Eureka houses. Mike Harris left LA, hoping to move into "an old log cabin in the redwoods," such as he remembered from a visit as a teenager. He found out those cabins had long been plowed under, and 4,500-square-foot minimansions now tower over tiny, subdivided plots of land. So he shifted his gaze to the Victorians. "In LA I felt like I was in a little cubby hole. I guess because I couldn't get the land I wanted, I decided to get as much house as I could," Mike says.

He chose a 1904, "Colonial Revival" three-story, 2,400 square-foot, plus basement, house with never-painted, carved and lacquered hardwood trim, and a solid cherry mantelpiece. "It wasn't a very fancy Victorian, but a middle-class house," Mike explains. It had sheltered just two families in its first eighty-eight years. "They probably had about as many people per square foot as our family has in an apartment."

Mike and his wife Debbie moved in and started renovations. Their son Kevyn was born. The house was large enough to set up a tent inside, build a giant cardboard ship, or even roller-skate inside (all of which they tried). Who wouldn't love such a house?

Debbie began noticing drawbacks. The kitchen was planned for servants, dark and closed at the back of the house. She couldn't cook and keep track of her toddler at the same time. Sunlight, especially in winter, did not penetrate several of the rooms. The heating bill was outrageous, the household to-do list endless. When fourteen people stayed over at Christmas, the house was warm and happy, but once they left, it felt haunted again. Debbie and Mike could pass the whole day in the house, and hardly see each other. "We were two people lost in a maze of clutter, and all we spoke of was the work to be done," says Debbie. After five years, she was ready for drastic change.

So in 1998 Debbie bought herself a two-bedroom cottage on the other side of town, in a neighborhood where she could "park my little car in front and fit in with the neighbors." She moved there with Kevyn. Soon, her mother, two sisters, and niece, who were new to the area, joined them. How could they all fit? I asked.

"Well," she replied, "when we speak of our nation's multiculturalism, we find each family has its own culture. People who are committed to their families find that the love that exists is greater than the inconveniences that arise from a situation that brings a family closer together. Our family's motto is 'Make do with what you have.' We always shared bedrooms, so it wasn't an issue for us. We were taught success was about doing, not having, good things. It sounds like a cliché, but that's the way it is."

For a year, they slept like this: Granny with her granddaughter in one bedroom, Debbie with Kevyn on the fold-out bottom bunk in his room, one sister on the top bunk, and the other on the living room couch. The arrangement varied depending on who went to bed first. "Basically, it was 'Sleep wherever there's an empty spot!'" Debbie recalls. The kids loved it. Kevyn and his cousin are both only children, and now they are like siblings. Debbie lived far from her sisters for years, so she cherished the chance to be close again.

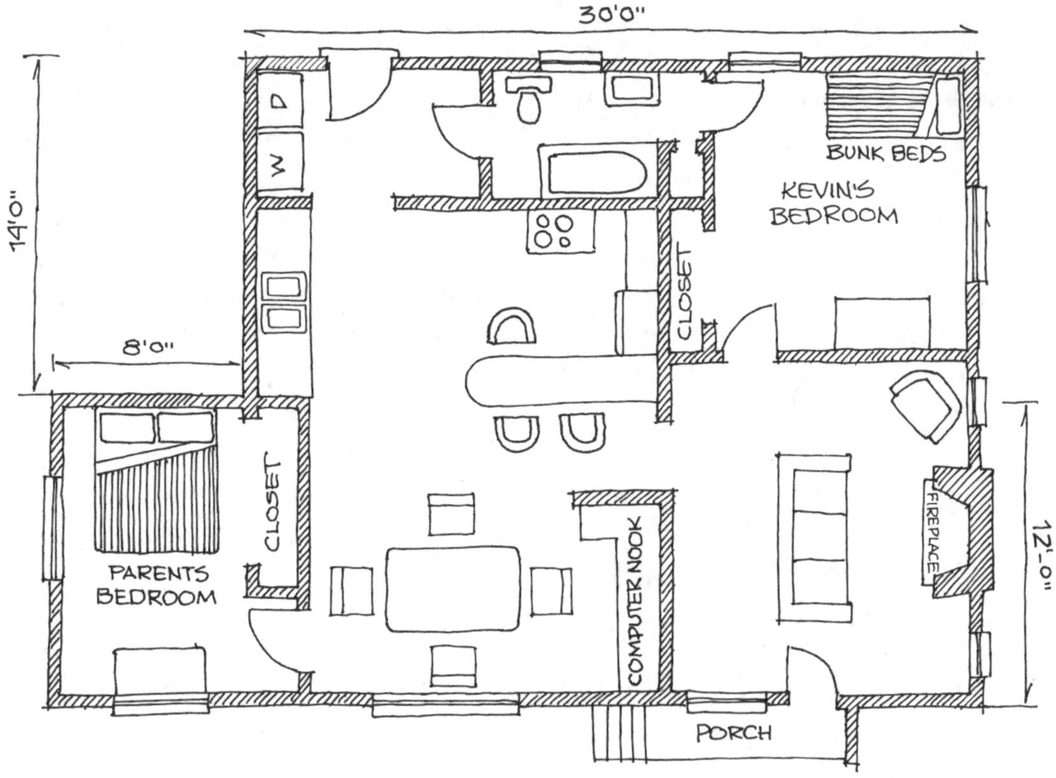

FLOOR PLAN

“I was happy in my home, and Mike saw that, and wanted to be near me. In the past, our conversations were pretty much, ‘Did you fix that yet?’ Now the nagging is over. We enjoy each other. I identify with Hestia, the goddess of the hearth. She’s all about keeping the fire stoked and creating a place of warmth where people can come. I’ve created my space and brought Mike into the fold of what I have created.” —Debbie Hart-Harris

After a year, Debbie’s mother and sister found homes of their own in nearby Arcata, and Mike was ready to move back in.

Mike rented the big house out to three separate households—a top-floor apartment, a painting studio on half of the first floor, and a recycling warehouse in the rest. Although he insists he’d be equally happy in a cardboard box or a mansion—“It’s the state of mind you have, not where you are”—he appreciates his new home. “It takes the same amount of time to paint the entire exterior of this house as it takes to paint one wall of the other. The Victorian was not intended to be maintained by one person.”

Natural light flows through every room in their little house. The arched doorways, 10-foot ceilings, and high kitchen cabinetry prevent any boxed-in feeling. Debbie, working in the kitchen, in the very center of the house, can watch the action on the street, or in her backyard, and can call out to Kevyn wherever he’s playing in the house. The counter space seems minimal compared with modern homes, but Debbie, who cooks two meals a day, insists that between the breakfast bar, the sink counter, and an old-style pull-out chopping board, there’s plenty of room.

Debbie removed the closet doors in the bedroom and replaced them with fabric, so there’s no need for swing room. One of the doors she reused as a desk, placing it on file cabinets in the dining room alcove. “Everyone needs a little space—it doesn’t have to be a room, but a little corner, a bed, some place that no one else in the house disturbs,” she explains. “We may convert the garage into a bedroom for Kevyn when he becomes a teenager or into a workroom for Mike.”

As Kevyn pounded on a keyboard 5 feet away, and Debbie carried on a conversation across the table, I asked Mike if he hoped to have a workroom, a place of his own. He replied, “You find your place inside yourself. Everyone has psychic space inside their head. Nobody can be inside my head but me. If you are happy, you just occupy your psychic space. It’s only when you project outwards and start claiming physical space that all these problems arise.”

Debbie, who describes herself as a “typically practical Virgo,” appreciates her tidy home. “If you have extra time, you tend to procrastinate. Same thing with a house. If you have space, you fill it up with junk.”

Mike likes the cottage and the Victorian for the same reason: it’s a bit of living history. “Clothes wear out, TV sets break, but if you maintain a house, you own a piece of the past. That’s real.”

“Stuff just occupies space. You have to lug it around. It competes with people for space. The best part about living in the big house was when we didn’t have anything in it.” —Mike Harris

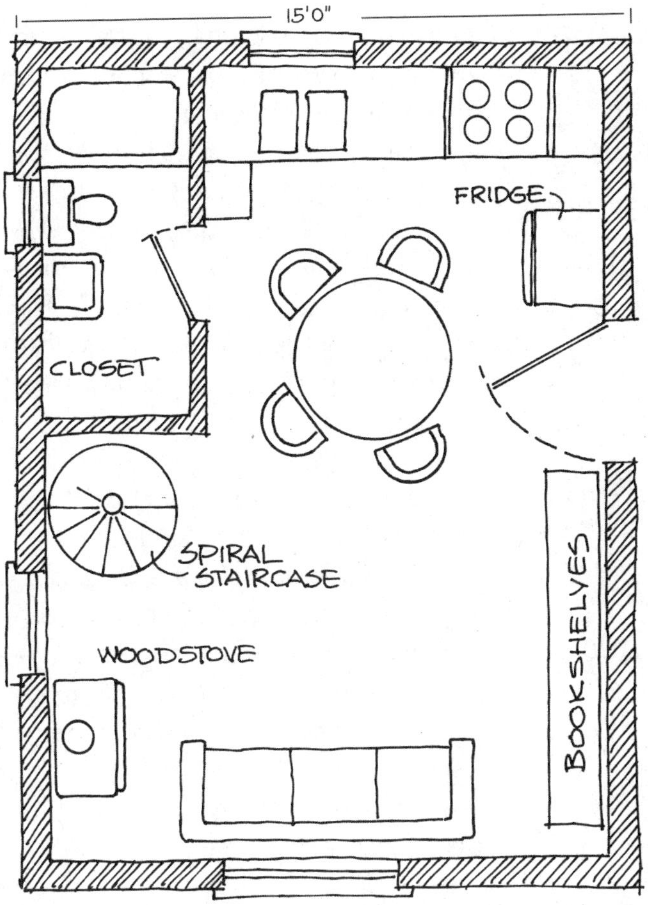

JUDY AND GARY RAYMOND, MABEL AND KENNY
Built 1880s, renovated 1980s

AREA:
300 plus 150-sq.-ft loft, on 40,000 acres of owned and leased land

INTENDED NUMBER OF OCCUPANTS:
1-4

COST: RENOVATION COSTS:
$2,670

UTILITY COSTS (MONTHLY):
Propane and electric, about $120/winter and $35/summer

LOCATION:
South Central Wyoming

John Mahoney, an Irish-born engineer and former

cavalry officer, spent much of the 1870s and '80s acquiring riparian areas, especially watering holes for livestock, until he controlled huge swaths of the territory that would, in 1890, become the state of Wyoming. He acquired Ferris Mountain Ranch in 1880. Mr. Mahoney and his hired men found an old schoolhouse a few miles away, put it on skids and horses pulled it to the new ranch headquarters, to use as a cookhouse. They dragged logs down Ferris Mountain to build a small cabin for a tack and harness house. They dug irrigation ditches, plowed fields for hay, and brought in cattle and sheep. Today it is a ranch so wide the livestock look like tiny insects in the distance.

In 1949, Kenneth and Roy Raymond, and their father, Burdette Augustus, purchased the ranch from an individual who had held it for less than a year. Kenneth's father-in-law set up a sawmill on the site and milled boards from more logs, and the men divided the cookhouse lengthwise, down the middle, and built two additions, to make a T. The brothers brought their brides, and a newborn baby in 1950.

One hundred years after Mr. Mahoney's arrival, Gary Raymond, who was born on the ranch, decided to move out of the bunkhouse and into

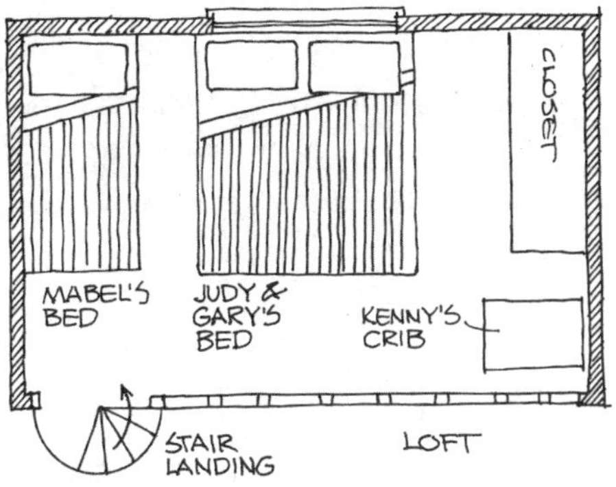

ABOVE: FLOOR PLAN

"There is something about this life, lived so close to the land, without pampering, that is really worth preserving. We see the irrigation ditches that settlers dug, moving boulders by hand, to bring pasture to this area. We see the marks on the logs from hand tools. Everything that's here is a testament to the people who went before us, and their work. Legend has it that Butch Cassidy stayed in the Harness House." —Judy Turner Raymond

the Harness House. He spent his midthirties jacking up the walls to dig out plumbing lines and add a concrete foundation, then jacking up the roof and adding four layers of logs—old power line poles— to make room for a loft. He replaced the old chinking between the logs, and cement, and reroofed the cabin with $200 worth of hand-split cedar shakes his mother heard about on a radio "swap shop" show. He installed a bathroom in one corner and a Heatilator fireplace in another corner. This bachelor had no need for a kitchen.

Gary, a devout Christian, prayed that he'd find a woman to marry, but living 40 miles from town in the least populated state in the U.S., he wondered about the likelihood. "She might just have to fall out of the sky," he predicted. Once, in the nineteen seventies, after an especially bitter winter, Gary's uncle had proclaimed, "If someone offered a million dollars for this place, we'd be fools not to sell," and Gary replied, "I'd never sell it, not for ten million," a comment which made Gary's grandmother beam and let Gary himself know that, God willing, his place was on the ranch, with their 450 cows, their calves, and the open sky. Gary imagined that if he ever did find a wife he'd "have to build her a big new house to convince her to stay."

Then Judy Turner bicycled past the road to the Raymonds' ranch. A college math instructor and environmentalist, she had figured out the exact cost of cars, and so she vacationed by bicycle instead, taking months to cross the country, sometimes leading tours. Wyoming had special appeal for her, and she made friends with the owner of a bed and breakfast. Three years later Judy married Gary, and moved into the Harness House, bringing her lightweight bicycle stove, which she used until the kitchen was finished.

The house opens to the kitchen on one side, and the living room on the other. Opposite the front door is a spiral staircase that Gary made out of metal from a nearby oil field: treads from the derrick platform, stringers out of sucker rods, and an oil well casing as the center post. The stairs lead to a loft bedroom. Off of the kitchen is a bathroom. And that's all.

No garbage truck visits the ranch, and instead over the years the inhabitants have stored extra items outdoors, next to the Harness House, in a kind of open-air museum of farm and home implements: plows and combines once dragged by horses, a belt-driven circular saw, scythes, old plates, and bottles marked "2 cents." This junkyard is also practical: with the next hardware store about an hour away, it usually makes more sense to weld something from what they already have. "It's amazing," says Gary, "What a welder can do with an old piece of metal, to make it something new."

Gary likes to quote Hebrews 13:5 "Let your character be free from the love of money, being content with what you have" to explain the source of his happiness. He says that nothing has come to him by accident, but because he is blessed by grace.

EPILOGUE

Judy and Gary built the straw bale walls and steel roof of an addition onto the Harness House, but before it was finished, at the end of 2002 Gary's Aunt Mary passed away, leaving her half of the cookhouse. So the family moved in. The 2,100 square foot "mansion" is more difficult to heat, but it offers a separate home schoolroom for the kids, and more storage.

The family plans to build a hearth around the fireplace in the Harness house, out of stones brought from each geological "time zone" layer of Ferris Mountain. They rent the house to hunters in the Fall. Sometimes they dream about moving back.

OUTDOORS
WINDOWS
MULTI-USE
STORAGE
BATHROOMS
LOFTS
NOOKS

PHOTOS: OUTDOORS

A

B

F

G1

G2

H

A

B

C

D

A. A BOX FOR SHOES DEFINES THE ENTRANCE.

B. CLEAR JARS REQUIRE NO LABELS.

C. A BOOKSHELF ON WHEELS TUCKS UNDER A COUNTER.

D. A DRYING RACK ABOVE THE SINK MEANS DISHES ARE ONLY MOVED ONCE.

E. DRAWERS TUCK UNDER THE SLOPE OF THE ROOF.

F. A DRAWER FILLS THE KICK SPACE UNDER THE CABINETS.

G. THICK WALLS HAVE SPACE FOR A COOL BOX.

H. STORAGE CAN BE CREATED UNDER THE A FLOOR.

I. COOKING PANS HUNG OVER THE STOVE ARE AN EASY REACH FOR THE COOK.

E

G

H

F

I

A

B

C

D

A. A TUB SHARES THE PLUMBING WITH THE KITCHEN.

B. A DEEP TUB IN A FORMER CLOSET OPENS TO THE BEDROOM ON ONE SIDE AND A "WATER CLOSET" ON THE OTHER, AND CAN BE CLOSED OFF FROM EITHER OR BOTH SIDES.

C. THE TOILET SEPARATED FROM THE BATH DOUBLES THE USEFULNESS OF BOTH.

D. AN OUTDOOR SHOWER SHARES PLUMBING WITH THE INDOOR BATHROOM ON THE OPPOSITE SIDE OF THE WALL.

E. A SKY WINDOW CREATES JUST ENOUGH HEADROOM TO ALLOW A TINY BATHROOM IN THE ATTIC.

F. MARLEY AND LYNN'S BATH, WITH SUNDECK ABOVE.

G. WHEN THE WHOLE ROOM IS TILED, A TINY BATHROOM FITS IN JUST FOUR BY FOUR FEET.

A

B

C

A. POLLY SEPARATES THE LOFT FROM THE LIGHT AND VIEW OF THE DOWNSTAIRS ROOM WITH A SIMPLE WHITE CURTAIN.

B. A LADDER TO THE LOFT IN FOX HAVEN.

C. LINDA AND IANTO'S BAMBOO LADDER IS SO LIGHT IT CAN BE LIFTED AND STOWED IN THE LOFT.

D. THE ROBERTSON-GIBSON HOUSE.

E. MARGARET'S LOFT IN THE MAXWELTON CREEK COHOUSING COMMUNITY.

F. A READING NOOK TUCKED IN A SPACE TOO LOW TO STAND IN.

A

B

C

D

A. CAROLE'S BED ALCOVE.
B. QUINN IN THE GUEST BED ALCOVE.
C. ANNETTE IN A WINDOW SEAT.
D. BRIGITTE AND ELYSE IN A DINING ALCOVE.
E. FURNITURE CREATES AN ALCOVE.
F. A BED ALCOVE AT ONE END OF A CABIN.
G. HELEN'S ROOM, TUCKED INTO THE ATTIC.

POPULATION:
62

ALTITUDE:
1,430 feet

LOCATION:
Flint Hills of Kansas

Kansas is the place where hamburgers come from.

Driving through on Interstate 70, or on many of the smaller, straight highways, you can see your meal in acres: a mile of wheat, then a mile of sorghum for fodder, then maybe a feedlot full of steers eating that fodder, then more wheat, or corn for fodder. The fields are extremely productive: a small billboard reads, "This farm feeds 374 people." But for something as exotic as tomato or a leaf of lettuce for your bun, you might have to turn down an older road and find a retired farmer with a kitchen garden. This is a land of monoculture, and the economic law of comparative advantage rules that it's better to just let sunny California and Mexico grow those tomatoes.

ABOVE: **THE COMMUNITY CHURCH**

MATFIELD GREEN: THE RED BRICK SCHOOLHOUSE

Alternatives to this farming method have been suggested. One couple claims that taking down all the fences and running buffalo, free range over untended grasslands, then hunting the buffalo, will more efficiently produce meat than the current method.

Another theory questions the desirability of annual grasses. The Land Institute in Salina, Kansas has spent twenty years—an eyeblink in evolutionary time—answering the basic "problem of agriculture," that it extracts food from the earth, depleting and sacrificing its source as it grows. By selectively breeding perennial grain crops, including sorghum, wheat and sunflower, that can be planted as a polyculture and harvested like fruit, without any need to plow and disrupt the rich life of the soil, the Land Institute believes it can transform prairie agriculture from an extractive industry to a more sustainable pattern.

Would perennial agriculture lead to perennial human settlements? How could a town rely on renewable, instead of extractive economies? And how can people, like grain crops, become native to a place?

With these questions in mind Wes Jackson, a founder of the Land Institute, drove down the winding roads of southeastern Kansas, and in the early 1990s purchased seven houses in the town of Matfield Green for 4,000 dollars. A group of friends purchased, for 5,000 dollars, the vacant, brick, 10,000-square-foot schoolhouse; and the Land Institute, for 4,000 dollars, purchased the high school gymnasium. In 1918, when war made it impossible for Europeans to farm, wheat was at $2.85 a bushel (it sold for under $3/bushel in 2005), and Matfield Green may have had 400 people. Later, an oil field supplied work for townsfolk, but when the oil dried up, the town shrank again. In the early 1990s about 50 people lived there.

Tom and Barbara Armstrong now live in one of the houses that Wes bought, a house that was moved from an area closer to the oil fields, perhaps in the 1950s. "Just about every house in Matfield Green has moved at sometime or another," says Barbara. After a life of moving around the country, following Tom's career with the Park Service, the Armstrongs retired to this house in 1996.

Tom serves on the five-members-plus-mayor town council. Matfield Green may have the most direct democracy, with the highest ratio of representation, we've ever visited. The townsfolk pay sales and property tax, and see it returned to them in the form of

BARBARA AMSTRONG AT EMILY HUNTER'S HOUSE

A CORNER CABINET

wages for a part-time town clerk, treasurer, and, most importantly, a manager for the town water system, who monitors the tank on the hill and the two well pumps that feed them, tests the water daily, and reads each house's meter.

The brick schoolhouse is open five days a week and hosts a self-service library. On Sundays a local minister abandons her denomination and offers an ecumenical service. Emily Hunter, an educator, organizes gatherings that bring visitors to Matfield Green. A bar is the only establishment that regularly charges money, though a few people sell eggs and produce to each other. "The town is about 60 percent old-timers, and 40 percent more recent arrivals. There aren't any strong disputes between the two groups," Tom reports. "We've lost three or four people in the last decade, and gained about a dozen."

LESA'S BEAUTY SHOP

7
Live at Home

My life goal is to be
a house husband. —MICHAEL SHUBERT

DO YOU OWN YOUR HOME BUT YOU'RE NEVER HOME? Today if you spend four hours awake at home each day during the workweek, you're home more than the average North American worker. Over a third of male college graduates spend more than fifty hours per week at work, and parents, especially mothers, work a double shift that often involves spending as much time driving their children to activities as being with them awake at home. Millions of houses stand unpopulated all day, appliances heating and cooling their furniture.[1]

In contrast, many of the people most committed to living in less space spend most of their time at home. Their home is the happy focal point of their lives. They have been able to cut back on their work hours by making their house pay for itself, either by dividing it up and renting out the space they weren't using, or by working at home, at their own business or telecommuting. They are rediscovering an older pattern of life, one that makes home the center, and outside work its support.

A Brief History of How We Left Home

Not so long ago, home and the world were not so distinct. Five or ten thousand years ago few people had sturdy, year-round residences. Most either migrated with the seasonal weather changes or lived in places where they did not need strong shelter, and could live without clearly separating the inside from the outside. At that time, and still today in some societies, "home" meant family and tribe, language, tradition, location, and landscape—something quite different from a roof and walls.

Two hundred years ago, most North Americans still lived very close to where they worked. Farmers, slaves, merchants, and teachers slept next to barns, stores, and schools. Homes produced food, clothing, medicine, and entertainment, as well as products sold for cash. Many couples and whole, extended families spent the day working near each other.

In the nineteenth century centralized industry began replacing home and farm production, urban

“Working at home used to be a ‘girl thing’: mothers who were trying to earn a little money, or women who started businesses out of their homes until they could afford office space. No one serious would work from home ten or twenty years ago. But now that the boys realize the advantages of working at home, it’s gained prestige.” —Carol Venolia

and suburban population grew, and most men and some women left home to join large factories in centralized warehouse districts. The dream home was born: refuge from the rough male world of industry, a tiny castle enclosing just the romantic, nuclear family, surrounded by a moat of lawn and tended by a virtuous woman, with no help nor hindrance from her extended family. Most new houses built in the twentieth century reflect something of this dream.

By 1976 that virtuous woman was on her way into the paid labor force. She was unlikely to have more than two or three children,[2] and the word “housewife” had begun changing from an honorable title to a nearly embarrassing term that evolves every few years (“homemaker,” “household manager,” “stay-at-home mom”), in an attempt to reclaim respect. In 1965, U.S. and Canadian minimum wage standards enabled one worker to reasonably finance a family of four, but ten years later the buying power of the minimum wage began a decline that has not since reversed. Aid to Families with Dependent Children, a U.S. federal welfare program begun in the 1930s, depended on the idea that homemaking was an essential occupation, and therefore single women with children should not be forced to hold jobs outside their home. By 1990, most families believed two incomes are a necessity, and single parents were expected to hold jobs. By the end of the twentieth century, even our babies were leaving home: in 1995, 44 percent of infants spent at least thirty hours a week in childcare.[3]

In the 1960s and ’70s social scientists predicted that thanks to technology, a new era was about blossom, a time of less work and excessive leisure. We planned to be burdened by our idleness, our leisure, and too much time with our families. What happened to that dream?

WILL WE EVER RETURN?

Since 1950, worker productivity has more than doubled. That means, roughly and theoretically, that if we could somehow maintain a 1950 standard of living today, we could each work forty hours per week for less than six months each year, or twenty hours a week for a full year. But we have chosen instead to channel the benefits of increased productivity into more consumer goods for workers, and higher profits for corporate executives, directors, and shareholders

Trade unions and a variety of civic organizations are working to lighten our load, but in the meantime, unless you move to Europe (where work hours are a bit shorter), or take a time machine back to a prehistoric era or at least the fifties (anthropologists believe that many prehistoric people worked only a few hours each day), you’ll have to be creative if you want to live more of your life at home.

The Pleasure of Working at Home

One way to spend more time at home is to work at home. If you choose this route, you’ll be in good company: Stay-at-home humans list a variety of advantages to working at home. There’s no commuting, no rush hour, and less dressing for work. They can count part of their mortgage or rent payment as a business expense. They are home to greet children after school, or are able to juggle home-schooling and adult work. They avoid office drama, work more efficiently, make friends with their neighbors, eat a healthier, inexpensive lunch, watch their garden grow, and benefit from home improvements they’ve made. At-home workers can take frequent breaks to exercise or nap without any raised eyebrows from coworkers. The autonomy of working at home is a badge of honor among some who do it, who insist they “Can’t imagine how I ever worked in an office.”

Of course, there's a flip side to each advantage. The basic one is this: once you've mixed home and work together, how do you separate them enough to create a productive, focused workplace, within a restful home? These are the basic two problems you will wrestle with if you work at home: how will you get to work, and how will you get home?

HOW IMPORTANT IS YOUR RESUMÉ?

Will anyone take your work seriously if your office is at home? Will you take yourself seriously? And how will you progress up the ladder if you aren't in the office to make the right contacts?

The stereotype that anyone who works at home just isn't professional is slowly eroding. With the emergence of computer gurus who can telecommute from a remote Caribbean island to a Palo Alto office, working at home is becoming more prestigious.

Some clients and customers prefer visiting a home office. Some therapists and health-care providers say their patients are comforted by the neighborhood location, and some parents seek out home-based daycare. Builders, gardeners, and artists use their home to show off their work. Would your work be enhanced by a more intimate connection to home life? If so, you're a good candidate for working at home. If not, there are ways to emphasize separation between your two domains.

Carole Fournier solved some of the work-at-home dilemmas when she and Jacques Belanger purchased a Grow Home a seven-minute walk from the center of Montréal:

Five years later, Carole got her wish. Carole and her family inhabit a 1,500-square-foot, three-story Grow Home. The front door opens to a small (4-by-4-foot) foyer and stairs leading straight up to their home, which occupies the top two floors. The door to Carole's office is on the left. Originally, the family planned to rent the bottom floor out as an apartment, but Carole's business, translating food labels and advising companies about Canadian and U.S. food laws, grew so quickly that before they had time to build a kitchen downstairs, Carole needed the space as an office.

"As a young mother, a home office is the best. I was able to fit my two work schedules around each other. When Alex was little and napped or played quietly, I was just a few steps away from my office. Now, I am here when he comes home, but after his bedtime, I can come downstairs and finish. If the courier arrives with a package at a quarter to eight, or a European company needs to call me at six, here I am." No one need know she is still in her pajamas. And for companies who care about such things, she has a downtown address.

Her only complaint is occasional loneliness. "It's nice to share successes with others." She recently hired one employee, and hopes to hire a second soon.

Making Home Work

A SEPARATE ENTRANCE

If you work at home and don't have a separate office, eventually you may yearn to have one, ideally located a few steps across a small, lovely garden or on another floor. A converted garage or a shed works for some. To convert an extra bedroom, consider adding an exterior door and then closing

"The studio actually was easier to arrange than my current, somewhat larger home because it was one long, rectangular room, without so many windows. I used bookcases to delineate one end of the studio as my office; I knew when I was walking into and out of it. I figured clients shouldn't really be looking at my bed, so I put my bed in the kitchen breakfast nook, which had a partial wall, and I added a screen. It worked." —Carol Venolia

off the interior door. This will create a better sound barrier between your work and home space and enforce the ritual of going to work. Your family will have a clearer understanding of when you are at work, and since your clients will no longer walk through your home, you'll be able to cut back on cleaning and discussions of family photos you've left on a counter.

THE MULTIUSE SPACE

But what if you don't have the luxury of a separate office, or even a separate room? Some serious small-housers who work at home say that they don't need it. For ten years, Carol Venolia maintained a home office in her 450-square-foot studio apartment (see above).

You might use file cabinets, bookcases, or screens to create a partial wall, and put your office near the front door if you intend to host clients. Thanks in part to the minimization of computers and other office tools, a utility room or even a small closet can be converted into an office, or a partial office, with a desk inside and a chair placed in the doorway when the office is in use, then removed when the office is closed. You can save floor space by building a high desk and chair, which will allow storage below and give you the option of shifting between sitting and standing at your desk. A closet that is next to an exterior wall can be given a window to extend the sense of space.

THE DISCIPLINE OF MULTIUSE

You may find that the physical design of a space doesn't affect your work habits as much as your internal discipline, and the relationships and social agreements around you.

When Jennifer and Dag Munter of Los Angeles, California, married, Jennifer decided to give up her larger, more expensive Santa Monica apartment and move to Dag's 544-square-foot place in East Hollywood. "The smaller apartment, and its lower cost, fit the new life that I wanted to create," she says. Jennifer had just ended her career as an art director for film because she wanted to work from home, making and selling garden art, counseling clients about their homes, and writing.

Early on, the couple decided they'd use the main, 180-square-foot room of their one-bedroom apartment for creative endeavors rather than for "entertain-

When Cecile and Paul Andrews (see Chapter 10) decided to rent out their upstairs floor as an apartment, Paul needed to move his office to their main floor. Cecile decided to let him have her office, and instead placed an armoire in the front room, which she can close up when company comes. "I rarely went in that room before during the day, but it's the most beautiful room in the house, the only room with a nice view of Grand Lake. For $500 I have a whole office, and it folds closed. Plus it's small enough that it doesn't let me get as disorganized as I used to."

ment." Jennifer sews, refinishes and builds furniture, makes cosmetics and candles, bakes bread, and writes. She estimates that her usual workspace takes up less than 30 square feet. Simultaneously, her husband, who is a musician and a composer, uses the space as a studio. He's discovered that the closet works well for recording vocals. Typically, Dag wears headphones, but, "He can't for mixing. So I take a few deep breaths and remind myself how much I love him. Then we have to discuss schedules."

Dag's musician friends visit often. "Our friends don't mind that they are coming into a workspace—they come to see us. Besides, we have windows on three sides, and the building is old enough to be a little charming, so it's a nice place to be," says Jennifer. Jennifer usually sees her clients in their homes (some of which are five to ten times the size of hers), but she thinks her apartment has had a positive effect on the few who have seen it. "They may see that a creative space gives more pleasure than a consumptive space."

Jennifer and Dag, like other couples who share workspace, negotiate and schedule time to support each other's focus. Doors, curtains, written signs and schedules, a hat worn by the worker, or an agreement not to make eye contact during work hours—there is a long list of ways to indicate to those around you, "Please let me work."

But how do you get yourself to work? You can no longer rely on the imposed discipline of a daily commute. Author Dan Chiras uses a kitchen timer: fifty minutes of writing, then ten minutes of exercise. Other people rely on a scheduled ritual, a prayer or meditation, or a daily pattern such as washing the breakfast dishes, walking a dog, or putting on work clothes. These activities send a message to the self: "I'm going to work now."

Nancy Peacock was used to working in complete silence and isolation. She discovered, when her partner Ben moved into her cabin, that the most profound change required to adapt to the new situation was to recognize "That my quiet psychological space is my own responsibility."

Focus and Balance

If your childhood and adolescence were spent in school, you probably learned to comply with an existing schedule, not how to create your own. You may know how to be motivated by a teacher's goals. How can you reach your own? Creating a visible structure or pattern helps, but subtler techniques may also be necessary.

On days when Jennifer Munter resists work, she tricks herself: "Okay, I won't work today. I'll just get ready to work, and sit down at my desk, but I don't have to do anything."

If you are used to being available to others at all times, you may find working at home provides a psychological challenge to your self-image.

Barbara Hubert Baiardi has worked from her home for almost thirty years. Initially, she slept on her cutting table at her small lower east side New York wool cape factory, to save on rent and protect the store from vandals. Barbara offers this advice:

"Eat three meals a day, at the same time each day. Take a walk, even just a block, at the end of your workday. If you demonize your body by neglecting it, telling it in effect, 'My head is more important than you,' when you lie down at the end of the day, your body will fight back."

WORK AT HOME, WORK ALONE

Carole Fournier's complaint of loneliness is common. Workplaces offer a culture of support, education, friendship, and drama. Working at home can be lonely, and boring, and you might miss out on information and training. If your work is your joy, it's easy to maintain a pattern of working and sleeping, and leave the house too rarely. Peter Lee, a therapist, says that he structures his time so that he spends at least three days a week away from home, taking classes or doing volunteer work, and he travels to conferences for a few weeks each year. Deborah Brady (see profile) says she never felt lonely working from home

Nina Schmidt designs wastewater systems from her home office about twenty-five hours a week. She says of her toddler, "The good thing about Ella is that if she's around, I just can't work. She keeps me from overworking, and when she is away with her father or across the street at the neighbors, I know I'd better squeeze efficiency into those few free hours that I have. She's made me more productive, at least per hour."

When Ella was born, Nina restructured her work so that now she doesn't speak directly to clients but acts as a subcontractor, receiving calls only from two people who understand that she can't always get return calls right away, or might have to suddenly leave the conversation.

because she became close with her neighbors, and someone dropped by each day. Parents of young children are less likely to complain that they forget to stop working.

Mark Brandenburg, a personal coach for men, who himself works from his home, encourages his clients to try it. "Men, at the end of their lives very rarely look back and say 'I wish I'd spent more time at work, and less with my kids.' It puts your work in perspective if you stay home."

HIRE A BOSS

Personal coaches, or an uncertified equivalent, give some workers-at-home the structure they need.

Sigi Koko was in a funk. A young architect, she worked nonstop for six years, out of her home, where work was in her mind every minute of every day. Her work spilled out onto every surface, so instead of having a home with an office, she had a large office, where she slept. "I never stopped. It was too easy to see the laptop in the evening and say, 'I'll just answer the e-mail.' I erased all boundaries." Visiting a friend in Vermont, she realized she had become a workaholic. Her friend gave her the name of a life coach, Helaine Iris, a former midwife who now "helps people to be born into a new life."

Helaine started by asking Sigi, "How does this fit? Does this work for you?" Answering these questions, Sigi found out how she works best, which, it turns out, is switching each week: one week she has only meetings, away from her office, and the next only design work and writing, in her office. She's strict about this division, and never schedules a meeting during her creative, concentrated, office time.

She's now also strict about rest time. To remind herself, she made a papier mâché sculpture of socks and sandals. "My parents are German, and socks and sandals are what they wear on vacation. When I put out that symbol, it means No More Work."

Helaine also helped Sigi discover what she wanted in an office. Despite her many years designing for others, Helaine suggested a writing exercise that allowed Sigi to see what she herself needed. "I wrote, free-form writing, pretending I had the ideal space, noticing all the aspects of it. I found I wanted to be able to roll around on my chair and reach everything in my office. If I ever have to stand up, I know I won't put it back." Her office is 7 feet by 13 feet, one long rectangle. The books are on one side, and a long desk is on the other. "I knew I wanted light, and space for plants, which I have. It's perfect, now that it's arranged correctly."

TRADE WITH A NEIGHBOR

A few people have found a way to have a separate workspace, along with the psychological balance of a collegial relationship, by trading places with someone else.

Sarah and Pat, who both work as translators and live about six blocks from each other, traded home offices. They now each walk at least a mile each day, and appreciate the change of scenery. Sometimes they arrange to eat a meal together and they enjoy having someone else who understands the work.

By exchanging offices, Sarah and Pat may also be less likely to become sick from their houses, a potential drawback of staying home. There is some evidence that changing environments gives your body a rest: for example, you might show allergic symptoms to cat dander if you are around it 24/7, although you tolerate it well for 8 hours. Environmental illness—extreme sensitivity to common chemicals and other environmental factors—appears to be triggered by being at home at least as easily as being in workplaces.[4] You'll be wise to be especially mindful of the substances in your house.[5] Dividing your workspace from your home space will also help you avoid the homeworkers trap of forgetting to leave work, and go home.

MAKE YOUR OWN SABBATH

Choose a date, and a beginning and end time.

Make up rules about what you will and won't do. The rules will define what is rest. People make rules varying from "No shopping" to "No screen time" to "No dieting" to "Stay in bed all day" to "Whatever I feel like."

Unless you've made the rule "Complete solitude," find a friend or friends who will agree to the rules and the time set. It's best if everyone plans to play for the whole time.

Prepare ahead of time two rituals: one to begin the Sabbath and one to end it. Some people say prayers, or eat a specific food, or sing a certain song. Choose something that will stick in your mind and help make a clear separation between the work time and the Sabbath time.

Try out your noncreation.

TIME FOR SABBATH

How do you get home? If working at home has lengthened your day, you're tired, and your projects have piled up, it's time for a Sabbath.

Sabbath is the moment when work time stands still, and humans marvel at the creation that is, without tampering or scheming. It is the difference between doing and being. It is a simple, free way to convert a workspace into the luxury hotel that is your home. It has the magical power to expand your home into an oasis of immense dimensions. Free people have practiced the Sabbath forever, weekly or seasonally, or whenever the harvest allowed it. It can last as long as a week or as short as an hour. Sabbath is the antidote to greed, the well of contentment. It is your home.

A friend introduced me to the Sabbath by inviting me and other friends to his home, for a 24-hour completely restful conversation, eating, and sleep fest. The rules were that we couldn't go away during that time, and that we should try to do our best to relax, and to please ourselves, and that we weren't to speak about work or the troubles of the week. I can't describe well with words what happened—you will have to try it yourself— but the altered state of time and communion with friends that the Sabbath encourages is a good balance for the loneliness you might feel if you work at home. Leaving the lonely state is the subject of the next chapter.

BOB THEIS
Built 2000

AREA:
27 sq. ft.

COST:
$250

LOCATION:
Richmond Heights, California

When architect Bob Theis says his office measures 5½ feet by 5 feet, some

people immediately understand. They spread out their arms a little, and something lights up in their mind: "Oh, so everything is at your fingertips," they nod, seeing the convenience in their mind's eye.

Like many good designs, it was by accident that Bob's office is so perfectly small. He and his partner Barbara Baiardi had bought an old, poorly built house and were in the midst of rebuilding it when Bob decided to move his architectural and planning office home. The only space that was ready was one they originally intended to use as a laundry room: four framed walls underneath the exterior staircase that leads up to their residence. The stairs had needed new supports, but instead of just putting up new posts, they put in a room, under the landing. "So now we say I am the troll under the bridge," Bob says. "And when Barbara comes out of the house, onto the landing, I know, because the ceiling shakes."

The west wall of the office is a pair of mostly glass French doors, which open out toward a small yard and, when thrown open, give Bob the advantages of being outside, without the disadvantage of no roof. "Everyone thinks they want a window in their office, when what they should be demanding is an outside door. A door puts you right on the edge of inside and out, and like they say in permaculture, 'All the richness is on the edge,'" says Bob. The doors provide most of the light Bob needs, and since he sits facing south, it pours in over his right shoulder. The scene outside is pleasantly distracting, and when he turns 30 degrees to rest his eyes on the faraway view, he's likely to find a robin or squirrel at his feet.

Across the room from the doors is an 18-inch square window, which is used mainly for ventilation, particularly when Bob decides to ban the neighbor's cat for a bit but wants a breeze. But more often the cat lies on his lap, and between the cat, the thirty watts of drafting lamps, the computer, and insulated (R-19) walls, the room stays warm enough in the winter without additional heat for all but the rainiest, gloomiest two or three weeks. When the temperature outside drops below forty, a few minutes of a tiny electric heater cuts the morning chill.

No wall space goes unused, and Bob can reach everything from where he sits, on a stool, in the middle. On the east wall, on either side of the window, is an 11-inch-deep shelf, which stores current files on the left, and drafting tools and the computer hard drive (the compact Apple G-4 cube) on the right. Beneath the window is a 20-inch-deep counter that runs the length of the wall and holds a printer, scanner, and paper. The bottom shelf holds 5 feet of reference books. On the south wall, above his 5 feet of drafting table, is a flat-screen monitor, fit into a 5-inch-deep wall cabinet in the center, with wall-mounted drafting lamps on either side. After work, the computer hard drive hides inside a decorated box, and the monitor cabinet door, which hangs from the ceiling, swings closed, to discourage thieves. Above the doors on the south wall, a long, narrow, 4-inch shelf carries just compact disks, work disks on the left, and music on the right. A wall phone hangs to the right of the door.

Opposite the drafting table, the north wall holds two rows of finishing nails. Bob attaches bulldog clips to his works-in-progress and hangs them on the wall (next to a few drawings by his favorite nephews), so he has a hanging file, and a visual cue of his progress. But what about the wide tables architects need to display and review their giant plans? If he's working on a complex project that requires "reference surfaces" (a place to put extra, related drawings), he sets up an ironing board, loaded with heavy paperweights, outside the doors. He finds that although he's worked in large offices with many tables, he doesn't miss them now.

"This idea of wrapping the wall surfaces around you, working with everything so close, has made me understand what the essence of an office is. I now encourage this kind of office for my clients. It's like being in a cockpit, or like wearing an office like a suit, that enables you to work, with all your tools right there, in your hands." Barbara, who also works from their home, has noticed, "I may walk by fifty times in a day, but he rarely looks up. The compactness of that office, with all his helpers gathered near him, concentrates his attention."

LESA PERRY AND LARRY CORNETT, CANDACE, JAZMINE, DA'LESA, AND XAVIER
House built 1998, addition added 2001

AREA:
2,100 sq. ft., including beauty shop

INTENDED NUMBER OF OCCUPANTS:
6 plus 3-7 clients in shop

COST:
$48,000 (main house)

ADDITION COST:
$35,000 material; $7,500 labor

UTILITY COSTS 2006 (MONTHLY):
Electric $100; gas $50/summer, $150/winter; water $50

LOCATION:
Indianapolis, Indiana

ABOVE: THE PERRY-CORNETT FAMILY

In 1999 beautician Lesa Perry was told that her

"booth fee"—the rent charged by the shop where she worked—would be going up to $500 per month. Lesa had bought a house the previous year, and appreciated the benefits of owning over renting, so this announcement prompted her to wonder, "For $500 a month, couldn't I do better?" She'd never liked punching a time clock. She dreamed of staying home.

Lesa and her three school-age daughters were no strangers to construction: they had helped build their own house, so they had some idea of how to budget and build a home-based shop. They added on to their house a 300 square foot beauty shop, plumbed for sinks and with its own restroom, and then added an extra bedroom and bath to the main house, in anticipation of a new baby, and Lesa's marriage to her fiancé, Larry. Larry and Lesa scraped together their savings, and charged up their credit cards. In 2001 she opened her doors to business and in 2002 she paid off her loans.

Her clients don't come just for a cut. The elaborate designs that Lesa styles from people's hair can take an hour or two. During that time, the room, which fits up to seven clients, is filled with laughter and friendly advice. "You'd think we were on Oprah's talk show, when you hear the problems these women come in with," says Lesa. "No one is a licensed psychologist here, but the solutions they come up with wouldn't be any better if you paid for them. Everyone is very honest, and instead of just one person's opinion, you usually get at least three to choose from."

The shop has a separate entrance. Lesa is lucky to be near the entrance of her neighborhood, so extra cars can park outside the residential area, on a more major street. The shop has its own bathroom to deflect clients' "natural curiosity to come see what your house is like." Lesa insists, "You have to have a line that keeps your house private," and the door between the shop and her house opens to a hallway that blocks the view into the living room and Larry's office, where he works as a private investigator. People ask them, "How do you spend all day together?" and they reply, "I guess we're friends."

In 2005 they considered buying something "bigger and better," but then they did the math: "Did we really want to trade a $358 mortgage for a $1,300 mortgage payment? We have everything we need. I walk my kids to the bus stop every morning, and we're home to raise our baby boy." Instead, Lesa's cut back to 2–3 days of work, and has invested her excess time in acquiring real estate properties.

Lesa's mortgage is low because she partnered with Habitat for Humanity to build her house. Habitat, an ecumenical Christian organization that works worldwide, is the seventeenth most active homebuilder in the U.S. Habitat affiliates honor three basic guidelines: a) sweat equity (homebuyers pay most of their down payment by working on their own and other Habitat houses), b) no profit (buyers only pay the actual cost of the house, and c) no usury (Habitat doesn't charge interest on their mortgage loan). Habitat has built well over 200,000 houses in the U.S. and Canada.

If Lesa had bought a house in a typical new subdivision she might have faced CCRs (see Chapter 10) restricting home businesses. Habitat affiliates must fit in with local laws, but since they are motivated by a desire to help families succeed, they avoid placing additional restrictions on new homeowners, and instead encourage them to be good neighbors.

Habitat does have guidelines for maximum house sizes, based on number of bedrooms. "We are here to house people, not stuff," explains Habitat's Director of Construction, Mark Van Lue, so normally 2-bedroom houses are under 900 square feet, 4-bedroom homes are under 1,230 square feet and children of the same gender are expected to share rooms. He notes, "Our sizes allow for all necessity and even a little luxury." Because Habitat works worldwide, in areas where a four-room house, or even just a four-walled house is a luxury, their perspective is global. Habitat's founder has always lived in modest houses, and Habitat employees tend to follow his lead.

Affiliates must balance the construction cost of houses with the long-term cost operation and maintenance cost. Some affiliates, anxious to build, neglect the long-term energy cost. Recent partnerships with large companies allow Habitat to provide better insulation and more efficient appliances to their homes. A few affiliates have decided that unless a home is superefficient, it isn't affordable; high utility bills eat away at families' abilities to pay for food, medicine, and other necessities. The National Affordable Housing Network (NAHN), based in Butte, Montana and directed by Barbara Miller, has partnered with Habitat to produce houses that use less than half the energy of comparable houses, saving 11,000 kilowatt hours of electricity per year, and costing occupants less than $500 (in 2005) in total utilities, annually.

These superefficient houses rely on nationally available industrial products, and in northern climates offer R-60, usually fiberglass, insulation in the ceiling and R-40 walls made of insulated panels or "double stud" construction. This means that the insulation completely envelopes the house, with no "thermal bridge"—no hardware or wooden frame that can conduct heat between the inside and outside. In addition, the houses often use a "heat recovery" system in winter that exchanges inside for outside air, but doesn't allow heat to escape with the air. Correct solar orientation improves efficiency by 15 percent, and careful crafting of details—even the hole under the bathtub is sealed—ensures that the houses are weather tight. So tight in fact, that NAHN is careful to prescribe no-VOC paints, and to limit or eliminate carpeting to maintain good air quality.

"The special quality of the NAHN plans are their replicability," says Jennifer Langton, of Habitat's Construction and Environmental Resources department. Since Habitat's volunteers and employees move and share ideas all over the continent, replicating the same plan saves on work. Critics might argue that houses should be designed with local aesthetics and materials in mind. Barbara insists, "We can drop one of our houses into almost any region in North America and they will perform well. These homes display the art of the possible."

DEBORAH BRADY, MICHAEL SHUBERT, AND QUINN BRADY-SHUBERT
House built 1946, most recent remodel 1996–2001

AREA:
1,400 sq. ft. (main house 950 sq. ft., plus 450-sq.-ft. apartment)

INTENDED NUMBER OF OCCUPANTS:
4–5

PURCHASE PRICE
$65,000 (1992)

REMODELING COST:
Under $3,000, materials (no labor costs)

UTILITY COSTS:
Electric and water, $30–$40/summer, $80/winter; wood, about 1 cord scrap/scavenged (free)

LOCATION:
Eugene, Oregon

ABOVE : **THE FRONT STEPS WERE TURNED 90 DEGREES.**

The first time that I met Michael and Deborah,

they had just finished converting their family room into a studio apartment. Michael spoke excitedly about the details. I asked him, "So once you've rented this out, I suppose it will make it possible for one parent to stay at home." He paused for several seconds. "Actually," he answered, "we're doing this so that both parents can stay at home."

In the space of nine years, Michael and Deborah managed to purchase and pay off their house; remodel it, creating on the same footprint an extra, rental apartment; run a home-based daycare; and organize nearby neighbors into a "virtual cohousing" group which joins to share tools, babysitting, food, and entertainment. And they pulled it off while living "like kings," below the U.S. poverty line. How did they do it?

When they met, they both hoped to live in the country, perhaps as part of a cohousing group. They joined groups, attended meetings, and discussed dozens of possible futures. Eventually, their son, Quinn, prompted a decision.

"We had a baby coming," recalls Michael; "we had to leave the meeting stage, and settle down." So they bought their house, in Eugene—a three-bedroom, 1,400-square-foot stick-frame, split-level bungalow built so quickly in 1946 that the builders didn't bother to put an overhang on the roof. The house was dark—the former owners had shrunk or removed all the windows—and too large, like a cavern. The walls echoed. But it was on a half acre of the best agricultural land in the county, which enabled them to become "country bumpkins, but in the city." They planned to stay five years.

The house cost $65,000. Their combined savings at marriage was $23,000. By living rent free as apartment managers, and saving every penny during their first year of marriage, they put together $40,000 as a down payment. Because they had never used credit cards, and have been primarily self-employed, no bank would offer them a loan for the balance. So with a $5,000 gift from a relative, they financed the remaining $20,000 with loans from a wealthy acquaintance. They paid off the mortgage in 1998.

For four years while Quinn was very young, Deborah ran a preschool in their family room, but as Quinn grew older, and wanted to go to school, they were no longer using their whole house.

"Creating a separate apartment, that was 100 percent Deborah's idea. I looked at how much work it would take, and I wasn't excited," says Michael. But by scavenging most materials from construction burn piles (Deborah is a consummate dumpster-diver) and mining the house itself for lumber (Michael used the thick boards from the old staircase to build the cabinets in the new kitchen), for less than $3,000 they have an apartment they can now lease. "There's a housing crunch in this town. It feels good to be able to offer someone—an artist, or a student—a nice place to live, at a low price."

One of the first changes they made was to jackhammer out the concrete front steps, which faced north and were always slimy in winter, and replace them with slightly wider wooden steps, which they turned 90 degrees, to the east, and covered with a small awning where they "sit with a cup of coffee and watch the kids bicycle off to school." It's a small change, but now they exchange greetings with their neighbors each morning.

They converted the dining room—a clumsy passageway they rarely used—into a shared entryway, storage, and laundry area for both units. They shrank the stairs, which lead up to a dormer, and moved them from the south wall, where they were blocking the winter light, to the center of the house, and they

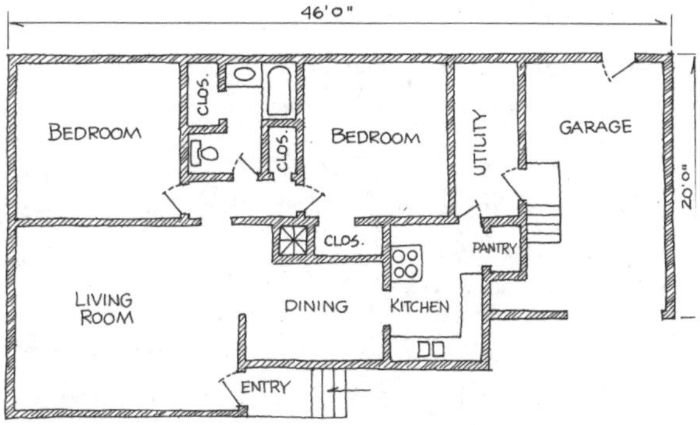

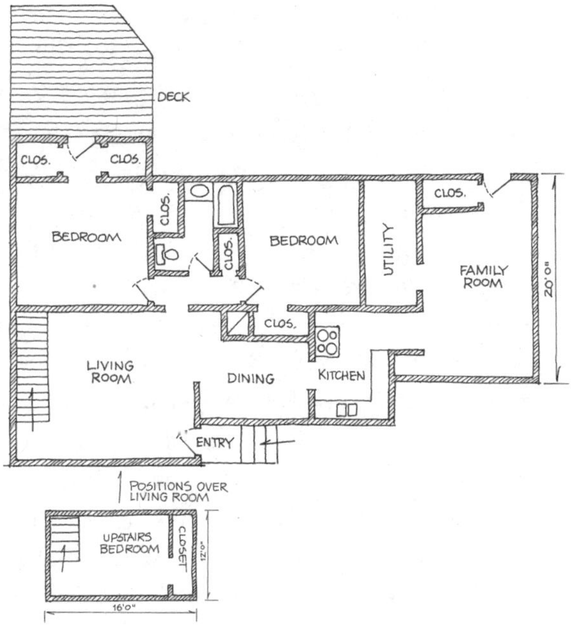

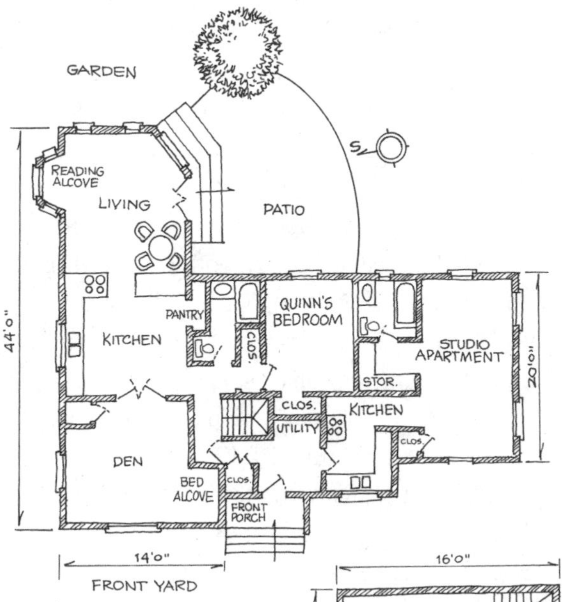

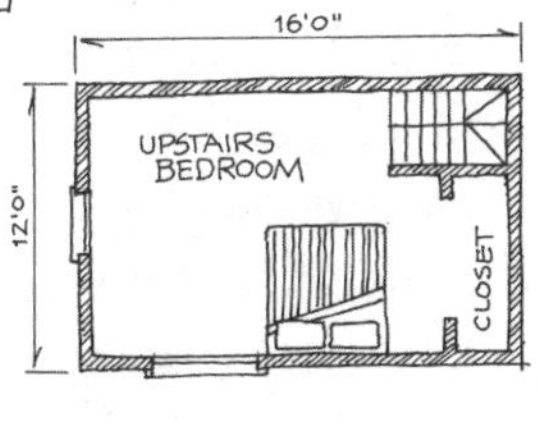

ABOVE: FLOOR PLANS, TOP, CIRCA 1949, MIDDLE, CIRCA 1972; BOTTOM, CIRCA 2006

converted the utility room into a large bathroom and storage area for their new tenant. A few years later, the new apartment became particularly important when Deborah's grandmother needed to move to a more practical dwelling, "If we hadn't had this apartment, Grandma would have had to go to a foster home with strangers," Deborah says.

On their own side, the couple enclosed the covered deck, a space that had been too cold to use, and converted a bedroom and its closet into a kitchen with pantry. The new kitchen is a little large for Deborah's taste, "too much walking back and forth," but Michael (who dreams of house-husbandry) thinks it's not wasted space, since they regularly preserve garden produce, make wine, and bake bread. Five gallons of delicious blackberry wine was on the counter.

The kitchen, den, and living room shine with sunlight from windows on two or three sides. Because it's foggy during the coldest part of their winter, the house does not precisely follow passive solar design; glass doors on the northwest side offer a wide view of the vegetable garden, the walnut tree, and the grazing chickens. Michael used reject (less than 3 feet long) floorboards, which give the floor a pretty, mottled pattern. The hand-cut kitchen counter tiles are made from recycled auto glass, and the kitchen table itself was built from lumber Deborah found. The hand-planed, carefully sanded recycled-wood surfaces—table, doors, cabinets, countertops—glow pale orange and ochre.

The den includes a bed alcove, a private space perfect for a guest. The three rooms together form something like a "great room," but much better, in Deborah's eyes, because they are three distinct spaces. The ceiling (raised) and the floor (slightly sunken) of the living room separate the space from the kitchen. If Deborah is writing, or holding a meeting in the den, she can close the doors, creating a completely separate space. And in winter, they save fuel by heating only the parts of the house they are in.

In Quinn's bedroom, they left the door to the adjacent apartment intact, and covered it with shelves, to create an "accordion house." If Quinn moves out to go to college, they will be able to rent out a larger apartment, without changing the main living space at all.

Quinn has the larger bedroom, filled with toys, and his parents imagined he would play in it, but at his age (nine) it's too far away from the common living space: "He takes whatever he wants to play, and sets up in the living room. He wants to be near us." So much so that at night his room becomes the guest room, since Quinn prefers sleeping upstairs on a cot near his parents.

Upstairs, via a staircase just wide enough to squeeze a queen-sized bed through, is Michael and Deborah's dormer bedroom. With small windows on only the east and south sides and a closet built under the eave, it's a cozy retreat quite separate from the rest of the house.

Wooden hooks on the wall store half-dirty clothes. "Often my clothes aren't really dirty enough to wash, but putting them back in my closet with clean clothes is dangerous—clothes moths like the oil in dirty clothes. I'm not a frou-frou kind of gal, but if you were, you could cover your hung clothes with pretty scarves."

Deborah was adamant about "no second bathroom." "Face it, when you have kids, your house is dusty part of the year and muddy the rest. The last thing I need is a second bathroom to clean." Her solution upstairs? "A half-gallon yogurt container, with lid. It's a modern chamber pot. And a gallon jug for him." It turns out, the nitrogen in their urine is excellent for their garden compost pile and as long as they don't have typhoid, or another serious disease, urine is essentially benign—the Romans used it as laundry detergent. Deborah expects that as they age, they will pee more often, and may prefer to move downstairs, into the den.

The couple meant to keep their "five-year plan" to move out to the country. But as the years passed, they noticed their friends who had moved out were moving back to town. "Our friends in the country were commuting for jobs, for schools, for kids' playmates. Town is where the people are. It's the place for us."

While staying put in town, they still held on to many of the ideals of cohousing. Deborah realized, "Here we are, each in our own house, and we have to have our own of each little thing, and we have our TVs to entertain us. " So six years ago she started "dispersed cohousing," by meeting her neighbors and calling friends and acquaintances who lived nearby.

Six households came together. They started by buying food and fruit trees in bulk, at a reduced price. They also care for each other's children: "That way you don't pay for a babysitter, and you really know who

DEBORAH, QUINN, AND MICHAEL

is taking care of your kid." Entertainment nights at people's homes have become popular. "For instance, leading up to the holidays we made handicrafts, and some evenings we read passages from favorite books to each other. People love that."

The group swaps garden produce and seedlings. (Our interview was interrupted by neighbors stopping by to drop off squash and potatoes.) They keep a list of who has what tools to share. "It's better than a tool library. You know better whom to trust with what." One man brews beer, and a woman makes wine, and they taught the others how. "If someone has surgery, we make meals, or if someone has a baby—whatever happens, we are there. You have relatives from out of town, well, one of us has a minivan. People love it."

The weekend before the interview, the couple hosted seven people for a work party. They stacked a year's supply of firewood and weeded the entire garden. After trying various methods, the group has settled on a credit system for work parties: neighbors get a credit for every hour worked. The house with the most credits in the black cashes in and calls the next work party. This way, people can choose how much they want to work, with no guilty feelings when they don't come.

Michael and Deborah managed to achieve their dream of community and country living, in a way they hadn't expected. Their son, Quinn, is happy with how things have turned out. I asked him if he envied his friends with big houses, and he replied, "We are usually outside, so half of their houses go to waste. Kids don't need a big house. They need a big yard.

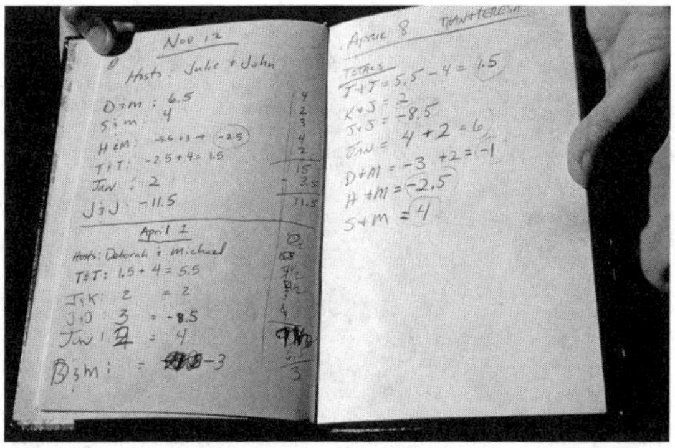

THE HOUSE WITH THE MOST CREDITS CASHES IN AND CALLS THE NEXT WORK PARTY.

PRAG'S CHORE LIST.

8

Give Up Your Loneliness

The most daring thing is to create stable communities in which the terrible disease of loneliness can be cured. —KURT VONNEGUT

A RESEARCHER NOTICED IN A VILLAGE WHERE HE LIVED that people coated their babies' bellies in dung right after birth. I asked him, "Didn't they get tetanus?" He said, "Occasionally." "Couldn't they see the dung was causing it?" He replied that there was no way to know: it might be the dung, or it might have been that they didn't use enough dung, didn't coat them as thoroughly as was right. There was probably something good about the dung.

So it is with loneliness. As we spend more time segregated in cubicles, and among people we don't know, we imagine that what we really need is "some time alone." The answer to a couple's fighting is "give me space" and the cure for children's misbehavior is "time out." Our newest prisons offer their high-risk inhabitants twenty-three hours of solitary confinement every day.

If we each spend enough time alone, will we evolve into a species of enlightened saints?

We won't find out soon, because most of us don't spend much time in true solitude. Nor do we spend it together, but instead in the gray zone of neither really alone nor in close company. Shopping and commuting, and jobs where we greet a quickly passing public, or workplaces where employers discourage casual talk are part of this gray zone. An advertisement for a computer program that keeps employees from "chatting" on the Internet reads, "From chit-chat to Ka-ching!" and reminds us how hungry many of us are for interaction, especially sustained conversations. Is there any surprise that many college students keep a cellphone glued to their ear? It's a reliable source of companionship, and maintains an ongoing conversation, unlike the other students in the bookstore line.

THE LONELY AMERICAN

Somewhere along the way, many of us lost the habit of being comfortable and present with each other, of spending long hours, just enjoying company. Some believe that loneliness is the natural state of human existence. Old proverbs reflect this assumed fate ("Born alone, die alone"), and our

English teachers divide our stories into "man against nature, man against man, and man against himself." How very lonely.

But loneliness is a choice, not our fate. "Born alone and die alone" expresses fear more than a fact. Look at that proverb again: The first half reduces the mother (and anyone else in attendance) to a ghost. The second is a choice. Families and friends often sit with the dying, and many people know that their ancestors and god(s) accompany them in the afterworld. At times we imagine our feelings at birth or death or other important events are uniquely ours, but we have no way of knowing whether others don't feel exactly like we do. Here's a different proverb: "Deep inside, our feelings are the same." How can we know which way it is? The evidence is contradictory. Our belief in uniqueness is a choice.

Our dwellings reflect that choice. Doors to our apartments are placed to avoid interaction. Houses face out like a stage set, instead of around like a folk dance. The newest houses have more than one private room per occupant, in addition to private bathrooms.[1] They are, says real estate agent Candy Aguilar, "designed to anticipate a divorce." What does a dwelling look like when it encourages companionship and intimacy?

Coming Back Together

Eighteenth-century Americans complained of loneliness if they had to spend one night alone in a bed. Three generations, long-term visitors, and boarders were common to many households, and especially in winter, people joined together to stay cozy. Today, most of us sleep every night alone, with a whole room or even a whole, large house to ourselves.[2] The large sizes of modern rooms make some people uncomfortable: Elizabeth Harmon found moving to a tiny apartment made her "Less lonely, because there is not a whole lot of empty space yawning around me here."

When we live alone we each have our own appliances, utilities, walls, paint, decorations.... When you consider in detail the minimum necessary for any dwelling, it's easy to see why it's hard to construct a home for a single resident that is as efficient per person as shared space. In other words, even if three people share a house that is three times the size of their previous, separate, smaller houses, they are likely to use less energy as a group. Some people choose to conserve by keeping their dwelling close to others, and some double (or triple, or sextuple) up. After making some adjustments they realize the benefits of the new intimacy they've added to their lives.

SHARING WITH A PARTNER

Have you ever had the romantic dream to live with a beloved in a tiny cottage? On our travels we met a number of people living that dream. They seemed happy. Happier than other happy couples? There's no way to know. A tiny house may not save a marriage any more than a bigger house will, but at least these folks weren't fighting about finances. Happy small-house couples seem to have similar habits to other happy couples, but maybe a little more so. These is what they say makes their life work:

- They can be comfortably silent when they are together.
- They are tidy, or they share an identical standard of cleanliness.
- They take time apart, with friends, and totally alone.
- They have signs or codes that indicate, "Don't talk to me right now."
- They like being outside.
- They each have their own, separate small area that is private and exclusive.
- Their love is central to their life.
- They talk about problems soon after they come up.

This last habit is the most important, according to Carmen Velarde, a deacon who has taught prenuptial classes and has herself been married for fifty-seven years (see profile in Chapter 11). "If you believe as I do in marrying for life, there's no point in waiting to talk, because unattended problems just get worse. Do you want to spend your whole life this way? When problems come up you need to deal with them *now*." Others agree that small dwellings tend to force them to work out disagreements because there's nowhere to avoid each other. "There's literally no void in our space," said one, "so we can't avoid things."

THREE GENERATIONS UNDER ONE ROOF

For some people, the leap from living alone to sharing with a partner or spouse is enormous. Yet living alone, although very common now, historically, except for a few monks in caves and trolls under bridges, was almost unheard of. What has precipitated this enormous dive in density, this flight from shared life?

Many people point to the creation of the nuclear family. Its natural habitat, the single-family home, some say, was an invention to force us all to buy more stuff.[3] They say a smaller family unit increased mobility, making it easier for ambitious employees to move around the country in pursuit of better jobs, instead of staying home, developing loyalties within the community and developing mature local economies. Some people suggest that the shrunken modern family is a product of a spiritual, cultural shift that allowed personality development outside the constraints of tradition. Whatever the cause, the move away from extended families has had an enormous effect on our density, maximizing our resource use and minimizing our sense of social support.

But some families never divided into nuclear units, and others are coming back together. Children benefit from their grandparents' childcare, and grandparents benefit from their children's health and hospice care.

Tami Schaff (see right), from Jackson, Tennessee, admits that her situation only works because the members of her extended family all get along very well. For families who'd like to be closer, but maintain some household autonomy, the perfect balance—although it's not quite as energy-efficient—can be separate quarters in very close proximity:

"I don't know why people are living with so few people in their home. Maybe it isn't the norm, but I say, do it! Before my mother moved in with us, my husband had to mow her lawn, as well as ours. He had to do all her house repairs, as well as ours. Now that we all live together, in one house, everyday life is so much easier. My husband handles our one lawn and house repairs, I handle the cooking, and my mother does the laundry. We all pitch in on cleaning. We all spend less time doing work, and we have much more free time, plus we save money with this arrangement. My mother pays rent (which is a lot less than it was when she had her own house), so we will be able to pay our mortgage off faster. We only have one electricity bill. We waste less food. Saving money and having less work to do really makes life more enjoyable.

"With my mother living here, our life is more peaceful. I no longer worry whether she is lonely—I can just go in the next room and talk to her. If I can't play with the kids, they go see Grandma, so it is good for the kids too. My mother is an insurance adjuster, and her customer files are on the computer, so she doesn't need much space even though she works at home. The worries we felt before this new living arrangement are gone. Having my mother here makes our house more of a home. If we ever do crave being alone, all we have to do is go on a walk." —Tami Schaff

NEW FAMILIES

If you don't have an extended family, or one that you want to live with, you can build up your

Fumiko, like about half of her ancestors before her, has spent her whole life in the same house. A traditional Japanese person, she assumed that when one of her two sons was grown, his wife would join the family and share her kitchen. The bride, it turned out, had different ideas. Eventually a deal was struck to rebuild the house, adding a second floor where the newlyweds have a top-floor apartment with its own kitchen, a mezzanine that shares the acoustic space with the downstairs parlor, and a staircase with shallow, wide steps so future children will be able to run between the two spaces.

own, making roommates of friends and friends of roommates. You may enjoy the pleasure of shared experience and threads of conversations that last for days. People share space to reduce costs; share child care; have someone to feed the dog when they are gone; because they enjoy eating dinner with friends, or because, "It just doesn't feel right, keeping all this space to ourselves."

Many people can tell you about drawbacks, complete with a story of a "housemate-from-hell," whose most redeeming quality was that subsequent housemates seemed easy as pie. There's a skill to choosing others to live with, and a skill to living with them that is hard to learn without giving it a try. Seasoned house sharers say that compatibility is key, but finding it is tricky. Most of them say that friends work out better than strangers, and that agreements about noise, guests, cleaning, energy use, departure rituals, morning routines, bedtimes, and so forth help, but don't eliminate surprises. A visit to potential housemates' current dwellings will tell something about their habits, and a trial week, or a trip taken together prior to move-in, may reveal incompatibilities.

Gerentologist Jane Porcino[4] suggested that older people in particular benefit from communal living for many reasons, but especially because being exposed to a "wider spectrum of thinking" encourages us to continue growing.

Fran Allison, age 89, lives with her daughters in a cooperative, rural community in North Carolina. Their house includes space for volunteers who come for a few months at a time to work in construction or gardening. The community is designed with young people in mind, and it's more dangerous for Fran to walk her dog on the rocky paths than it was in town. However, Fran says, she's never lonely, there's always someone to eat with, and most of all she's happy to be supporting a larger community that is part of an educational mission.

Cohousing specifically designed for seniors is an option, and one such community broke ground in 2005. Single mothers are another group who see the advantage: in its first months of existence, thousands of single moms joined "Co Abode," (see profile) an Internet-based matchmaking service for single moms who want to share a house with another single mother.

"Intentional communities" is the phrase given to a wide array of living situations that vary from students sharing a house for a few years, to long-term, income-sharing cooperatives that have lasted for decades or generations. North America has a long tradition of "utopian" communities, and through the centuries they have offered an alternative, a solution to whatever the ills of the day were.

MAKING IT LEGAL

You might be surprised to learn that at one time, unmarried people or unrelated families living together was illegal in your state. *Unrelated adults* is the legal term used by municipalities and subdivisions who have rules against such arrangements, rules that were typically created to make it difficult for homosexual or unmarried couples to shack up, or to prevent groups of students from renting houses in an expensive neighborhood. Luckily, few areas enforce such restrictions, these laws appear to be unconstitutional,[5] and often they only restrict more than four unrelated adults from living together in a single-family dwelling. A more important legal consideration is

Ma'ikwe Ludwig and Marqis Rotenberg were not married, but they were about to have a child together. At first they hoped to marry, but it became apparent that they weren't compatible. Still, they wanted to raise the child together. Because they lived in a cooperative community, they were able to have separate bedrooms but see each other in the kitchen, and work with each other in the garden. "We were a broken family at heart," says Ma'ikwe, "and normally that would mean meeting each other in a parking lot to pass off the kid. But because we had neutral, nurturing places to be with each other, we were able instead to evolve past our anger and disappointment into honest friends. The community helped because they knew both of us, and couldn't afford to take sides. They didn't encourage us to hate each other, like some friends do." Marqis agrees, "In a community house, there can be more motivation to deal with a conflict, then to just walk away. Which is good because for eight years now our son has had both his parents nearby, and he hasn't had to choose."

how groups can share property ownership.

Tenants-in-common (TIC) is one way a group of two or more people can share title to a property. The group places into the deed or addendums any number of agreements (typical TIC agreements run twelve to forty pages long), including the percentage of the property that is held by each member, and/or a physical description of which parts of the property the member has access to, or specific ownership of. This form of group property ownership is particularly popular in the San Francisco Bay Area. A Marin-county based financial institution was the first in the nation to finance shares of a TIC property, instead of financing the whole property at once. Typically, however, a single bank holds the whole mortgage, and all member/shareholders are considered as the borrowers. "You should do it with people you trust, and who know their intentions," says Geetha Tamaroon, a TIC house co-owner, "because any single owner can force a sale of the property." TICs are under some judicial scrutiny in San Francisco currently because money-motivated individuals are using them as a way to purchase property, divide it up into shares, and profit by selling shares to investors who don't live on the property and may not even know each other.

If you turn the property into condominiums, each owner will have rights similar to a TIC, but with clearly defined separate dwellings. Your group can incorporate, as either a Limited Liability Company (LLC) or a for-profit corporation, and distribute shares among your members, or form a nonprofit cooperative, or a community trust, like the Evergreen Land Trust that holds Prag House (see profile). The bylaws you write when you incorporate will determine how and whether the group can ever decide to sell, the rights of heirs, your decision-making process, and anything else you want to ensure.

There are plenty of other legal options, which you can research locally. The crucial point is to choose some kind of legal agreement, one that all the members understand thoroughly, or consciously decline a legal agreement and understand that you are living in a tenuous and temporary situation.[6]

Brinda spent a decade of winters in a women's community, on a few acres of desert land, owned by one woman, who rented spaces for trailers and tents. Eventually, some of the women built small houses for themselves, and planted gardens. None of the women were wealthy, and depended on the

Cedar Rose owns "Building for Health," a natural and nontoxic building materials company in sunny, snowy Carbondale, Colorado (elevation 6,200 feet). She's also a designer and contractor, building houses of straw and earth. She and her family live in a concrete-block town house. Does this make sense? It sure does, once you know that the town house is a short walk from her business. Its ceiling is well insulated, it shares its sidewalls with neighbors, and its ample south-facing windows are perfectly oriented and far enough away from the next row of town houses to capture the winter sun, so the only supplemental heating needed is a small woodstove, with a flue that runs up through the second floor.

Cedar knows that, per unit, the town houses, which were built in the 1970s in the center of this old mining town, took down less of the forest, and use less energy to operate than many of the natural homes she's built for clients. She enjoys the proximity of her neighbors, and the shared property maintenance. So although she isn't going to recommend building with concrete blocks, now that she's covered the cement walls with more natural finishes, she feels perfectly at home.

low cost of the space. When the owner fell suddenly fell ill, and became thoroughly incapacitated, the residents realized they had no legal claim to anything there. As I write this, the relatives, who have arrived from out of town, are debating what to do.

COHOUSING

Cohousing developments have some of the cooperative qualities of other kinds of communities: shared workdays, meals, a consensus-based decision-making process, some outdoor space, a community room. Many cohousing groups meet for years, ironing out agreements, visions, and designs before any building begins. A few groups create relatively "instant cohousing" by buying an apartment complex or a series of houses, and retrofitting them to better suit a community. Cohousing is described further in the next chapter.

THE MULTIFAMILY LIFESTYLE

Because multifamily dwellings share walls, and are closer together, they use less asphalt, land, and energy in their construction and operation.

THE UNEXPECTED PLEASURES OF APARTMENT-COMPLEX LIVING

Part of why Cedar Rose (see left) likes her home is that she sees her neighbors every day, when she walks past them to work. Bob Theis, a consultant for village and neighborhood planning points out that in modern times many of us see more strangers each day than most of us would have seen in a lifetime a thousand years ago, but nonstrangers are more rare: "I'd guess it takes about ten nonstranger contacts on average each day to keep most people sane. Tribes and old villages provided that." Friendly apartment buildings, mobile home parks, and town houses do too. Many apartments share amenities, such as swimming pools, laundries, gardens and clubhouses, where residents can meet casually. Apartment dwellers eat out more often, spend more on entertainment, and have more friends than their counterparts in single-family homes, either because their dwellings are too small to host guests, or because they have more free time, since they aren't spending it on home maintenance. The net result, according to some apartment dwellers, is less loneliness.

The National Multifamily Housing Council reports that the

TORONTO SEMIATTACHED HOUSES ARE COMMON IN TORONTO'S CORE. BECAUSE THEY SHARE A WALL, HEATING BILLS ARE REDUCED, AND LOTS CAN BE NARROWER. NEIGHBORS OFTEN MAINTAIN A UNIFORM FAÇADE, BUT SOMETIMES INDIVIDUAL OWNERSHIP IS CLEARLY EXPRESSED.

fastest-growing segment of apartment dwellers are people who could easily afford to buy a house but prefer the amenities that new luxury apartments offer—no maintenance, jacuzzis and gyms, twenty-four-hour concierge service, prewired Internet and cable service, movie screening rooms and pet care. While luxury town houses and apartments aren't intended as a showcase of environmental sustainability, they are far more efficient than a subdivision of McMansions, each with its own amenities and maintenance needs. A brief look at New York shows how apartments can be most ecologically efficient.

IS MANHATTAN AN ECO-VILLAGE?

Can a forest of human beings and concrete pillars be environmentally benign? Relative to other North American settlements, it sure can be. New York City residents use (depending on the study you read) about one-half to one-seventh the resources of other Americans. Manhattan is particularly "green." Forced to grow up instead of out, with 1.5 million people covering 33 square miles, Manhattan Island has the highest human density of any place in the United States, about 800 times the national average.[7]

Over 80 percent of people in Manhattan get to work without using a car, compared to about 20 percent in Milwaukee and Miami and 10 percent in most towns and cities west of the Mississippi. The cost of delivering and maintaining services—garbage pickup, mail delivery, utility services—is lower per person because distances are shorter. Even though many New York apartment buildings are verging on antique and not well insulated or outfitted for efficiency, with poorly regulated, overheating furnaces requiring some residents to open their windows in winter, shared walls and ceiling/floors mean that less heat is used, in part because escaping heat makes its way to neighboring apartments. The average New Yorker uses half as much electricity as other Americans. The fact that buildings are old and "reused" means less construction waste, and lower embodied energy. Small apartments make it difficult for New Yorkers to acquire as much excess stuff. No one has yet studied New Yorkers' overuse of Chinese restaurant take-out boxes, and shoeshine, but the research concludes that in most respects Manhattan is a model green community.

The central core of Toronto, primarily because of its strong mass transportation system, is one of very few North American[8] cities that rivals Manhattan for energy efficiency. Both cities suffer from poor air quality—instead of spreading out their pollution and letting wind carry it away quickly, their waste lingers—and Toronto unfortunately imports extra air pollution from nearby coal-fired plants. There's some irony that two areas that produce the least pollution per capita end up living with more than their share. Like commuting bicyclists who eat smog and risk dismemberment each day they ride, from afar they seem to be more concerned with life in general than their own private health.

The five boroughs of New York City cover 309 square miles, including over 1,800 city parks and playgrounds spread out over 28,000 acres, giving it acre-for-acre more public green space than most cities. Add to that acres of public squares, museums, and cafés, and a visitor has an idea of how a combination of plenty of public space and a minimum of private space inside apartments combine to encourage a sense of shared, common place. When New Yorkers meeting for the first time ask each other in great detail the exact location of where the other lives, they are not (just) placing the other in an ethnic or economic category, but are looking for a common place where they have both dined, or walked, or watched, a sense of a place where they both lived, at different moments, but otherwise together. This sense of shared place, and how it affects our ability to live compactly, is the subject of the next chapter.

While many Detroiters fled their town for the suburbs, Mary Nelson chose to stay put. In 1966 she moved into her current home, and six years later she began buying it from the owner. "On this street, we've established ourselves, we've created our neighborhood," she says. "When Joe Louis was the world heavyweight champ, his house was down here. The Borden milk family lived in my house fifty years ago. We have history that you can't get from moving around. We've all known each other for decades. I've known some of my neighbors here on Helen Street since they were in diapers. No one wants to move now."

When the suburban fashion turned to antiques in the late 1980s, Mary found she could no longer safely leave things on her front porch. Old doorknobs, light fixtures, even trim became booty for export. "Everyone who had moved out now wanted a little piece of Detroit. Someone even stole my birdbath!" But with rows of deserted, boarded-up, and burnt-out houses just a few blocks away, Mary's street, with its well-maintained gardens, lawns, and façades, is an oasis of relative security, and proof that strong neighborly ties can create stability even when the larger trends threaten the city around them.

MARY AND CHERYL NELSON

JAMES AND CEIRROME

Built 1912

AREA:
2,264 sq. ft.

INTENDED NUMBER OF OCCUPANTS:
3–8

COST:
$16,950 (1972)

UTILITY COSTS (MONTHLY):
$500 gas /winter;
$110 electricity; $100 water

LOCATION:
Detroit, Michigan

ABOVE: **MARY AND CHERYL ON HELEN STREET**

MARY AND CHERYL AT HOME

Solidly built of clay brick and hardwood in 1912 by people optimistic about their city's future, Mary's three-story home was designed to house several generations. The ground floor, meant for newlyweds, has a reduced, simple kitchen, while upstairs the main floor's kitchen is slightly larger. The warmest apartment, the attic, was reserved for the grandparents. "As you matured in this house, you moved up," Mary explains. "I believe this house was built for an Italian family."

Mary's daughter Cheryl, after living alone, then married with children, then divorced, and losing her new boyfriend to homicide, found herself leading the harried life of a single mother. When Mary's downstairs apartment vacated, she invited Cheryl to move in. "I did realize at the time I was getting a tenant I wouldn't be able to kick out," she smiles.

Mary says it's worked out well: she helped raise her two grandsons, taking them on excursions and being home for them after school. When the older boy turned sixteen and wanted his own room, he moved upstairs with Grandma, until he left for college. Cheryl says that since she lived away for some years, when she moved back her mother treated her with adult respect, and she appreciated her mother's help. With the money Cheryl saved on babysitting costs, she was able to send her sons to private schools for a few years. On the downside of the arrangement, Mary lists that she worried about them if they came home late, and they sometimes took her cooking pots or ate the last piece of cake from her kitchen. And she had to remind them every Thursday to put out the garbage, "even though they were old enough to remember." On the positive side, she feels safe when they are home, and never lonely. "Payback time will come soon enough," she says; "I think they'll take good care of me if I need it."

Once upon a time, down a long, windy road, past a

burbling brook, in a cloud of Oregon mist, lived a young man from the East. He had moved west to help others organize their own housing, and in a few years he found himself seeking his own lodging.

He happened upon a dark, old hunting cabin, on the homestead of an acquaintance. He restored the old cabin, in exchange for free rent, and set about tearing up rotten floorboards, replacing small windows with larger ones, adding a loft and a porch in the process. Kiko lived alone in his little cabin for five years.

Kiko is an artist, as the handsome details in the house proclaim. He's also a bread baker, a sculptor, and a builder of magical mud bread ovens that are shaped like animals or historical beings. His ovens bring a kind of bread normally only found east of the Atlantic to North American backyards.

The bread ovens brought Hannah to Kiko. "I had quit my job in England as a baker, and I took a trip visiting organic farms. In British Columbia, I saw a mud bread oven and the man who built it showed me an article about Kiko's ovens. I decided to look him up and buy his book."

Hannah married Kiko, and moved in without furniture. A second spice rack appeared in the kitchen, and they built a desk at the foot of the bed, 4 feet high, with storage underneath and above. Hannah's desk is at the opposite corner of the bedroom from Kiko's, and with the difference in desk height (Kiko's desk is low; he sits on an exercise ball to write), and with their backs turned away from each other, even though they share the room, there is a sense of privacy and separated quietness when they write. "We respect each other's solitude," says Kiko. "When we want privacy, avoiding eye contact helps."

Recently, Hannah made another small change: she gave away the armchair that used to sit between Kiko's desk and the bookcase, which she found they used to pile up half-dirty clothes. She converted the space to "a beauty corner," an uncluttered space with a bit of art on display.

HANNAH FIELD, KIKO DENZER
Original cabin built circa 1948, renovated September–November 1994

AREA:
220 sq. ft. plus 352-sq.-ft. art studio

INTENDED NUMBER OF OCCUPANTS:
2 adults

RENTAL COST:
First 5 years, 918 hours of labor; currently $225/month rent

CONSTRUCTION COST:
$865 in materials; landlord provided hauling, roofing, and other materials per agreement

UTILITY COSTS (MONTHLY):
$11–14 electric; less than 2 cords wood per year

LOCATION:
Central Coast Range of Oregon

ABOVE: **KIKO AND HANNAH'S STUDIO**

AFTER THE SCREEN IS FILLED WITH SLICED APPLES FOR DRYING IT WILL BE HOISTED OUT OF THE WAY, TO THE CEILING.

"Dad will miss that chair, when he comes to visit, but now we put our clothes away," she says.

The loft has no windows, and was long ago abandoned as a sleeping area, once Kiko noticed the darkness made him sleep late. It's used for storage now, and is accessible by ladderlike steps permanently attached to the wall.

The house wastes no time in admitting visitors to their favorite room: the only door opens into the kitchen, which is appointed like the cockpit of a plane; a single step takes the cook to the wide variety of implements and materials. The wall is stacked with clear glass jars of dried herbs, grains, and fruit ("Jars are best when they explain what they hold without words," says Hannah), and every corner and cranny is filled with a cabinet or shelf ("The only drawback to the shelves is that this is a seismic zone," worries Kiko). Both the built-in booth and its table have storage underneath.

"Shelves not only store stuff," writes Kiko, "but also testify to the life of the occupant." The shelves and hooks in their home display a life lived with art (small sculptures and mosaics rest here and there), and books (including Kiko's own, *Build Your Own Earth Oven*), and good eating (over half the house is dedicated to some aspect of cooking). The contents hint that a giant garden is just outside the door (which it is).

A screen door hangs from the ceiling, flat, and on a pulley. The first task after breakfast the day of the interview is to slice eight pounds of apples and lay them on the screen to dry, and raise the door back up to the ceiling. This system could work well for drying clothes in winter, as well.

The next task of the day is to knead a few loaves of bread. A countertop, stored in one corner, is moved to the sink to create extra workspace. In a few hours, the bread will be placed in the cob oven outside and by late afternoon fresh bread will be ready. In the meantime Hannah harvests peas and tomatoes from the garden, and then takes her guest on a lively march up through the forest to harvest blackberries, which she'll boil into delicious preserves in the evening.

If the cabin is a tidy triumph of well-divided content and function, the studio, just eight steps away, is its complement: a gallery of uninterrupted space and light, with enough room to assemble a 12-foot sculpture, and wide doors to let the artwork out. The studio is hand-built, of cob, with vaulted window openings, and smooth, white plastered walls.

Between the studio and the cabin is a porch, wrapped around the south and western sides of the cabin. The west side serves mainly as a mudroom and storage area (for seeds, more artwork, and garden produce), while the south is the best place for a guest to sleep, as it looks out towards forest pasture, and the neighbors' horses, and is just 20 feet from a perennial brook.

I asked Hannah if it bothers her that they don't own the land where they live. She replied, "My father was a farm worker in England, so we always lived on our employer's land. It was a beautiful place." Kiko adds, "By accepting the offer of tenancy, by living as though we are staying, we make ourselves part of a family ranch that has been going since the 1860s."

Children seem like a possible outcome of this union, and people have asked them, "When you have children, won't you move into a larger house then?" To which Hannah jokes, "We've heard that small children fit in a low drawer and sleep quite nicely."

EPILOGUE:

In fact, a child did join the couple, about two years after we made this visit. They found themselves trading spaces with the studio, which gave them 30 percent more living space than they had before, and a spacious, spread-out feeling. The cabin has become their office, spare bedroom, and storage. In 2006 they were expecting a second child.

PRAG HOUSE
Built 1908

AREA:
9,500 sq. ft.

INTENDED NUMBER OF OCCUPANTS:
13-16

UTILITY COSTS (MONTHLY):
$770 electric, gas, and water

PURCHASE PRICE:
$48,000 in 1972

LOCATION:
Seattle, Washington

Prag House has been a successful cooperative

house for thirty years. The solid twenty-four-room residence was built in 1909 as home for a family of five, plus servants, and later it served seventeen years as a convent. In the 1960s it reached its lowest point of human density ever when Mrs. John W. Barnet and her husband filled "every corner, wall, and bit of floorspace" with pre-T'ang vases, African masks, ancient Greek footed jars, Renaissance furniture, and so forth. In 1966 Mrs. Barnet told the *Seattle Times* she was "addicted to beauty," attributing it to her childhood in industrial Chicago, where she "didn't see grass until I was three years old."

In 1972 the building had most recently been used as a halfway house for women fresh out of prison when the "Provisional Revolutionary Action Group" (the name, they now say, has always been tongue-in-cheek) moved in. The community evolved toward stability, experimenting along the way with methods of communication, decision-making, and social change. The land trust created to hold the property now holds one other house, and three farms as well. Currently, politics are not the house focus, but Prag did manage to send one member to the Seattle city council. Nick Licata, a founding member, attributes Prag's success to "never getting stuck on one single ideology."

Typically, about fifteen adults and two children share eighteen bedrooms, one kitchen, a formal dining room, an office, two living rooms, an exercise room, a laundry room, a workshop, a tool shed, a darkroom, basement storage, a large outdoor deck, a porch and a balcony, two stairwells, three full bathrooms, and one water closet (less than one-quarter the national per-capita bathroom average). They use one refrigerator and

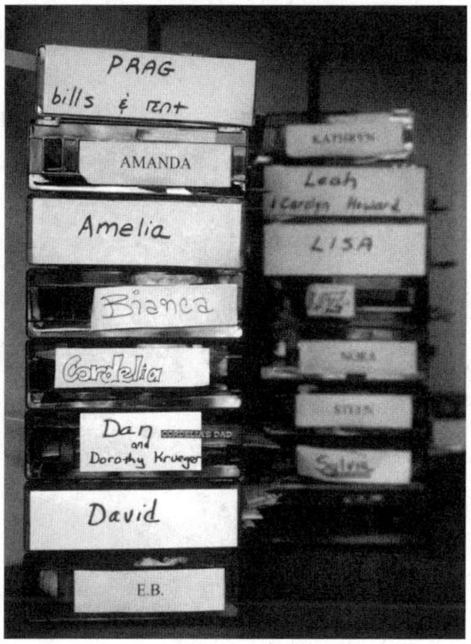

ABOVE RIGHT: **PRAG'S KITCHEN HAS TWO DISHWASHERS.** **ABOVE:** **PRAG MAILBOXES**

one deep freezer, two dishwashers, three televisions, twelve telephones, one toaster, and seven cars. "What we don't have here is the one basement per three or four persons that many households fill up with unused exercise machines and the remnants of hobbies given up years ago," says resident Dan Nord.

At the time of the interview, residents included a teacher, a social worker, a lawyer, two students, a computer programmer, a new mother, a firefighter, an audio engineer, a college administrator, an Americorps volunteer, an international businessman, and two counselors. "Here, I can walk into the kitchen any time and find an adult, and hear an interesting conversation," reports Lisa Keith, the new mom. "They might even take the baby for a few minutes. Other mothers never wonder why I live here, just how I found it," she adds.

Members typically pay about $500 per month in rent (rent varies slightly with income), which includes all food; soap and toothpaste; lightbulbs, cleaning supplies, etc.; all utilities including a phone; and a housekeeper who cleans the public spaces once a week. The group meets monthly and goes on retreat once a year to determine short- and long-term plans. Members are considered equal except in room selection, where seniority rules.

Members work four hours per month on a home-maintenance project of their choice, and do two hours per week of chores (sweeping, shopping, recycling). "Maybe the best thing about Prag," says Sylvia Jones, "is coming home to a full refrigerator every day, even though I never shop."

The dark and clumsy Victorian kitchen, seemingly designed to discourage servants from enjoying their work, was endured by the community until 1998, when builder Dick Patterson completely remodelled it. A central chopping block (with spaces for compost, trash, and recycling underneath), two sinks, two dishwashers (one for clean dishes, one for dirty), and 14 feet of counter space make it easy for several people to cook simultaneously. The remodeling was financed by borrowing from members, with only an amortization schedule as a note. "We operate with a maximum of trust and a minimum of paperwork," says Dan Nord. "It's remarkable how much folks are willing to contribute despite not having an equity share."

With about 530 square feet per person, 12-foot ceilings, broad hallways, and a giant entrance foyer, life at Prag, though more compact than the middle-class average, does not feel the least bit cramped. Most bedrooms are separated by closets, the walls are solid, and the floors are thick with some carpeted, so sound doesn't travel between rooms easily.

If memory is serving the current members correctly, only one resident has ever been asked by the others to leave. Such an action requires a unanimous decision. "In this case, the fellow took years to leave." Sylvia explains, "If you are considering joining a cooperative house, never do it for the cheap rent. And don't do it if you really like to control what's planted in the yard, or what color something is painted. Some of the loveliest people should not join co-ops."

New members are selected slowly, after interviews and checked references. Political beliefs, they all agree, don't matter as much as annoying habits. "You need people who take the garbage out, and do their dishes," they explain. An ability to communicate directly is crucial, while people who "worry constantly about what other people think of them might drive themselves batty here," says Lisa Keith.

The members support each other in their quest to live according to their values. Recycling and gardening may seem daunting for many busy people living alone, but at Prag it's worked into the chore list. Residents return from their work in the competitive world, and are cheered by the sight of their ideals in practice. Lisa says, "The kids who have grown up here have an openness that I hope our child will have."

The house is now assessed at well over $2 million. Because it's held in trust, there is no incentive to sell, but if Prag were starting out new in 2005, assuming a low selling price of $2 million, with a 10 percent down payment, each adult resident would have to pay about $13,000, plus take out a $125,000 mortgage to buy it now. That's comparable to what it would cost for two people to buy a small single-family house in Seattle (if we don't take into account the savings on appliances and household goods that come from sharing). However, the average homeowner gets tax benefits that Prag residents don't share. "So while I really like collective living," says Dan Nord, "we do have to remember that our place works financially only because we are getting the benefit of a very old, already paid-off mortgage. It's thanks to the founders' vision that we are here."

Single mothers are one group who sees the advantage of house sharing: in

its first months of existence, thousands joined "Co Abode," an Internet-based matchmaking service for women who want to share a house with another single mother. Currently about 20,000 are members. Co Abode was founded by Carmel Sullivan, who suddenly became a single mom after 17 years of marriage:

"The loneliness was so profound I started having anxiety attacks. I made my living as an artist, so I was used to being alone. It had been wonderful to be at home with my son, Cooper, while he was little, but suddenly Cooper, now eight, was in a Sudberry-style school, that the students love so much that even though it doesn't get out until 5 pm, they don't want to come home at the end of the day.

"So that's when my loneliness kicked in. It's strange to be totally alone, not to hear anyone else moving or breathing. I was born in Ireland and I grew up with seven brothers and sisters, nine of us all under one roof, until I was a teenager. So here I was alone in my house and even my son didn't want to come home. I went back to California one weekend to visit my sisters. After a two-hour meditation, a very lucid meditation, I had an image, a strong message: "Find another single mother." I decided to move back to California, and I decided to look for another mom.

"I interviewed 18 single moms. One matched me well, an Australian woman with two girls. Then I looked at the list and started matching other people, like two women who each had a young daughter. One woman was living with her two kids in a garage. Housing is an enormous problem with single moms. A single mom with her kids in a one-bedroom apartment—the kids in the bedroom and the mom on the couch—is typical. Younger children sleep with mom. Millions of moms and their kids are living like this. That's why a three-bedroom apartment works well for many of our members—the moms each have a room, and then the kids share a room, as long as they aren't adolescent kids of different genders. We try to match people who have kids close in age. But single moms have more in common than just the ages of their kids. They understand each other." —Carmel

With over 11 million single mothers in the United States, and over half of all children living with a single parent for at least some part of their childhood, it's clear why Co Abode has become popular quickly.[1] At least two thousand mothers have found their match, making commitments of everything from short-term support for other single mothers who fled hurricanes in the South, to matched women who now own a house and have

THE CO-MOMS
Started 1998

INTENDED NUMBER OF OCCUPANTS:
About 20,000

UTILITY COSTS (MONTHLY):
Usually drop by about 35%

COST:
$29.95 to join

LOCATION:
The United States

“What we really emphasize is that it isn’t a quick fix. It takes time to choose the right person. Don’t just jump into it. Of course, some people have—I did—and it worked, but it’s better to take a trip together, spend some months or more getting to know each other, and think about who would be a good match for you. Two people with giant egos are just not going to work out well together.” —Carmel

agreed to stay together at least until their children turn eighteen.

One pair of mothers bought a duplex. They knocked out part of the dividing wall, so they have one big kitchen, and living room, and bedrooms and bathrooms on their respective sides. Another group of three moms owns a brownstone in Brooklyn. On the first floor they share a kitchen and living room, and the lower and upper floors have bedrooms for the families. In one case, Co Abode negotiated with the owners of a new apartment complex and received a reduced rent for 10 apartments, reserved for single mothers, creating a kind of instant cooperative community on two floors of the complex.

About 25 percent of single moms have a house they kept after a divorce. They may look for another mom to share, so they can maintain the mortgage payments. This doesn’t work as well as when two women meet and then go look for a place together, because there are more questions around furniture, and old patterns, but it can work. One woman, a 22-year-old who thought she’d have to give her baby up for adoption, for financial reasons, was so relieved to find Co Abode, she stopped the adoption process. Soon enough, she found a place she could live with another mother in exchange for housekeeping and childcare and was able to keep her child. More than one woman has found the courage to leave a man who beat her, after realizing that with Co Abode she might be able to support her children financially, by pooling resources with another woman. To the over 30 percent of single mothers who live in poverty, sharing household expenses is an interesting proposition.

Male postmarital participation in housekeeping is slowly on the rise in North America, but at this rate it will be a long time before men reach equality with women.[9] Co Abode members remark that with their new co-mother, suddenly “everything is cut in half—cooking, cleaning, helping with homework.” Carmel reports, “Our preliminary analysis shows that mothers gain about 52 hours of free time per month once they are matched.” Barbara, a single parent of boys, Tyler, 11, and Kevin, 15, testifies:

“For me, there’s been a tremendous sense of relief in house sharing with another mom and her child. At the end of the day we get in there together and tackle what has to be done; ‘You do the dinner—I’ll help the kids get their homework done.’ We have a mutual respect and admiration for each other. My kids have a playmate and are easier to manage. I now have more money to spend on them too.”

Single fathers (there are at least 2 million in the United States) have asked to join the network, and they will be accommodated, says Carmel, “As soon as our program is fully funded.” Senior citizens who live alone in large houses have asked to join as well, and a few couples with only one child have used the website to find a mother and other children to share their house with.

The matching process is important and the website offers advice. Matches works out best between single moms because they understand each other. It doesn’t work as well between single people plus a mom—they just don’t have the same interests at heart. Carmel explains,

Carmel and Cooper’s Co Abode mom gained full custody of her two daughters, and moved back to her native Australia. The transition was hard, but Cooper, who is now a teenager, still sees his “cousins” at least once a year when they visit on vacation.

PAMPER YOUR GUESTS

Fire is needed by the newcomer
Whose knees are frozen numb;
Meat and clean linen a man needs
Who has fared across the fells.

Water, too, that he may wash before eating,
Handcloths and a hearty welcome,
Courteous words, then courteous silence
That he may tell his tale.
—Hávamál, (Traditional Icelandic Poem)

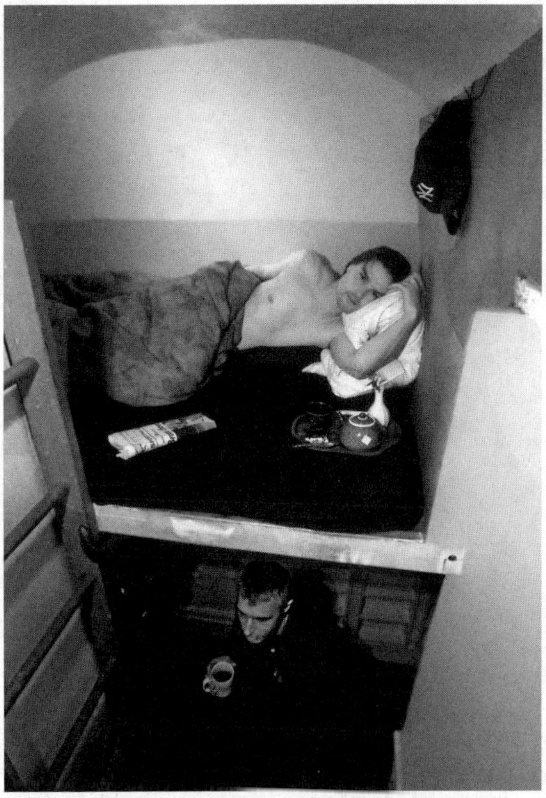

A TINY LOFT BUILT IN THE EMPTY SPACE ABOVE THE STAIRS IN THIS SHARED HOUSE IS LARGE ENOUGH FOR GUEST LOGI TAMAROON, BUT SMALL ENOUGH SO IT WON'T BECOME PERMANENT RENTAL SPACE.

As we traveled around the country visiting small-home dwellers, we were surprised and delighted to discover that the size of your house has no bearing on your ability to be hospitable. Indeed, we found ourselves pampered by our small-house hosts who displayed their generosity not so much by the amount they had, but more by the proportion of it they were willing to give away.

Some of them hosted their guests by giving up their own bed, or their children's bed, (which their children perhaps wouldn't sleep in anyway—more on that in Chapter 11). Some had special alcoves, or lofts, or porches that double as guest space. Some use a trailer. A few have guesthouses larger than their own tiny house. One woman wrote to tell us that when she did the math she found that by trading in her oversized house for a smaller one she saved so much annually that when friends visited she could insist on paying for them to stay in a bed and breakfast near her. My small house neighbor, Rose Catalán does something similar, but when her friends visit, she goes with them to a motel. "Then there's no cleaning, the kids can run around and swim in the pool, and I can focus on being with my guests."

The focus Rose refers to creates the pampering that welcomes a guest. The knowledge that the host cherishes the guest's presence creates a space that special soap and fluffy pillows may enhance, but can't create on their own.

A GUEST ROOM MADE FROM A CONVERTED CHICKEN COOP

JUANITA NEWTON IN HER GARDEN

9 Reclaim the Commons

When we were kids, there were no fences, no privacy walls. We could play all around the block, without touching a street. —ANTHONY J. GARCIA

HOW MUCH OF THE WORLD IS YOURS? More practically speaking, where can you go right now, outside your home, where you can breathe, watch life, "loiter," play, talk, just be, without paying money? These places are your free dominion. They are the common places, where edges meet and offer action, social life, and new relationships. They are the location of equal rights. Keep these places close, and they will widen your home.

When neighborhoods don't have relaxing, joyful common spaces, families try to replace them with "entertainment centers," large kitchens, and huge children's play areas in their own homes. Or we drive all over town, patching together a communal life from a series of planned and timed events. Some of us expand our sense of space by watching television or the Internet—our virtual marketplace and national commons—but the connection we feel from video screens is ephemeral, and if it isn't balanced with a real reality show of friends, it can be maddening.

WHEN SOCIETY IS NOT OUR FRIEND

Without good common space we restrict our friends and acquaintances to a narrow selection of intimates and colleagues whom we welcome into our homes or see at work. There may be people we'd be happy to know casually, in a public space, but since there are few public spaces to meet them, they remain strangers. The gray area of neither friend nor stranger, but fellow citizen, fades into an abstraction.

Perhaps people can develop national and community ethics through solitude or a small family circle. But what if healthy moral connection depends on conversation and shared experience with a wide variety of people? When we are limited to a small circle, it's harder for us to feel empathy and understanding for the wider group. We may be less likely to intervene when a stranger is in need, and more susceptible to all kinds of prejudice and unkind behavior toward the unfamiliar. Children who grow up knowing that other humans are not far away, but always excluded from the group can internalize a kind

“The location was right, the house was nice, but I was visiting downtown with my five-year-old, who seems outgoing in our home and at school, and I noticed she was terrified of people she saw, especially if they didn't look like us. At her school people look pretty much all the same. I don't want her growing up scared. Now we're looking for a new place to live, in a regular neighborhood. We really hadn't made friends in our subdivision anyway.” —Jamie

of caste system, and the notion that society exists to protect property, not to promote the common good or the national character.

Jamie (above) grew up in New York City, moved around during college, and settled with her husband and two young children in a gated development in a suburb of a southeastern city.

MAKING COMMON SPACE COMMON

The desire for community is so popular, we hear the word in advertising, grant proposals, and politicians' speeches that decry the decrease of common values, common space, and common sense. We see related words—"village green," "plaza," "marketplace"—added to improve the appearance of apartment buildings and strip malls. In some places the desire is answered by huge construction projects, designed by imported consultants, with mixed results: some oversized or poorly located "town squares" are filled with empty benches and walkways sized for elephants, rather than the tiny flow of human traffic they actually host.

In general, our cities and suburbs weren't originally planned to maximize civic interaction. Some people are retrofitting our built environment, making common space more common. What they've learned along the way are two principles about happy common spaces: first, they require a common sense, from a common history developed slowly by longtime residents who share the space. Second, if they are to encourage new social interactions, they have to be dense enough and interesting enough to encourage people to come so close together that their city or neighborhood starts to resemble a series of friendly, safe dens.

THE SILENT NEIGHBORHOOD

Right now, no solid ground is legally public to every human. Every square inch of the Earth's land has been claimed and mapped and is owned by a political entity that applies its laws, drawing a circle around the allowed people, separating them from the others.[1] Inside the nations, smaller judges make smaller circles, regulating city parks or building clubhouses only common to the inhabitants of a gated neighborhood. North America in particular has been surveyed and platted (which literally means "flattened") into square blocks made of lines that mostly disregard bumps and grooves in the geography, to make land easier to parcel out and sell. In an era when everyone's time is on the meter, it's harder for a large group of people to retain an ambiguous, common, nonmoney-making area than for a small for-profit group or individual to figure out a way to sell or rent the commons.

Who is served by neighborhoods quiet as a morgue? Just as the hyperwhite of hospital walls turned out to be an aesthetic decision, not a sanitary one, a silent neighborhood does not protect residents from crime, and certainly not from loneliness. Peace and quiet aren't always allies: there's evidence that messy, lively, intricately layered spaces are less likely to be affected by crime, since there are more eyes on the street.[2] Some people who measure their wealth by the price tag on their house have connected that price to the quiet emptiness on the streets. Maybe it's simply because it seems easier to measure something that is dead than something that's alive.

Finding Common Ground

Meanwhile, other people are discovering that a walk in the forest, a park filled with children, or a

A self-storage company hired consultants to get neighborhood compliance with the zoning change they'd need to build eight acres of facilities. They followed the rules: a neighborhood meeting and notice of the council meeting. At the neighborhood meeting, attended mostly by second- and third-generation neighbors, the consultants showed aerial photographs, elevation and plan drawings of the proposed site, graphs of crime statistics, surveys of "positive responses from other subdivisions where our company has successfully operated for over five years." They promised to build a high fence, then upped their offer to a wall around the perimeter. They promised "bright lighting."

The neighborhood listened respectfully, with just a few questions from the younger folk. The consultants looked pleased. It felt like time to go. But a woman in the back, flanked by her two middle-aged daughters, stood up. "You keep telling us how quiet it's going to be, this thing you want. How little crime there will be. How tall the wall is going to be. That land you want, that used to be farmland, for at least 400 years. People shared the part that was grazed. We had a swimming pond at one end, fifty years ago. It was full of life, then. Now I live alone. I'm tired of quiet. I can't drive, so I watch the street. I like noise. I like to watch the people, walking, driving, whatever. It's life. This isn't a subdivision. It's a neighborhood. Whatever goes on here, it's our life. Give us a park, or something else with action, but not some quiet storage."

The neighbors fought and won a battle against the rezoning. One consultant predicted, "They'll get something worse now." Two years later they could not prevent the construction of a high-priced, walled, new subdivision that covered the lot with tightly packed, oversized snout houses, a roof-town with a "common area" composed mainly of an asphalt cul-de-sac. "We fought stuff storage and we got people storage instead," quipped one. "Now we have neighbors who never leave their houses, except in a car, and are walled off from us anyway. We expect them to start complaining about the noise our farm animals make any day now."

shared common house with daily meals is worth more to them than empty rooms in their house, and a big empty yard.

GO WHERE THE WILD THINGS ARE

Citizens of the United States and Canada do share some huge common spaces, in particular, national forest or crown land. Small-housers benefit by visiting, vacationing, and living near this land that is already ours, and that we all pay to maintain. Most national forests

COHOUSING RESIDENTS PARK THEIR CARS ON THE EDGE, AND WALK HOME THROUGH THE COMMONS.

The homeowners who created Maxwelton Cohousing Community on a 21-acre parcel in semirural Washington State built eight houses, including one house attached to the common house, on about 3 acres, around a quarter-acre green. Incorporated as a Planned Residential Development, they cannot build outside their residential ring, so they have about 17 acres left as open space for agriculture or wildlife. In addition, they agreed to build no house larger than 1,500 square feet, and park their cars in a single lot, at the entrance to their tiny village.

allow stays of at least a week, so it's possible to build a life meandering park to park, walking or driving with a tent or a trailer. Others, living near a forest, have restricted the size of their own homes, out of respect for the natural beauty that surrounds them. They want cabin fever to force them into the forest often.[3] A few miles down most wilderness trails in North America you'll find few or no humans, and a sense that your home is as wide as the world.

If you don't have the time to enjoy the public forests, while you're not there someone with time and money might figure out a way to sell them:

The treaty of Guadalupe Hidalgo, through which Mexico ceded about half its territory to the United States, made provisions protecting the property of Mexican citizens, including the preservation of common land, land that had been free for locals to graze animals, hunt, fish, and harvest wood. Land could be sold, but if it included land that had been common, access to the land had to remain open.

In 1960, Jack Taylor bought a million-acre ranch in Costilla County, Colorado, and he slowly started building fences and closing access. In 1981 local citizens filed suit, and after a twenty-one-year battle they finally won back their rights. However, in other areas, where towns had been drained by emigration to the city, and people lost their knowledge of the old treaties, common land was more easily converted to private land.

On the opposite side of the country, in Maine and other parts of New England, huge tracts of forest held by paper and lumber companies have become more immediately profitable to sell as lots for luxury housing than to maintain for future wood use. As woodlots, they provided habitat and recreation for moose and deer, and their predators, cross-country skiers, hikers, snow mobilers, and the general public. While a collaboration of for-profit politicians and real estate developers welcomes this change in the real estate market, other, non-profit groups and local governments are working to convert the woods to national forest or state parks or hold them in land trusts and conservancies as wildlife refuge. This kind of struggle is active all over the continent, as national governments collaborate with multinational corporations to privatize common land.

Some small-house groups are helping to reverse the trend, making private land a little more public at a smaller scale: they purchase rural land they love, and show their love by clustering small homes in a tiny area, closest to an existing road, and preserving most or almost all of what was there.

TAKE TO THE STREETS

By far the most popular common space North Americans share is our intricate network of asphalt, concrete and gravel roads, streets, avenues, boulevards, highways, freeways, parkways—the many names we have for them attest to their importance in our lives. They are where we share the most common experience and common sense, of how to turn and park and signal, and our schools offer whole courses in proper driving etiquette. They serve a social purpose: we eye each other from our cars, sometimes even smile or scowl, and draw moral and psychological conclusions from each other's driving patterns. In some areas, teenagers still promenade and court each other from their cars, and race, and park, and party. And where else do we see political and theological beliefs expressed so publicly, but on our bumpers? The road is our common ground, and we spend more of our money on it than on any other.

Alongside our interstate freeways are thousands of rest areas, some of the only free public places where any one of us may sleep, as long as we have a car. Sam Walton's stores offer free overnight parking in hundreds of locations, and a number of municipalities will allow travelers to park on their streets. The simplest way to access our largest fount of public space is to live in a vehicle.

But with the rising insurance costs, gas and oil prices, and pollution levels, some people have started rethinking how they want to use their asphalted common space. In some areas, neighbors have changed their streets to *woonerfs*—a Dutch word translated as "street for living"—by adding speed bumps, basketball courts, and circular or odd-shaped tiny gardens or art installations in residential intersections to beautify the view and slow down traffic. A few European traffic engineers have experimented with eliminating signs and lights that regulate speed, and found that the lack of instruction provokes drivers to act more responsibly, think for themselves, and have fewer accidents. The key is creating the sense that the street is for people, and cars are an intrusion.[4] Others have narrowed the road, some by parking cars perpendicular to the sidewalk, and some by planting edible fruit trees, so they can eat fresh fruit "from the same ground where trucks used to run, importing it."

The first time I visited Lois Arkin, she invited me to step outside into the street. Right on the asphalt, near the intersection, she set up a card table, a few chairs, a large umbrella, a teapot, and a bright sign encouraging people to slow down. A friend of

THE SIMPLEST WAY TO ACCESS OUR LARGEST FOUNT OF PUBLIC SPACE IS TO LIVE IN A VEHICLE.

hers appeared, and so we sat in the street, chatting with each other, and with anyone who happened to drive by. "We're trying to encourage people to see the street, and our neighborhood, as something other than just a place to pass through." Her neighborhood in central Los Angeles is near some of the most trafficked intersections in North America, and many drivers cut through it on their way somewhere else. "If we want to gain a sense of safe, friendly neighborhood, we need less driving, more sitting, more visiting," she explained to one driver who couldn't imagine what a table was doing in the middle of the road.

When I visited her twelve years later, she had lost her house when the local public school needed to expand. Luckily, the LA Eco-Village, a project her nonprofit organization started in 1993, had acquired a forty-unit and an eight-unit apartment building across the street, and she lived there now. An ample lobby furnished with comfortable furniture, bulletin boards, and mailboxes greets visitors from the street entrance, and opens to an interior garden courtyard. An inviting open stairway leading up from the lobby is carpeted in rich purple recycled tire material. Small and large groups often occupy the courtyard, lobby, and community room at the top of the stairs, and residences are right next to these areas, so to dampen noise every floor has a layer of Homasote—a sound insulator made from recycled paper—below its cork, bamboo, Pergo, or linoleum finish.

The apartments range from 400 to 800 square feet each, and their large windows and some French doors open to the garden spaces, which are busy with dozens of fruit trees, vegetable plots, innumerable flowers, herbs, and two pet rabbits in a 400-square-foot animal enclosure woven from neighborhood plant trimmings. On the south end of Eco-Village, a 500-foot section of the street has been transformed into an eco-park with native plants, a streambed that cleans storm water, a small children's playground, and benches where teenagers happily loiter.

Since the weather is normally idyllic, the lobby is typically open, giving the apartments the feeling that the street is also part of the complex. Eco-Villagers work toward including the whole neighborhood, and in 2005 all the neighbors on one block agreed to park in a nearby lot so the street could be closed off for a two-day festival. Lois reports,

"We do still eat in the street from time to time. Since we've created the plaza in the intersection, we are now doing 'car retraining.' It's an extension of the idea of the traffic calming. Here's how it works: we have a meeting in the middle of the intersection—sometimes just standing around, sometimes sitting around a table. I like the standing, because we're all so used to moving out of the street when we see cars coming. But the car retraining activity is about staying put, with good energy and smiling faces, until the cars figure out they have to go around us, rather than us moving for them. People love it and are astounded at the results. Mostly drivers smile back and go slowly around us."

Front porches can help turn a street into a friendlier common ground. They are making a comeback on the façades of new houses, either instead of or alongside the garage. They widen the view and help you meet your neighbors, but only if you actually sit on them. Elaine Boyer, a native of New Orleans (speaking two years prior to the 2005 catastrophe), lamented about her new home in the North: "At home the porch was busy—people visited each other that way—but here no one goes out, so I'm not sure why they built porches."

The automobile is blamed for all manner of ills. In Elaine's case, her neighbors drive to work and the garages are in the back, so people don't even walk across their porch after they've parked. In general, we blame the car for the dullness of the modern city grid, although the grid predates the automobile. It was clearly evident in Babylon and a dominant aspect of the Roman empire, whose *castra* were built square and walled. Mark Lakeman and Erica Ritter, members of the Portland, Oregon group, City Repair, explain it this way:

"The Romans conquered villages by force, razing the buildings. They enslaved the villagers and then rearranged their typically circular or irregularly

shaped villages into the straight, square, walled grid of the castrum. Two intersecting main streets, the cardus maximus and the decamanus maximus, divided the village into four quarters with just four gates, and the forum, the only meeting place, was at its center. Once they controlled common meeting ground and forced houses into rows, a small group of soldiers could subdue a much larger population: from just a few intersections they could monitor the movement of the whole village.

"When the empire fell and the villagers overthrew their captors, in many cases, villagers moved outside of the castrum to build a new village, using materials they mined from the Romans' buildings. Archaeologists wonder why they left such sturdy structures behind. They left because the grid did not fit their culture, did not reflect their spiritual and social beliefs. From 600 A.D. until the late seventeenth century, European settlements were not built on the grid, not until the Napoleonic era. Bastille Day, France's national holiday, celebrates the destruction of the Bastille, a fortress used by the empire to imprison political adversaries, and to control public access to one of the gates of Paris. It seems highly symbolic that a public 'Place de la Bastille' now occupies the location the Bastille once commanded.**"**

CITY REPAIR ENCOURAGES BLOCK PARTIES IN THE STREET.

The challenge of City Repair is to create common ground in our gridlocked cities, without leaving the city behind. To this end they have promoted the designation of common space in neighborhood intersections, initially through the creation of a mobile "T-horse," a huge, multi-winged public teahouse, mounted on a small truck, which they joyously drive to parks and intersections, offering homemade chai to everyone on the street, and creating a party wherever they go. They have worked with the city government, first through a pilot project in 1997, and later via Portland's city ordinance #17220, the "Intersection Repair Ordinance," which allows and funds each neighborhood to convert one intersection into a plaza. Mark recommends that people who want to create common space try it where they live or work, where they have support and know people. In this way an intricate culture can grow up imbedded in the space. City Repair discourages imposing common space on strangers' neighborhoods.

On a trip around Portland, midday, midweek, we visited a few intersections that had been "repaired" via the addition of tea kiosks, community bulletin boards, benches, and gardens. They were pretty and pleasant, but unpeopled. At present Portland's neighborhoods have too few people to fill them everyday. On weekends and in summers they are busier. Even empty, the decorations and plants add a sense of neighborhood pride.

TEAR DOWN THE FENCE

If you look around, you may discover places nearby that could expand your common space. One place is your neighbors'.

Frieda Foreman has lived in her Toronto semi (Canadian duplex) for about thirty years.

"I've immersed myself in foreign cultures that have common space, and what I was told by the people I met is that if you have to ask an authority permission to have common space, it isn't common space. Real common space doesn't come with a list of written rules. Time has made the rules. For example, in Italian towns everyone knows when they can drive into the piazza, and when they can't. They don't need a sign. People live the rules, having grown up with the rules. Their common understanding creates the space." —Mark Lakeman

She shares a wall with her neighbors Rusty Shteir and Griff Cunningham, and a driveway with her neighbor Jane Jacobs. There has always been open passage between the three backyards, but fifteen years ago Rusty suggested they take down the fence and replace it with a pergola that spans the two property lines, with a pebble floor and a grape arbor above. "They could have asked me fourteen years sooner," says Frieda. "It takes absolutely nothing from me and adds something beautiful. I worried because Griff spends so much time gardening, and I do so little, but Rusty said, 'This just expands his palette,' so now I just feel lucky." Twelve years later, on the other side, Jane's fence had been disintegrating, so she decided just to take it down. Frieda's son Gideon reports: "Now the grandchildren have several distinct places to explore: Griff's greenhouse and garden, my mother's raspberry bushes, and Jane's 'Enchanted Garden'"—a patch of what formerly was called weeds, but thanks to the wildflower seeds Griff tossed around can now be called wilderness.[5]

A PERGOLA REPLACED THE FENCE BETWEEN THEIR BACKYARDS.

Another way small-housers expand their home universe is to build strong friendships, and share house keys. That way they have a place to rest, in another part of town, and they might get to see each other, without scheduling an event. Or they leave their doors open, and let people know they can drop in. As Raheli Gai explains, "I love it when friends drop in. It's like where I grew up; no one calls first."

THE BUSY-NESS OF MULTI-USE COMMONS

Why are many of our common spaces often empty? In some towns, the common space is too spread out, and we just don't have enough people to fill it up. We're busy, and we like to stay in our comfortable homes. Also, many public spaces are essentially unipurpose: they allow a few forms of recreation, but little else. Public spaces that border commercial enterprises, allow free enterprise, or are shared by schools or other programs like Dufferin Grove Park, or the community gardens in Detroit (see profile), are more likely to be busy. Arcosanti, an icon of high-density life with plenty of common space, embodies the

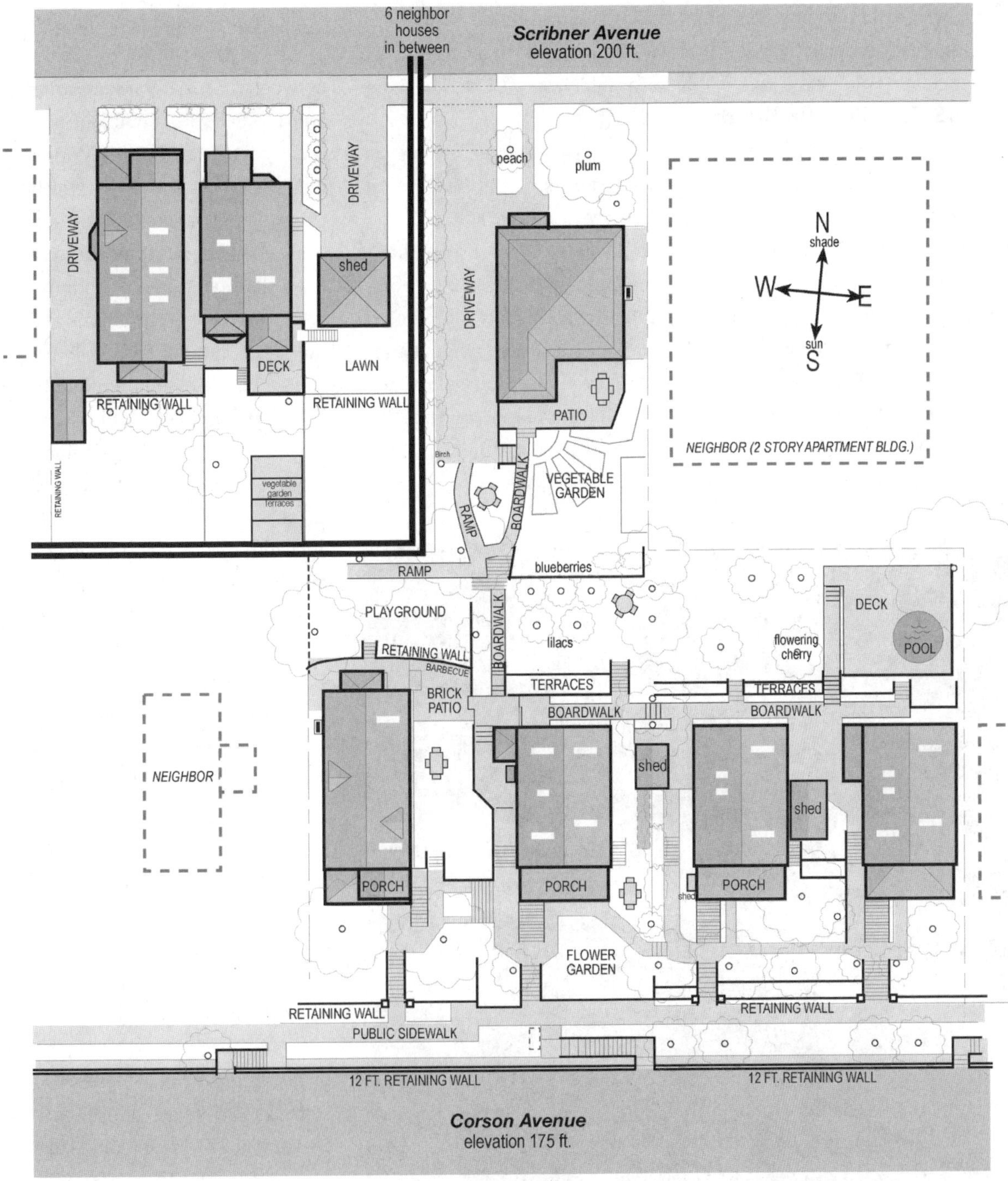

GANAS COMMUNITY IN STATEN ISLAND: GANAS, A COMMUNITY WITH ABOUT 90 RESIDENTS IN STATEN ISLAND, NEW YORK, HAS ACQUIRED A NUMBER OF HOUSES, SOME OF WHICH SHARED AN ALLEY. THEY TOOK DOWN THE FENCES BETWEEN THE HOUSES AND CREATED AN OPEN AREA.

principle of layered, multi-use common space (see right).

Busy common space also allows us the pleasure of being with others, without talking.

CLUSTERS AND COHOUSING

If you're building or buying new, you have the opportunity to consider housing settlements that share common land or facilities. About half of the new houses built in the 1990s were built in "communities" that have "neighborhood associations." This means, depending on your perspective, that you'll be subject to a list of extra rules, administered by a small group of very busy bodies; or you'll have the opportunity to participate in a democratic process, and can make friends with your neighbors through the shared use of a clubhouse, pool, or other common space.[6]

Close to a million of our newer settlements are walled, sometimes with a guard stationed at a single gate. So far, no one has a real moat with alligators.[7] Some gated residents feel more neighborly, because they no longer are worried about their safety, and they let their children run free, inside the walls. Other residents worry that escape during a fire or other disaster might be difficult, and some people outside the gates complain that walls ruin the civic sense of the greater community.[8] To increase the connection between the greater community and a walled settlement, one citizen's group in southern California built a tall viewing platform, which they placed so that passersby could climb the steps and see over the wall into the gated community.[9] Most new developments are not gated, but when they share exclusive use of common facilities, they may seem to drain the greater community of its common sense. A miniscule percentage of these developments share their common space with the larger public. Cohousing communities sometimes do.

GRACIELLA AND ANGUS LIVE ABOVE THE FOUNDRY.

Built new, or retrofitted from existing apartments or houses, cohousing is consciously planned by the residents to maximize interaction in common spaces. Typically, a number of functions—the mailboxes, common house, swimming pool, bicycle shed, laundry, bulletin board—are placed near each other, and sometimes a single path leads to them, to maximize the chances that residents will bump into each other during the day. In some developments, the setbacks that create odd, difficult-to-use space between houses are eliminated, by sharing exterior walls, so that livable outdoor space is maximized. In rural and suburban areas cohousing may have rings of common space: play space near the houses, and kitchen gardens; land for agriculture; and forest, pasture, or wildlands.

Currently populated primarily by about one hundred students, artists, and builders, Arcosanti is an educational experiment in centralized planning. The built environment, which is restricted to twenty-five acres and planned for a village of 5,000, descends down the south side of a hill toward a creek and about 4,000 acres that are reserved for agriculture and wildlife. Typical planning rules don't exist here: cars are left outside the village; no place is numbered, but instead known by a name; and pathways between locations are irregular and often vertical, providing a stair-step exercise program for the whole community.

The intricate layering of complex, miniaturized functions is inherent in evolution, according to Arcosanti's master planner, Paolo Soleri. Just as a brain would function poorly if all its synapses were spread out to their maximum width (a twenty-square-mile patch, in Mr. Soleri's estimation), society functions poorly when it sprawls.

Arcosanti doesn't sprawl but climbs, with miniature living spaces and large common areas. Although Arcosanti is under construction, and therefore underpopulated, the common spaces are well used, because the inhabitants enjoy company, many apartments are tiny (some of them 8-foot cubes), and common meals are prepared three times a day. Working, sleeping, playing, eating: all spaces are interwoven. Angus Gluck and Graciella Pazzanese, for example, live in an apartment with convex walls that lean out and look down over a small foundry. "You'd think it would be noisy, but they are very quiet, lighting their propane in the morning, waking us up gently. We have to wake up for work anyway," says Graciella. Angus, who works in construction, sees just one drawback to the close proximity of all the spaces: "Our culture needs to develop a respect for the trades, and the discipline they require, so that people can see others working and not distract them by chatting."

The cohousing common house serves prior to construction as a source of much discussion, as future residents plan it. Minimally, it provides residents a place to share meals. Sometimes it expands to include space for childcare, offices, meetings, guests, storage, movie-watching, weight lifting, ping-pong, craftwork, or anything that the community would like to do together.

A few housing developers are beginning to mimic some design aspects of cohousing, including adding a central common house to clustered developments. "Cottage housing–" new houses built smaller and of higher density than the houses near them—in particular lends itself to shared common space. For more details about the Cottage Housing ordinances which allow these developments, please read on to the next chapter.

COBB HILL COHOUSING
Common house built 2001

AREA:
3,000 sq ft

INTENDED NUMBER OF OCCUPANTS:
3 full-time, 5-50 part-time

Cobb Hill Cohousing, in Hartland, Vermont, is home to fifty-three people

who live in six duplexes (twelve units), seven detached homes, and three apartments, which range in size from 400 to 1,600 square feet, giving them a little over 450 square feet per person. They also share a common house designed by architect Jeff Schoellkopf, with the collaboration of the residents. At 3,000 square feet, the common house is smaller than many McMansions, yet seats them all comfortably the few times a year that everyone comes to dinner.

The most popular entrance to the common house is through the mudroom, the community's "nerve center," which holds mailboxes, a bulletin board with announcements, a sign-up sheet and a calendar, and eggs for sale. It is adjacent to a small den, which can hold meetings of about fifteen people, and offers the only open fireplace in the community; and to the dining room, which typically seats twenty-five. The south wall of the dining room is mostly glass, so the space is flooded with sunshine in winter. The room can be noisy, but carpeting is not ideal in a dining room, so the residents hope to quiet the space by hanging fabric panels from the ceiling. The kitchen, at one end of the dining room, has two stoves, and two refrigerators, and 40 feet of counter space, allowing a few cooks to work side by side. A shout away from the kitchen is a playroom that also opens to the outside.

Past a public washroom and down a short hall, two small apartments and a guest room share the main floor and use its kitchen. This plan was originally designed with the first founder, the late Donella Meadows, in mind. She was paring down her life and didn't see a need for her own kitchen. The ambiguous line between private and public kitchen space in the common house has been confusing for other apartment dwellers: it turns out that some people don't like to have a tour march through while they are eating breakfast in their pajamas. This issue has been clarified by scheduling and better communication.

Upstairs, in the attic, are a third apartment and a second guest room, and a 20-by-40-foot community room, which serves as a movie theater, dance and meeting hall, and a place for the older children to socialize. The 45-degree, cathedral ceiling under the steep, 12:12-pitch roof is "perfect, acoustically," magically allowing everyone to hear each other's viewpoints during discussions. Shelves for a library have been installed on the east wall, near the popular south dormer, which is a large sunny alcove. The residents insisted that the two dormers be large enough to stand in, even though it meant they were pushed up to the roofline—aesthetically less pleasing to the architect—so now when the Sustainability

Institute hosts seminars in the house, fellows can break out into small groups and confer comfortably inside the 70-square-foot dormers.

The mostly unfinished basement has enough space for woodworking; a ping-pong and a pool table; storage for a puppet theater and the beekeepers' honey; two root cellars; and production space for a cheese company.

While they were planning the development, the residents worried that the common house would be underused. If anything, the opposite has happened, and the only tragedy of this common space is that it wasn't built quickly enough: Ann Armbrecht who lived at Cobb Hill in its first year theorizes that the reason a few families switched suddenly from the 1,400- to the 1,600-square-foot model is that they didn't realize how much the common house would expand their sense of space. "It's difficult to get bank financing for something that no single individual owns, so it took us some time to put it up. Ideally, cohousing communities would put the common house up first."

Cobb Hill residents share more than the common house. Perhaps the most essential common space they share is the giant "garn," a forced-fan, Minnesota-built, super-efficient woodburning stove that heats every Cobb Hill residence, via a piped water radiator system. This district heating system, which burns 2.25 cords per residence each winter, means that the residences spend no space on a furnace; that they built supertight houses without fear of being poisoned by the fumes from a woodstove; that they had one more reason to build the houses close together; and that every hour from 5 a.m. to midnight an adult resident must visit the furnace and stoke it with wood. "Some of the people who live here who aren't used to working with their hands were excited to learn precisely where their heat was coming from," says resident Phil Rice. "And there's a feedback loop: if someone misses a shift, the propane backup kicks in, at an extra cost to everyone."

Prior to 1996 Cobb Hill was farmland, and the cohousers intend to keep it that way. They built their cluster of houses on the side of a hill and preserved the good flatland for fields. One house is reserved for a farming couple that runs a community-supported-agriculture market garden with a dairy, laying hens and meat chickens, and a sheep flock on the community's common land. In a 15-acre portion of the 210 acres reserved for forest, bright plastic tubes run between the trees, collecting sap for maple syrup each spring. There's plenty of room for family vegetable gardens. Phil explains, "Although legally we are each on a zero lot line, like a condominium, the Land Use Committee decided that if there's a natural barrier, like a rise in the hill near your house, you can use it to mark your garden space. When we first moved here there was a sense of scarcity as people claimed garden space, and people argued a little over it, but later we all realized there was plenty for everybody."[11]

EXERCISE: IMAGINING THE COMMONS

1. Notice during your day whenever you enter or pass by a location where you don't need to pay nor work to be there.
2. Notice places that aren't common space but could be. Imagine what you would do to change them.

DUFFERIN GROVE PARK
Park founded: 1890s

AREA:
14 acres

INTENDED NUMBER OF OCCUPANTS:
25-600

Garrison Creek runs through Toronto, but mostly underground now.

Nineteenth-century immigrant settlers used the creek, then above ground, to discharge sewage, and by the turn of the century it had become so polluted, it was covered and converted into an underground sewer. For sixty years it was mostly ignored, subtly suggested by dips in the road, better-watered trees, and foundations that crumbled under houses built in its path. Then, in the 1980s, as Toronto sewage outgrew the sewer's capacity, and a new sewer was built, a variety of citizen and government groups began rethinking how best to occupy the creek bed. At present a plan exists to create more parks along the path, and perhaps daylight the creek in some areas.

The creek meanders below Dufferin Grove Park, a fourteen-acre city park established in the late nineteenth century on land that has been public since before European settlers arrived in the area. The park is surrounded on three sides by a neighborhood that is composed mostly of two- and three-story "semis" (known in the U.S. as "duplexes") and a few small apartment buildings. One block north of the park is a subway stop and an avenue with stores and offices.

"The sandpit cost the FDGP $3,000, and was completely worth it. When kids are building in the sandpit, the way they treat their creation, it may as well be grains of gold they are building with! Every once in a while a parent says, 'This sandpit is a liability issue.' We invite them to take their child to a safer place. In fact, the biggest injury we ever had was in the sandpit, when a teacher brought her class of twenty-five, and told them they couldn't run around the park, that they had to stay in the pit. Of course the kids felt the lack of freedom, and rebelled. I read a study from England that showed that highly supervised playgrounds have more injuries than unsupervised ones. Kids who are always waiting to be told what to do don't know how to play safe." —Jutta Mason

Dufferin Grove neighbors have modest homes and small yards that can't be expanded to create entertainment centers or private volleyball courts. Instead, many of them have extended their homes by turning their local park into their "huge backyard." Although Toronto's weather is hardly tropical, it is, smiles one neighbor, "arguably the warmest city in eastern Canada," and many residents hurry outside whenever the weather is clear.

In the 1980s the park was neglected and had become a "bland open space," where, as one park visitor described it, "You see some people looking cowardly, and other people looking menacing, and the washrooms aren't functioning so the homeless have to shit in the bushes." The Dufferin Grove neighbors wanted something different. In particular, one neighbor, Jutta Mason, had the time and energy to become a spokeswoman for the "Friends of Dufferin Grove Park" (FDGP), a small, unincorporated group that "usually doesn't have meetings because we see each other in the park and communicate that way." In 1992 Jutta began to organize activities and connect people with resources. Jutta explains, "It's pretty easy to be a great park: just have a washroom that isn't filthy, and a drinking fountain that works."

But the park offers quite a bit more than that. Our tour began at the huge ice-skating rink, large enough to host two hockey games at once. Artificially cooled by compressors and pipes under the ice, it opens December through March, seven days a week for skating and shinny hockey and hosts special events such as ice basketball, and the locally famous day-long "Bikes on Ice" tournament, a display of bicycle courier talent. In summer part of the rink becomes a basketball court, and the rest is used for the local farmers' market. The rink house contains arts, crafts, and breadmaking supplies, an office, equipment storage, and in winter, a café, which serves dinner to about forty people each Friday night.

Next to the rink house a large vegetable and herb garden produces pizza toppings and soup ingredients, including tomatoes, tomatillos, oregano, basil, kale, and corn. We pass a basketball court packed with players and continue around the wading pool, which, more like a deep plate than a bowl, is a wide circle of concrete that gently slopes from its dry perimeter towards its 16-inch-deep center, so there are no steps to worry about. The pool has recently been drained (it's early autumn) and the activity has shifted to a 20-by-40-foot sandpit, surrounded by a few logs—Jutta calls them "Flintstone furniture"—where parents sit.

A loyal group of dog lovers built a fence around the playground after neighbors pointed out that some doggy activities don't mix well with small children's health and safety. There is no special dog area, but the occasional friendly, unleashed dog is normally welcome. Outside the fence two women picnicking with their children looked up nervously as a light mist began to fall. Jutta called out to the women, suggesting they wait out the mist in a nearby rain shelter. Walking on, she muttered, "People are such wimps about weather. What drives them outside is their kids."

At one edge of the park, past the volleyball net, is a small old brick building, the original park clubhouse which Jutta says served in the early 1990s mainly as a meeting place for the "Stupid Marijuana Club." When she heard the puppet theater "Clay and Paper" was looking for a space, Jutta told them she knew of an orphaned clubhouse. Jutta explains, "We had some kids using that building who thought they were in a movie about the Los Angeles Kryps and Bloods—they even dressed the part—so we changed the scenery, and now the club has changed." Across the park from the clubhouse the puppet theater was setting up their giant puppets on a small hill for this evening's performance, their third in a six-week run.

In the distance several Filipino and Latino families are picnicking, some with hibachi stoves set up. Watching them, Jutta notes, "Immigrants still understand parks. Most Canadian-born families are too busy making money to spend a whole day here. Even the Italians aren't coming as much." The stoves and other fires are encouraged by the FDGP. Jutta reasons, "If you want a park to be safe, it has to be popular. To be popular it can't be banal. It has to be beautiful and surprising. There has to be a reason to go. That's why we have a year-round fire permit here."[10]

Eighty-year-old Muriel Simutis is celebrating her birthday with forty friends. Her daughter, Judy, is the FDGP's garbage queen. Each weekend Judy walks the park for an hour, picking up trash. It's inconvenient during winter to properly clean up after dogs, so Judy's also organized special spring cleanups for dog owners that end with a party, a "feast for both man and beast." In the 1980s leaks and breaks could be overlooked for weeks, but now they are noticed quickly, since eyes are on every square foot of the park. In the distance we saw a city worker repairing a leaky irrigation line. Jutta comments:

"It's been a battle at times to do some simple things here. It's a common story— the history of public space is a history of mismanagement. From 1981 to 1993 the city parks' budget tripled, yet not a single new park was built. They forgot they were the parks department, and built offices instead.

"There ought to be a simple way to staff a park, but nothing is simple. When we had staff, the job was so narrowly defined and with so little power the employee couldn't do anything. We're better off without full-time staff. The only way to get anything changed here is by a nonemployee, who is not beholden to the bureaucracy. The position I have doesn't exist. Since I have no public liability, I can actually get things done. Some city administrators are glad I'm here because they want to see things happen, but they would lose their job if they did anything interesting. This way they can blame it on me, and everyone can enjoy it.

"We once had a change at the upper level of park management. The new people decided to give me the silent treatment, so I said, 'I give up. I can't work like this.' The neighbors organized a meeting with the commissioner, a pizza party, and invited the top staff. They told these people, 'You need to understand that Jutta is just a messenger. It isn't her. She speaks for us.' So now the city has given up trying to change us. They say, 'We can't do anything about the way that park is—the people want it that way.'

"There are so many people now who consider this park their own. We have a 1980s play set, solid steel. We made it clear to the city that they dare not take it away and replace it with those bright plastic things they are selling everyone. It's fun when people are willing to mobilize to stop something just because they think it's a dumb idea. If the city came with a silly, expensive plan, the neighbors would stand in front of the bulldozers."

Some of the guests at Muriel's party are preparing to bake pizzas in the park's fifty-loaf, 4-by-6-foot brick oven, which has a low, domed concrete ceiling, and was designed by mason Allen Scott. Visitors pay two dollars for a ball of dough, tomato sauce, and herbs and vegetables from the garden. They bake their own pizza in the oven themselves. The wood fire in the oven burns so hot that only a small coat of ash is left, and after the firing, the oven can bake up to six hours without additional fuel. On Fridays, the FDGP hosts a more elaborate meal, but always with fresh bread. Recently, four other parks and the local community food bank have built their own bread ovens.

Back in the rink house a group of teenage summer hires sing as they mix bread dough. They are missing part of the melody, so Jutta marches in and sings along, then encourages them to get the loaves in the oven soon. "We rely on high school students, but sometimes it's hard for them to work because at this age they must talk to each other incessantly."

When the bread is done, Dan Dematteis, the puppet theater's cook, will roast spicy marinated chicken, wrapped in banana leaves, with potatoes, peppers, and garlic. By selling dinner the puppet theater can sometimes turn a profit on their production, and even if they don't, the cast will enjoy the leftovers. He admits, "Our food activities are in the shadow of legality. A public health worker told us that there's an old exemption for church suppers. A politician in one province tried to change that rule and almost lost his seat over it, so we feel pretty safe having 'church suppers.' "Judy Simutis says that a few neighbors complain, saying there should be more organization, more committees, more meetings, "and less fun. They are sort of missing out. The Friday dinners are fantastic. Student artists and chefs try out their new, delicious creations. And when park volunteers like me try to pay the fee for dinner, they won't take my money. You can't buy community."

EPILOGUE:

Three-and a-half years after my visit. Everything has expanded: A second bread oven was built, as the bakers struggle to keep up with demand for fresh bread. The garden has grown to include fruit trees. The park now has a staff of fourteen part-time workers, the FDGP an email list of 500 members, and park activities have become so popular the FDGP has been helping nearby parks to become more interesting, so they can attract some of the crowd.

In winter, hungry skaters dine seven days a week at the Zamboni Café, inside the rink house. In summer, eating and preparing food has become so popular near the playground that the health department asked the park to add sinks and counters. Builder Georgie Donais appeared in 2005 and posted her drawn plans to build a cob courtyard that would incorporate the health department requests. "This is how all our projects have started—an individual has an idea that they want to implement, and we encourage them," says Jutta. That summer, after two months of discussion of the plan, 400 volunteers built the 50-foot curved wall that forms the courtyard, plus mosaic sink countertops, four sinks, cabinets, a fireplace and a diaper-changing station.

What would you do if most of the supermarkets in

your city closed shop and left town? What if the ones left specialized in alcohol, snacks, and two-week-old iceberg? What if, due to factory closures, house arson, and abandonment, an increasing amount of rich, rain-fed land was cropping up all around you? If you are like 10,000 of inner-city Detroit's hardiest residents, you might try homegrown.

Detroit began deindustrializing in 1956, when the ninety-five buildings of the mile-long, four-story, Packard Automobile Plant closed, initiating a pattern of downsizing and relocation that other industrial North

ABOVE: AS VACANT BUILDINGS FALL TO DISREPAIR AND ARSON, THEY ARE REMOVED AND DETROITERS HAVE MORE GARDEN SPACE.

ANIMALS—INCLUDING CANADA GEESE—THAT FLED DETROIT AT THE HEIGHT OF ITS INDUSTRIAL PERIOD, HAVE STARTED TO RETURN.

American cities would later follow. The Packard Plant was the largest of about 200 Detroit factories that closed between 1949 and 1980. Each closure emptied not just the factories themselves, but also the structures of community that had supported the factory workers. Thousands of houses now stand empty. With almost 10,000 acres of open green space, pheasants, raccoons, and foxes run wild through a landscape of broken bricks and lush pasture, surrounded by skyscrapers in the distance. There's room for anyone who wants to garden.

Juanita Newton can show you how. She should know. A Detroit resident for sixty-six years, she was born in Lagrange, Georgia, and has harvested over 300 gardens in her life. Her family—first when they were enslaved, later when they owned their own farms, and even when they became blacksmiths and masons and began moving north in the 1920s—has always maintained a garden. "There's been no break in the generations. We have gardening in our blood," Juanita explains.

Like thousands of Detroiters, Juanita's garden has expanded into her neighbor's lot. She enjoyed her neighbors' company for ten years, watched them move away in the 1970s, and then watched their house deteriorate from lack of maintenance and tenant carelessness. Eventually the city condemned and demolished the building, and she purchased the lot in 1990.

Beets, broccoli, Brussels sprouts, carrots, cantaloupe, cauliflower, collard greens, corn, hot and bell peppers, mint, okra, onions, parsnips, pumpkins, radishes, salad greens, spinach, squash, tomatoes, turnips, white potatoes, zucchini—most vegetables that you can find in a store and many things you can't, grow in Juanita's garden. All her produce is organic, and some have won ribbons in the Michigan State Fair, including the prize for largest sunflower head.

Juanita's efforts extend beyond her own plot. To extend the growing season for herself and her neighbors, she started a grow lab for seedlings in the basement of the local, historic, Duffield Public Library. Then, when Juanita retired from her position as director of social work at a local hospital, she expanded her gardening efforts throughout her city. On a trip around town she points out a twenty-two-story apartment building for senior citizens. "I had the students plant 400 tomato and hot and bell pepper plants in Styrofoam cups, and distribute them for people's balconies." The program was such a success that the next year they added cabbage, marigolds, sunflowers, lima beans, and Italian sweet peppers. "With no stores in the area, they appreciate them. That's the power of children!" she exclaims.

Our next stop is at the home of Jennifer Michelle Lee, a twenty-year-old college student whom Juanita has mentored for six years. Inner-city Detroit now has some of the most active 4-H clubs in the state, and in 1999 Jennifer became the first African-American 4-H queen in Wayne County. Juanita's insists that children make the best gardening students, "The younger the better. At three, children are still undistracted. They focus so hard on the seed, they make it grow," she smiles. At times local gardens have suffered because parents and children are afraid to go out. Sometimes people are afraid of waves of violence, or a disease—most recently, people fear the West Nile virus. But staying inside just increases the fear and rage, so that's exactly when Juanita makes sure to go outside, with her great-grandchildren, and keep gardening. "These children began by loving the flowers. Pretty soon they start walking through, breaking off a piece of cauliflower, or pulling up a carrot to eat it."

Juanita also helped initiate a horticulture program at the Winsett School for developmentally disabled youth. It's become a kind of vocational prep program, where students learn watering and seed propagation, and research methods. One student, who after years of schooling was assumed incapable of speech, uttered her first words to her teacher, in the garden: "Look Mrs. Massengill, it's a radish!"

After lunch at Aknartoons, a restaurant with very urban customers and very country cooking (Cornish hens, gravy, collard greens, yams, sweet potato pie), we made our last stop at the home of Charles Simmons, a professor of journalism at Eastern Michigan University who also credits Juanita with getting him out into the garden.

"Today many of us live for our personal achievement, usually defined as monetary success but Juanita personifies the old ethic of 'Lift as you climb,' meaning the success of one must signal success for the whole group. I wouldn't have gotten involved if I hadn't hooked up with Juanita. The young people think 'mass media,' but our people, you have to go to their door and talk with them if you want their involvement. That's how Juanita does it."

Dr. Simmons worked as a journalist overseas and around the country before returning home to care for his ailing aunt. Across the street from their house lay the ruins of a factory building that had once served as a dry-cleaning facility. At night trucks from the suburbs, with their license plates covered in tape, dumped waste in the lot. "The kids were playing in it. The rats were getting big," he remembers. Soon he joined a fight to get the lot cleaned up.

Establishing ownership of the mess was difficult. The city insisted it did not own it. The local judge explained that the fee for legally disposing of toxic waste is so high, it's cheaper for companies to pay the occasional fine. After three years of complaints, demonstrations, and with the support of the local Sierra Club, the city finally cleared and cleaned the lot. Now it's a community garden.

Charles and Juanita are members of the Detroit Agricultural Network, a voluntary association of a few hundred people who share seeds, educate new gardeners, and lobby the city to maintain gardening services, such as free tilling for elderly people. Their gardens grow in backyard plots, libraries, churches and soup kitchens, and on ten acres of city lots farmed by schoolteacher Paul Weertz.

Paul teaches teenage mothers at the Catherine Ferguson Academy. Originally a biology teacher, he expanded into gardening, then acquired chickens, bees, and finally goats, which graze on empty lots. Last year his students harvested 3,000 bales of hay from local lots, which they store in a barn they built themselves. They feed and milk the goats daily, and they've begun processing cheese. Paul estimates there are 40,000 empty lots in Detroit, and the city spends about $75 per lot mowing the grass, so the city is glad to have him harvest as much as he wants. "We baled $9,000 worth of hay, and saved the city thousands of dollars. Why wouldn't they be happy?" he asks.

Farming is not a new phenomenon in Detroit, Paul reports. The old garages were once barns and chicken coops. "My uncle raised rabbits in the city, and sold the pelts. Our generation is kind of lost, but just a generation ago people knew how to farm, and harvest and preserve their own produce."

THERE ARE WELL OVER A HUNDRED COMMUNITY GARDENS IN DETROIT.

who were proud of their work and optimistic about the future, young people from the suburbs and around the country are buying up vacant houses and renovating them. Some of them simply like old houses, but others are part of a wider movement that hopes to watch a self-reliant village grow, built not by the force of a centralized vision, but through interconnected, parallel projects.

Students at the University of Detroit–Mercy, initially studying with architect Kyong Park and now with professor Will Wittig, have mapped one ambitious vision that includes a multitude of small businesses, three major farms, a community sawmill, tulip farm, ethanol refinery, cattle grazing on the common green, pedestrian-only pathways, the renovation of the old Packard plant into a three-dimensional city, and daylighting the river that has been rerouted underground since the early twentieth century.

One of the biggest concerns of DAN members is that most community garden land is leased year-to-year from the city. As the city promotes redevelopment of its interior, it may donate or sell large tracts of land to builders, without regard for the human and microbial effort that has built up the topsoil on a particular vacant lot. Similarly, people who have maintained their homes over the years sometimes receive a notice from the city explaining that their house lies in the path of a new development. "People say, 'I stuck on through the Depression, and the plant closures, and the riots, and now they are making me leave?' It's mostly elderly people," says Paul Weertz.

A new wave of urban homesteaders takes a different approach to the city's redevelopment. Appreciative of the sturdy brick houses, finely crafted seventy to a hundred years ago by new Detroiters

Meanwhile, hundreds of other Detroiters who are working out their own home-based details of a more sustainable Detroit feel connected to a greater plan, which they have called "Adamah," a biblical name for "Earth."

Some of them invite us to join them. "Detroit needs all of the smart, hardworking, altruistic people it can get," says John King, who relocated from Boston "because it's exciting to be in a place that is truly post-industrial, to start rebuilding from the ground up." Jim Embry, coordinator of the Detroit Summer program, which brings youth from all over the country to plant community gardens and paint murals, echoes him. "Every American should come to Detroit, and treat it like a pilgrimage. This is where the first Ford rolled off the line. This is Motown, the first motorized city. Detroit is where it all began."[12]

PARKLAND AS A PERCENT OF CITY AREA, 2002

A lecturer reported that Northeastern cities in the U.S. have more parkland than Western cities. I couldn't confirm the statement with the speaker, but a little research shows that while there are some exceptions, it is easy to find cities west of New York and Washington D.C. that have a much smaller fraction of their land dedicated to parks:

CITY	LAND AREA (ACRES)	PARK AND PRESERVE LAND AS PERCENT OF CITY LAND AREA
Washington D.C.	39,297	19.3%
New York City	194,115	18.9%
San Diego	207,575	18.3%
Boston	30,992	17.6%
San Francisco	29,884	17.2%
El Paso	159,405	16.5%
Philadelphia	86,456	12.3%
Seattle	53,677	11.2%
Oakland	35,875	10.7%
Los Angeles	300,201	10.0%
Milwaukee County	154,880	9.8%
Las Vegas	72,514	7.5%
Kansas City, MO	200,664	6.9%
Denver	98,142	6.6%
Tulsa	116,891	6.0%
Louisville County	246,400	5.8%
Houston	370,818	5.7%
Indianapolis	231,342	5.4%
Honolulu	384,000	4.0%
Atlanta	84,316	3.7%
San Jose	111,910	3.2%
Tucson	124,588	2.5%
Fresno	66,791	2.0%

SOURCE: THE TRUST FOR PUBLIC LANDS

Park planners sometimes look instead at amount of park acre per resident, which matters when people want to swim laps in a pool or play tennis on a court. But to a kid who wants to find others to play with, a dog who likes to sniff other dogs, or a jogger who feels safer in a busy park, high park acreage per resident is less important than having busy parks within walking distance of houses and businesses. When the percentage of parkland is low, it's unlikely that people are walking to parks. Western cities have more of their parkland paved over for parking lots.[13]

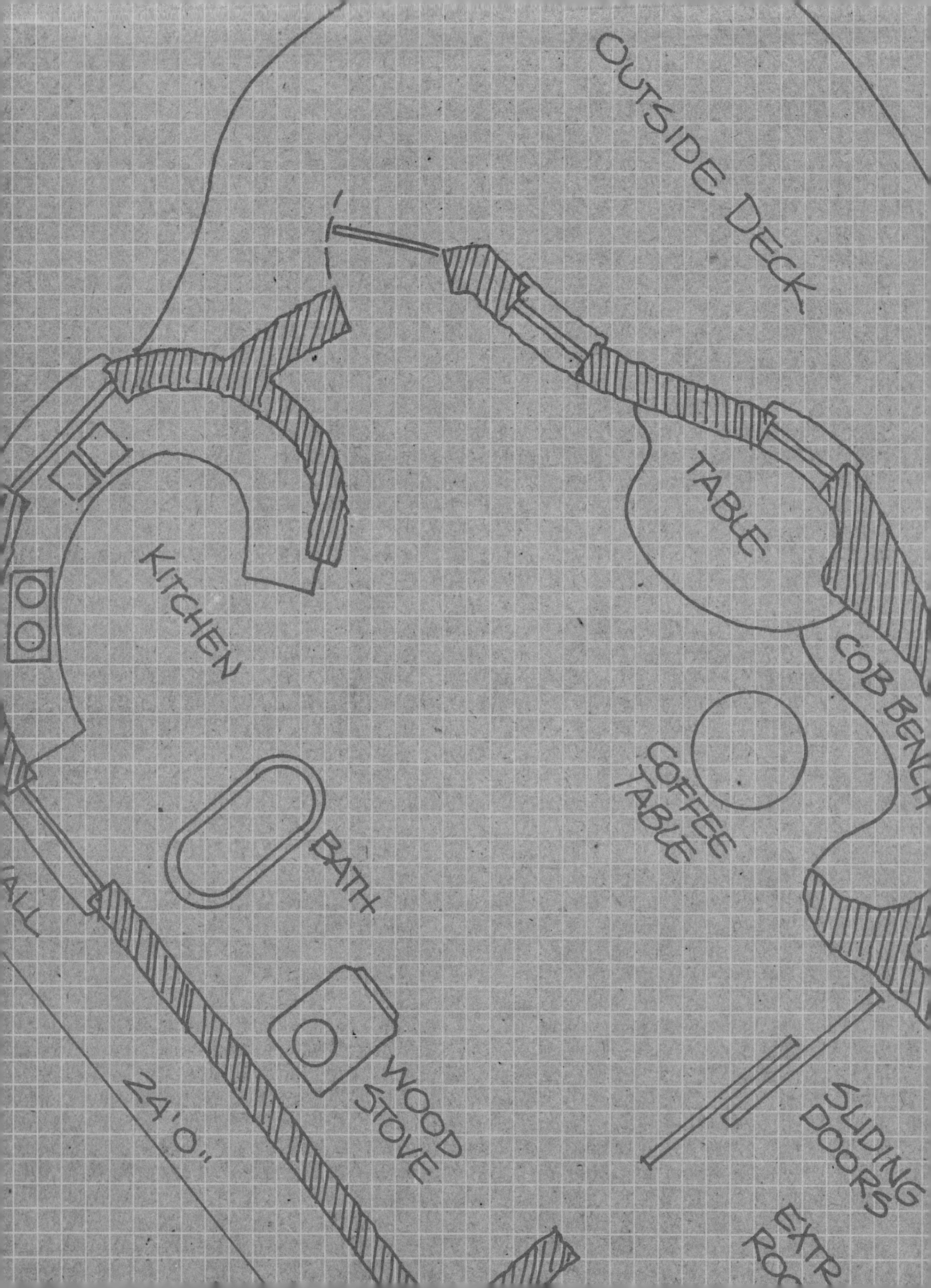
OUTSIDE DECK
TABLE
KITCHEN
COB BENCH
COFFEE TABLE
BATH
WOOD STOVE
24'0"
SLIDING DOORS

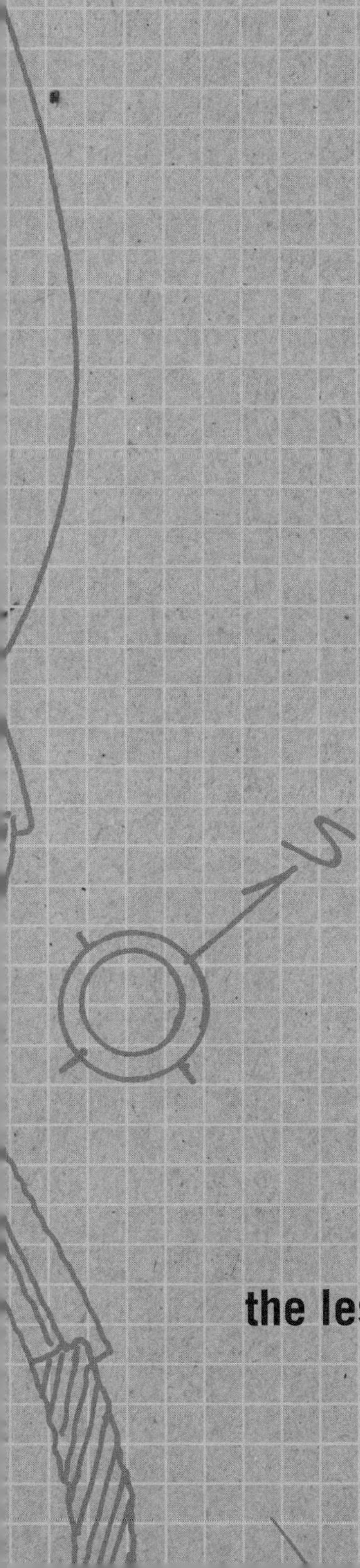

PART THREE

re•lax

the less tangible outer and inner forces that shape our experience of the domestic environment

CECILE AND PAUL DIVIDED THEIR
HOME INTO THREE APARTMENTS.

10
Know the Codes

"Well, I shan't go at any rate," said Alice; "besides, that's not a regular rule: you invented it just now." "It's the oldest rule in the book," said the King.

—***ALICE IN WONDERLAND***

EVERYONE BLAMES THE BUILDING CODE FOR SOMETHING. Developers hate the regulations that drive up their costs.[1] Environmentalists say the code requires us to use toxic, wasteful materials, and blocks the development of alternatives. Homeowners say it's illegible. Down at the permit review office you can sometimes find a contractor sweating while laborers wait idly back at the site, their work stopped by an inspector's ruling.

You can blame the building code for forcing you to use toxic, CO_2-producing materials (such as cement and steel) in greater quantities than you might think necessary; for wasting your money (for example, on a $1,000 nationally-approved composting toilet that you could have made from a plastic tub and a light bulb); for being beholden to commercial interests (certain companies seem to have a near-monopoly on certain code-approved hardware); for lacking a sense of location (the code book is sometimes accepted wholesale by local officials, with very limited regional variations); or for hegemonic tendencies (our building code is named the International Building Code, although it's currently read only in Canada and the U.S. and its authors are trying to encourage its adoption by developing countries throughout the world). But it's quite unfair to blame the building code for large houses.

Are Large Houses the Rule?

The building code has certain ceiling height requirements (most ceilings must be 7 feet 6 inches or higher), and staircases must be 36 inches wide; many local building codes require you to build an indoor bathroom. It's difficult to meet code with a primary house that is smaller than 350 square feet, but precious few people (see Jay's profile, this chapter) are trying to build detached houses smaller than that. In fact, building small is one of the simplest ways to reduce all costs, while still meeting code. Many cities and counties assess permit fees based in part on house size, and charge you a little less for building less.

FIREWALLS BETWEEN HOUSES THAT SHARE EXTERIOR WALLS ARE REQUIRED IN MANY AREAS.

The building code has a first cousin, though, sometimes enforced from the same office, and a necessary step in the permit process: planning and zoning ordinances. A sense of collective planning in human settlements seems to date to prehistory. Late empire Romans passed "sun-rights" laws that forbade one building from blocking the solar gain of another. In the United States in the 1920s, state governments gave themselves the power to legislate zoning. One major zoning goal at that time was to separate dwellings from the smokestacks of industry.

Current zoning ordinances have carried the general theme of "better life through separation" farther than initially intended. Most regions require placing new houses back from the property line ("setbacks"); prescribe a number of parking spaces; and require wide roads and driveways. Some make it difficult for "unrelated" people to share a house, and forbid home businesses and/or guesthouses. Because they spread us out, requiring more asphalt and sidewalks, and longer water, sewer, and telephone lines between us, zoning laws are credited with increasing housing costs and commuting time for all of us. What is a citizen to do?

LIVING BELOW THE RADAR

Leave town. There are still places where very little of the code is enforced, or there are few zoning ordinances, and some counties have a special code for owner-builders. Some people specifically seek out such places. If the full code or new zoning is ever adopted, usually existing structures will be "grandfathered" in. In any case, before you buy a house or land, check with the planning and permitting officials to make sure what you want to do will be permitted.

Be dumb. Some people successfully ignore ordinances. This only works in areas where neighbors are either out of sight, or are themselves opposed to regulations. Make friends with your neighbors, and find out what the penalty will be if you are discovered. If you seek bank financing, you will be required to meet all regulations, and if you sell your house to someone who uses bank financing you may be required to alter the house.

Your neighbors are the main determinant of how codes and ordinances will be enforced in your area. Unfortunately, even if sixty out of sixty-one neighbors are fine with your structure, one neighbor (as Jim and Mindy Phypers discovered) can make your life miserable.

Ignoring the rules works best for projects that have a low investment.

Inside the zone. If a building lot already has a main, permitted house, it is often possible to build one or more "storage" units. If they are kept under a minimum size (typically 100 to 200 square feet), these "outbuildings" don't require a permit. It is theoretically forbidden to sleep in an outbuilding, but thousands of North Americans will tonight.

Some municipalities do require (through zoning law, not building code) a minimum house size. One man got around such a requirement by showing plans for a "complete" structure, but only building part of his house. In other areas it is the reverse: buildings under 1,000 square feet may not require an architectural review or engineer's stamp, so some people build 900 square feet and later add an addition. There is always some risk involved when you choose a semilegal route.

I convinced a group of visiting Senegalese economists to give me a ride to a community near Emily Dickinson's hometown, in Massachusetts. We drove through the thick woods, down a long dirt road. Getting out of their car, the North Africans were shocked. "This is like our grandparents' homes," said one. "But smoother and nicer," said another. "I'd rather live in this than in the fine apartments of Dakar," said a third. They all agreed that it was one of the most beautiful homes in the world.

My friends Jan and Suzanne had built a work of art. Suzanne, a skilled carpenter, and Jan, one of the first cob builders in the U.S., used the earth below their feet and the trees in the woods to create a smooth, sculpted haven, a nest with two small lofts above, and a tiny office, kitchen, and sitting area below.

But Jan and Suzanne never lived there. A building inspector found out about their work and insisted on a myriad of structural tests that were prohibitively expensive. Then the local Board of Health said that without an indoor toilet and full septic tank (they had a composting toilet and the community shares a modern, luxurious bathhouse), they would never allow them in. The cost of complying with all these regulations would have been over four times the $6,000 Jan and Susanne spent to build the house. This they could not afford, so after over eighteen months of petitions, they gave up the fight and moved away. They sold the building. It is now used as a part-time office.

A few years later, the same building inspector became very supportive of cob and alternative building structures in his area. Jan now believes, "My mistake was not going to him from the start and asking for his help. I was too filled with rebellious idealism."

Jim and Mindy Phypers literally ignored zoning: they lived in a way-out-of-the-way, unincorporated area where half of their neighbors, like them, lived in single-wide mobile homes. They had no idea zoning did not permit these homes. Over the years, they carefully remodeled their home, adding insulation, building a large, semiattached greenhouse, installing photovoltaics and wind power, and decoratively stuccoing the façade. Their inexpensive, off-the-grid masterpiece won an award and became part of the National Solar Home tour. But then a real estate agent convinced a wealthy out-of-state investor that the subdivision was about to become "the next Vail," and sold him the property adjacent to theirs for above market price. When the man finally visited, after the sale, surprised at all the trailers, he called the county and discovered trailers were only allowed temporarily. He "cleaned up" the neighborhood by convincing officials to force Jim and Mindy to tear down their house, and build a new one.

BECOMING PART OF THE RADAR

Zoning variances. Getting a zoning variance usually involves consulting neighbors, holding a public meeting, and a city or town council or county commissioner hearing (or your local equivalent). For some special people, offering a bribe or political contribution works. Variances are not impossible to obtain, but if the neighbors don't support you, unless you have strong political influence you're probably out of luck.

JAN AND SUZANNE'S

“All seven of those projects [which were celebrated in a design book] required a variance. Now, a variance is supposed to be given in very unusual, hardship circumstances, particular to a specific location. In those seven instances, the variances were just because they are the right thing to do. It wasn't specific to the site. It's too bad that the most sustainable, intelligent thing to do often requires a variance.” —Charlie Deans

Landscape architect Charlie Deans (below) has been successful gaining zoning variances, some for projects that went on to win awards.

Unfortunately, just because you get a variance doesn't mean your neighbor will too. Instead, they will have to start the process themselves, from scratch. [3]

Rules inside rules. Individuals and corporations may write restrictions into the deed of a house before they sell it. The Nature Conservancy, for instance, buys up land, places “conservation easements” on the title, and then sells it to buyers willing to comply with Conservancy policy. Many developers create special “covenants, codes, and restrictions” for the subdivisions they market. CC&Rs are usually designed to keep house prices high and preserve certain characteristics of a neighborhood. CC & Rs are private laws, for private property.

For over a century, until they were challenged in the U.S. courts, CC&Rs in some subdivisions denied home ownership to Catholic, Jewish, Irish, Portuguese, African, Mexican, Puerto Rican, and/or Italian-American families. Current CC&Rs can prescribe such details as house color, pets, and lawn ornaments or ban any changes that can be seen from the street, including solar panels and vegetable gardens. Others regulate behavior, such as whether you can hang laundry outside, eat barbecued chicken on your front lawn, or kiss someone in your driveway. CC&Rs commonly enforce minimum house size and require garages.

Buyer beware: as long as they don't discriminate by race or religion, CC&Rs seem to be holding up in court. You can only change them by getting involved in the homeowners association, and then only if your neighbors agree.[2]

Changing rules. Some energetic citizens join together and change the rules. In the 1970s citizens in northern California lobbied to create a special code that would allow owner-builders more freedom to design their own house, as long as they weren't building it to sell. In the 1990s petitioners in many states convinced officials to add straw-bale to the list of acceptable building materials. Composting toilets, gray-water irrigation, tire foundations, and traditional adobe are a few of the many provisions local activists have convinced code officials to accept in local areas.[3]

Zoning is regulated by city and county ordinances, which are created by elected officials. It is therefore theoretically easier for citizens to change zoning laws. "Growth Management" legislation passed in various areas has provoked discussion as it mandates some changes in zoning ordinances.

"Form-based" zoning is one of the current visions for city planning. Promoted by the "New Urbanism," it prescribes physical and spatial characteristics for neighborhoods, emphasizing that form is at least as important as function and encourages developers and remodelers to match their buildings aesthetically with the rest of the neighborhood.

North American form-based zoning doesn't eliminate building code requirements, and so far typically it is laid over the old zoning rules. However, in some pilot programs, old land-use restrictions have been relaxed, so that owners have more control over how they use their buildings, but less control over how the outside shell of the building looks, how it is shaped and sized, and where it is placed on the lot, in relation to the street. "Form-based zoning opens the question, 'What exactly do we want to regulate with our rules?'" says Theresa Lucero of Denver's Planning Office, adding, "At least it may inspire debate."[4]

"Inclusionary Zoning" is another conversation sparker. IZ ordinances are developed by governments who notice that their own employees– teachers, secretaries, firefighters and so forth– can't afford to live in the town where they work. IZ mandates that new subdivisions include a minimum number of housing units that are affordable to people in the middle- and lower-income ranges, and provokes debate about private property rights, whether poor and rich people should live near or far from each other, and how the growing housing gap affects us.

"We will be building 2,000 square feet. Why? Because that's the minimum size the CC & Rs here require. Sometimes there isn't a choice—we couldn't find any other land in this area. In other ways, however, we are doing our best to be as environmentally sound as possible."

—California couple

A visiting French builder gave a presentation about his work. When asked how he convinced local officials to allow him to build with stone, straw, and earth, he was confused and replied that as long as the building didn't clash with the style of the local church in his small village, why should they care? Further pressed by questions, he said, "Well, if someone builds a house and it collapses on his head, that's his problem, but the rest of us don't want to have to look every day at someone's ugly façade."

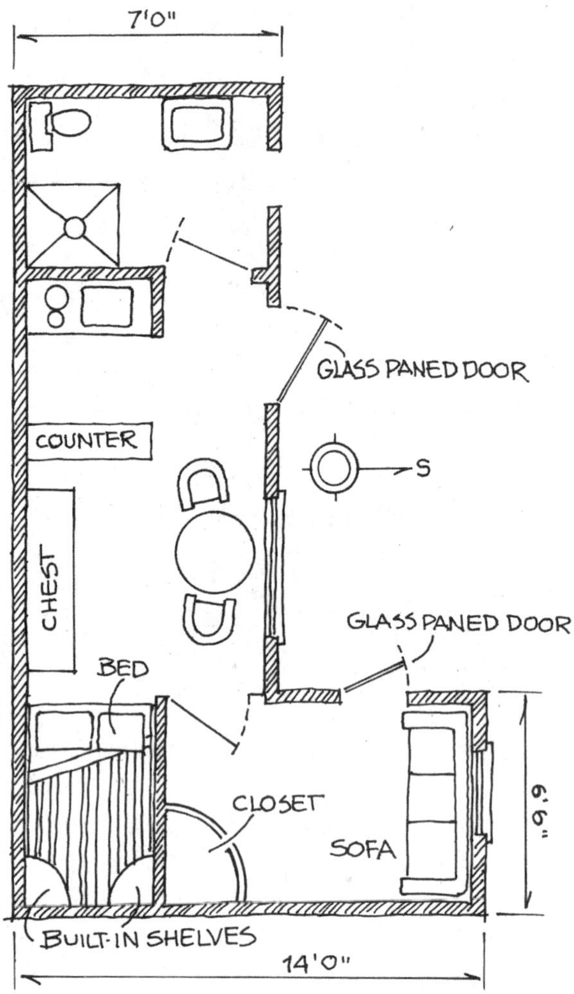

RUTH SHARONE DESIGNED AND BUILT AN ADU THAT WRAPS AROUND THE OUTER EDGE OF HER GARDEN, IN A NARROW L-SHAPE. IT IS CURRENTLY USED AS A GUESTHOUSE.

Encouraging Developments

THE MANDATE TO LEGALIZE GRANNY'S FLAT

In the past fifteen years, coalitions of transportation planners, environmentalists, architects, mass-transportation passengers, and home dwellers who would like to build structures in their yards or divide their house into two apartments, have come together in various parts of the country to legalize the construction and rental of "granny flats" (a.k.a. "coach houses," "mother-in-law apartments," "second units" (a.k.a. "accessory dwelling units," or "ADUs"): small dwellings, either detached or attached to the main house, and usually inhabited by extended family or friends.

ADUs are a clear solution to a chain of problems: small families or single adults in large houses too expensive for even two-income couples to maintain happily by themselves; lack of reasonably priced rentals in some neighborhoods; separation of generations and extended families; and the absence of sufficient urban density to operate cost-effective public transportation. If they are placed near the back of a lot, ADUs can also add what some call "eyes on the alley," which is thought to discourage crime. ADUs are such a good idea that tens of thousands of otherwise law-abiding citizens built them illegally in the 1980s and '90s.

In the last two decades many cities have worked to legalize and promote ADUs, both to expand their source of tax revenue and to facilitate enforcement of fire and health codes. California, Florida, and Washington, in an attempt to create more affordable rentals, while lowering greenhouse gas emissions by discouraging sprawl, have enacted state legislation allowing or requiring municipalities to make it easier for owners to build ADUs. Dozens of cities and counties from Virginia and Massachusetts to Ontario and Idaho have passed similar ordinances. The American Association of Retired Persons (AARP) promotes ADUs, both as a way for grandchildren to live closer to grandparents, and as a source of postretirement income: Grandma moves into her guesthouse, rents out her main house, and voilà, her house makes money instead of costing.[5]

Opposition to ADUs comes from some neighborhood residents, who say they oppose change in the "neighborhood character," and fear a drop in the price of their property. Perhaps some are nostalgic for a time when more single-family homes were filled with nuclear families, or perhaps they are simply afraid of any change: Brian H. Wert, president of the Cranmer Park-Hilltop Civic Association in Denver, reflected a common worry when he said of a proposal to change a zoning ordinance that prohibits people unrelated by blood, marriage, or adoption from sharing a house, "We've taken the position for no change in the ordinance because we don't know what the results would be."[6] Some people think the existence of lower-class renters in the neighborhood will lower the sales price of their house. For people who have no other savings, or who have never lived near people outside their limited social sphere, the fears are strong.

Before you create an ADU, check your local zoning office. You may be a lucky resident of one of the many areas where they have always been legal.

COTTAGE HOUSING ORDINANCES

Some areas are platted for sprawling development, and zoned for low density. Homeowners in these areas currently assume that increased density in their neighborhood will harm them. But in areas where housing is in short supply, and citizens would like to preserve the last bits of forest and farmland, planners are looking for ways to encourage a little higher density. Some planning departments are encouraging "cluster developments" that construct houses closer together, then leave a larger, continuous, unbuilt area, sometimes as a shared park. A few municipalities have Cottage Housing ordinances (see profile this chapter) which allow the construction of two, or sometimes just one-and-a-half small houses (meaning three on two lots) where otherwise one mansion might have been. In other places, on a limited number of lots per neighborhood, four or even six tiny homes are allowed where just one or two might have been before. Sometimes they are restricted to a certain part of town—the university area, for example.

BANNING MCMANSIONS

A few small-house citizen groups, instead of trying to make a little more space for tiny houses, have gone right to the crux of the matter, and passed zoning laws to

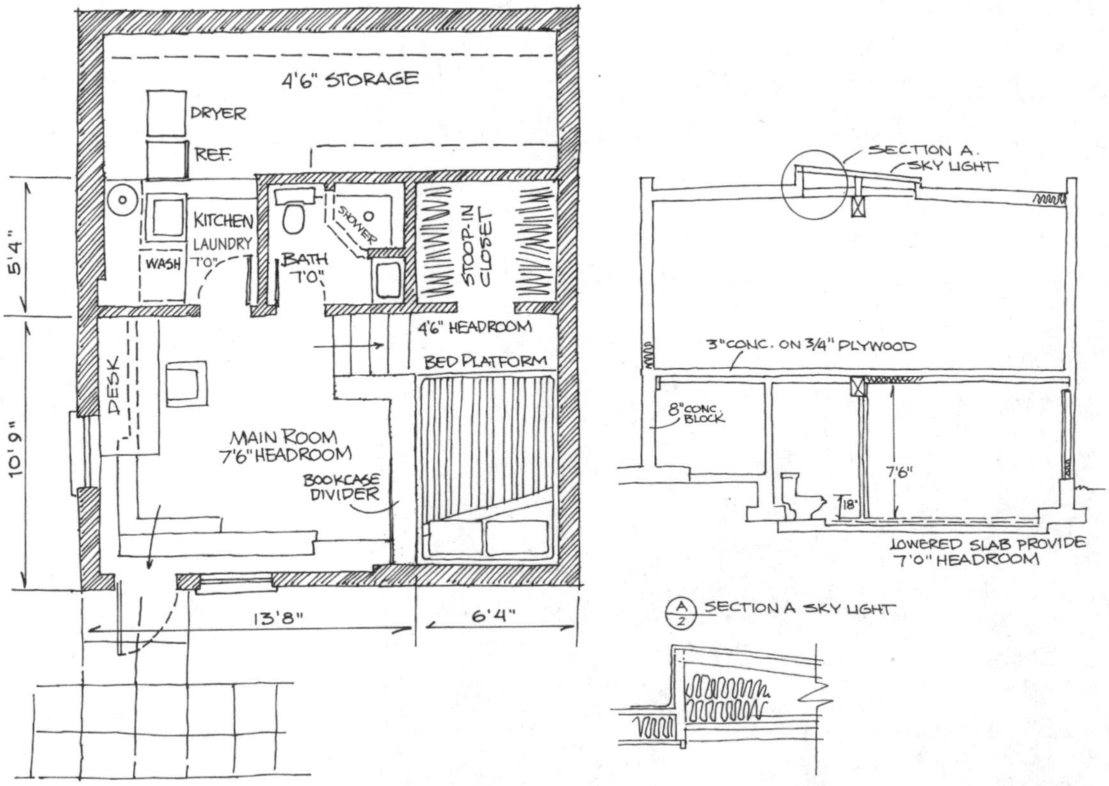

DESIGNED BY ARCHITECT DAN SMITH, THIS DAYLIGHTED BASEMENT APARTMENT CLIMBS UP THE RISE IN THE HILL WHERE IT IS BUILT, CREATING A COZY SLEEPING AREA IN THE LEDGE UNDER A LOW CEILING.

limit other people's home size. Residents of Crestone, Colorado, passed a law banning the construction of houses over 4,500 square feet because they were afraid they might otherwise become like their neighbor Vail (an elite ski resort that has displaced all the old families in the area, and has no space where the non-fabulously-wealthy can live). Palo Alto, California, during a year when 300 houses were torn down and replaced with McMansions, passed a similar ordinance. Marin County, California, passed a rule that any house over 3,500 square feet must prove it uses no more energy than a typical house of 3,500 square feet. Chicago, Illinois; Gainesville, Florida; Chevy Chase, Maryland; Portsmouth, New Hampshire; and Los Angeles and Santa Cruz, California, are a few of the municipalities that have passed temporary or permanent ordinances restricting "mansionization."

Codes and zoning laws are agreements among people about how to live. They were designed to protect tenants and buyers from callous landlords and developers, and to protect everyone from the dangers of the environment, built and natural. Almost all of us live within the code, but up to now a small group has determined the rules, defining for everyone what is a danger and what is safety. As more people with new perspectives enter the conversation about the code, maybe we'll turn our built environment into space that's more comfortable for all of us, present and future.[7]

CODES ARE AN AGREEMENT BETWEEN PEOPLE.

JAY SCHAFER
Built 1999

AREA:
130 sq. ft.

INTENDED NUMBER OF OCCUPANTS:
1

CONSTRUCTION COST:
$40,000

UTILITY COST:
$150/year propane for heating

LOCATION:
Iowa City, Iowa

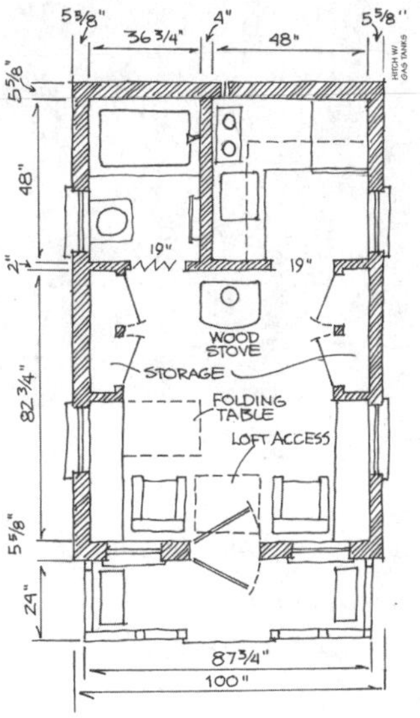

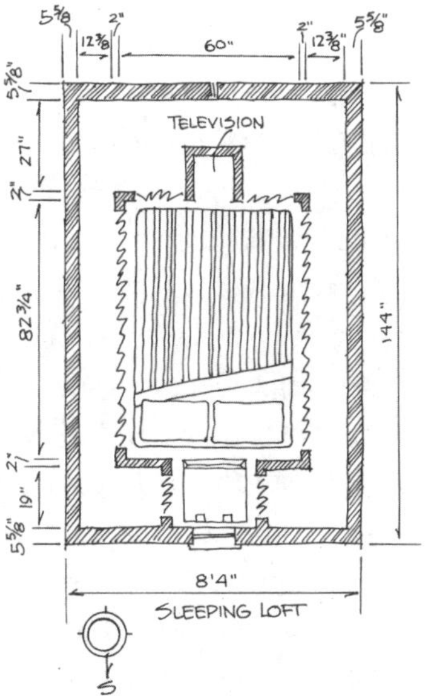

ABOVE LEFT: **"ROLLING GOTHIC"**
ABOVE: **FLOORPLAN**

One cloudy, wet day in the spring of 2000, a flatbed

trailer made its way up a 100-year-old cobblestone street, with Jay Shafer's most recent artwork built on top. As the truck slipped and turned in the grassy backyard, positioning the piece in its new location, the neighbors came out to watch. "What most surprised me," remembers neighbor Monica Martin, "was how normal it looked, like it was meant to live next to the other houses on our street. Except of course it was much, much smaller."

Jay's creation, his 130-square-foot, cedar-shingled and -sided, clapboard cottage, is the most recent in a series of installations that allow participants to experience the pleasure of economy of space. Earlier work includes a 3-foot-deep by 8-foot-diameter sweat lodge Jay and artist Jenny Ansley

"ROLLING GOTHIC"

JAY'S DESK.

dug in the ground and topped with a domed willow-hay-earthen roof. This grotto, named "Anodyne," soothed the souls of the eight people who coinhabited occasionally for about a year, until the roof collapsed. Jay recalls, "Eight was pretty minimal for that hole. Thirteen would have fit comfortably."

But for this project, which is his own home, Jay decided to stick with traditional, European-inspired, Midwestern forms, using the local building material of choice (milled lumber), square and vaulted multi-paned windows that offer the symbol of the cross, a heating hearth in the center, and a peaked ceiling over the sleeping loft. "I didn't see any reason to dilute the message of this work by straying from the acceptable, vernacular forms," Jay, an art instructor at the University of Iowa, explains. "Every great work of art shows this principle: if something is unnecessary to a composition, it weakens the composition."

Jay has been paring down tiny homes on paper since at least 1985, perhaps since childhood. He's not sure where his interest came from—certainly not from his father, who favors giant houses, and has yet to cross the threshold of Jay's. Jay imagines his houses stem from a series of Madonna icons he was painting and sculpting in '85.

"The lap of the Madonna, and her throne, is the archetypal form that led me to begin experimenting with domes." Jay explains that the dome of the Church reflects the Madonna, the balanced whole, and that ultimately the gabled roof found in his home expresses the same duality principle: the coming together at one point of opposites, fear and desire in balanced opposition. "Once you get through these opposites, you are in nirvana, divine. With symmetry you enter at the center, in peace."

Each year Jay drew more plans. "It became kind of perverse, an obsession. I drew small-house plans as a way to procrastinate my artwork. There was some shame around the plans. I never mentioned them to my family or my girlfriends. Then I started to open up. I showed one plan to a girlfriend." At the end of the year 2000, Jay won the *Natural Home* magazine Home of the Year award. Suddenly, Jay received inquiries from all over the country, and now people are buying his house plans. Jay says he's been shocked to evolve so quickly from shame to national recognition.

Jay's first full-time foray into small living came in 1995 when he spent three years in an Airstream trailer six miles outside of town. After gutting the trailer and rebuilding it to fit his tastes, he was content in his womblike abode. But living in the countryside was too solitary. He longed to be close to friends and the university, and he knew that any ecological savings accrued by living small was offset by his fuel consumption, driving into town.

So he sold the trailer and set his sights on building a tiny home on a lot in town, but after consulting with the building department, he gave up. "The code does not easily allow a home smaller than 200 square feet," explains local plans examiner Bill Timms. "They are probably unconstitutional, these laws, but I didn't see a way to change them," says Jay. However, he did find out that it is legal to park a trailer in your backyard. So Jay bought a house, rented it to a friend, and put his tiny creation on wheels, renaming it "Rolling Gothic." He now lives in his own backyard.

A stone path from the street winds around the front house and descends slowly through maple and walnut trees, showing a view of the home against the backdrop of the 160-acre county cemetery adjacent to Jay's backyard. The visitor is welcomed via a minuscule front porch, complete with railing and two 3-foot-wide benches. The house then maintains its dedication to symmetry, violating one common rule of small-space design: the 23-inch front door is set at the center of the façade. To the right of the door are bookcases, with a narrow ladder stored in the corner. On the left is a removable dining/writing table the length of Jay's forearm (17 inches), and as wide as the space between his elbows if they rest normally on a table (24 inches). The table is flanked by two chairs, 9 inches wide at the shoulder and 12 inches wide at the knee, tapering to just 7 inches wide at the waist, designed to accommodate Jay's narrow frame.

A CD player, meant for an automobile, and thus able to draw power from a car battery, is set into one bookcase, while across the room a cellular phone hangs from a hook, in a small carrying case, ready to travel as necessary. Exposed stainless-steel decking screws at most joints, along with cold sheet-metal

JAY'S HOUSE: EVERYTHING FITS

A CD PLAYER IS SET INTO ONE BOOKCASE.

STEEL DRAWERS BALANCE THE WARM PINE BOOKCASES.

drawers (decorated by punch holes) holding house plans and clothes, balance the warm pine bookcases and tongue-and-groove fir boards that clad the interior.

A shower, currently used as a closet (Jay bathes in the basement of the main house), fills the northern corner, opposite an immaculate, square and simple kitchen "L." Based on standard kitchen design, just shrunk smaller and not spread over a long counter as in many trailer kitchens, Jay believes the kitchen is perfectly adequate to prepare most meals. It's yet to be proven: a large bowl of packaged high-protein bars affirms this bachelor's confession that he has never used the kitchen to cook.

A VAULTED WINDOW GIVES THE SPACE THE SOLEMNITY OF A CHURCH.

With the front door closed, the narrow ladder is moved from its storage to an opening in the ceiling. Upstairs, under the peaked ceiling, a fluffy white queen-sized bed fills a cozy loft. Four-inch muslin curtains hang where the ceiling meets the edge of the bed, covering shallow storage space tucked into the corners. Also hidden by muslin is an exhaust fan designed to draw heat up and out of the house in summer. A 9-inch television with video recorder is set into one gable end, opposite a vaulted double-paned window with lead mullions that gives the space the solemnity of a church. Jay didn't skimp on details: these windows cost $600 each; downstairs, the solid mahogany front door is hung on hand-forged iron hinges.

With R-15 3-inch extruded polystyrene in the walls, R-20 in the floor, and R-30 in the ceiling, the house stays warm through the cold Iowa winter with about $150 of propane burned in the heating stove each winter. Although it takes up space, Jay offers the hearth the respect of the center. "The house is designed to offer the basic sense of shelter—fit to the human scale of the home dweller at the center, at the fire." Jay's plans for his next project? "I have a new design that shaves off another 3 inches."

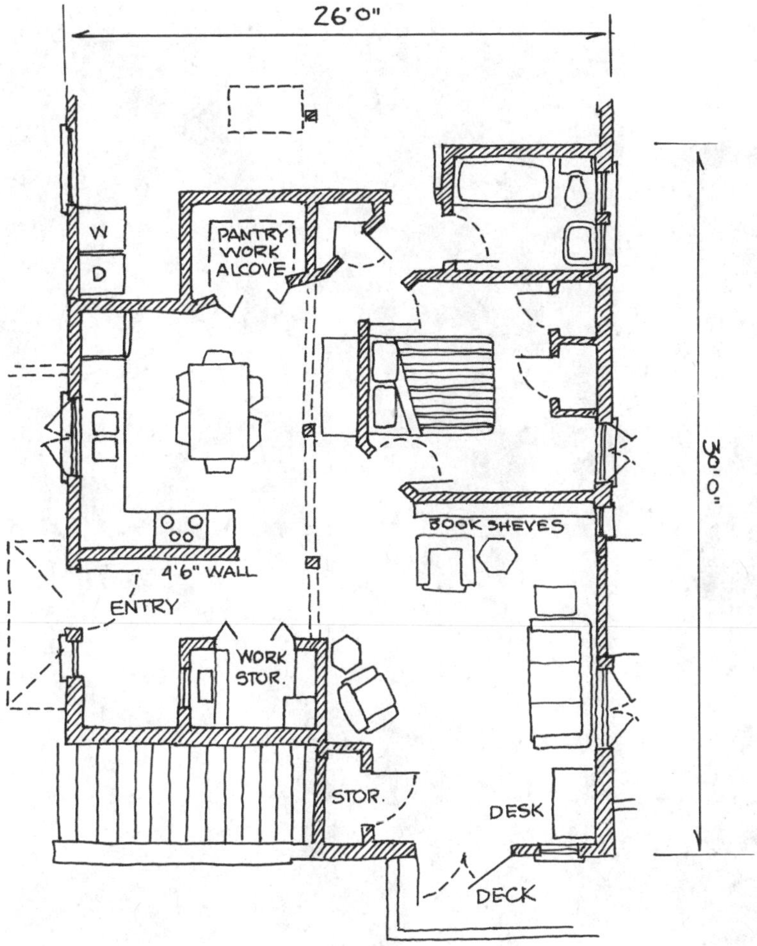

CECILE AND PAUL ANDREWS
Built 1927; basement remodeled 1996

INTENDED NUMBER OF OCCUPANTS:
4–8 in the entire house

AREA:
2,800 sq. ft total, between three apartments

PURCHASE PRICE:
$143,000 in 1988

UTILITY COSTS (MONTHLY):
$70/apartment

LOCATION:
Seattle, Washington

Cecile and Paul are an odd couple: she writes

books about the simplicity movement; he coauthored a biography of the richest man in the world. When they decided to divide up their house and live in just part of it, people asked Cecile how she convinced Paul to do it. "Actually," she told them, "he's the one who never spends any money. He was very pleased when I *discovered* simplicity."

The Andrews bought their two-story-plus-basement home when their teenage children left home. They loved it as soon they walked in, figuring they could put the extra room to use for studies and home offices. But they eventually found themselves estranged in their large house. Paul's giant upstairs office was so remote, he felt like they were living in separate houses. Paul remembers, "The office was beautiful to walk through, but that's all I did with that space. It wasn't worth it."

Paul moved his office into a bedroom on the first floor, and Cecile moved her office into the spacious front parlor, a room with a gorgeous view overlooking a lake, that previously she rarely enjoyed, particularly in daylight, since she reserved it for hosting guests. "Now I'm in the nicest

ABOVE: **FLOOR PLAN**

CECILE AND PAUL'S ANTIQUE KITCHEN

room, all day," she reports. Cecile tends to spread out as she works, and piles of paper accumulate, but now that she's near the front door, she finds, "The mess can't go on forever, like it used to. I'm forced to clean up." She bought an armoire that now contains computer, files, dictionary, and desk space. When company visits, she just closes it up.

[Q] How did you overcome your fear of living in less space?

[A] PAUL: Actually, I missed living in a smaller space. When I had the upstairs office, I would get home from work and go up to my computer, and it was almost as if we were living separately. The space was big, and my work sort of sprawled out. I didn't need all that space.

[Q] Some people say that two people just can't live in a small space together. We've become such strong individuals; it just won't work.

[A] PAUL: I think if you do that, what you're doing is avoiding the issue, rather than working on the relationship. We get along better when we do spend time together.

CECILE: What a nice declaration of love!

PAUL: We've noticed over the years that the more time we spend together, the closer we feel. In fact, the amount of time you spend together increases exponentially the depth of the relationship, while absence has the opposite effect.

CECILE: We bicker a lot . . .

PAUL: We do. We have a very contentious relationship.

CECILE: . . . so it was easier, when we first got married, for Paul to run away. If you'd give him the space, he'd just run away. It's a male thing to do. But now, he can't avoid me. We're almost in the same room.

PAUL: You need strong communication skills. People don't really have them—we haven't fostered them. No one teaches it in school.

CECILE: The research shows that it's always the woman saying, "Let's talk more." I remember that when we first got married, if I got angry you'd run away to bed, I'd have to come and roust you out.

PAUL: Yep, you'd chase me.

CECILE: So I think it must be good for men and women to have to live in a small space. It forces them to talk. Of course, the real key to happiness is our dog. We just love our little dog. Did you take her to see the chickens tonight? He's the one who spoils her. Three chickens is all that's allowed in the city, and Maggie loves to see them.

In 1994, when the City of Seattle began passing ordinances to make it easier for homeowners to create "granny flats," Cecile and Paul hired architect Jack Baker, took him on a tour of their home, and said, "Design us a place that we would want to live in." They are so pleased with the resulting basement apartment they think they might move downstairs one day. Paul took his plans to the building department and they ran them right through. He remembers, "Before the '90s, the city strictly opposed accessory dwelling units, but when the housing crunch hit, they started to open up, and now they encourage them."

When an apartment becomes available, the Andrews hold an open house on a Sunday afternoon, and they ask interested parties to write a brief description of themselves. "The process is like an essay contest," Cecile, a college professor, jokes. The results have been excellent, and the Andrews have no complaints about their tenants. Cecile particularly enjoyed the Mexican family who lived upstairs for three years. "Roxana, the wife, suggested I paint the kitchen these beautiful, bright colors. I used to apologize about my kitchen—it's never been remodeled—but one day a visitor said, 'This is an *antique* kitchen, from the time when kitchens were workrooms, and not made for magazine covers.' Between that kind comment, and Roxana's bright colors, I love this kitchen now."

Another perk of having tenants is that when they move out, they leave behind heavy items. The couple has acquired a sturdy bookcase and a gas barbecue so far. And when Paul travels away for work, Cecile is safely sandwiched between friends, upstairs and down. Instead of fearing the sound of unknown stirring outside, she enjoys the "human noises" of her tenants moving in their apartments.

When Paul received an advance for his second book, the Andrews decided to pay off their mortgage. A financial advisor told them they could make more money investing in the stock market. "This was right before the dot-com bomb lost investors millions," says Paul. Cecile says they are happy they chose to pay off their mortgage. "You aren't always able to switch jobs. Gas for your car, utilities for your house, these will always cost. But if you own your house, and have rental income, that's one more way you create autonomy. We don't want a ton of money. We want to be free."

12 COTTAGE HOMES
Built 2004

AREA:
12 houses 1,000 sq ft each, clustered on 1.5 acres of a 9.5 acre parcel (a second phase is planned that will add 13 more houses on 1.75 acres)

INTENDED NUMBER OF OCCUPANTS:
12–18, currently 15

PURCHASE PRICE:
$400,000 (land and site improvements cost $182,000)

LOCATION:
Redmond, Washington

ABOVE: **A LAYERED SEQUENCE SEPARATES PUBLIC AND PRIVATE REALMS**
ABOVE, RIGHT: **FLOOR PLAN**

Architect Ross Chapin and Developer Jim Soules

of the Cottage Company, say that Conover Commons, and their similar cottage home developments in Washington State, are similar to cohousing, "but without all the meetings." The twelve 1,000-square-foot, 2-bedroom, 2-bathroom, carefully-designed Craftsman-style houses at CC share a common green, landscaped like a park, in the center, and a small forest on the north side of the site, which is a buffer area near a stream and wetland.

Residents also share a common house that has space for a sit-down dinner, and a bar sink and cabinets filled with paper plates, but has no kitchen, so there are no dishes to clean up after gatherings. The space typically hosts potlucks, business meetings, and birthday parties, and has a small library of gardening books and current magazines. Attached to it is a public bathroom that guests and workers can use, "so they don't have to walk into the private homes," says Jim.

Cars are parked in a cluster on the perimeter, with a garage for each home and unassigned open spaces for guests and second cars, so no greenspace is taken from the front yard for parking. Instead of dividing the space between the houses in half, and creating two shady, useless sideyards, each house has a 10-foot-wide yard on one side, and a zero lot line on the other. Each house also has a private front yard, separated from the common green by a 2-foot split rail fence, and large enough to allow a bit of personal expression, be it a pea patch garden, a birdbath, a Japanese bonsai, or a rose garden. These circles of garden, commons, and private outdoor space offer the development a greener appearance than some more sprawling detached single-family homes with large concrete or asphalt drives and streets.

The development offers a layered sequence that separates public and private realms (see right).

"We locate the parking areas intentionally so that residents and guests walk through the commons to the front door. This raises the number of "chance interactions" among people— the friendly chats among neighbors—that provide the seeds for a strong sense of community. There is a passage/implied gate from the parking into the commons. At the edge of the commons there is a perennial hedge and low fence to delineate the realm of the private yard. The porch is a couple of steps up from the walk, and is large enough to be a usable outdoor room. It has a low "perchable" railing—enough to provide a sense of enclosure, but not so high to be a barrier. The active areas of the house face the commons, while further back and upstairs are the private realms. Because the layers of personal space are delineated, a person is more likely to engage with others in the commons.

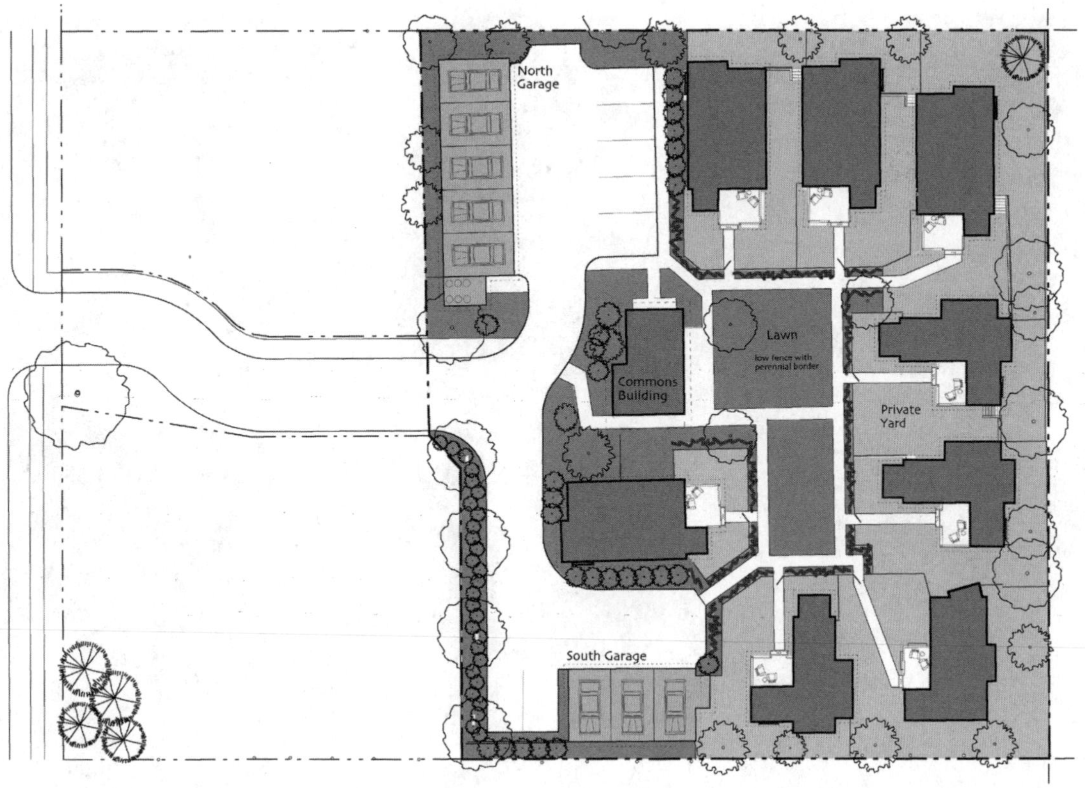

"This layering of realms, In my opinion, is the most important element in courtyard developments. Yet because it is subtle, it is the design principle most likely to be overlooked. "Cottage style" is alluring, but it's not essential to "cottage housing" development.” **—Ross Chapin**

A board of directors, elected from the owners, interprets and refines the bylaws, ensuring, for instance, that no one install a plastic hot tub in their front yard (one neighbor, in a previous project, tried to) nor sneak in a room addition in violation of the municipal Cottage Housing code.

Cottage Housing codes allow developers to build up to 100 percent more detached houses on the same amount of ground, as long as each unit is not more than 1,000 square feet. For example, if four contiguous lots that add up to an acre are zoned R-1, instead of allowing four 3,500-square-foot houses, the cottage code provision may allow a community of eight cottages, each permanently restricted to 1,000 square feet, and subject to other site design requirements such as a limit on building height, covered front porches of at least 80 square feet, front doors oriented to a courtyard, private yards and open space in front of the house.

"We build the cottages to a high standard, with high-quality finishes, details, and craftsmanship, so it will be understood that they are just another kind of single-family home, and completely appropriate for most suburban neighborhoods. If they are built right, they provide a little variety for the neighborhood, and the larger neighborhood is fine with them. There's a tremendous demand for this new option," says Jim. The Cottage Housing code was developed by the King County Partnership in Washington State and has been adopted by a number of municipalities.

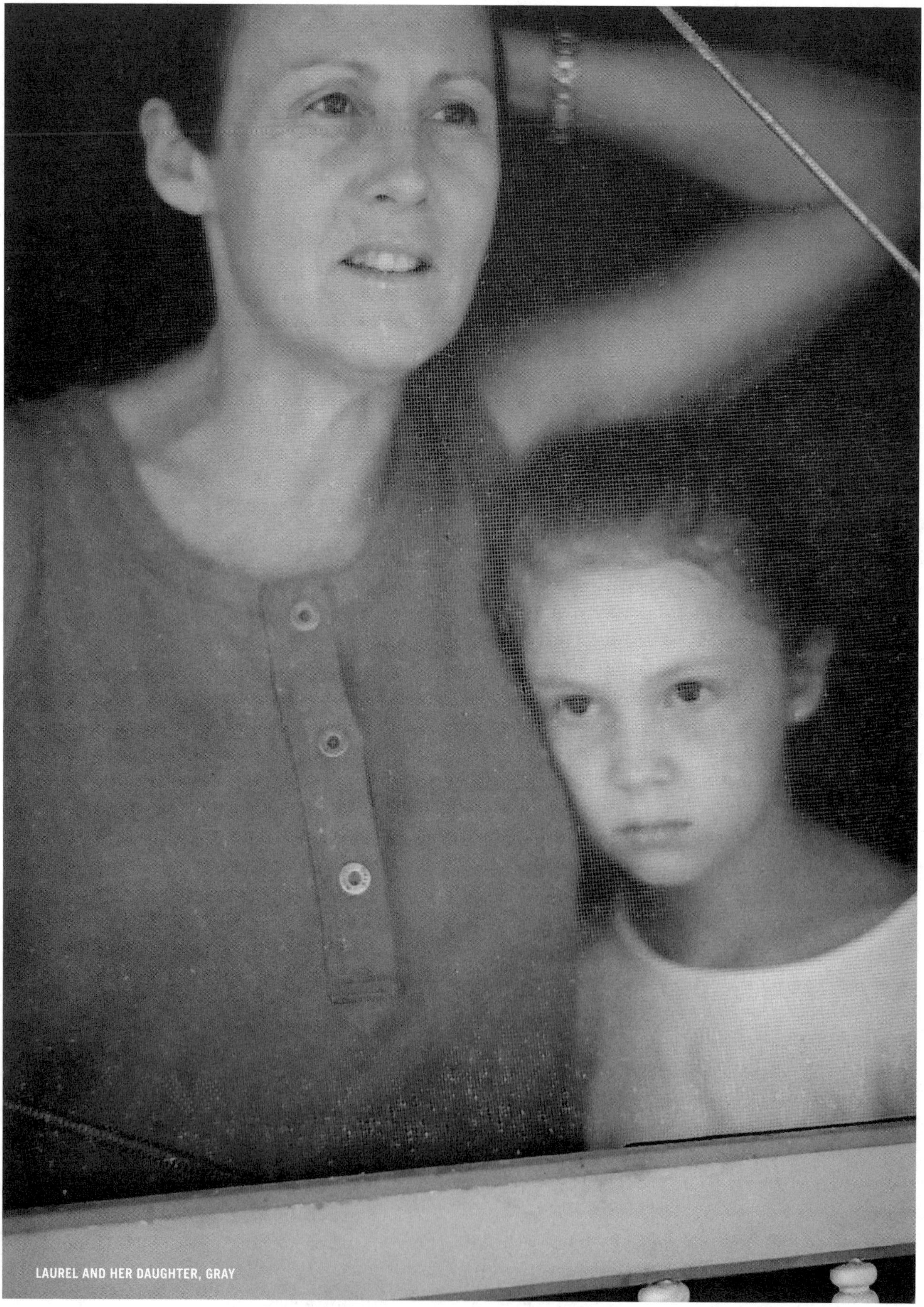

LAUREL AND HER DAUGHTER, GRAY

11
Love Your Children

In my father's day, if you kept your children warm, dry, and fed, you were a very good parent.—HELEN SEAGRAVES

DOES LIVING SMALL HARM YOUR CHILDREN? If you simplify your life, and your children have fewer things, will they grow up feeling inferior to their companions? Will they endlessly crave in adulthood what they wanted in childhood, if they don't get it? Parents work overtime trying to provide for their children "what we didn't have." Some say, "Simplicity is fine for single people, but I don't want my kids to feel deprived."

No sane person intends to deprive the next generation of a happy childhood. But what is a happy childhood? Mountains of books, research studies, and experts vigorously address this question, offering a rainbow of contradictory theories. Maybe many theories all apply, or maybe no one knows. This childless author certainly won't enter the fray. All I can assure you is that we met many children who seemed to be quite happy growing up in little space. We heard a number of adults attribute their current well-being to having spent childhood in close quarters with others. On the other hand, it's difficult to find an adult who says her present or past happiness depended on the large private room she had as a child.

What Do Children Really Want?

The obvious things that children want are plenty of food, clean water, and a safe, warm home. Once these basic needs are met, children's happiness isn't so influenced by material gains. Small-home dwellers who have raised children agree on two things: "Children want their parents to be happy," or more specifically, "They want their parents to be glad they are parents," and, when they are small, kids want to be near adults. As Judy Turner (see Chapter 6) says, "Even if your kitchen is two acres long, your young ones will want to stay right near you." Most, but not all, agree that adolescents need some kind of space of their own.

STAY HERE, MOMMY, DADDY

Many small-home dwellers figure that a lower mortgage, enabling part-time employment and therefore more time spent at home, means more to their children than a bigger house. Specifically,

“Our culture [Thailand] is changing, and our families are now smaller, but people still like to sleep near each other, either inside the house or outside on bamboo platforms, where the breeze is refreshing. No privacy is good for a couple because we have more fun that way. Sometimes a few couples share one house. People aren't so romantic in my village. Sex isn't such a big deal, and we don't have so much. Our rate of divorce is very low. People can always find a way to have sex, but the point is how to enjoy other people. X-rated movies show so much sound and action, but traditionally sex is very quiet, and there is a different way of expressing emotion.” —Jo Thandai

they ask themselves, “Will our children prefer having their own room, or having an adult home after school? Is there a way to give them both a large college fund, and a parent to help them with their homework? Would they benefit more from a more expensive neighborhood with a prestigious public school, or a family that can take two months off in summer to camp?” These are difficult questions. Regardless of the answer, a small house can be very cozy for children.

A Child's Place

THE FAMILY BED

For the period of infancy through toddler-hood—and sometimes for several years beyond—many parents determine that their young child only needs her own space as a way of storing clothes and toys, and thus all she really needs is a closet, or even just a chest. Although the U.S. Consumer Product Safety Commission has announced that “co-sleeping” is dangerous[1], almost every infant sometimes sleeps with adults, and the majority of babies spend every night with their parent(s). Some parents lower their bed to the floor, to avoid the fear of their baby falling out of bed, and pull the bed well away from the wall so an infant can't get trapped in a crevice. Others attach a “side car”—a crib or bassinet with one open side—to the side of the bed or hang a baby hammock over the bed. Some nursing mothers report, however, that typically the nursing baby stays next to the breast for most of the night, and mother is too tired or too afraid to wake the baby to move him back to a different sleeping place.

Especially if the child has no siblings, no cousins, and no grandparents to sleep with, most children prefer to stay with their parents, sometimes until they reach puberty: we visited a number of families who, in confidence, told us that their school-aged child had yet to sleep in his own room. Parents sometimes reply with a separate bed, at the foot of theirs, or a loft, or a sleeping cubby built on the side of the room. Most North Americans find the idea of making love while a child lies within earshot unappealing or immoral, but it must, very discreetly, be happening (see left).

Some parents try musical beds—one parent falls asleep with the child in one room, then joins the other parent later, after the child is fast asleep. In the wee hours of morning, the child wakes up and joins the two parents.

A CHILD'S ROOM OF HER OWN?

The ranch house of the 1950s was usually built with parents' and children's bedrooms far away from each other. A recent ad for a huge house in California suggested that the third-floor suite, two floors away from the kitchen and backyard, is an “ideal location for the nursery.” If your children will be raised by a nanny whom you don't want to bump into, or if your strongest value is independence, it might work to have a child's bedroom far from the core, but small-housers tend to take an opposite approach, locating the child's room adjacent to the parents', and also close to wherever adults spend the day; a corner in the kitchen, or a closet off of a home office might be designated as daytime childs' play or nap space. Of course, in a very small house nothing is very far away.

Laurel Robertson and Charles Gibson found enough space in their 710-square-foot house to build a room for each of their three children:

"The kids' rooms are 12 foot by 8 foot, just big enough to squeeze in a single bed, shelves, a dresser and a desk. We get extra floor space by using a top bunk (without the bottom) and putting the dresser and closet beneath. In a small room, a small amount of stuff seems like 'enough stuff.' We had to train the relatives to not send giant stuffed animals for Christmas. Toys get rotated periodically from high shelves to lower ones, creating new interest in old toys.

"The younger kids like having Mom and Dad close at hand. For a while our seven-year-old wouldn't do her homework in her room because she felt so 'far away.' I had to convince her that as long as I could still hear her breathing, she wasn't too far away."

Currently, children's bedrooms are conventionally between 10 by 12 feet and 12 by 14 feet in size, but many children find that an alcove or loft room two-thirds or half that size, and built to a child's scale, is very comfortable.

An 8-by-10-foot add-on with 6-foot-4-inch ceilings was sized just right for Manon and David's three-year-old daughter. It was furnished with a tiny desk, twin bed, mirror at three-year-old height, and 4-foot door that opened to the outside. When the couple moved to France and rented out their home to a woman and her teenaged daughter, everyone was surprised to discover the tiny room was also perfect for a teenager, even when she grew to be 6 feet tall and acquired an array of snowboarding equipment. Now in college, she remembers, "My friends loved hanging out in that room. It was tight."

If you look around your existing home, you may find a small space—a large closet or a corner of the attic or basement—that may suit your child as well as a standard bedroom would have.

Why do children crave small spaces? Of course, children also enjoy wide-open fields and gymnasiums where they can run wild, but for most daily activities—sleeping, reading, playing with dolls or board games, talking with friends—they'd rather snuggle up in a cubby. A small space feels safe and is a space they can control.

A TEENAGER'S LOFT ROOM

Helen Walters, age thirteen, has a room that is 12 feet long and 4 feet wide, with a 7-foot ceiling. It is tucked under the attic ceiling, and at one end an alcove adds an additional 4 by 7 feet of bed space, under a ceiling that slopes to 2 feet on one side and climbs to 5 feet high at the opening to the alcove. Helen's parents, Terese and David, placed a 44–by-42-inch roof window over the bed, which can open as a vent, even when it's raining, swings in for cleaning, and potentially serves as a fire escape. Helen watches the stars through it as she falls asleep. At the other end of the room a closet and drawers fit into the sloping space, for more storage.

Helen's brothers, Samuel and Kevin, share a more normal room, next door, at one end of the attic. Terese explained that Helen's room was built before Helen's sister Margaret, now six, was able to sleep away from Mom and Dad. "We built it thinking, 'Helen will grow out of it in a few years,' but she hasn't." Currently, Margaret has the largest bedroom in the house, next door to and more than thrice the size of Helen's, but the room is so big that Margaret prefers to play in her closet.

Terese has tried to convince Helen to move in with her sister, so the alcove can be converted to a sewing room. Helen replies that she'd rather figure out a way for Margaret to move into her room. Helen's room is the favorite play space for Samuel, Margaret, and school friends when they visit, so popular that Helen has installed a doorbell, and dedicated a drawer in her room for each of her younger sibling's stuff. Terese admits it's the coziest room in the house and when her whole family is away, Terese sleeps in Helen's room.

This sense of control is something everyone agrees that children should have in their special place. Parents offer this sense by resisting the urge to design or decorate a perfect bedroom for their children, and instead allow their children, as parenting expert Elizabeth Pantley suggests, "to choose a few new things, such as bedding, curtains, and wall decorations."[2] Some parents go farther and designate a room, a wall, or an outdoor location that children are free to rearrange and decorate in absolutely any way they please (we'll explore this in more detail under "At Home Outside"). If it's outside, children will have only the natural limits to restrict them.

SHARING ROOMS

Until fairly recently, almost all North American children shared rooms, with a sibling or a relative, and some people still believe that children who don't grow up sharing rooms will have a difficult time living with a spouse, and will learn to be roused by every snore and sigh in a room, and fall prey to insomnia in the future (see Aleidria's story, this chapter).

Some children who share a room meticulously divide it, using furniture, a curtain, or an imaginary line on the floor. Others prefer sharing a bed, but still having a private space for their things. Parents can help children divide

KIDS IN SMALL SPACES: LEFT AND CENTER: **A CLOSET CONVERTS INTO A TODDLER'S ROOM.** RIGHT: **HELEN'S ROOM**

their room into private cubbyholes and shared play space, a balance between public and private, and a microcosm of the larger house and world. (see Barbara Tognocci on page 198)

A PARENT'S PLACE

Parents develop a number of ways to enjoy living in close quarters with their kids, and to control the chaos of clutter. Laurel and Charles built a 710-square-foot guesthouse, intending to build a larger main house quickly. The house, and the much-lower mortgage payment worked out so well that they stayed for ten years, and only started on the second house when their kids were teenagers. Laurel writes,

My initial fear was that my husband and I would never have any privacy from our three kids. But they each have a room of their own to retreat to (or to be sent to), and once they're in bed asleep we have the entire living room, kitchen and our bedroom to ourselves, which is ample (okay, that's 400 square feet total, but we're not playing basketball).

Daytime racket can be worse in small spaces, especially if everyone is home most of the time. My husband runs a business from his desk in our living room, so a portable phone has really saved some situations; the front porch is 2 feet away. Our kids have also learned to respect the need for 'indoor voices.'

I imagined the kids might not have enough space to spread out into involved games of pretend or make big art messes, but one 5-by-7-foot living room rug has comfortably accommodated countless block constructions and games. It just has to stay on the rug, and get cleared away before bedtime.

Family members have their own place at the kitchen table, and as I go through the day I stack stray belongings at the owner's place at the table. Before they can sit down for dinner, they have to put away their stuff. I have a designated place near the front door for "Things Going Out" to help remind me to get them to the car.

We have a tall ceiling in the kitchen/living room, so I hang baskets from pegs in the rafters for extra storage, using a hooked pole to reach them. I keep several stepladders to make easy use of high shelves.

Part of the success of Laurel and Charles' house is that they live in the countryside, in a climate with fairly short winters. "Big art and other messy projects are outdoor activities," Laurel explains. "We're outside a lot."

At Home Outside

CHILDREN'S SHRINKING RANGE

Recently my sister overheard neighbors commenting with surprise about an unaccompanied(!) nine-year-old boy seen bicycling around the local park. A generation ago, most school-aged children were allowed to walk around their neighborhoods, alone or with friends, or even take public

Barbara Tognocci raised four children—aged two, four, six, and eleven when they moved there—in a four-room cabin in the woods of Vermont. The attic was warm, and Barbara divided it into three alcoves by hanging walls from the struts (bracing designed to help the roof hold heavy snow loads) that were already there. There were no doors, but a kind of privacy, with three walls for each "stall" and a 12-by-24-foot shared space that faced a bank of sunny southern windows. At one end of the shared space, her seven-year-old slept in a "room" defined just by a line on the floor. "I might have tried harder to make him his own space," she recalls, "but he didn't seem to mind, and it was only a short time between the youngest moving upstairs and the oldest moving into a colder but private room we converted from a shed in the back.

"I had a contentious relationship with my sisters growing up and I wanted it to be different for them, so I tried to coach them to take care of each other. They still enjoy each other's company, and at Thanksgiving even though they have their significant others with them they insist that we all crowd into this small house together."

transportation alone. Two generations ago most North Americans lived in rural areas and children could run to the forest, prairie, or beach to play. Our fears about each other have shrunk our free world. Even in areas where crime has declined, most parents are reluctant to let their children run unsupervised anywhere.

Part of the reason is the lower numbers of children per household. Although children sometimes hurt each other, it usually feels safer and more fun to play in a park or on a sidewalk with many children, instead of a desolate one. Another problem is that many new houses have been built so far apart that children cannot reach a common park easily.

Parents who regret that their children's free range is limited compensate by making their home a particularly free place to be. They may also locate themselves, for example, in a cohousing community or apartment complex that has shared play space with many children. Children who spend their days running from house to house or playing outside have little interest in a large private bedroom.

THE TEEN-BUILT HOUSE

Many teenagers want to get away. They sense their range is too limited. In some cultures, they are sent away, to initiation rites, on religious missions, to herd animals, or to war. Few families in the industrialized world have the social networks to send teenagers safely away, but summer camps, boarding school, exchange programs, and extended stays with relatives sometimes mimic these older traditions.

One rural or suburban solution to the teenager who is ill-at-ease in the small family home is to encourage her to build a tiny house outside. If this outbuilding is properly constructed, it might become a guesthouse, a cottage the parents retire to later, or rentable space when the child moves away.

Annette Bader moved with her two boys, Jamil and Ahren, into the Maxwelton Creek Cohousing community in Whidbey Island, Washington, in 1998. For a year they lived in a trailer while their house was built. Jamil, who was three, slept with his mom, while Ahren, age nine, slept in his own room, as he had in their previous house.

In the new house, Jamil and Ahren shared a bedroom. Parallel loft beds lined the walls; Ahren kept his drum set below his bed. Ahren, who wasn't used to sharing a room, said he and his brother fought "about all kinds of details."

Outside, behind the house, Ahren had his getaway fort. Before the main house was finished, Ahren's godfather helped him build it, pouring four small concrete footings in a 6-by-9-foot square, placing 2-by-6-inch boards around the perimeter, and building a platform of salvaged lumber that grew into a 4-foot-tall cabin with a gable roof made of planks that let the sun and moonlight in, and the rain through. In spring and summer, Ahren sometimes camped out in his fort.

In late 2001, the family raised the roof, to a 7-and-a-half-foot peak and 6-foot walls, and laid a reused accordion wall divider (wood paneling joined by rubbery plastic) over the roof structure, nailing it to the walls on two sides, and capping it with a metal ridge. A window and a weather-tight door were added. On the inside the walls received an R-11 layer of fiberglass insulation covered by egg cartons for soundproofing, and then carpet, and on the outside roofing felt and antique cedar shingles scavenged from the local county fairgrounds' burn pile.

By the spring of 2004, Ahren, age fifteen, had moved in full-time. His sound studio equipment dominates the space. He sleeps in a sleeping bag on the floor in the area that is "walking space during the day." Although the ceiling is uninsulated, outside temperatures rarely drop below freezing, and the space is small enough to stay toasty with just a small electric heater.

In 2005, after four years and 118 inches of rain, the accordion roof had developed just one small leak, which a friend "repaired" by tucking a dirty sock behind the ridgepole. At the end of the year the family built an

JAMIL AND AHREN IN THEIR SHARED ROOM

AHREN'S SHACK, BEFORE IT EVOLVED INTO A SOUND STUDIO/BEDROOM

8-by-12-foot more conventional "picnic shelter" roof over the whole structure, but slightly higher. Made of four 4-by-4-inch posts and 2-by-4-inch rafters, the roof is sheathed in plywood and covered with felt and asphalt composite shingles, left over from the roof of the main house.

In 2006, Ahren said, "We drove by a kiosk last week, and I realized my place isn't much bigger. I don't know how I do it." He says that he and Jamil now have an "excellent sibling relationship," and Jamil says he's happy to have his own room, in the house.

Other families take an opposite approach. Figuring that adolescence is both the last chance to influence children, and a dangerous time for teenagers, they pull the family close together by, for example, taking a year-long camping trip.

When Cedar Rose and her husband divorced, her family was living in a beautiful, 1,200-square-foot house in the woods, her dream house. After the divorce, Cedar realized that her attempts to maintain the house on a single income were taking a terrible toll on her life. So she moved with her two children into an RV for a few months, and later, when winter came, into a studio apartment. "To get our life back in order I had to accept that I was a person who could afford $400 a month. I said, 'Let's figure out how to have a really good time with it."

For three years Cedar shared a 210-square-foot studio apartment with her thirteen–sixteen-year-old daughter, April, her fifteen–eighteen-year-old son, Summer, a dog, a bunny, a hedgehog, and an aging hamster. For extra fun at night they let the bunny and hedgehog run around with the dog in the center of the room.

Cedar insists, "The best thing, hands down, that I ever did for my kids was to get everyone into a single room for three years, while they were teenagers. We learned how to sleep with the lights and TV on, and while others are talking. I managed construction crews during that time, and sometimes I'd bring six people home for dinner—that's fun. We found out that when you live that close you just can't afford to be grumpy for long. You have to get over your problems quickly. And you don't have to pry into your teenager's life to know what she's up to, because it's right there in front of you."

To ensure that each of them had private space, Cedar lined the sides of the room with bunk-bed alcoves that had private shelves inside. Each alcove could be curtained off from the rest of the room. Fortunately, the bathroom

was private—it even had a door—and the kitchenette had a partition that separated it slightly from the rest of the space.

Cedar's son, Summer, clearly has mixed memories. He agrees it was probably good for him, but remembers he was shocked at his loss of freedom. At his dad's larger house there was no curfew, and, he admits, he could have moved back there if he'd wanted to, but preferred life in the studio. April, who is quite achievement oriented, sees it as a family accomplishment. "I learned that when you work for something, and get it, it's just like a gift, but better." Nine years later, Cedar's business is thriving. Summer and April have their own web design business and live on their own. Cedar lives in a 1,100-square-foot town house and wonders daily what to do with all the extra space.

CHILDHOOD SPACE

This exercise may be impossible for parents of young children to do, since it ideally involves taking at least an hour—or two or three—to themselves. You can do it alone or with a friend, or even with your children. You'll need paper, pencil, crayons, or paints, and perhaps a tape recorder. If you are with a friend, try to spend the first hour or so in silence.

1. Spend some time getting comfortable, and relaxing, however you like.
2. Recall details of your childhood. Remember, if you can, going to bed. What were the rituals? How did you feel about it? Where did you sleep? Write down a description, draw, or speak into the tape recorder your memories.
3. Remember happy times spent with other people. Where did they happen? What was the quality of space, the distance between people? Record your memories.
4. Remember if and where you had special places, secret places, or places that were just yours. What were they like? Record them.
5. As a child, did you make drawings or write stories about dream houses, schools, or villages? What were your fantasies? Record them.
6. If you are alone, study what you have recorded. If you audio-taped your ideas, listen to them. Be gentle with yourself when bad memories come up. If you are with a friend, it's time to talk with each other about what you discovered.[4]

Family Values

IS TV A HUMAN RIGHT?

In retrospect, Cedar was glad that she had to move into such close quarters with her children, because it made it more possible for her to influence them. Although parents hold enormous responsibility for their children, they find their influence is often limited, compared to the influence of peers, school, and the media. A British Broadcasting study that has followed twenty-five children since their birth in 2000 asked them at age five to look at two houses, one modest, and the other a huge "Georgian pile," and then describe the people who lived in each one. Two parents, who themselves were dedicated to a modest, small-house, "vegetarian, Buddhist" lifestyle, were shocked to hear their son explain to researchers that the "good" people lived in the bigger house.[3]

What's a parent to do? Many are glad they've eliminated broadcast television, or all television, or even all "screen time" (videos, computer games, Internet surfing), from their lives, although it doesn't seem to completely solve the problem. "We don't want to cloister our son," writes one parent, "but we realize that just a trip to the supermarket traps him in a weird kind of contact high that takes an hour to cool down from. He's only five." It's unlikely you'll eliminate all shopping from your life.

THE DELICATE DANCE OF NEED AND GREED

Parents who live rurally have less trouble maintaining a family life consistent with their values. Even if rural neighbors don't prize family and learning over possession, the space between houses allows

Jean-Baptiste and Jeannette raised three girls in a three-room apartment that was tucked into one end of a converted, seventeenth-century, stone sheep barn. As part of a Gandhian, ecumenical, monastic community, they renounced many of the typical trappings of modern life. I asked them if their daughters rebelled against their parents' vow of simplicity. As adults, all three daughters have adopted a humble, Christian lifestyle, but the couple agreed that material desire is an ongoing question, throughout childhood. Their family unity was enhanced by the fact that all their immediate neighbors had similar values. Ultimately, they insisted, "Children are content when their parents are content," and then added, "But we did finally give in when the oldest wanted a radio."

parents to shield their children from ideas they dislike. But even rural families eventually have to face the question that urban families never escape: How to raise happy children in an atmosphere filled with advertising and peer messages their parents are at odds with?

Advertisers, recognizing that minds are even softer when they are young, devote enormous resources to creating psychologically sophisticated messages. Successful parents, although they may not recognize it at the time, intuitively respond with an equal level of sophistication, and a superior level of devotion. Just as they discipline their own inner dialogue to "resist the urge" to indulge in "needs" that have high-priced side effects, they maintain an endless conversation with their children, interpreting, accepting, and rejecting the world as they pass through it.

Parents can model the life they want to promote, and they can model contentment. Barbara Tognocci remembers that when her children went to school, they saw they didn't have the things other children did, "but they knew we were mostly happy at home, and that's what counted." At home, small-house parents try to expand their children's sense of safety by building a nest, parallel to the one they maintain in their own psyche, protected from the outside winds of bad thoughts and deeds. They are well aware, however, that their nest is only as strong as the tree that holds it. That "tree" is the subject of the last chapter, and something they hope will stay secure for many generations to come. In the meantime, parents can also try their best to ensure their own balance and sanity—"children are happy when their parents are happy"—a subject the next chapter addresses.

Four Children

ROWAN

Before their children were born, Rowan Swanson's parents lived for two years in an Airstream trailer, which they parked on their site, near Story City, Iowa. They spent the trailer years planning their future house, never rushing. "They were very stable about the process," says Rowan.

The result was 950-square-foot, open-plan, earth-bermed house, with precast concrete walls underground, and brick walls above ground. Well-oriented for southern, winter solar gain, it was designed as a Department of Energy test house, and proved that even in the harsh Iowa winters it's quite possible to heat a family house with about one-and-a-half cords of wood per year. The house was designed with two woodstoves, but it heated so easily, the family gave one of them away.

Rowan shared a bedroom with his sister for six years. When they were eight and ten they placed a wardrobe between their beds, and eventually their dad built a sweet-smelling cedar wall so they each had a 90-square-foot private room. "Dad was particular about the materials he used—we had a redwood bathroom. Of course, an environmentalist can't really have a redwood bathroom anymore," Rowan smiles.

"Sometimes I'd have a burst of envy for a friend with a normal, split-level wood-frame house. My parents listened carefully to my arguments about how we should move. Eventually I would argue my way out of the idea."

—Rowan Swanson

ABOVE LEFT: **ROWAN**
ABOVE RIGHT, TOP: **ALEIDRIA AND ANJA**
ABOVE RIGHT, BOTTOM: **SYLVIA**

The children's bedrooms doubled as guest rooms whenever, Rowan says, "the guests were older than us." The family shared a single bathroom, but "it was no problem. It helped me learn about timing and schedules. Sharing helps promote family values."

Rowan, who is a senior at the University of Iowa, says his current dream is to build a house with his friends, where they can all live together, and have lots of visitors.

SYLVIA

Sylvia was born in a tent—a big, plastic dome that her parents built—in a rural community in New Zealand where her American parents moved in their search for the perfect place. We met her in Seattle, where she moved after college to spend the year working as a radio producer.

For the first two years of Sylvia's life, the family didn't have running water or electricity. They did laundry on an old washboard and cultivated a large organic garden. Because she grew up around neighbors "who didn't spoil their kids," her childhood seemed normal to her at the time. She and her three siblings stayed home for schooling until her parents started a school. When she was twelve her family moved to a new community, and Sylvia opted to attend public high school.

Sylvia's parents both quit their careers because they believe that children need two parents at home. Sylvia reflects, "I can honestly say that I prefer having my father around the house to having my father's money. My dad taught me carpentry, and car repair. It's more precious than money."

When she was fourteen, Sylvia got a bedroom of her own in her neighbor's house. Others her age in their community had their own little rustic cabins. Just before she graduated high school the New Zealand government changed its free education policy, so she took out $7,000 of loans to get through college and then paid the loans off in one year, while she was working in Seattle. "It would have been nice if they had money for me," she says, "but in a way I feel glad that I did it myself."

Sylvia is contemplating the options for her future. None of her siblings leads an ostentatious lifestyle, and two of them are homesteading. Now that land is so expensive, sometimes she's disappointed that her parents were ethically opposed to private ownership of land. "Because they had this ethic they donated their land to the community, and we each have to start from scratch." If she raises children, ideally she'd return to a rural area.

"Everyone at the school wore uniforms, so there wasn't much competition. I had after-school jobs, and made my own money. I was aware that others had more, and I never felt quite in fashion, but we were all farmers' kids, so it was nothing like kids in the city here. I grew up valuing education and travel, but not clothes. I don't remember feeling deprived, not materially. "Many parents at the new community were involved in a personal growth kick. We weren't abused in any way, but there were times when the parents were so absorbed in their own problems that they didn't pay us much attention. That's the only deprivation I felt, but I guess it wasn't much." —Sylvia Jones

"It's hard to pull kids out of consumerism once you're in it. Kids are crying out to be outside more. Kids are fascinated with nature. Everybody loves to be on a raft, or play in a swamp or hang out with the goats. I think if you don't have nature, you need a video game to fascinate you."

ALEIDRIA AND ANJA

Aleidria shared a room with her sister, but she didn't understand her, as she explains at right.

The bedroom they shared was like a long, wide hall that their parents walked through to get to theirs. They had two twin beds on opposite sides of the room and they would often rearrange their beds or switch sides of the room. They argued about who got which side of the room. Aleidria can't remember "why it was so important other than just having something to argue about, something to stake our claims on."

On good days, after school the girls ran across the length of their room. Aleidria would try to snap the back of Anja's training bra and Anja would try to squirt hairspray in Aleidria's eyes.

"When our friends came over we played a favorite game: we lined our beds up parallel and we shot each other over to the other bed by using our legs as a catapult. I remember how I would fly through the air to the other bed thinking that there was no place in the world that a girl could feel more free. Other times I would sweat in loathing at night as she snored away on her side of the room. I would try everything to shut it out. I would count out loud, shove my fingers in my ears, and sing songs to myself.

When I grew up I went to live on a ship, where I realized that if you don't have space in your head, you crave more physical space. If you can't learn to make a home in your own head you might find yourself sweating and loathing your neighbor for their lights, their noise, even the shrubs they have in their yard."

Aleidria now sleeps alone in a room and likes it, but she's fond of her memories. She says, "I wouldn't trade the moments we shared flying across our room together for all the space in the world."

"She was taller than me and interested in watching her silhouette in her bikini on the wall of our room after school. Sometimes we would bond by watching television when we were not supposed to. In fact, that was the most frequent time that we bonded—when we were doing things we were not supposed to." —Aleidria

SHANNON AND MATT FEDEROFF
ISABELLA, KERIAN, LIAM, NOAH, TATIANA, THADDEUS, PAVEL, AND ZOE
Built 1999

AREA:
2,100 sq. ft.

COST:
$28,000 land; well, septic system, and construction: $112,000

UTILITY COSTS (MONTHLY):
$90 (electric), no gas; well water

LOCATION:
Vail, Arizona

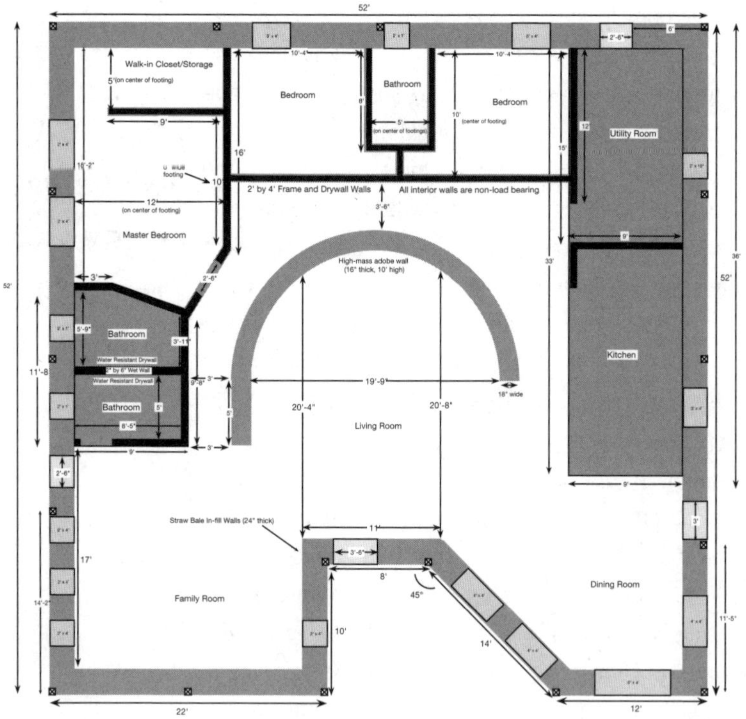

According to columnist David Brooks, natalists

"are more spiritually, emotionally, and physically invested in their homes than in any other sphere of life, having concluded that parenthood is the most enriching and elevating thing they can do."[5] Matt Federoff is happy to identify as a natalist, and adds to that definition that a natalist is someone who "embraces and encourages life in all of its forms." He says he is an environmentalist who loves human beings, and adds, "Living a simple, modest, family-centered life is gentle on the environment."

Over the last fourteen years Matt's wife Shannon has given birth to eight children. Despite their large population, Matt has evidence that his family uses less water and energy than a typical family of four. Citing Saint Francis, he explains the family's environmentalism stems from their Catholic dedication to frugality and modesty. The energy efficiency of their home stems from fairly good passive-solar orientation, superinsulated straw-bale walls, and R-40 fiberglass-insulated ceiling, solar water and radiant floor heating, and rainwater catchment. In addition, they buy very little new, own no video games, and drive less than the average family because Shannon, a former public school teacher, schools the kids at home.

The front door opens to their classroom, a 220-square-foot room that includes a comfortable reading loft for the older kids only, with a ladder too difficult for the younger kids to climb. Left of the door is a bathroom, so the children can run straight to it from outside without tracking dirt across the house. High on the wall, above the door to the bathroom, is 9

ABOVE: THE FEDEROFFS AT HOME
ABOVE RIGHT: FEDEROFF FLOOR PLAN

WHEN THEIR OLDEST DAUGHTER TURNED TEN, THE FEDEROFFS DIVIDED ONE OF THE BEDROOMS INTO TWO, TO SEPARATE THE GIRLS AND BOYS.

by 4 feet of schoolbook storage that requires a ladder to reach.

The classroom flows into the living room, a semicircular area that is marked by sofas with patterned upholstery (to hide stains), and a round carpet, and encompassed by a curved adobe partition wall that rises 8 feet high toward the 12-foot ceiling, allowing both air and the shout of a child in need to flow easily. The living room is open to the kitchen and to the dining room, which has a 10-foot-long table and two long benches to match. The house was designed to allow an easy sight line for a cooking parent who must keep an eye on the children.

With a design inspired by Don Aslett's book, *Let Your House Do the Housework*, the large utility room houses guinea pigs, a carpentry workbench, cleaning supplies, and the washing machine, and includes 12 feet by 5 feet of wide shelves, built for twelve plastic 2-by-3-foot tubs, with labels like "infant" and "boy church clothes" that hold extra clothes. The Federoffs believe that having no hidden storage and therefore knowing exactly how much they have keeps them honest about how much of creation they are taking for themselves.

Well over two-thirds of the house is common space, which was a problem when the Federoffs sought bank financing. They had planned to build just 1,600 square feet, but were required to add an extra 500 square feet to obtain a mortgage, because a bank won't finance a "too-small" house it doesn't believe can be resold. An appraiser told Matt that modern houses are "designed for a blended family. It's assumed people don't want to be near each other, so there's a lot of private space in the corners that people run to as soon as they get home." Matt is disturbed by that trend. Shannon prefers that her children spend their time in the company of others.

To that end, the Federoffs started out with just two bedrooms in their house and, when their oldest daughter turned ten, divided one of the bedrooms into two, to separate the girls and boys. The children's bedrooms each have a bank of metal lockers (with locks for those children who want them) and four closets, each one uniquely decorated to suit its owner. A narrow spiral staircase leads to a steel loft with a 5-foot-6-inch ceiling furnished with three beds. Each bed has drawers underneath. The girls have divided up dominion over the wall space, so that each has a

"When they upset each other, I tell them that life is about other people and people annoy each other. They'll be annoyed by their college roommate, and by their spouse, one day and by everyone who is important in their life. This is how we grow. As we rub against each other, we become polished."

—Shannon Federoff

section to decorate. The older boys have a shelf for their tiny warrior dolls that hangs on the wall opposite the loft, out of the younger boys' reach. The baby sleeps near his parents in an "apartment" crib, narrow enough to easily pass through the parents' bedroom door to the classroom each day. Shannon, who has enough children to generalize, says that by eighteen months children want to leave the parents' room and sleep with their siblings. Currently, the two-year-old sleeps with his four-year-old brother.

In retrospect, the two parents wish they had planned for a quiet nook "where two adults can have a conversation." Their fourteen-year-old daughter may agree—although she obviously enjoys her sisters' company, she seemed a little wistful as I told her the story of a boy her age who built his own bedroom in his backyard. A small addition is planned for the northeast side of the house, for Shannon's grandmother, who is expected to come live with them soon. Above the addition will be a loft, where the older girls may make a quiet retreat. Currently, the younger children say they find a place for themselves in their bed, in a nearby creosote grove, and, for one, in a huge hole the children dug in the backyard and roofed with plywood. The four-year-old suggests "covering your ears" if you need some time alone, but generally the younger kids associate time alone with punishment, not pleasure.

Considering that eight children shared one large space with their parents, the photographer, and the interviewer, the constant patter of little feet and chatter of little voices was not loud—certainly no louder than the sound of a television. I wondered if this is the background noise level people are trying to achieve when they leave on an unwatched television.

BRIGITTE MINER, ELYSE DICKIE, LARRY CHASE
Built 1994, addition 1999

AREA:
About 400 "round feet" plus 250 sq. ft. upstairs and a 40-sq.-ft. playhouse outside

NUMBER OF OCCUPANTS:
2–3

LAND COST:
Free

CONSTRUCTION COST
$5,000 including family's living expenses during construction

UTILITY COSTS (MONTHLY:
$15

LOCATION:
Rural Oregon

The dreams started when Brigitte was pregnant

with Elyse. Dreams of mud houses, hand-built, no bricks, no mortar, just mud and hands. The same dream came every night.

Brigitte asked old friends, new acquaintances, everyone she met, what they knew about mud houses. Her husband started to think she was crazy. "This is about the time," she recalls, "I first felt my inner strength."

Three years later she found herself divorced, with her young daughter, a car, and $4,000. At a welcome-back party in Oregon, Brigitte, as usual, started a conversation about hand-built mud houses. "Go visit Ianto Evans," a stranger told her. "He has wild ideas like that." Two weeks later, Brigitte met Ianto, and convinced him to teach his first workshop about "cob," the earthen building technique indigenous to his native

ABOVE LEFT: **ELYSE AND HER MOTHER BUILT "THE BURROW," A COOL SPOT IN THE MIDDLE OF A VERY HOT GARDEN. INSIDE, A BOOKSHELF IS SCULPTED IN THE SHAPE OF A GIGANTIC BANANA SLUG. THE FOUNDATION IS CINDER BLOCKS, THE WALLS COB, AND THE ROOF IS "LIVING": IT'S PLYWOOD, COVERED WITH TAR PAPER, THEN WITH A WATERPROOF MEMBRANE, THEN SOIL, AND PLANTED WITH GARDEN WEEDS AND BULBS.**

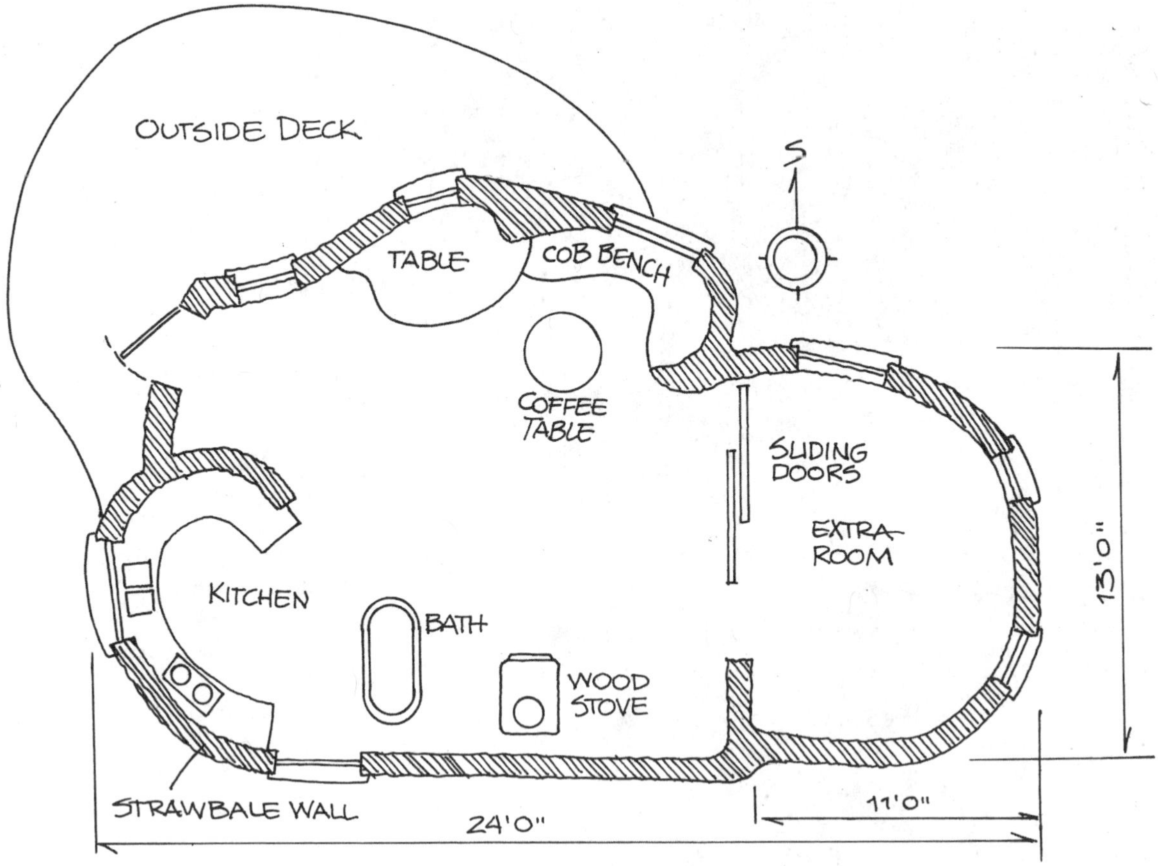

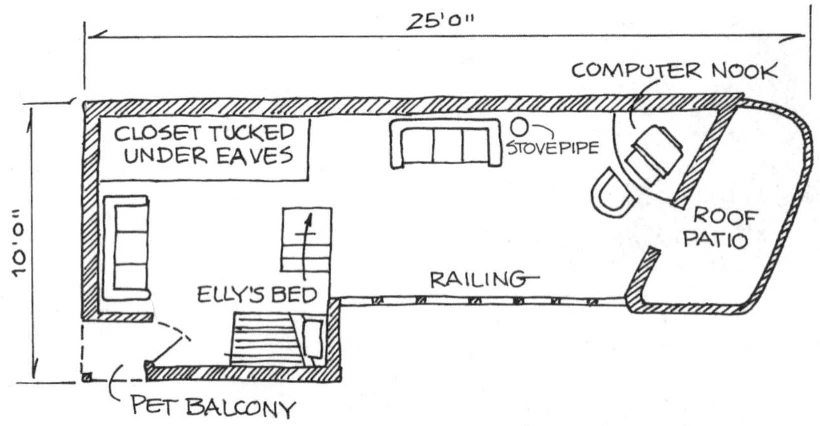

BRIGITTE'S FLOOR PLAN

Wales, which he really didn't know too much about, yet. "He used us as guinea pigs. Everything developed out of that first workshop."

Brigitte immediately began looking for a place where she could build her own cob home, and homeschool her daughter. Her parents invited her to live on their ten-acre woodlot. Skeptical about cob, they suggested she park a trailer on their land, and while they brought up Elyse, Brigitte could resume the career she had prior to marriage. This was not Brigitte's plan at all.

"My father was a great motivator," she recalls. "He said the cob house had to be finished by fall, or I'd be living in a trailer. I believed that if I failed, every dream that I'd ever had, everything I felt so strongly inside me, was not true. So I worked hard. I loved that time."

Brigitte made a papier-mâché model of her future home. She made two little dolls and put them inside. On her birthday, May 5, 1994, she "took a stick in the dirt, and drew out the foundation, just how I wanted it, about like the model," and then she started to dig along the line she'd drawn. The next day, she filled the trench with rocks from a nearby quarry, and then began stacking larger rocks to build a low stem wall. The next week she began to sculpt lumps of earth mixed with straw into walls. Meanwhile, Elyse spent her days with her grandmother wandering in the forest, picking blackberries, and then coming home to play in the mud.

Two months and 5,120 (she counted) lumps of cob later, with the walls almost finished, her parents stopped doubting. "I was standing on a little protrusion of cob, high up on the wall, still building. My father suddenly realized how strong this material is." Soon her mother, father, and boyfriend all joined in to build the roof and door frames—"Lucky for me," says Brigitte, "since I didn't even know how to pound a nail straight." In September 1995, Brigitte and Elyse moved into their cob cottage.

Two rooms were added to the house in 1997: a storage/art room on the west side (which now seems "bigger than we need"), and a loft with a bedroom upstairs for Elyse, complete with a tiny balcony where her guinea pigs live. Where the stovepipe exits the house, under the slanted ceiling of the loft, it warms two no-standing-allowed nooks: on one side is a couch for reading, and on the other a computer desk. Next to the desk a window provides passage to a tiny sundeck on the roof. The open loft allows Brigitte to throw items upstairs instead of climbing up herself.

Downstairs, the bathtub is conveniently located near the woodstove and the kitchen, so the hot water is all in one place: "It's a treat in winter to be able to warm up by the woodstove right after a bath," her boyfriend Larry reports. The kitchen features nooks and niches in the cob for spices and grains. The window over the sink opens to the compost pile, so it's a convenient toss from the cutting board, out to the pile.

Reflecting on the evolution of her house, Brigitte says,

"I'm different from many people. I just take the first step without seeing the whole plan. When I need something, it will come. For instance, when we needed a lot of hands to move rocks, visitors showed up. I learned to trust the inner feeling and the house turned out all right. It's about having faith rather than being mental. I didn't dare think about money, because I had so little. The day we moved in, we had spent our last pennies, so it was time to look for work."

Brigitte found work that takes her away just a few days a week. On those days, Elyse studies geography with her Bompa (grandfather), has wild horseback adventures with her Biss Biss (grandmother), or visits friends from her home schooling group.

At nine years old, Elyse and her mother built Elyse her own cob house, just large enough for two small children to sleep in. At ten, Elyse began attending to her own fortune, making mail-order, ready-to-assemble silk "flowerina" fairy dolls. "I saw them in a bookstore, being sold for $8, just pipe cleaners and a few silk flower petals, and I said, 'I can do that!'" In 2000 her business grossed about $6,000 per six months (she prefers to work just half the year). Elyse now employs her mother and grandmother part-time. I asked Brigitte if Elyse wants things that she can't afford.

"Sometimes, but she doesn't see television commercials, so she's pretty content. It's easier for a parent to make these choices when children are young, or before they are born. If kids are brought up on plastic toys and too much stuff, after a certain point it's hard for them to change."

Originally, Brigitte's parents insisted that this would be a temporary living arrangement only. "My dad said, 'Just two years.' But now that Larry is moving to take a job two hours away, Dad says how much he'll miss him. It's not like my dad to express emotion. For years he was hoping I'd pursue that all-important career, but eventually both of my parents grew to respect my lifestyle and choices. They began to see the results of raising my daughter with the 'Less is more' attitude. Now my dad talks as if he'd like us to stay until he dies!"

"This life is a spiritual choice. You reduce your needs because you have something more fulfilling inside. But be careful. I've known people who suddenly make a spiritual discovery, and they tell their kids, 'Now we're going to go to church, or to meditate all day.' If you change your child's lifestyle suddenly, drying up the child's options, they will resent you. That said, it's fine for every parent to quietly go in that direction." —Brigitte

EPILOGUE:

Elyse is now sixteen, has a driver's license, and is a lifeguard. She is still home-schooled, but attends college classes as well. Brigitte and Larry got married. They still live in the cottage, and it remains their dream home.

"I went to San Luis, in fall, and got boxes of potatoes and flour for bread, and dry grains. We grew corn and beans. We had apples and peaches, and I dried the fruit myself. We slaughtered a pig and smoked it, and we had lard and ham all winter. I hunted deer, and fished. We had hives for honey, and we made our own brooms, soap, and candles. You can still do a lot of these things yourself. I still use soap made from lard and lye to wash my blankets, and ash to keep the bugs off my squash." —Carmen

ABOVE: **CARMEN AND HER GREAT-GRANDCHILD**

Carmen Velarde has been a fireplace builder for sixty-eight years. She and her husband have built rooms onto their own home, and as a *mayordoma* of her church she helps with the replastering of the church's exterior walls, a tradition that is at least 200, perhaps 400 years old. She became so famous for her fireplaces that she was twice an exhibit at the Smithsonian Institution in Washington, D.C., building a fireplace and *horno* on the mall in front of a crowd. A psychiatrist on a museum panel asked her if it wasn't "out of insecurity as a woman" that she had become a builder. She replied that he obviously didn't know anything about her culture. "In my town alone six women are trained as fireplace builders."

The descendant of Apache, Taos Pueblo, and Spanish people, Carmen inherited a way of life developed by people who stayed in the same area for generations and centuries. Her grandmother was born in northern New Mexico, in a house with fourteen rooms, built around a courtyard, and shared by what modern Americans might call four families, and that they called one. Her grandmother answered and encouraged her questions. "In this way I learned how to work, and grew to believe I could do anything. She taught me the old ways, and took me to the Kiva to learn the Indian ways. In this way, I grew up fearless."

At five Carmen began learning mud work from her grandfather, who took her to work with him everyday. A few years later, Carmen's father fell ill with cancer. The oldest of nine siblings, Carmen took on the task of feeding her siblings (see her comment, left).

Carmen spent her teenage years building, and gained a reputation as a hard worker, which won her eleven marriage proposals. "Some of these men had maids, and didn't want me to work, but I wanted a partnership," so she married her good friend Ernest and, aided by her sisters, started work on her own house. The largest expense was a $600 well, dug years after the house was started, when the *acequia*, the water canal near her house, stopped running as reliably.

[Q] What do you suggest for other people?

[A] Start with a single room, 16 or 20 feet by 40 feet, and close it in well before winter. Later, you can divide it, into a kitchen, a bedroom, and when the kids are bigger you can divide the girls and boys.

A modern couch was once in Carmen's living room, but when her boys broke its springs she replaced it with solid adobe bancos, large enough for a guest to sleep on, and with storage underneath. "When my kids were teenagers they said, 'Mother, why don't you get a regular couch, a new one?' I told them there'd be more children soon." Twenty-two grandchildren and twenty-eight great-grandchildren later, the bancos are still in use.

Until they were ready for school, Carmen's four children came with her to work, where they played in the mud. She says that getting your hands dirty works better than reading books, if you want to learn to build. Because "children grow so fast you have to do something by the time they start growing," she bought each of her children an acre before they were teenagers and told them, "Start making adobe bricks. You'll be married soon." Ernest taught them plumbing and electrical work and all three of her sons became builders.

Her sons lived at home when they were first married, while they built their houses, but her daughter and son-in-law opted for a new trailer, and a mortgage. Later they moved to an adobe house two blocks from Carmen and Ernest. "Those trailers are usually dull and broken before the mortgage is paid off," she laments, and adds: "A mother wants to interfere, naturally, but the secret to my success with my family is that I have so many interests of my own—I'm on the chamber of commerce, and I paint, and volunteer at the battered women's shelter—that I don't have time to get on their nerves." Currently Carmen and Ernest have four children and two grandchildren living within two blocks of them, on the acres they gave them so many years ago.

THE FOX HAVEN RETREAT CABIN

12

Make a Room of Your Own

I hold this to be the highest task of a bond between two people: that each should stand guard over the solitude of the other.... Only those are the true sharings which rhythmically interrupt periods of deep isolation. —RAINER MARIA RILKE

SUSAN MUDD OF THE MILWAUKEE, WISCONSIN, GROUP, Citizens for a Better Environment, was relating to a conference of city planners and environmentalists one of the more surprising points researchers discovered when they asked the question, "Why don't people ride the bus?" They found: "Women love their cars because it's the only place in their lives where they can think, sing, cry, control the music, and talk to their kids one-on-one, undistracted."[1]

The automobile currently serves not only as a dressing table, a dinette, a telephone booth, a home theater, and of course as a form of transportation, but it is also the modern boudoir. I wondered whether Henry Ford or Virginia Woolf ever anticipated this development. In 1928, about a year after the 15,000,000th Model T Ford rolled off the assembly line, Mrs. Woolf composed and delivered a speech that would later be titled and published as *A Room of One's Own*, in which she discussed the effect her own, sudden inheritance of a modest but guaranteed income had had on her own writing, and predicted, "There will be women Shakespeares in the future" just as soon as women have the freedom of reliable income, and a simple room they can retreat to, that is theirs alone.

Wondering whether the word "car" can be found on the pages of her book, I reread *A Room of One's Own* and was struck most of all by the paragraphs, as long as my forearm, built of sentences that snake through layers of images, creeping down the page, decorated with a few commas, terminating at the half dozen periods allotted for each chapter, and I recalled a conversation I was lucky to have with the venerable author Jane Jacobs,[2] who said that the main change in writing in the last forty years is that sentences have become so short, there's hardly an idea per sentence, rarely more, a situation she attributed to the speed of computer word processing: Handwriting and typing encourage the author to think out a full idea before she begins to compose, while word processing leads to just throwing words on the page, and sometimes

"It is a cottage of quite a peculiar kind, for it is only ten feet square and less than seven feet high, and as I did not decide to fix it in any definite place I did not choose the site by divination as usual. The walls are of rough plastered earth and the roof is of thatch. All the joints are hinged with metal so that if the situation no longer pleases me I can easily take it down and transport it elsewhere. And this can be done with very little labor, for the whole will only fill two cart-loads, and beyond the small wage of the carters nothing else is needed[3]."

—Kamo no Chomei, Japanese hermit, circa 1210

neglecting to return to fix them up later. Word processing shortens sentences. But I think our modern brevity is especially a product of the time/space conundrum: indeed I thought, reading *A Room of One's Own*, "Who has the time anymore to read, much less write such long sentences?"

So even though we have more than one bedroom per person, and many of us have incomes as reliable as incomes can be, it's still very common to hear adults complain, "I just don't have space for myself." How will we find this space that we crave?

Making a Retreat

WHEN WALLS MAKE A SPACE LARGER

Women complain widely of the no-space phenomenon, and this chapter is prejudiced toward them, but men also suffer. Architect Ross Chapin echoes the opinions of many when he laments, "The modern house which has neither basement nor attic is a prescription for divorce. Men used to have a workshop to escape to, but now there's nowhere to go." Some people blame the open plan, which gives a strong sense of open space by allowing people to live in a small area while they look out on most of the rest of the house, but sacrifices the intimacy of tiny rooms, and requires subtle understanding between people if they want to share the space and engage in different activities. Most North Americans need strong visual cues—doors, or walls, and distance—to be able to take time alone.

So, some people are retrofitting their open plans, or houses with many rooms but no room for the self, by physically creating a room of one's own. "ROOOs" usually share the following characteristics:

- They are on the edge of the domestic space, away from the center of activity.
- They allow the inhabitant audio control, or as Kathleen Dean Moore says, "Control to choose which voices we will hear."
- They have a focal point—a large window or a tiny "Zen" opening, a desk, or a shrine—that directs the inhabitant to look inside at an image, or outside at a view, but, conversely...
- ...they are hidden, or semihidden, and it is difficult for the inhabitant to be seen, even if she is able to look out.
- They provide security for the inhabitant—security for possessions, and a shape and small size that makes the body feel safe and protected. They may be cloistered, and so assure the mind that what will be seen in the location is predictable.
- They require or encourage a ritual when approaching or settling into the place.
- They are often beautiful.

The private car fills these qualifications to a surprising extent: it is, almost by definition, on the edge of things, since it exists to provide passage between edges; the stereo provides audio control; tinted windows allow looking out, but not in; the trunk in particular is very secure, and there are locking doors on the cab; the pattern of finding keys, opening the door, buckling the belt, adjusting the mirrors provide a ritual of settling down into the space; and designers, restorers, and some drivers work to make them beautiful. But perhaps you don't want to live in your car.

A final quality of the ROOO is debated: is it a static location, or a set of materials that can be easily moved and erected? For some, a particular location where they return regularly, either on a whim or as part of a particular ritual, provides the sense of place that settles their mind. For others, a ROOO that is mobile like a car works fine.

SHALL WE RUN AWAY?

Kamo no Chomei hid his cottage "deep in the fastnesses of Mount Hino." He retired to "the shrilling of the evening cicada" and was inspired by nature around him toward metaphor: "the snow as it piles up and melts seems like an allegory of our evil Karma." Architectural theorist Ann Cline compared eastern mystics, who embraced nature as inspiration, with medieval Christian monks who rejected nature as a distraction from God, and with some eighteenth-century English gentlemen who, instead of escaping to a small hut of their own, installed bearded, old men—"ornamental hermits"—on their estates. "Nothing, it was felt, could give such delight to the eye as the spectacle of an aged person with a long gray beard and a goatish rough robe, doddering about amongst the discomforts and pleasures of Nature."[4]

Modern westerners have mostly embraced the eastern view of nature as inspiration. But what about the "ornamental hermit"? Plenty of weekend getaway cabins see their owners just a few times a year. Is it worth it to have a ROOO if you never go there? And what of the environmental impact of so many of us building our ROOOs out in nature that, as Kathleen Dean Moore writes, "No matter how far you go, 'there's no away away'"?[5]

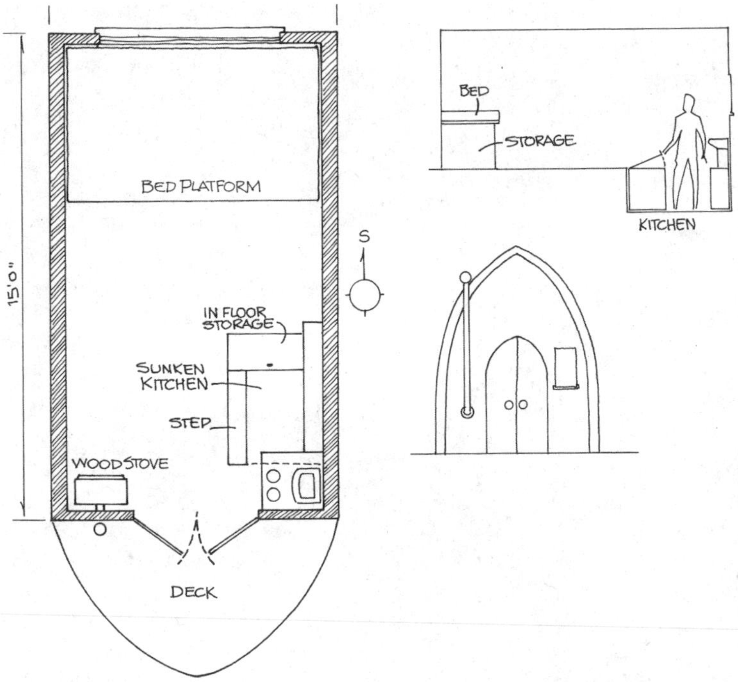

TWELVE RESIDENTS OF A SPIRITUAL COMMUNITY IN LAMA, NEW MEXICO, ROTATE USE OF THIS 140-SQUARE-FOOT HERMITAGE AMONG THEMSELVES, AND RENT IT OUT TO VISITORS. BECAUSE THE AREA IS DIVIDED INTO THREE DISTINCT SPACES, AT FOUR DISTINCT LEVELS: RAISED BED, SUNKEN KITCHEN, AND WOODSTOVE/LIVING ON THE "MAIN" FLOOR, THE AREA SEEMS LARGE AND IS VERY FUNCTIONAL. THERE'S AMPLE STORAGE UNDER THE BED AND A PANTRY/CABINET SUNK INTO THE FLOOR NEXT TO THE KITCHEN THAT KEEPS MILK AND CHEESE COOL DURING MOST OF THE YEAR. AN OUTSIDE DECK IN FRONT MIRRORS THE INTERIOR SPACE AND FACADE.

Is there a way to find this space without leaving home?

The Home Refuge

A CORNER OF THE GARDEN

Anyone with a yard has room for a tiny retreat, a hammock hung in a tree, or chaise lounge behind a screen.

Architect Rick McDermott was asked by client—a doctor in charge of a ward of babies born prematurely—to design an addition to his house, and to landscape the gardens. Rick thought about the demands of his client's occupation and decided to give him a gift: a simple place where he could rest, undisturbed. His crew installed a comfortable bench on the edge of the larger backyard garden, enclosed by vines and bushes that allow in winter sunlight, and open to a narrow view of a small pond. "We wanted to give him the opposite of a hospital environment. He can read there, or he can just sit. As long as he gets out there, he will relax."

"Getting out there" is usually the main challenge; giving yourself a specific comfortable destination can help. Tony's T-Houses offers simple wooden structures, made of Douglas-fir and redwood, with a durable fabric roof that people typically place in their backyards for use as a meditation,

LINDA MATHEWS IN HER T HOUSE

prayer, exercise, or guest room. The kit is built in California, or in Indonesia, and the basic T-house at 6 by 6 feet or 6 by 8 feet requires only four level foundation stones as its base. Tony Gwilliam, the company's founder, says,

"I had lived in Bali, so I had spent considerable time sleeping and watching the clouds and chatting in their traditional, airy, bamboo structures, seeing the stars, waking up to nature. Back in California, I was working at the computer too much, and I needed some balance, a break from my work. Everything here is so time and money oriented, we tend to overlook other things, so I decided to build a 'teahouse' for myself, but with American materials, something that would wear well, that would last, just for myself. I didn't mean it to be a business.

"Other people wanted them, so I built a few designs. I use some hardwoods, which will last for a hundred years, but it's a precious material so I use them in precious ways. If people move they can take the structure with them. Our philosophy is 'Do the maximum in any space.' The kotastu table is an excellent example; have that, and need no other furniture. The idea also is each person can have one, and if two want to join together there's their bigger house, or if twenty want to join together.... Everything opens to the outside, so in a rural area you have a maximum view of space with a minimum construction of space.

"Most of the people who buy our T houses are women who want a space for themselves. Women with kids don't have any space in their house—it's all taken over. These women need spiritual space, psychic space. I myself move around currently and my Airstream trailer works as a T-house for me, so I don't need it so much."

With a retreat in your backyard, you can leave the dirty dishes, ringing phone, and stacks of bills in the house and in fifteen seconds be somewhere else.

RETREAT INSIDE

Inside your home there is some corner where you can create a little space, just large enough for you. Consider putting the washing machine in a shed and moving into your laundry room, or taking over a walk-in closet.

Consider creating a space that can easily be converted to a peaceful retreat, and then quickly converted back.

In his own small home, architect Jack Baker placed an antique twenty-eight-pane, 4-by-5½-foot window between the din-

ing room and the dojo/study so light can pass through but a sense of sacred separation is achieved. When the altar in the dojo is closed, the cushions are stowed away, and the hinged desks are open, the room is a home office, but when the altar opens, the desks close and the dojo returns to a state of calm, with any distracting paperwork hidden inside its walls.

IS BEAUTY A HUMAN RIGHT?

Household shrines show that a "room" can be created without extra floor space. Beauty that focuses the attention away from everyday habits can be as apparently minor as a picture on a wall, or a bell hung in a tree, but if an inhabitant treats the view, or the sound, as a resting point, it can serve as room. Women (and men) who find their time is swallowed up in attention to others, if they can't "take" time for themselves, may be able to "give" time to God, or a ritual practice. A shrine, a clock or a calendar that reminds you to pray or meditate can be as relaxing as a physical room. Even if you have a whole room to yourself, a ritual, triggered by a schedule or by a sign you watch for, will make your retreat room useful, instead of ornamental. Kris's story shows that even if you live alone, you may find you need a room of your own.

A few months before Kris Barney moved into her new one-bedroom Virginia apartment, she decided to make the focus of her home her yoga and meditation practice. Her regular job absorbed most of her energy and

Chet Phillips and Debbie Hawkins, in anticipation of a baby, built Chet a 6-by-8-foot minioffice by adding two short walls opposite one corner of their living room. The walls that separate the office from the living room are lined with bookshelves, and tightly packed with books, which increases sound insulation. A window is on the exterior wall and a computer screen is on one end of the rectangle. Chet plans to be the primary caregiver for the child, but since Debbie only works three or four days a week, he anticipates that on her days off, his ability to shut himself away in a fairly soundproof office for a few hours each day will be a joy to his mind.

CHET'S OFFICE

A SHRINE CAN BE AS RELAXING AS A PHYSICAL ROOM.

creativity, so she wanted home to be a sanctuary. After reflecting on how she had once lived in one room for four years, the solution became clear: She put her yoga mats, blocks, pillows, and blankets in the bedroom, with two small tower shelves in the corners to hold small special objects. She added nothing else. "So the space is very clear and quiet. I close the door to the rest of the world, and I have my space."

Her family and friends were surprised when they found Kris had moved her bed to the main room. "I felt resistance in myself as well, because a bed doesn't belong in a living room. But I actually prefer sleeping out here. The bedroom was a little claustrophobic, as a bedroom. I've been happy in a studio apartment, and this is similar, except I have my own beautiful meditation space next door."

At Thanksgiving Kris hosted twelve guests. Everyone loved the space, especially the toddlers who could go wild in the yoga room because there was nothing to break, and then return to the living room and entertain the grown-ups with a game of "climb the mountain" on the bed. Kris says, "I know the way I've set up my place has improved my health. My home feels whole, balanced, and integrated."

Some of us blame each other—our children, our spouses, our colleagues—for the lack of sacred solitude in our lives. Many creative people—Alice Walker and Doris Lessing come to mind—decided they had to divorce if they were to produce masterpieces. Can we help each other grow in solitude, without separating permanently?

THE COMPARTMENTALIZED FAMILY LIFE

In an historical museum in Korea I saw a diorama of an old, thatched house. It showed three rooms: a man's room on the right (with a male doll, who appeared to be writing), a woman's room on the left (with a woman doll banging clothes with two short wooden poles—an equivalent of ironing), and a shared room in between them. Outside in the courtyard was food storage, including a kimchi jar, and a cookstove that could also heat up the house via a flue that ran underneath the raised floors. I was reminded of this scene when I heard Paul and Raquel's story:

Paul and Raquel live next door to each other, but in the same house. This is their solution to what they feared were "irreconcilable differences." Paul, a meticulous draftsman, lived by himself for sixteen years before he and Raquel, a gregarious schoolteacher, married. Within a year their different ideas about cleanliness provoked problems. "Raquel convinced me that I probably had Obsessive-Compulsive Disorder, so I went to a therapist who didn't really agree—his desk was very neat—so now I say "liking order is not a disorder." Paul's clean bill of mental health didn't solve their problems.

After a year of fighting, Paul suggested they divide their 1,250-square-foot house and each live in part of it. Raquel got the two bedrooms and the full bathroom: the couple put a small kitchen in one of the bedrooms, and they added a gate so Raquel can easily go from her car to the sliding glass door of the master bedroom. Paul got the open plan living/dining room/ kitchen area, the utility closet, the office nook, and the half-bath. They added a Murphy bed to one end of the living room. Paul uses an outdoor shower in warmer months, often showers at his gym, and in a pinch visits Raquel's shower. They converted the hall between the two parts of the house into a closet for Paul.

"At first I was heartbroken—I didn't admit to my family what we were doing—it wasn't my dream to live like this," Raquel remembers, "but it's been three years, and I see the benefits: I come home to my place, and I can dump my stuff on a table without anyone glaring at me. Most nights, I go over to Paul's. He cooks dinner, and usually he's happy to clean up without my help. It's like a date at a restaurant. When we have guests, they stay in my room and I go stay with him. I've started to learn guitar, which I don't think I could have ever done if I knew that Paul could hear me practice. I still think he's a control freak, but I no longer hold that against him. I have to admit we're getting along very well."

THE FRIENDLY CREATION OF SACRED SPACE

Jane Jacobs, who faulted the computer for the shrinking of the modern sentence, also credited her husband for guarding her solitude, so that she could write. Some couples and cooperative households take a "word fast," and spend a day in silence together, turning off the phone and the television, avoiding eye contact and supporting each other's deepening thoughts, from afar. Some people do this alone, but among others, by announcing their intention. We can learn from people like James whose ability to focus is so strong, they require very little physical space (see above).

If you haven't yet developed a superior ability to focus, you

James is a technical writer, and all he needs is his laptop and an Internet connection to work, so he has no office, and instead lets his partner use the spare bedroom for hers. He has one bookshelf that takes up about 5 square feet of floor space. Otherwise his "office" is wherever he sits or stands, plus the support under his computer. When he needs a wider space he goes to work at a coffee shop.

A SHARED HOUSE FOR A COUPLE FROM A KOREAN HISTORICAL MUSEUM

might practice by spending time alone. "No woman, especially no mother, will ever get any free time alone, unless she steals it," proclaims Deborah Brady, who takes her time two weeks a year, when she stays at home while her husband and son visit relatives or camp. "I try not to tell even my friends that I'm here, so I can hole up and find myself at home." Or perhaps you'll take your time by escaping to an island—just don't build anything there.

For fifteen years every summer near the end of June, Carmen Mills has spent a week on an empty beach on a small island. "I don't know why everyone goes to the other side of the island. I'm just lucky they do." For the first seven years she went with friends, but on the eighth year her companion suddenly couldn't come, and she decided to go alone. "What a surprise treat it was," she remembers. "Now, each time summer comes, a little voice tempts me, 'Let's invite so-and-so!' I have to be disciplined and say 'No' to myself—or I guess it's 'Yes' to myself and 'No' to the voice. When I arrive, and my feet touch the sand, I remember why I came alone."

The ritual begins with a seven-hour bus ride, a short hitchhike, a ferry, a water taxi, and a two-mile hike. As she passes the familiar signposts, the layers of her regular life begin to fall off. Carmen is learning what to bring with her: light, dehydrated food, jugs to fill with water at the outdoor spigot of an empty house, a small tent, a sleeping bag, and maybe her bicycle. "At first I took art supplies, stationery, books, my journal.... Now I'm down to one novel and my journal. Maybe next year I won't bring the novel. I love being able to lift with my own hands everything I need."

She buries her watch—which she'll need to catch the bus home—at the bottom of her bag, and lives instead by the long tides of the shallow beach. Only once she looked at it: in the middle of the night when she saw the edge of the waves were inches from her tent. She dug out her watch to compare the time with the tide schedule, which told her the tide had turned, and she didn't have to move her tent.

"It takes several days before I really settle in. The first two days I mostly sleep and cry and I wonder, 'Why isn't this fun?' Then the high-frequency motor in my head shuts off and I slow down to a natural pace. It takes serious effort to stop trying to do anything. My current goal is to unitask: If I read, or I walk, that's all I do. I don't cook dinner and watch the sunset at the same time, but do one and then the other. If I could give anyone a gift, it would be the gift of a week alone."

ALICIA ALLISON

AREA:
154 "round feet," plus access to a kitchen in the main house

INTENDED NUMBER OF OCCUPANTS:
1

COST OF TIPI:
$1,500, plus $150 for gravel base

LAND RENT:
$400

LOCATION:
Santa Barbara, California

Alicia Allison couldn't find her center. Five years out

of college, she had gone from being a professional golfer to teaching children's special education classes, to being, as she puts it,

"Completely spun out, my life was chaos—the typical girl story of compromising to the point of sacrifice. Suddenly I woke up wondering what the heck is my path? I was going so fast I couldn't see that I was on someone else's path, certainly not mine. I wanted to sit down, learn from my mistakes, and rediscover myself."

In this new state, Alicia was extremely sensitive. She couldn't share space with anyone else, since she could no longer distinguish herself and her problems from others and their problems. After visiting a tipi at a friend's house, she saw a way to create a refuge, a way to literally ground herself. "It sounds strange, but I've noticed that whenever I've lived on the second story, my life falls apart." A friend offered her space in the backyard, which she slowly cleared and leveled by hand, working an hour each day for two months, with occasional help from her parents and friends. She purchased a 14-foot-diameter, 11-foot-6-inch-tall Sioux-style canvas structure from Nomadics Tipis for $1,500.

ABOVE LEFT: **ALICIA'S TIPI**

Nomadics' tipis are made of cotton canvas, imported from India and treated with polyvinyl weatherproofing in the U.S. The vertical structure is four 7-inch-diameter pine posts that lean on each other at the top, in a spiral arrangement, and splay out at the ground, creating a tilted cone, as the back is slightly less slanted than the front. Traditionally the door faces east, and the back or side faces the prevailing winds. The door is an oval opening with a flap that's attached inside at the top, but hangs outside at the bottom, like a shingle, so it sheds rain. A modern liner wraps the interior to about 5 feet high. Since the tipi canvas doesn't touch the ground, but the liner does, outside wind is funneled up the space between the liner and outside canvas. This airflow cools in summer and encourages a steady draft from the fire to escape through the firehole at the top. Harry Janicky, who for twenty years has managed Nomadics, reports:

"Although we encourage it, most people are too busy to cut their own poles, so they buy ours, lodgepole pine culled from the U.S. national forests in Montana and Oregon. Twenty years ago, most people bought them to live in, but now we sell mostly to Scout clubs, resorts, and RV parks, and to people who have a big house, but can't find a peaceful place inside, so they buy a tipi for their yard, and use it as a meditation space.

"There's something about the space—maybe because it's round, or tall in the center, or the hole at the top—that quiets the mind. Adults who enter quickly assume the posture they'd have in a church or library. Noisy children hush. A few teachers have them in schoolyards, and use them for reading classes. Children who were having problems focusing do better inside the tipi. When I lived in one, I loved hearing the wind outside, but being inside and protected."

When Alicia's clearing was ready, friends of hers gathered acquaintances, rock climbers from the local college, to haul two tons of pea gravel by wheelbarrow to lay beneath the structure. Then they raised the tipi poles. "We called it an erection party. Maybe not such a serious spiritual feeling, but very happy." Afterwards they ate chocolate and drank tequila, and since the sloping walls of the tipi favor reclining over standing, six partiers sat, and then lay down together inside, while Alicia's future boyfriend serenaded them. "Maybe he was trying to lay some claim to the new space," she thought.

But when everyone went home the next day, the tipi was Alicia's alone, and she grew to love it that way. Furnished with just a bookcase, a low table and a bed, the space allowed Alicia's mind to move away from chaos and toward a meaningful reality. Hidden from the main house and the city views by high bushes and separated from the neighbors by no fences but instead by small orchards, she lay on the ground and felt a deep calm surround her. Above her she saw the sky through the open smoke flaps.

During this time, Alicia reinvented her life as a golf coach and rock climber. Golf may sound incongruent with tipis and rock climbing, but there are similarities: all three offer instant feedback—when your mind wanders away from the present, you are quickly brought back by reality—and all three require staying close enough to the earth to notice its waves and ripples.

"I imagined I was swimming through the earth, or lying on the belly of a living, breathing animal. Animals visited me—owls and skunks, and an albino raccoon. A doe regularly made her bed a few feet from my head."

In her tipi, Alicia found that listening to her breath, which sounded loud through the canvas walls, calmed her.

[Q] Did you ever think of moving into an apartment with your boyfriend when he suggested it?

[A] No. I was in my tipi for thirty months.

[Q] What do you suggest to your clients?

[A] Find a place, a natural place, and go there every day for at least half an hour. Sit with yourself and breathe.

Patrick has plenty of space—he lives in a

40,000-square-foot complex, a former factory, in Rochester, New York, which he shares with other artists, famous and local works of art, antiques, classic automobiles, and motorcycles. His private studio section is about 14 by 21 feet, but he realized that that wasn't small enough or private enough, since every day of the week visitors passing through the complex for art shows and performances stray into his space, or come to see his work. "It just isn't right to be dozing off on the couch when the public walks in." He needed a place to hide, sleep, and relax, and his tools needed a home as well. The ceiling height of the building exceeds 20 feet. "After contemplating the height of the room," Patrick says, "I knew which way to go."

Construction began on one side of the room with an armoire 5 feet wide by 3 feet deep by 7 feet tall with mirrored double doors, which holds his tools. The back of the cabinet stands away from the wall about 13 inches, giving him enough room to store plastic and metal milk crates. On top of this cabinet he built the bedroom.

"From my reading of books on feng shui, I knew that the bed area should be used just for bed activities and nothing else, so my bedroom could be small: 5½ feet wide—the width of my futon—and 7 feet long by 4 feet high, tall enough to comfortably sit up and read and to stretch out my limbs. Three of the walls of my bedchamber have either windows or small wooden doors, all of which hinge open for cross-ventilation and as a means to peek out and look around.

"I enter through a hatch at the foot of the bed via a tilted ladder I keep behind the armoire. Inside is a recessed shelf, which holds the television, video recorder, stereo, video game console, banker's lamp, and samurai sword with an adjacent recessed shelf for book and CDs.

"To store my clothes, I built a wooden cube on top of the bedroom. This closet cube is approximately 6 by 6 by 6 feet and its framework is composed of different levels of shelving as well as a long clothing rod for hangers. Access to the closet is a 2-foot-square hatchway on the ceiling above the bed. I simply stand up in bed poking my head and arms through the opening to have a 360-degree view of my clothing selection. To enter the closet completely, I hoist myself up and sit with my legs dangling in the bedroom or climb all the way up to sit or stand in the closet itself, about 12 feet up from the studio floor.

"Close to 100 percent of the structure, everything except the metal screws, comes from salvaged materials. This small dwelling has given me a great level of comfort and efficiency even while in its perpetual state of construction. Its hodge-podge aesthetics of reused material offers a visually impenetrable camouflage as to the contents of the structure itself. I can doze or read, while the public walks by."

PATRICK S. DOYLE A.K.A ROGUE STEVEDORE
Built in 2001 (still in process)

AREA:
573 cubic feet, inside 40,000-sq.-ft. shell

INTENDED NUMBER OF OCCUPANTS:
1 with up to 2 guests

COST:
$300 plus hundreds of hours spent scavenging materials and remodelling

STUDIO RENT:
$350

UTILITIES:
Included

LOCATION:
Rochester, New York

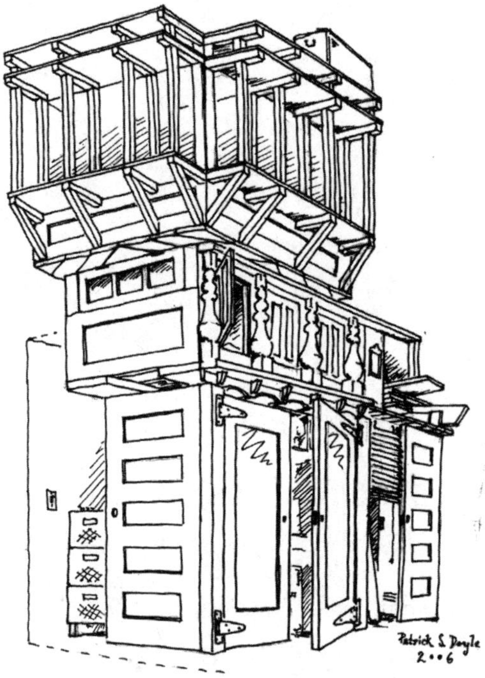

ABOVE: **PATRICK'S TOWER**

KATHLEEN DEAN MOORE
Built 2006 (in process)

AREA:
56 sq. ft.

INTENDED NUMBER OF OCCUPANTS
1 plus an occasional guest

COST:
(design and materials) $10,000

LOCATION:
Southern Washington State

Kathleen Dean Moore is a philosopher and nature writer. On her first week-

long solitary writing retreat, she discovered that while other people fuel her mental fire, only with time and space away from others can her ideas lengthen, strengthen, and become complex enough to write, for example, a novel, instead of a brief essay. "I find that thoughts fragment and dissipate around other people, but they gather in nature." So she sought a refuge away from the assault of other voices, a place where her thoughts can be undivided, "all-one," which is what she hears when she sees the word, "alone."

Kathleen and her husband enlisted their daughter Erin Moore, who is trained as an architect, to design a refuge, a minimal writer's shack, to be placed on fifteen acres of forest that they own. She didn't want a place that encourages solitude to the point of solipsism, but instead one that keeps a door open to the provocations of nature. "When listening is your spiritual life, a refuge is where you can choose which voices you are going to hear." But she can't choose what nature will say, and from this tension her creative fire is kindled (see her comment, below left).

The forest is, arguably, always better off left alone and possibly a better inspiration to the writer if she doesn't settle there. What could a nature writer and her biologist husband build in a forest without ruining the qualities that brought them there? They started with a $10,000 limit, and the idea of a boat on water. A house typically shelters people from the land, through separation. In contrast, a boat, if it's small enough—an inner-tube float was their ideal—keeps people in touch. Erin had already pondered the "implied hierarchy between the ground and the structure built on it." Must a building, like a master, seem to survey the land beneath it, or can it be part of the land, changing with the land instead of changing the land?

The result was a 7-by-8-foot wooden shack, built on four piers, with a steel roof and walls of "certified sustainably harvested western cedar" posts, with tongue-and-groove boards hung horizontally in

“I studied the concept of refuge in history, the concept of sanctuary, places of pardon where no harm can be done. Medieval European churches offered sanctuaries: whatever guilt people had, they could go to a church and be safe. The Greeks and Hebrews, the Hawaiians—many cultures had locations of refuge that could not be profaned by the presence of any person, that were open to everyone, where people in some cases by just entering the space were purified, and no longer guilty. In modern times we have wildlife refuges.” —Kathleen

between, attached to dadoes grooved into the posts. The walls and roof have no insulation, and the inhabitants, who are used to camping for weeks at a time, intend to keep warm by dressing in thick clothes, and through the occasional use of a propane heater. Outside temperatures rarely drop below 45 degrees Fahrenheit or rise above 85 degrees.

The building is located on the side of a natural opening in the forest canopy. A window on the south provides light, and warmth on the few occasions when the winter sun shines through. Windows were minimized—there are just two—because they promote separation, providing a connection much like the one between a museum specimen and a spectator. How can a human vessel not be just an object to be looked at and looked from? In part by being so small that it forces its inhabitants to exit, to cook on the outside fire, or to socialize with other beings. Underneath, between the piers, the ground is arranged to encourage snake habitat. On the exterior walls are boxes where birds are encouraged to make nests.

Inside the walls thick rods fit horizontally between the posts. The desk hangs from two rods, eliminating the need for table legs. Catty-corner from the desk is a 3-by-6-foot platform, that has beneath it a second drawer, which, when pulled out, creates a bed platform wide enough for two. "If Dad visits, he's like a passenger, on the bed, with Mom at her desk. The window above her is a windshield," says Erin. Inside the bed/drawers are inflatable mattresses and sleeping bags. "It rains every single day, almost constantly in this forest," explains Erin, "so anything that can mildew, will. So we planned for marine conditions. Trying to keep water out is almost impossible, especially when you're avoiding using industrial chemicals, so instead we've built no place for water to pool, and nothing that is harmed by getting wet." The sleeping bags are safe from the rain within the drawers, and go home with the visitors.

MOUNT GILEAD FRIENDS
Land acquired 1996;
hermitage built 2002

AREA:
200 sq. ft., plus 92-sq.-ft. loft

INTENDED NUMBER OF OCCUPANTS:
1-2

CONSTRUCTION COST:
Under $32,000

LAND COST:
$93,000

UTILITIES:
Kerosene for lights, woodstove for heating: less than $0.40 per night used

LOCATION:
Near Bloomington, Indiana

Sometimes the most powerful room of your own is one you share

with others, but not simultaneously. Over the last three years the Mount Gilead Friends' Retreat cabin "Fox Haven" has been shared by about a hundred people.

The cabin is heated by a woodstove in winter, and cooled by opening windows to the shady forest in summer. An antique pitcher and washbowl serve as a sink, and a modern composting toilet is in the washroom. The twin bed downstairs is covered with a patchwork quilt. A kerosene Aladdin lamp lights the writing desk.

Retreat co-coordinator Donna Eder, a sociology professor at the local university, was inspired to help others start the retreat after her mother's difficult illness and death. On solitary retreat she dreamt "of swimming through snow," which she interpreted as a desire to be completely immersed in spiritual work and the ideals she cares about. She joined with Janette Shetter, who shared a similar leading, and six other Quakers to move forward on their vision.

Janette believes the retreat provides a place for the practice of "centering down, to seek that of God within." Although Janette has always enjoyed solitary walks in nature, it was after she joined the Religious Society of Friends (the Quakers) that she understood how nature can lead us to discover what we are called upon to do in life.

Janette and Donna worked with several others to found the nonprofit organization that manages the cabin and the sixty acres of forest that surround it. Most of the funding to pay the land's 10-year mortgage comes through donors, and from the $30 per night charged to retreatants.

Hundreds of people visit the land each year, either for contemplative, outdoor group activities and celebrations, or more likely, just to spend a few hours walking along the creek. The hermitage area is secluded and not open to day visitors.

"The uncluttered space is an incarnation of the four Quaker testimonies of simplicity, harmony, community, and equality. Our goal as Quakers is to live our beliefs, and Fox Haven offers a model of simple living. We hope to show how nice simple furnishings can be, and how comfortable and refreshing it is to have very little, surrounded by nature." —Donna Eder

The group used a slow, consensus process over two years to develop a few guidelines for construction: Use local materials, well insulated, no plywood, no electricity, small living space, and situated to use natural light and southern solar gain. They choose to use a steel roof, to allow for

THE BED, THE DESK, AND THE STOVE AT FOX HAVEN

nontoxic rainwater catchment. They hired builder Jason Hobson, who was aided by a group of volunteers. For this project Jason chose to use hand tools, almost exclusively, to maintain the quiet and add to the sense of sacred space.

The structure is timber frame, with walls of cordword, made of logs of cedar that fell near the property during a storm. Stacked a bit like bricks, with their cut, ringed side facing out on each side of the wall, they are mortared together with a cement–based mixture. The mortar joint is insulated in the center of the wall with sawdust treated with lime. The group first built a llama shed on the property using cordwood, and noticed that some gaps developed between the cordwood and mortar joints, from both materials shrinking after construction, so Jason changed the mortar mix slightly, using more lime and less cement, and the walls of Fox Haven are quite solid, with just a few hairline gaps. Joe Davis, one of the organizers of the project, wonders whether a cob mortar might work better, since cob can be dampened and reworked after it's dried, if gaps appear, but, he adds, "Since the space is so small, even if there is a tiny gap or two, it stays warm."

The cabin has a loft, with a second bed, for those few retreatants who prefer to come with a friend. Solitude is a learned practice that requires patience to master, a skill we shouldn't expect to know before we start doing it. "Some people think about it a long time, gear up for years before they are ready to try a personal retreat," says Donna. "We aren't used to being alone. Some people find solace knowing that it's here, even though they aren't ready to take a retreat yet."

"OUR GOAL AS QUAKERS IS TO LIVE OUR BELIEFS."

PEARL AND DAVID'S DESERT YACHT

13
Remember the World

Every spirit builds itself a house, and beyond its house, a world, and beyond its world, a heaven. Know then that world exists for you. —RALPH WALDO EMERSON

THERE'S A MOMENT ON BUILDING SITES WHEN the tensions have risen. It can happen with new construction, or a renovation, or just a parent fixing a leak in the bathroom. The job has gone on longer than expected, the day is late, and a small group of people are beginning to feel trapped together in a very stuffy space.

Sometimes it's the sun setting that provokes the builders to go outside—maybe to pick up the tools before dark falls. Maybe the builders were already outside, but suddenly they look up. What is it about this golden, bewitching hour that can soak us in tension, and then wash our fear away in a simple change of light?

On some enlightenment-bound worksites a bell is rung, or the time is noted regularly, by union or religious decree, and people take a break, rest, eat, or maybe sit in meditation. Often when they return from that break, the nail that wouldn't pry loose, loosens, or the paint color that wasn't right, is now drying nicely, and the misplaced tools reappear. It's a handy habit to keep near you when you're working, this habit of perspective.

Wider World, Smaller Planet

At some point you will be done with your house, done building, or repairing, or just done obsessing. Prepare to welcome that moment. The world will have waited for you, ready to feed you what you've been missing. If you have set yourself up with what David Omick (see profile) calls a "thick margin of extra time, resources, and energy," you'll have the power to create a wider, safer home in the world than you could have imagined in your own separate house. As your perspective grows, your house shrinks in significance, and you might rediscover your soul floating safely in the universe.

KEEPING UP WITH THE LEES

The most common way small-housers remember the world is in a persistent thought they have about the Joneses, which is "it's not the Joneses anymore. It's the Lees, the Singhs, and the Garcias."

“I must point out that although it’s smaller than my friend’s houses, our house isn’t small in my eyes. I don’t compare it to the other houses in Canada; I compare it to houses on this Earth, so it’s more than plenty, and I even feel spoiled.” —Jacinte Wikow

Jacinte Wikow (see Chapter 4) voices this thought, above.

International and moon travel, television images and radio news, the constant trade of objects across borders and the conformity of façades as corporate branding decorates the landscape—many things seem to wrap us together in a tighter web of interdependence and common experience. Really, the world has been small to humans for a long time: for thousands of years, people have migrated by foot around the forested taiga crown of the Northern Hemisphere; or by horseback across the plains; and paddling canoes and sailing boats across the oceans.

Today the world is shrunk with speed: whereas Odysseus sailed for twenty years, now a modern warrior sometimes climbs into the cockpit at Whiteman Air Force Base in Missouri—“Home of America’s Bomber”—on a Wednesday morning, flies to the other side of the world, drops bombs on a village, and is back home for the weekend, where he might discuss with his wife whether their kids are old enough to walk the half mile to school alone.

Or, by guiding robot-planes from an office at the base, the pilot never need leave his town. Technology has reduced the distance between a pilot’s willpower and a village’s fate down to zero.

This connection, the connection between one person’s power and another person’s fate, leads many people to share Rowan Sherwood’s sensibility. She says, “I know when I don’t use something or buy something that I don’t need, there is one less child going hungry today. In a globalized world, no one is separate.” Put differently, if a soldier can press buttons to destroy a village, can’t the rest of us save at least one life with some other apparently small push?

In part, this thinking is magical. Clearly, switching to solar from gas water heating won’t revive a child who has passed out from dehydration, and driving less today won’t literally stop a war tomorrow. But making these connections restores a sense of power and community in our overwhelming, broken world.

Some people clarify the connection by tying their lifestyle change to a specific donation. They sell some furniture and give the proceeds to a beggar, or they skip a meal, and send the cash cost of the meal to a hunger organization. One small-houser, a physically disabled woman who prior to her disease dreamed of traveling abroad as a volunteer, reliably donates half her salary to an orphanage, providing over half their annual budget. Now they depend on her good health, and she on theirs.

Beyond these charitable connections are the apparently magical, but entirely material connections we all share, through the weather, the economy, and our energy and water supply. If it’s true that a butterfly’s wing can provoke a windstorm, then a house that exhales more oxygen than carbon dioxide can cool an ice cap. The changing climate is a worry common to the whole world.

THE EQUALIZATION OF CONDITION

Alexis de Toqueville, the very quoted Frenchman, and other journalists who visited North America in the nineteenth century commented on the willingness of Americans to share resources, and the array of civic groups to promote the common good. In particular they noted the “equality of condition” of the citizens, relative to the more class-based societies of Europe, which were at that time dominated by monarchies and the notion of God-given inequality. De Toqueville offered America as proof that democracy and equality are irresistible, inevitable forces that will likely expand over time.

At present, equality is shrinking within North America. There are more people living in poverty and extreme wealth than forty years ago, fewer people control more land, and fewer people constitute the middle class.[1] Conversely, differences between some nations are shrinking: it's fairly common for a construction laborer on the south side of the U.S.–Mexican border to earn two dollars an hour; a few miles north in the U.S., a laborer earns six or eight dollars an hour for the same work. This 300- or 400-percent increase seems extreme until you know that the corporate executive who employs the U.S. worker earns five, or fifteen, or sometimes a hundred times what the laborer earns, so the differences within the company are greater than those between the nations.

Housing provides a graphic example of the gap: in both the U.S. and Mexico, the largest estates are sparsely populated by miniscule, wealthy families, while poverty housing is often densely packed. Here again, the gap between the living conditions of the working class of various countries is shrinking, while the gap within nations grows.

Into this pattern of simultaneous shrinking and growing equality enter Rowan and Jim and others who seek a universalist measure of consumption, such as the ecological footprint model (see profile) which imagines that all people count equally, and should have equal access to sustenance. Physically this means we should each have a fair, comfortable share of land, for housing and farming and everything else that we need. But how can we with so many people and so few resources?

POPPING POPULATION

We've been warned of the "population explosion" for decades, and it's happened. World population was at two-and-a-half billion in 1950, and now it's at six-and-a-half. However, the direst predictions were either wrong, or had the intended effect: population growth is leveling off more rapidly than predicted. Increased access to contraception, dropping sperm counts in all mammals, and self-determination for women to choose careers besides motherhood, are cited as some of the reasons. Some details are at first glance mysterious: China has a one-child policy; Taiwan, which doesn't, has a lower fertility rate. Densely populated Italy and expansive Russia both have extremely low birth rates (less than 1.3 children per woman). Some war-torn regions drop in fertility, and others rise.

The five largest nations (China, India, the United States, Indonesia, and Brazil), which constitute close to half of the world's population together, have an average fertility rate that is just above replacement levels, and two of those nations—China and Brazil—are well under. It's increasingly difficult to find countries where the average woman gives birth to more than three children, and in many countries with high birth rates, death rates from war and AIDS are so high the rate of increase is moderate: Zimbabwe, although it has a considerably higher fertility rate than the U.S., had (in 2006) a net annual natural increase of only 0.6 percent, compared to the U.S.'s 0.9 percent. South Africa went from having a net increase in population of 1 percent in 2000 to a net decrease of 0.4 percent just five years later. Delayed parenthood also has some effect: a thirty-eight-year-old new mother in a sense has half as many children as a nineteen-year-old new mother; if the family line maintains that pace, assuming identical life spans, half as many generations share the planet.[2]

Even when you've applied the brakes, you can still skid quite far: it's expected that in the next twenty or thirty years the population will increase by at least another billion, probably about two, and then level out.[3]

WHERE WILL ALL THESE PEOPLE LIVE?

While population levels out, millions of units of housing will be built to accommodate our newest additions to humanity. But much more significant to housing construction than population increase is migration. Without immigration, the U.S. would barely maintain its population level, and Canada would decrease. Inside our borders, as shown in Chapter 6, much of our new construction—arguably most—is due to internal migration, rural to urban, and toward whatever is the latest economic hot spot. Since the successful weakening of borders between European countries in the EEU, people around the world are questioning why governments should restrict human mobility. War, famine, and disastrous

A MOBILE BED

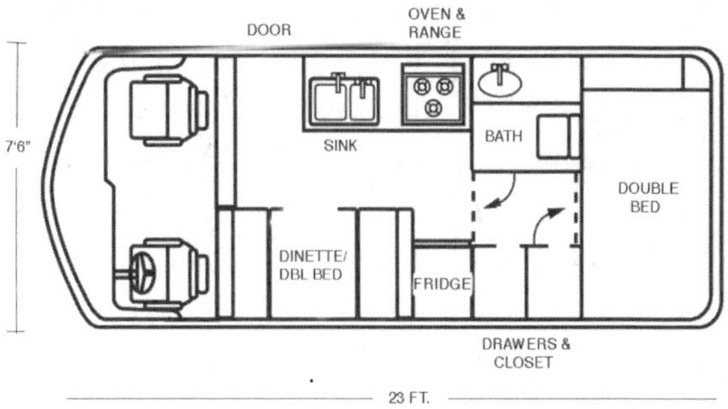

This book's photographer spent about two years living in a 23-foot 1973 GMC motor home. Because it was old, the GMC's interior had already mostly off-gassed, so he didn't worry about the effect of the harsh glues and varnishes used in its construction. The motor home's small size requires a compact, thoughtful design, and its interior heating, cooling, and maintenance costs are a fraction of those of a normal house, especially if it follows good weather. In his case, he never used the cooler, and used the heater less than two weeks per year.

The GMC used a gallon of gasoline per 12 miles traveled, while his car used a gallon per 26, so he figured that if he gave up his car and moved the GMC a little under half the miles he normally traveled in his car, his overall btu (including heating and cooling) use would actually be reduced. The EPA estimates that average U.S. vehicles travel 12,000 miles a year (at about 23 mpg,) so the motor home could have traveled from Vancouver, British Columbia, to Savannah, Georgia (a distance of about 3,000 miles), and back, and still use less gas than the average commuter.

Had he been more environmentally inclined, he could have followed the example of Claire Anderson and Shawn Schreiner, who purchased a 1976 Airstream trailer and towed it with a diesel truck, which they converted to run on used vegetable oil that otherwise would have been discarded. Stopping at restaurants around the country to refuel was a friendly way to travel. Inside, they retrofitted the trailer with bamboo flooring and a composting toilet. Many motor homes feature solar panels, and we even met one family who had a small garden growing just inside one of the windows of their rig.

weather are provoking huge movement, and new weaves of synthetic tent cloth are an increasingly popular material choice for world housing.

The small-house movement received a bit of press in 2006 when architect Marianne Cusato won a competition to design emergency housing for survivors of Hurricane Katrina in New Orleans. Visitors to the cute 308-square-foot cottage commented, "I could live here," and said it was a more dignified and pleasant option than the trailers that the federal government was offering. A tiny permanent house that can later be expanded seemed to many to be a better use of funds, and perhaps gives people more of a sense of security than something mobile and temporary.[4]

A minority of North Americans has the opposite view on how to best weather the changes. They prefer mobile dwellings, in which they can follow the best climate as it moves. Clearly, trailers clogging up the freeway right after an earthquake hits will not be a useful development,[5] but some kinds of weather—droughts and heat waves, and sometimes flooding and snowstorms—are predicted at least a few days in advance. Some people like to live ready to travel away from a crisis.

Another group, more concerned with economic and social changes, has migrated against the tide, out of North America. The U.S. State Department says that U.S. expatriate levels in 2005 were at a thirty-year high.[6] Enclaves of Northerners populate a variety of towns in Mexico, Costa Rica, Ecuador, and beyond. In 2006 Jim and Mindy Phyphers (see Chapter 10) wrote to say that their U.S. house was on the market; after eight months living in an Airstream trailer in a tiny village in Mexico, they considered their move permanent. Besides the benefits of a relatively strong dollar and a gently warm climate, they found their ideals of simplicity were considered normal in that part of Mexico, a relief from their former life where they'd felt like aliens in their own culture. Ex-pat developments are springing up around the world. Jim and Mindy add that they worry that the American luxury developments they've seen a few hundred miles away may someday pop up in their remote paradise.

Tony Gwilliam, who builds "T-houses" (see Chapter 12) in California part of the year, spends at least six months each year in Bali, building wooden houses, in the same style as a simple T-house, but expanded, as he develops tiny expatriate communities in one Balinese town. The price of his finely crafted, hardwood, airy homes is low for Europeans and Americans—around $40,000—and high for Bali, enabling him to transfer wealth to the village. The land under the house is only leased for twenty-five years, but the house is built so it could be moved, although most foreigners are happy to imagine their stay restricted by time, particularly if they retire to the area. Tony considers this a form of international, mutual aid.

ENVY

There is a downside to the kind of tourism Tony Gilliam develops (see above). Absolute income goes up, as the tourists arrive, but everyone feels poorer when they are suddenly surrounded by money-bought goods they hadn't known before. James Stark (see Chapter 5) worked as a consultant to villages threatened by the effects of tourism, and watched as villagers figured out how to resist trading everything they had for a radio, or an unlikely shot at a place in the world market. Betsy Hartmann and James Boyce wrote in *A Quiet Violence* how in Bangladesh, in the 1970s and '80s, local landholders began seeing the prizes of western industrializations—stereos, clocks, mopeds—only because they were visited by foreign aid workers. Previously their mango trees, the fat on their children, or a few inherited bands of gold seemed like plenty of wealth. In order to acquire the mopeds, etc., they had to figure out a way to convert rice and vegetables, which was their only product, to cash. This they did by raising the land rent for their neighbors, their tenants, in some cases literally watching them die of starvation, as they extracted enough coins to buy the new goods. How could they? The same way we all can.

Expectations around the globe are equalizing, and like gas stabilizing in a container, the trend seems unstoppable. In Kenya, future Nobel Prize Laureate Wangari Maathai organized women to plant millions of trees. Soon the groups also found a need to protest the development of new subdivisions of huge mansions, which the forests were being converted to. Why shouldn't the wealthy in Kenya live like the wealthy in the north? Indian software engineers can now leave Silicon Valley in California, and return home to American-style cookie-cutter subdivisions near Bangalore and New Delhi. Ana Ribas (Chapter 6) says that her parents in Venezuela, much like retirees in the U.S., added rooms to their house after their children left home—something that makes no sense to her siblings. In the Ukraine, huge private houses sprang up after the dissolution of the USSR. Now most stand empty. Too expensive to heat, they are offered for sale to foreigners for a fraction of their construction cost, while their owners return to apartment buildings and town

“These teens were trained to fire machine guns from motorcycles traveling 35 miles per hour. I would interview them in the hospital...most of the boys were killed during the course of the study. But their attitude was: ‘So what if I live only another two years or another two months? Right now I’ve got a Kawazaki and I can buy a house for my mom....’ In my neighborhood run-down houses became three-story buildings filled with the latest gadgets.”

—Hector Aristizabel, Colombian psychotherapist

houses.[7] In Colombia, where desperation is particularly high, some people are killing for fancier houses.

Antonio Espinosa, a Colombian architect writes:

“The extensive violence that rural Colombia has suffered in the past years has forced development to stay within the city. As refugees from rural warfare flee into the cities, architects and builders are obliged to produce housing and neighborhoods of truly small proportion.

“In this project of 480 houses we built 80 houses on each three-acre lot, leaving 51 percent of the land for communal space, including gardens and swimming pools. These green zones are important because the countryside is too dangerous for recreation.”[8]

Even countries that have stable populations and comfortable houses are influenced. In the Japanese countryside and suburbs, which has hosted largish, but densely-populated traditional houses for centuries, the importation of North American lumber, which is milled differently—its dimensions are thicker—has been accompanied by the importation of North American carpenters, to teach locals how to frame with this wood, and how to design subdivisions of American-style houses, often with cathedral ceilings and hard floors, and without the traditional tatami rooms or paper doors. Construction continues, even as Japan’s population declines. China is the most dramatic example of the trend:

Human housing, concluded biologist Jack Liu of the University of Michigan, is the reason the panda bear continues towards extinction. Despite China’s shrinking families and slowly declining population, internal migration and especially the switch toward western-style nuclear families in larger, suburban-style houses have translated into a housing explosion. Habitat loss is the main cause of extinction for any threatened species; our habitat gained is their habitat lost. Theoretically, larger Chinese families, living in the old style, with several generations under the same roof, and houses packed close together, might have served the panda better than the current lower population, but more resource-exhaustive modern families.[9]

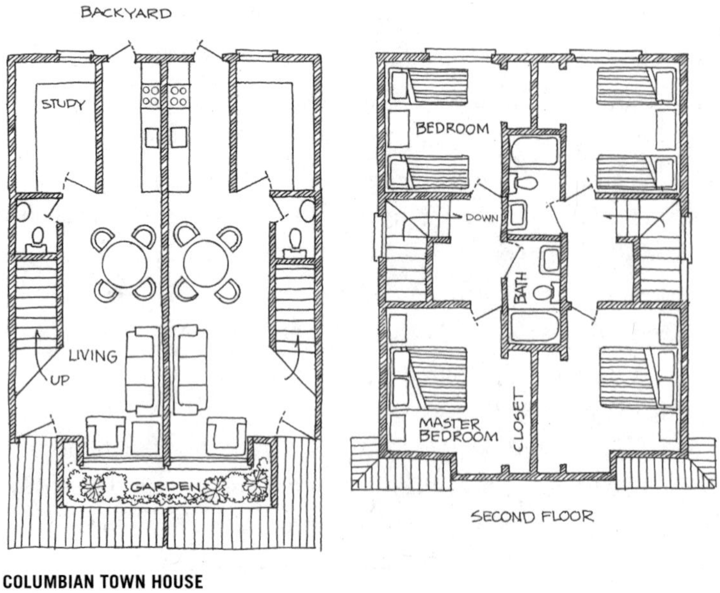

COLUMBIAN TOWN HOUSE

BACK HOME

Some small-housers prefer to stay home, reasoning it's where they can be of most use, and that there's no escape from world problems. Because they've streamlined their existence, they can weather economic change and continue to pursue what matters.

Some expand the skills they've learned building their own homes.

Tom Bowerman has spent thirty years "living in luxury." He built his own house for $3,000 (in 1979), and raised a family on less than $8,000 each year. He didn't give up his professional skills as a planner, builder, and businessman when he changed his lifestyle at age 29. Instead, he used them to acquire and renovate buildings, and rents them out to small businesses and organizations that create employment and pleasure for others, and charges them rent based on what they can pay. Most recently he's established a trust, so the affordability of the buildings will outlive him.

Others now find time to dedicate to a cause:

Tom Cahill describes his home, "Cozy and charming riverfront home; serene and rustic retreat in parklike setting; soaring wood-paneled great room with media, library, office, and entertainment areas; 3,600-square-inch flowing floor plan; picturesque outbuildings; facilities for the equestrian; fabulous views include elk and other wildlife; strikingly simple furnishings available. This home makes a unique statement."

TOM CAHILL AT HOME

What he means is that he lives in a one-room, 300-square-foot apartment over a barn, sharing an old farm with a number of other renters. It's meticulously furnished, with a mind-dazzling array of collected items. But Tom doesn't want to talk about his home. There's something much more important to talk about, something that if we work together, we can all change, and something that, ever since he lost his beloved wife and had time to reconsider the world in its complexity, he's chosen to spend every waking hour of every day working on, speaking on, and writing about.

The issue is prisoner rape. Common in U.S. prisons, it is also preventable— it is uncommon in many European countries—and in some cases allowed by sadistic or apathetic wardens as extra punishment. A large man, who never suffered from bullies as a child, Tom was surprised to find he was vulnerable to such a thing, when, as a college student, he spent three days in jail. He avoided his own memories for twenty-five years, then spent twenty years working with a group organizing for change. In 2003 he found himself in the Oval Office, while the President signed federal legislation to diminish the practice. This is what he wants to tell you about houses: "You'll never build one large enough or gated enough to protect yourself."[10]

Equality of condition suggests that if one of us is vulnerable, so are we all, and the right to safety is equal for all. We create social vulnerability through inequality, and then try to protect ourselves from it by distancing ourselves from the disadvantaged. But a spiritual life allows us to walk

As a senior in high school, Steve Beck was drawn to two disciplines: Zen Buddhism, and architecture. He pursued both in college, was ordained as a monk, and a few years later received a master's in architecture. Aware of the spiritual benefits of very small spaces, he also saw in them the potential to build universally affordable housing.

For the past thirty years he has inhabited, designed and built, and taught college students about dwellings that are typically under 160 square feet, and not over 1,000 square feet. Because restricted access to land is a primary reason housing is unaffordable to millions of people, his designs are mobile, so that people can live on land that is vacant, and keep their home even if they are evicted from the land. "To solve homelessness, it's essential to accept that the ethical right to live with dignity and respect supercedes the right to use space for profit or parking." The "suitcase" house that he's designed is easy to carry, and many of his designs roll, as they are adapted to a nomadic, urban life.

After years of contemplation, Steve concludes that the "mansionization" of North American housing is a subtle expression of the same trend that creates war and genocide. "It comes," says Steve, "from a 10,000 year-old human misunderstanding. It's this misunderstanding that created the clichés, 'might makes right' and 'it's a dog eat dog world.' Belief in these sayings creates that world around us. In reality, dominance, competition, and separation aren't necessary for survival." [13]

towards our fears, and find a deeper comfort beyond the paradox.

Does our social attitude echo our relationship with the greatest world, the environment? Is our vulnerability in it a figment of our social imagination, or is it an indisputable fact that we must subdue Nature to survive?

THE NATURE OF CONSTRUCTION

Imagine that despite our delicate hides and nutritional cravings, we aren't particularly vulnerable in the world, that our vulnerability in any case is no greater than that of other beings. Imagine that instead of subduing nature, we can somehow work with nature, as partners, or as students at the feet of a great teacher. This is a belief assumed by many "natural" builders, who try to mimic nature in their own creations.

They tend to build small, since few other animals build more shelter than they need. They notice in other animals a relative equality of condition within species, and a common (although not universal) aversion to killing one's kin. They notice specifics, such as which side of a tree a bird builds a nest in, or the relationship between the height of a beaver's dam and the river's water line. And they mimic habits: since the bees conserve energy in the winter, clumped together in the center of a hive, drinking honey, perhaps we might close off most of our house, and hole up in bed with a few delicacies, at least for a month or two?

When we look to Nature for advice we accept an invitation to be part of the limitless community that surrounds us. The Saguaro Juniper Covenant of the association where Pearl and David lived (see profile) recognizes nature to have the inherent right to evolve without "human interference," but also regards people as part of, and not apart from nature.

Where has the separation come from?

Just a few generations ago, we inhabited a material world more untouched than touched by human hands. It's now easy to go through a day, and never touch earth. But even in our built environment the cracks in the pavement, and the patterns of footprints on a stairwell begin to seem natural. One day soon, that face in the mirror may appear no less natural than any other fruit or flower.

Here's one key to making a comfortable dwelling: forget the dwelling. Make the dweller comfortable. Accept the human in the mirror as one more growing, struggling, dying part of Nature. A natural being who, for a few thousand years has been bent on changing, doing, building. Now more bent than any other being and maybe, hoping to change itself.

Hoping to change from a doing being to a being being. One who watches with its many senses and enjoys the glory of creation—not so much the creation of its own hands but the Glory of Creation. One who looks with kindness on the face in the mirror. One who sees the pattern in the cracked asphalt and knows

STEVE BECK

that it, too, is a kind of lovely. A being who knows it has done plenty. The world has been conquered. It's time to rest.

The circles of life that surround us, and the earth and the heavens that support us, body and soul, are the widest community we know. Eventually we leave our homes and retreat to their vastness. As we relax our sense of possession and domination, and enter that community on equal ground we may find peace as one part of a community of being.

ARTICLE 27
Artemisa and Antonio López

AREA:
36 sq. meters, plus 16 sq. meters in construction, and a 4 sq. meter outdoor room

INTENDED NUMBER OF OCCUPANTS:
2 or more

COST:
Land about $1,000 (U.S.)

CONSTRUCTION:
about $2,000 (U.S.)

UTILITY COSTS (MONTHLY):
$8/gas, $12/water, $35/electricity (all U.S. dollars)

LOCATION:
Nogales, Sonora

ABOVE: **ARTEMISA AND ANTONIO LÓPEZ WITH TERESA LEAL**

The line between Mexico and the United States is

one of the longest borders in the world—3,000 kilometers— and is said to host more travelers than any other. West of El Paso, where the Rio Grande turns, it abandons any natural pattern, and today, thousands of people in uniforms guard what is for many miles an imaginary scratch in the dust. This book has used the term "North America" to refer to Canada and the United States, although Mexico is also in North America. The southwestern quarter of the United States was, like Mexico, Spanish territory for about 300 years, and then was part of independent Mexico for about 30 years.

Starting in the 1960s both governments offered incentives to companies to build factories in Mexico, along the border. Currently most Mexican border towns have three to a hundred times as many people as their U.S. counterparts, and hundreds of thousands of Mexicans work in the factories. The location of these factories—called *maquiladoras*—makes shipment to U.S. markets easy. Money and things pass fairly freely in both directions, but northbound people are limited from entering the U.S. Near these border towns, the U.S. has in the last decade installed tall metal walls, barbed wire, and immigration police every few hundred meters. More recently many of these international factories have been quietly closing down operations and moving from this area to Asia and Central America, where they can pay workers less.

Factory owners, the local government, and the World Bank have collaborated to build subdivisions of duplexes and condominiums that offer workers many of the same amenities as in the U.S.: parking, greenspace, laundry rooms, and fake vigas or shutters on the façade. Company housing was so poorly built in the late 1970s that some developments remain empty now and people mine the old buildings for materials. Most workers live in houses they've built themselves. The hills of Nogales are half covered in handmade cardboard and tarpaper wooden houses that often evolve into concrete block houses, as workers accumulate wealth.

Artemisa and Antonio live in a handmade development on a hillside. Their land was acquired by applying Article 27 of the Mexican constitution. The U.S. government required this article, which concerns land reform, to be weakened, as part of the North American Free Trade Agreement (NAFTA), but most Mexican citizens still recognize access to land as a basic human right.[11]

Teresa Leal, who helps groups acquire land explains the process:

"We locate land that is held by someone who holds more land than the legal limit. The law states an owner may not hold more than 500 hectares in the city, or 5,000 in the countryside, and that they should be contiguous. We find a parcel that is not too far from city roads and services, but not so close that it is the best land the owner has.

"At the same time we locate a group of people who are "houseless" and can move to the land, who are willing to live without running water for probably about 5 years. They can't have a pending criminal record, and we perform a socioeconomic study to show that they constitute a family unit and need housing. That's not hard to prove in this part of the country, but it must be documented. We must do this secretly, because if the landowner finds out, he can have us jailed preemptively. We have the Napoleonic system here, so a person can be presumed guilty before a trial. Before we move on to the land we get a permit for occupancy from the government, but from an office in another city, so the landowner won't find out.

"We have to plot the land and divide it into sectors and numbered lots, so that as soon as people arrive they have a control number and site map. We

FACTORY OWNERS, GOVERNMENTS, AND THE WORLD BANK COLLABORATED TO BUILD SUBDIVISIONS THAT HAVE MANY OF THE SAME AMENITIES AS IN THE U.S.

need stakes, rope, and chalk ready, and the group needs to be able to make decisions peacefully and quickly. Of course we don't allow guns or violence, and we might make other rules if conditions require it. Onc late Friday afternoon, the whole group moves to their designated plots. The owner won't be able to file a complaint until the next Monday."

Artemisa moved to her land after the squatter group had been established for about a year. Eventually, the group negotiated a typical deal where the government compensated the landowner, and then charged each settler 8,000 pesos per lot. Each owner was allowed to apply for title after 7 years of occupancy, and was taxed to plow roads around each lot. There is some difficulty in surveying the lots, because they had to be drawn so quickly, and were made rectangular to comply with required city setbacks. The land, which is on a steep incline and has ravines, might have more naturally been divided slightly differently. After heavy rains mudslides have been known to move land and lot lines around.

Artemisa began in a trailer, and planted a garden of *nopales*. Eventually she accumulated enough cinder blocks to build a single room, 4 by 6 meters, and sold the trailer. With no money for ceiling joists, she invented a cathedral ceiling by attaching drywall directly to the roof rafters. Her neighbors like the expansive rise of the ceiling. A few years ago Antonio joined her, and built a bedroom, and is now adding two more rooms—for a bathroom and a shop for Artemisa, who is an artist. They won't expand further, they think, because they don't want to disturb the *nopales*.

Until 2005 they used a car battery to power her television, and neighbors came to watch. They wanted solar panels, but the city government forbids them, explaining the cost of bringing city electricity to the area is so high they want everyone to use it. In 2005 electric lines reached her neighborhood. They now share a line with three other families, which powers her microwave, refrigerator, radio, and television.

Artemisa has a sister in California, and wishes she could cross the border to visit her easily. She envies a few aspects of her sister's house—especially that her roads aren't dusty and that her water supply is reliable— but she doesn't envy her debt, and she doesn't understand how children sleep alone in one room to themselves. Antonio spent a few years working on the other side of the line. He said he was so lonely that he, a grown man, started to sleep with a teddy bear.

"To understand God's thoughts we must study statistics, for these are

the measure of his purpose," said Florence Nightingale about a hundred years ago. Joseph Stalin, several decades later, is said to have offered this instead: "A single death is a tragedy, a million deaths is a statistic." The amount of numbered information available to us about humans and the rest of the world has a numbing effect on some, and a chilling effect on others. In the quest for a fair world, how can we recognize true equity, if we don't count up our resources, and dole them out evenly, like children cutting a pie?

Jim Merkel was a young military engineer, selling weapons around the world. One evening, shocked awake by television images of *Exxon Valdez* oil spilled over the ocean and its creatures, he decided suddenly to change his life. He quit his job and exchanged his old desires for a new dream: to equitably share the Earth with the whole world.

Jim started by measuring his own resources, and determining mathematically what he'd need to do to earn and survive on less than a tenth of his former income. With his own sustenance secured on a spreadsheet, he turned to the world. What is an equitable share? To know this, he'd have to measure every single source, every acre, and divide by the population, a monumental task for a single engineer.

Luckily, humans have been taking measurements for innumerable generations, and by now we know much about the world. We know the surface area of our landmass, and we know the volume of the oceans, and we've counted the birds. We've even measured not just the air we breathe, but the molecules it contains; nations that have signed the Kyoto Accords (to reduce greenhouse gases) can now sell CO_2 "credits" to each other.[11]

Ecologists have taken a similar interest to Jim's. In particular, Mathis Wackernagel and Bill Rees have codified a method of measuring individual and national resource use, which they call the ecological footprint model (EF). When builders speak of a house's footprint, they mean the pattern and space defined by the foundation. EF counts not just the space that the house literally occupies, but the productive land needed to grow the timber, mine the copper wire, paint the walls, and so forth, and the power it takes to run and maintain the building once it's up.

EF calculators exist for every almost aspect of life, including transportation, eating, education, and telephone communication. The assumption is that the Earth holds a limited acreage of "bioproductive" land, and that we have now surpassed our limit (which is under five acres each), with a small percentage of our population using thirty or forty acres per capita (the average in North America is about twenty-five), and about 60 percent of the

ROWAN SHERWOOD AND JIM MERKEL
Built 1998–9

AREA:
180 sq. ft., plus a 120-sq.-ft. loft and a few shelves of storage in another house

INTENDED NUMBER OF OCCUPANTS:
2

COST:
$1,500 (Canadian dollars)

UTILITY COSTS:
Water, free (gravity fed); $18 electric (including $15 service fee); 1 cord of wood for heating, cooking and hot water.

LOCATION:
British Columbia

population using fewer than four acres (India's average is about three). When EF was computed for each nation, it correlated roughly to the World Bank's assessment of Gross National Product, so personal income is considered a very rough estimate of EF: generally, the more you earn, the more acres of earth you "spend" each day.

In 1996, Jim organized the Global Living Project (GLP). For five summers, small groups of researchers lived together for six weeks in British Columbia and carefully measured their resource use—counted miles traveled, weighed pounds of food swallowed and wood burned, measured the concrete in the building where they met, and the nylon in the fabrics of their tents, and measured every penny spent.

Rowan Sherwood joined Jim in 1998. Her path was "more subtle" than Jim's: "Some people have to hit bottom before they change. Others just tune into their freedom." Waiting for her leg to heal after a motorcycle accident in her twenties, Rowan had time to discover her freedom, as she sat in the garden of her house each day, reconsidering which life path would bring her happiness, and resolving to follow it.

The GLP researchers quantified the happiness and unhappiness they felt during their six weeks. Ultimately the study showed what Rowan had discovered in her own contemplation: that North Americans are capable of reducing their footprint significantly—the researchers averaged a little above three acres—without reducing their happiness. [13]

In the midst of these studies, Jim noticed his own house, which was only 400 square feet, but used two cords of wood each winter.

The couple resolved to build a smaller, straw bale cabin that would cut their wood use in half. They started in October of 1998. Struggling to keep the bales dry and slipping on the icy roof, they wished they'd waited until spring to start.

The whole south wall is glass, allowing a view of the surrounding wilderness. There are small windows on each of the other sides. The house could only be sited on a northern slope, so the solar gain is limited, but since the space is small, is warmed by two bodies, and the walls are made of R-38, firewood use is just one cord per winter.

"When I first got to BC I thought 'the wood in the forest is rotting anyway—why can't I burn it?' I cut nearly every standing dead tree near the house for firewood. Then I noticed the woodpeckers had left. Of course they left— they had no trees to bang their heads on! These big old trees stand for 200 years alive. One day they fall and rot for a few hundred years. They are nests for hundreds, and they rot into a sponge that holds more water than anything humans have ever created. These dead hulks regulate the creeks. The uncut creeks on our land flow fairly steady after five days of rain, but the pockmarked, cut-over creeks will rage during spring runoff then nearly dry up in the summer. There's no ecological free lunch." —Jim

The main floor is wooden plank, from a salvage yard, and the loft floor is from the land, chainsaw-milled by Jim. The walls are plastered in local earth. One corner of the dwelling has a shower basin drained out so they can bathe inside in winter, with water heated by the stove.

Jim saved receipts from the project, and also weighed a sample of each material: steel hardware, and wood, straw, and glass. The weight of each material was noted on a footprint spreadsheet (see the sidebar exercise) to calculate how much land area was used to supply the raw materials, the energy for production, and to absorb the wastes. The spreadsheet determined that if their cabin is used by two people for sixty years, it will have consumed about one tenth of an acre annually.

They lived in the cabin just four years, due to a "class 1 design error": it is located 3,000 miles away from their families. One trip home cost them more acres than living in their house all year. They could stop visiting their families, or move. In 2004 they moved home.

Their new house, which is long and narrow, is twice the size of the one they left, but somehow has less space. The layout "doesn't allow a circle of people to form inside," says Rowan. With time they will retrofit it. They've brought with them the same habits they had in BC. Jim says it's easier each year to live on $5,000. "Joe Dominguez told me that consciousness grows faster than inflation, and it's true. Each year I know how to grow food better, how to repair more things myself, and each year I have more friends, to teach me how to share more."

CALCULATING YOUR ECOLOGICAL FOOTPRINT

ITEM	AMOUNT USED PER MONTH	STANDARD UNITS/	METRIC UNITS	FOOTPRINT FACTOR (Standard)	FOOTPRINT FACTOR (metric)	ECOLOGICAL FOOTPRINT (in sq yards or square meters)
Dwelling (living area per person)*						
Age of home						
40 years	______	sq ft	sq m	12.2	109	______
60 years	______	sq ft	sq m	8	73	______
80 years	______	sq ft	sq m	6.1	54	______
100 years	______	sq ft	sq m	4.8	43	______
120 years	______	sq ft	sq m	4	36	______
Yard or total lot size including building**	______	sq yard	sq meter	2	2	______
Hotel expenditure	______	$	$	136	115	______
Electricity:						
From the grid (unknown source)***	______	kWh	kWh	31	27	______
Fossil fuel and nuclear	______	kWh	kWh	35	30	______
Large hydro	______	kWh	kWh	2	2	______
Small hydro	______	kWh	kWh	0.02	0.01	______
PV solar	______	kWh	kWh	0.3	0.3	______
Natural Gas, city	______	therms	sq m	232	76	______
Propane	______	gallon	l	208	46	______
Kerosene, fuel oil	______	gallon	l	389	87	______
Coal	______	lb	kg	35	64	______
Water, sewer, garbage collection	______	$	$	157	133	______
Firewood****	______	lb	kg	37	69	______
TOTALS		______	______	______	______	______

*Divide the total indoor living area by the number of people sharing it for a per-person number. If there are rooms that only some people use, account for this in your calculation. The system is calibrated to understand that the total area is entered each month.

**Do not include area that is used primarily for food production. Do not include land that is kept completely natural as wildlife habitat.

***A cord of wood is $128ft^3$ (4x4x8ft) and contains roughly 3,500 pounds of wood.

Worksheet adapted by permission from Radical Simplicity by Jim Merkel, New Society Publishers 2003[12]

YOU CAN CALCULATE THE MONTHLY ECOLOGICAL FOOTPRINT OF YOUR HOUSE USING THIS SPREADSHEET. FOR EXAMPLE, IF YOU SHARE 1,400 SQUARE FEET WITH ONE PERSON, IN A 40-YEAR-OLD HOUSE, YOUR FIRST ENTRY WILL BE "700 X 12.2=8,540 SQ YARDS." CONTINUE DOWN THE CHART, THEN CONVERT THE RESULT TO ACRES. 100 SQUARE YARDS IS EQUAL TO .021 ACRES. SEARCH UNDER "ECOLOGICAL FOOTPRINT" ON THE WEB TO LEARN MORE ABOUT HOW TO USE THIS CHART.

PEGGY REENTS AND JON THANDAI
Built 2004

COST:
20,000 bhat ($500 US)

UTILITIES:
Candles, $3/month; electricity (shared with another family), $4/month; firewood gathered for cooking

LOCATION:
Northern Thailand

Chiangmai is a tropical area with banana and mango and tamarind

trees, and the sweet smell of fruit souring is in the breeze. There are hardwoods in the forest, and the ground is gravel and clay of many colors, browns and yellows and light and dark purple. From this land, Jon Thandai, a farmer, builds houses.

Jon once took a bicycle trip through New Mexico and he stopped by accident in the Taos Pueblo, a 1,000-year-old low-rise adobe townhouse village. "It was so hot outside, but it was cool inside," Jon says. He couldn't read English, but he found a pamphlet about adobe and studied the pictures.

When Jon was a little boy, the long saw was introduced to his village. People stopped cutting bamboo with machetes to build their sleeping platforms, and instead sawed down the ancient hardwoods in the forest, and built houses, up on poles, with air circulating below and a tin roof on top. All 600 houses in his village have been replaced at least once in Jon's lifetime, and the forest is thinned of its trees now.

In the late 1980s the Thai government began promoting concrete houses, funded with mortgages. Many villagers, including Jon's sister, replaced their wood homes. In 1999 the Thai economy collapsed. "Many factories closed, and some rich people committed suicide. The government had loaned farmers money, but farmers don't know how to manage money. They bought motorcycles and concrete houses. They knew how to farm, so they didn't need any money for farming. They couldn't pay back those loans. The collapse helped us to start thinking about what we really care about."

> **"I built my first house working two to four hours a day, never more than four, in the late afternoon or early morning, when other people went out to play soccer or jog. I built bricks. The wood for the brick molds comes from the old hardwood houses. In three months I had a house. It's three rooms, 12, 9, and 18 square meters. I said, "Wow. It's so easy." Most farmers find it's not easy to get a house. If I have eight people working four hours per day for four days we make 2,000 bricks, enough for a single-story, small house. I've built about one house each year for a few years. So I am very poor still, but I have my houses. I let people stay in them."**
>
> **—Jon Thandai**

The concrete walls hold heat, and allow no breeze to pass, so many people use them as storage, and sleep instead on thatched bamboo platforms. However, the look of a concrete house has become fashionable, and having just a bamboo platform has become a sign of poverty, so when Jon began building adobe houses, the villagers were interested (see left).

In 2002 Jon attended an international workshop organized by a group of activist Buddhists and Janell Kapoor, a cob teacher from the United States. One hundred twenty-five people came, including several young Bangkok architects who abandoned their city lives and took up the path of adobe, and a friend who would introduce Jon to his future wife, Peggy Reents. Peggy was an American volunteer who had spent a year in the slums of Khon Kaen, and found, "Living there sure changed my ideas about space, and about what I need. In the city, people depended on their jobs, which weren't stable. Here they depend on each other. It's more hopeful."

"The Santi Asho movement promotes meritism instead of capitalism—the more merits you can accumulate from good deeds, the better you succeed. In our workshops we teach how to follow your consciousness, instead of only your feelings. We talk about how to live the easy way. Why build a big house and live in less than 20 percent of the house? Why make life hard? For many generations we lived the easy way. We did not have this word 'busy.' In the past people spent all day making a basket to take an offering to the temple. Now we use plastic baskets, and if someone makes a beautiful basket, we say they are lazy— how do they have time?" —Jon Thandai

The media has helped to bring knowledge of this technology to a wider public. According to Janell there are now at least 600 similar houses built in Thailand. Jon helps The Santi Asho movement, a fundamentalist Buddhist group, with trainings that they hold three times each month, with about 120 people in each course.

Soon, Peggy and Jon built their own home, designed by Peggy, and her brother, who was visiting, to be oval like a rice seed. They located it on the least fertile soil they could find, to avoid wasting farmland. The main door, on the west side has a bamboo terrace, covered in passionfruit vine, for shade. On the east side a second door allows a cross-breeze. Five windows shed bright light, which bugs dislike. Peggy mud-washes the earthen floor every day—"It doesn't take long once you know how"— and the walls are covered in brown clay plasters dug from nearby and sealed with tapioca starch. A researcher from Bangkok determined that although outside temperature varies between 38 and 10 Celsius, (100 and 50° F), inside the house stays between 24 and 26° C (75–78° F). The roof is thatch, which does attract insects if they leave the house unoccupied for too many months. "But that's how a house should be," says Peggy. "If it isn't being used, it should go back into the ground."

Peggy and Jon hope to spend part of each year in Colorado, and build a tiny village of earth houses there with Peggy's family, as an experiment in self-reliance. "People say it can't be done in the U.S.," says Jon, "but I think it can."

PEARL MAST AND DAVID OMICK
Built 1997

AREA:
128-sq.-ft. main house, 128-sq.-ft. porch, 16-sq.-ft. composting toilet, on a few square miles of wilderness

INTENDED NUMBER OF OCCUPANTS:
2

COST:
$3,000, including water line

LOCATION:
Southern Arizona

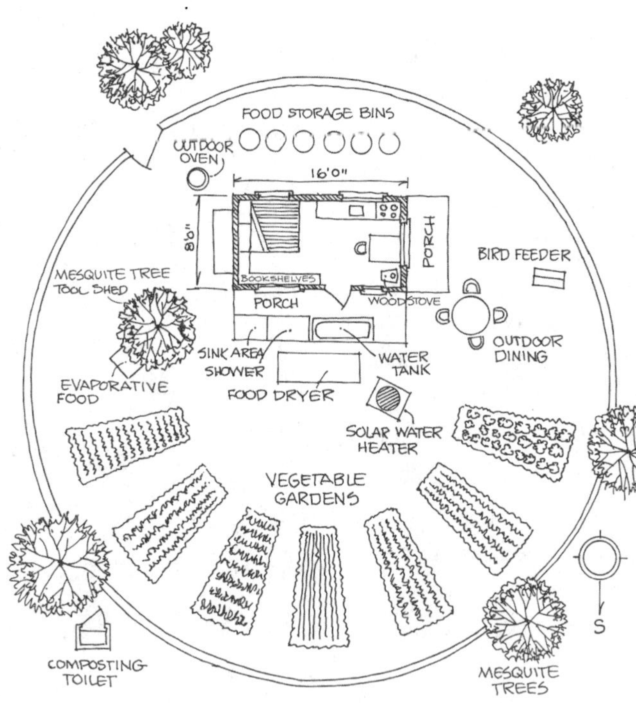

ABOVE: **SITE PLAN, DESERT YACHT**

There's a part of Arizona where the saguaro cactus

and the juniper trees meet with the mesquite, where three corners of bioregions overlap. David and Pearl moved to this land from south Texas, where they had lived with Catholic nuns developing and promoting appropriate technology and working in the immigrant community around them. They enjoyed their work in the greater community, but sought a situation where they could delve deeper into the questions of simplicity, balance, and alternative technology. David, who was formerly a sailmaker, had recently built a solar oven so hot it burned paper, and was beginning to build composting toilets. Pearl has always preferred the aesthetic of clean lines and a minimum of stuff.

Their cottage is indeed clean and smooth, like a tiny yacht somehow beached in a canyon, protected from flash floods beneath a spur ridge, with the land fanning in waves out around them. They built it of industrial materials: clad in T-111 exterior plywood, with a varnished plywood floor and a white painted ceiling. Some might fancy more natural materials, but since human circumstances and desires are subject to change they wanted something mobile. It needed to be light, and to fit on the axle that is under it.

“We had built with earth and straw, and enjoyed it, We did notice in Texas that an adobe house with a mud floor— well, it was typically the last thing the Mexican immigrants wanted. They wanted modern and bright. They wanted a concrete house, and they'd settle for a new trailer.

"We started to wonder for ourselves, could we build a trailer that was durable, aesthetically pleasing, and adapted to the desert? In any case, a 120-square-foot house is almost certain to use fewer industrial materials than a 1,200-square-foot house made of natural materials. Some of the developments of the industrial age—bolts and screws, for example—are just so adaptable. Unscrewing and unbolting allows materials to be reused and reinvented in different forms over time."

They built their home in a year of discussions, drawings and redrawings, three weeks building the shell off-site, and three weeks building in the cabinets, bed, porch, and composting toilet. They believe every joint, every cut in the design is easy enough for a handy, patient, but unskilled person to duplicate.

The details are ingenious. The doors are counterweighted with fabric bags filled with sand. The gates latch with simple bent pieces of metal strapping. A metal shelf, suspended directly over the oil lamp on

TOP LEFT: COUNTERWEIGHTS MADE OF FABRIC AND SAND. TOP RIGHT: METAL STRAPPING BENT INTO A LATCH. BOTTOM LEFT: THE STRUCTURE IS LEVELED ON NINE THREE-QUARTER-INCH BOLTS BOTTOM RIGHT: THE OIL LAMP WARMS THE KETTLE.

LEFT: GARDEN BEDS, A SOLAR WATER HEATER, AND A FOOD DRYER ON THE SOUTH SIDE OF THE HOUSE RIGHT: WASHING DISHES

the dining table, holds a kettle of warm water whenever the lamp is lit. The entire structure is leveled on nine three-quarter-inch bolts, placed on stones. The effect is streamlined, like a boat ready to float.

A breadbox-sized army tent woodstove, placed in one corner, is sufficient to heat the home. Opposite the stove, the bed is raised to window height, for good cross-ventilation, and storage below; the empty wall space behind is a backrest for reading. Bookshelves dominate one end of the space. Their priorities greet the visitor clearly: the *Encyclopedia Britannica* receives 6 feet of shelf space. Pearl insisted on 8 feet of kitchen counter space, which was no idle desire: besides cooking every day, she cans fruit and vegetables, and dries meat and herbs.

The south side of the house is lined with a porch, enclosed by a trellis, covered in vines in summer, and open to the sun in winter. The house is fed by a well, pumped by a windmill 700 feet away, and piped to a metal stock tank next to the dwelling. They could have a pressurized tank and a spigot instead, but they prefer scooping pails from the stock tank as it allows them to feel the water they are using.To ensure their drinking water is perfectly pure, they bottle it close to the source.

Dishes are washed outside, in a few basins on a table, next to the water tank. On the opposite side of the tank is a drip rack for wet laundry that allows water to drain to the vines. Next to the rack is the shower stand. A dark five-gallon container is filled with water, placed in the sun, then dumped into the shower bucket once the water is hot. The "tool shed" consists of garden tools held by the branches of a mesquite tree. "This way," says David, "we don't have to buy lumber for a shed."

Pearl and David often eat straight from their garden. Intrigued to see how much of their food they can grow and gather themselves, they dug twelve garden beds in a semicircle opposite the house. This design allowed them to hand-water with a minimum of walking, and made it easy to fence the area with one continuous circle of 4 foot high galvanized steel "cattle panels." Thirty steps from the entrance to the homestead, goats bleat at passersby. Beyond the goats, the land offers cactus fruit, edible salt weed, and most importantly, mesquite pods which the couple dries and then grinds into high-protein flour, which they cook into sweet pancakes and cover with homemade cactus fruit jam for breakfast. Behind the house the circle is completed with six fifty-five-gallon steel drums, outfitted with shelves that store hundreds of jars of fruit and vegetable preserves, dried meat and herbs, and flour, and topped with a steel cap that protects their food from ringtail cats, coati, raccoons, and a host of small rodents.

LEFT: THE TOOL SHED, WITH A ONE PLANK FOR A FLOOR RIGHT: FIFTY-FIVE-GALLON STEEL DRUMS STORE HUNDREDS OF JARS OF PRESERVES.

[Q] Do you have any suggestions for others?

[A] **DAVID:** Think small, think simple. Build below your means. Maintain a margin of time, of money, and of your energy. One promise we've made is whatever we have will be something we use daily or at least seasonally, things that actually work, and are easy to build, clean, and maintain. We've had experiments, like an evaporative food cooler, that could in fact cool food and looked intriguing, but the fabric rotted fairly quickly, so we abandoned that project. It's important to acknowledge when things aren't working.

[Q] Why have you chosen this life?

[A] **PEARL:** Because I like it. This is my favorite dwelling that we've ever lived in.

David thinks I should mention my Mennonite roots, but my siblings aren't living this way, so I'm not sure that's it. We like to be outside, and be connected to the world. It feeds us. This is not a life of deprivation. Self-denial just doesn't inspire.

I am inspired by the words of Jesus, "Heaven's imperial rule is like some trader looking for beautiful pearls. When that merchant finds one priceless pearl, he sells everything he owns and buys it." It's a lifetime quest. We both put a very high value on freedom and flexibility. Consider this: you might be freer without something than with it.

Then there's also the issue of how much of the world's resources can we justly lay claim to? My feeling, my gut feeling is that we are still using more than our fair share.

EPILOGUE:

In 2001 the couple started spending four months of summer each year with friends on a farm in Oregon, where they plant and harvest a big garden, and gather berries. In 2005, the riverbed near their desert cottage seemed to be slowly migrating, covering the wide, natural passageway to the road. They worried that eventually they would have to use heavy machinery if they wanted to move the trailer out. And after 8 good years in the canyon they wanted to live closer to friends and neighbors. So they disassembled their garden, bolted the tongue and wheels back on to the trailer, and with a friend's pickup truck towed their cottage out of the canyon 3 miles away to a friend's acreage, near the social "heart" of their rural community. They are happy to be a 5-minute bike ride from a large community garden, and they're happy to watch the land repair and erase the various indentations they made on the earth's surface at the old site.

Endnotes

INTRODUCTION

1. *Worldwatch Paper 124*, by D. M. Roodman and N. Lenssen, Worldwatch Institute, Washington, D.C., 1995.

2. *Building Codes for a Small Planet,* The Development Center for Appropriate Technology, P.O. Box 27513, Tucson, AZ, 520-624-6628, www.dcat.net.

3. "Effects of household dynamics on resource consumption and biodiversity" by Jianquo (Jack) Liu et al., *Nature*, January 12, 2003.

4. See Chapter 6, especially endnote 2, "Household Energy Consumption" table. See also *Revue de l'Energie*, 1996, p. 285, by L. Shipper, and "This New House," by Nathan Fox, *Mother Jones Magazine*, March/April 2005.

5. *A Golden Thread: 2500 Years of Solar Architecture and Technology*, by Ken Butti and John Perklin, Cheshire Books, 1980.

6. *More Work for Mother*, by Ruth Schwartz Cowan, Basic Books, 1983.

9. *Crabgrass Frontier*, by Kenneth T. Jackson, Oxford, 1985.

10. Crabgrass Frontier, by Kenneth T. Jackson, Oxford, and *Redesigning the American Dream,* by Dolores Hayden, W. W. Norton, 1983.

11. "Invasion of the Reluctant Renters," by Eric Dash and David Leonhardt, *The New York Times*, September 16, 2005.

12. "Home Builders' Stock Sales: Diversifying or Bailing Out?" *The New York Times*, October 2005. For a more thorough discussion see "The House Building Complex," *The New York Times Magazine*, October 16, 2005.

13. Forty vacant new luxury houses in a controversial Maryland development were set on fire in 2004 (see *The Week*, December 17, 2004). It's not an isolated incident. See also "Urban Sprawl," *National Geographic*, July 2001.

CHAPTER 1

1. *Crabgrass Frontier*, by Kenneth T. Jackson, Oxford University Press, 1985, p. 235.

2. "Invasion of the Monster Homes," by Maria Alicia Gaura and Carolyne Zinko, *San Francisco Chronicle*, 2001. DeKalb County, in Georgia (2006); Los Angeles, California; and Chicago, Illinois, are a few of the places that have placed restrictions on new houses that dwarf their neighbors. Aspen, Colorado, has entered the debate, by effectively banning houses over 15,000 square feet.

3. *The Millionaire Next Door*, by Stanley and Danko, Simon and Schuster, 1996, p. 147.

4. Lecture by Juliet Schor, Center for Popular Economics Summer Institute, 1999.

5. *The Overworked American*, by Juliet Schor, Basic Books, 1993; see also *The Wealthy 100*, by Michael Klepper and Robert Gunther, Carol Publishing, 1996;

7. **FLOOR AREA OF NEW HOUSES IS INCREASING WHILE FAMILY SIZE IS DECREASING**

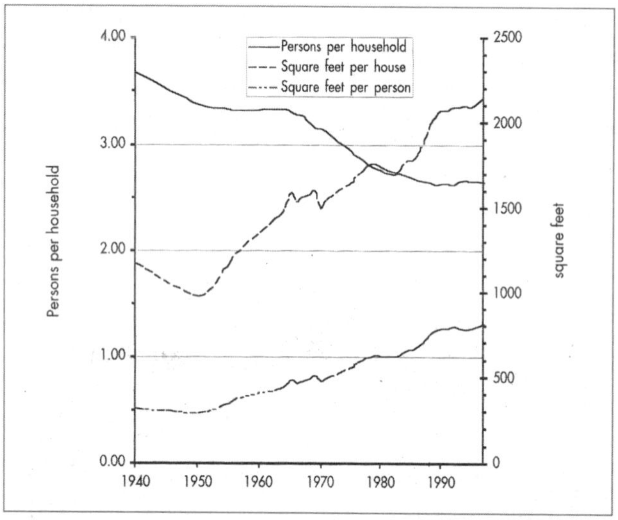

8. **COMPARATIVE ANNUAL ENERGY USE FOR SMALL VS. LARGE HOUSES**

House (sq ft)	Location	Energy Standards	Heating MMBtu	Cooling MMBtu	Heating Cost[3]	Cooling Cost[4]
3,000	Boston	Good[1]	73	19	$1,335	$190
1,500	Boston	Good[1]	35	13	$651	$131
1,500	Boston	Poor[2]	48	12	$891	$124
3,000	St. Louis	Good[1]	61	29	$1,134	$294
1,500	St. Louis	Good[1]	29	20	$543	$198
1,500	St. Louis	Poor[2]	40	21	$741	$206

Notes:

1. "Good" houses have R-19 walls, R-30 ceilings, double low-e (U=0.36) vinyl windows, R-4.4 doors, infiltration of .50 ACH heating and .25 ACH cooling, and R-6 ducts in attic.
2. Poorly insulated houses have R-13 walls, R-19 ceilings, insulated glass vinyl windows, R-2.1 doors, infiltration of .50 ACH heating and .25 cooling, and uninsulated ducts.
3. Heating costs assume natural gas at $1.50 per therm (updated 2006).
4. Cooling costs assume electricity at $0.10 per kWh.

Energy modeling by Andy Shapiro, Energy Balance, Inc. (Montpelier, Vermont) using REM/Rate Residential Energy Analysis and Rating Software. Adapted with permission from the January 1999 issue of Environmental Building News. *© BuildingGreen, Inc.*

quoted in *Luxury Fever*, by Robert Frank, Free Press, 1999, p. 15.

6. See "AOL Founder's Latest Lifestyle Choice," by Annys Shin, *Washington Post*, August 9, 2005; a receptionist at Jirka Rysavy's company said she believes he has a modest apartment in town as well.

7. "Do You Look Best Wearing Envious Green?" by Abbey Ellin, *The New York Times*, Sunday, January 20, 2002, Sec. 3, p. 11.

8. For a more complete treatment of these ideas, see *Luxury Fever*, by Robert Frank, Free Press, 1999.

9. See also *Poverty and Famine*, by Anyat Sen, Caredon Press, 1981.

10. For additional discussion of the phenomena of better schools in expensive neighborhoods, see *Graceful Simplicity: Toward a Philosophy and Politics of Simple Living*, by Jerome M. Segal, Henry Holt, 1999.

11. Data in Graph 11 was reported in *Advertising and the End of the World*, a video produced by Sut Jhally and the Media Education Foundation, 1997. Data in Graph 1.2 is from the Residential Energy Consumption Survey 2002, Congressional Information Service. See also *Energy Economics,* Vol. 6, Issue 1, January 1984. Researcher Sandra Hutton reports: "Income has little effect on Btu use once house size is taken into account."

12. Information about the Whitehall Studies is very widely available. I assume that the reason larger houses were correlated to better health is simply because they are related to higher status.

13. *Luxury Fever*, by Robert Frank, The Free Press, 1999, pp. 140–42.

14. There have been numerous studies that show this. One famous nine-year study in 1960s–1970s showed improved health and decreased mortality due to social networks. See "Social Networks Host Resistance and Mortality," by L. F. Berkman, *American Journal of Epidemiology* No. 109, 1979; and *Social Interaction and Patient Care*, by J. Skipper and R. Leonard, Lippincott, 1965. Similar, more recent studies have the same findings: "Australian Longitudinal Study of Aging," by L. Giles, *Journal of Epidemiology and Community Health*, June 16, 2005, Vol. 59. The Australian study showed that friendships contribute far more to health and longevity than do offspring.

15. *Ethica Nicomachea*, by Aristotle, translated by W. D. Ross, Oxford University Press, 1925, Book 8, Chapters 5 and 11.

16. Further reading: *The Simple Home*, by Charles Keeler, Paul Elder, 1904, reprinted 1979; *Downwardly Mobile for Conscience Sake*, by Dorothy Norvell Andersen, Tom Paine Institute, 1995; and *The Paradox of Choice: Why More Is Less*, by Barry Schwartz, HarperCollins, 2004.

CHAPTER 2

1. See *Storage Units: America's Creeping Menace*, by M. P. Dunleavey at MSN Money 9-30-2002, http://moneycentral.msn.com. See also "Self-Storage Demand Study," published by the Self Storage Association 2005.

2. *The Overworked American*, by Juliet B. Schor, Basic Books, 1992. For further thoughts on related subjects, see also *Affluenza: The All-Consuming Epidemic*, by John de Graaf, David Wann, and Thomas H. Naylor, Berret-Koehler, 2001.

3. *The Sun*, June 2005, p. 35, and verified through personal correspondence.

4. For information about the natural building movement, see *The Art of Natural Building*, edited by Joseph Kennedy, Michael G. Smith, and Catherine Wanek, New Society Publishers, 2002.

5. Due to zoning regulations, in many areas. "On a fifty-foot-wide lot, no architect is talented enough to overcome the requirement that two thirds of the façade must be dedicated to garage doors." *Suburban Nation*, by Andres Duany, Elizabeth Plater-Zyberk, and Jeff Speck, North Point Press, 2000. For general information about the effect of the automobile on the built environment, see *Asphalt Nation*, by Jane Holtz Kay, University of California Press, 1997.

6. A typical refrigerator built on the 1990s uses as much energy as leaving six small televisions on ten to twelve hours a day. One of the most interesting fridge upgrades we've seen is to unplug it, put it outside tilted toward the sun, and replace its contents with a water tank, taken from an old water heater (which you will no longer need). Put a sheet of glass on top, and presto! a solar water heater. An old deep-freezer works best.

7. Old copies of *Mother Earth News* are one source for further information; see "Good Food Without Refrigeration," by Miriam Bunce, July/August 1975.

8. See *Liquid Gold: The Lore and Logic of Using Urine to Grow Plants*, by Carol Steinfeld and Malcolm Wells, Green Frigate, 2005; and *Humanure Handbook*, by Joseph Jenkins, Jenkins Publishing, 2000.

9. Patricia Kerns wrote about her life in *The Last Straw Journal*, Summer 2000.

10. Simone Swan studied with and worked for Egyptian architect Hassan Fathy, who tried to revive the adobe tradition in Egypt in an era where concrete was replacing traditional structures. She trained Jesusita Jimenez and other people to build this way. *Simone Swan: Adobe Building*, by Dennis Dollens, Sites Books, 2005.

CHAPTER 3

1. One Protestant reader has pointed out that Puritans were not more anti-body than other religious groups of their time.

2. *The Silent Language*, by Edward T. Hall, Doubleday, 1966, p. 118.

3. To learn more about cob, see *The Hand-Sculpted House,* by Ianto Evans, Linda Smiley, and Michael G. Smith, Chelsea Green, 2002; *The Cob Builders Handbook*, by Becky Bee, Groundworks Publishing, 1998; and *The Cobber's Companion*, by Michael G. Smith.

For general information about design, I suggest *Japanese Homes and Their Surroundings*, by Edward Morse, Charles E. Tuttle Company, 1887; *If You Want to Build a House*, by Elizabeth Mock, The Museum of Modern Art Publishing, 1946; *A Pattern Language, by* Christopher Alexander, Sara Ishikawa, Murray Silverstein, et al., Oxford University Press, 1977; *Conran's Living in Small Spaces*, by Lorrie Mack, Little, Brown and Company Publishing, 1988; *Places of the Soul,* by Christopher Day, Thornsons/Harper Collins, 1990; and *The Earth House*, by Jeanne Dupreau, New Chapter Press, 1992.

CHAPTER 4

1. "Your Dream Home Brought Down to Earth," by Wainwright Evans, *Better Homes and Gardens,* May 1929.

2. See U.S. Census Bureau, Housing Tables "Homeownership."

3. Home Equity as a Percentage of Household Real Estate data, from the board of governors of the Federal Reserve Statistics of the United States. Chart from "For Middle-Class Families, Dream of Own House Drowns in Sea of Debt," by Christian E. Weller, Ph.D., Center for American Progress, May 2005.

4. Mortgage calculators are easily found on the Internet. You can calculate for yourself what a specific sum will cost over time.

5. See U.S. Census, Historical Census of Housing Tables Homeownership. See also "For Middle-Class Families, Dream of Own House Drowns in Sea of Debt," by Christian E. Weller, Ph.D., Center for American Progress, May 2005. "America" in this sentence refers to the U.S. Canada has a significantly different history and present. About half of Canadian homeowners carry a mortgage, which accounts, on average, for just one-fifth of

the household's disposable income. Government backing of mortgage bank loans in Canada began in 1987, unlike the long history in the U.S., and their share of the national debt is still below 10 percent. See *Where Credit Is Due: Residential Mortgage Finance in Canada, 1901 to 1954,* by Richard Harris and Doris Ragonetti, Kluwer Academic Publisher, 1998. Compare also Australia: About 30 percent of households in Australia have a mortgage, 40 percent own their house outright, and 30 percent are renting. See *Review of the Reserve Bank of Australia 2003* at http://www.aph.gov.au/house/committee/efpa/rba2002_03/interimreport/chap2.

6. See U.S. Census, Historical Census of Housing Tables Homeownership.

7. A variety of studies seem to show codes and zoning increase cost. See Chapter 10.

8. Some researchers trace the idea of interest to Sumerian times, when the loans included the loaning of domestic animals that were expected to reproduce. There's some evidence that something like compound interest existed in Babylon. Look for writings by William N. Goetzmann, and see *Accounting, Business & Financial History*, 8:2, Routledge, July 1998.

9. The value placed on real estate has outpaced U.S. National Income. Source: Federal Reserve and Bureau of Economic Analysis. Inspiration for this graph came from a marvelous set of graphs by economist Michael Hudson and artist Nigel Holmes, published in *Harpers,* May 2006.

10. *Snakes and Ladders,* by Gita Mehta, Doubleday, 1997.

11. "JAK, The Interest Free Savings & Loan" brochure, produced 1993. Address: Hälsans Hus, Fjällgatan 23A 116 28, Stockholm. For information about Islamic Banks in the U.S., contact LARIBA American Finance House, 750 E. Green Street, Suite 210, Pasadena, CA 91101.

12. "Green" mortgages are also called "Energy Efficient Mortgages" (EEM). Most of them are not based on actual performance, but on the acquisition of various new low-energy-use appliances and products—so if you reduce your energy use through home-made means (like sewing superinsulated window coverings, or shading a wall with a porch), even if you show your utilities bills have decreased, typically it won't be easy for you to refinance with an EEM.

13. The Allens credit their knowledge of irregular prepayments to *The Banker's Secret*, by Marc Eisenson, Villard, 1990; previously and subsequently published by Good Advice Press.

14. The majority of land in the United States is held by the federal and state governments. The Bureau of Land Management owns about 40 percent of the federal estate. The private land that is left over is held by a tiny group of companies and individuals. See *Planet Management*, by Alanna Hartzok, Robert Schalkenbach Foundation, January 1994. I don't believe the amendment to reclassify land as a financial instrument was yet passed, although it has reappeared in at least one other form, tagged on to other legislation. Banks would prefer it because it would eliminate the need to pay brokers and real estate agents.

15. Portland cement is made by burning clay or sand and limestone and other substances, in a kiln, at about 1,480 degrees Celsius. Petroleum is often used to heat the kiln, and a variety of waste materials, including car tires and hazardous waste, are sometimes used as a fuel supplement.

16. See "Conversion Factors for Pacific Northwest Wood Products," Institute of Forest Products, June 1957. David E. Kretschmann, of the U.S. Forest Service, verified that this conversion rate is probably approximately accurate. For statistics about cement, see "Supplementary Cementing Materials" Government of Canada publication, October 24, 2003.

17. Further resources: *Mortgage Free*, by Rob Roy, Chelsea Green, 1998; and *Home-Building Debt Free*, by Lynn Underwood, International Conference of Building Officials. "Optimizing Wood Framing," by Peter Yost and Ann Edminsterin, *Building Safety Journal,* is an excellent resource for minimizing wood use in conventional frame housing. Although they are not specifically about housing, I also suggest *Your Money or Your Life*, by Joe Dominguez and Vicki Robin, Penguin, 1999, and *The Joy of Simple Living*, by Janet Luhrs, Broadway, 1997. To better understand interest and money, see *Money: Understanding and Creating Alternatives to Legal Tender*, by Thomas H. Greco, Jr., Chelsea Green, 2001.

18. There's a kind of classic, *Passive Solar Energy Book*, by Edward Mazria, Rodale Press, 1979. See also *The Independent Home*, by Michael Potts, Chelsea Green, 1993.

19. See *Where Credit Is Due: Residential Mortgage Finance in Canada, 1901 to 1954* (see above, footnote 5).

20. For information about how builders and developers could build more affordably, see *Democratic Architecture*, by Donald MacDonald Whitney, Library of Design, 1996.

CHAPTER 5

1. Ninety percent is a common figure, cited widely, and usually attributed to the U.S. Environmental Protection Agency, which posts that figure on its website. The California Air Board found that Californians spend 87 percent of their time, or twenty-one hours per day, indoors. Specifically, they spend on average fifteen hours per day inside their homes, six hours in other indoor locations, two hours in transit, and one hour outside. Transit was thus counted as "not inside." See the reports, "Activity Patterns of California Residents," May 1991, and "Indoor Air Pollution: A Serious Public Health Problem," May 2, 2001, http://www.arb.ca.gov/research/indoor/rediap.htm.

2. Ultraviolet light, especially UVB, possibly protects against some forms of cancer. See "Commentary: Time for Public Health Action on Vitamin D for Cancer Risk Reduction," by William B. Grant and Edward D. Gorham, in *International Journal of Epidemiology* Vol. 35, No. 2, 2005.

3. Ayurvedic medicine is one tradition that emphasizes the importance of following the "circadian rythms," the daily, routine pattern of activity, especially sleepiness and alertness, which are regulated by the hypothalamus, in a twenty-five-hour cycle that, interestingly, readjusts itself to the twenty-four-hour daily cycle.

4. See "Am I Different Because I Have Allergies?" by Jacob L. Pinnas, M.D., *Tucson HealthStyle*, vol. 2, no. 1, January/February 1995, pp. 19–20; reconfirmed in personal conversation, May 2002.

5. For an explanation of the levels of carcinogens and some of the other nasty bits you're probably inhaling right now, see "Project Summary of the Total Exposure Assessment Methodology (TEAM) Study," by Lance A. Wallace, U.S. EPA, September 1987. Researchers examined people's breath each day after they had been in various locations for normal amounts of time, and found, "In all cases personal air values exceeded outdoor air values by ratios of 2-5.... The highest indoor concentrations exceeded the highest outdoor air concentrations by factors of 10–20." Note that this study focused on volatile organic compounds—gases that are likely to cause cancer. However, particulate matter, such as construction dust, and the black powder produced by tires moving on pavement, were not studied as thoroughly. Ozone, a dangerous gas, was not studied, since its source is outside (it's created by sunlight hitting a mixture of polluting gases in the atmosphere) and won't normally be found in your house. However, ozone is only very rarely present outside in dangerous levels. Matt Haber, a Deputy Director in the Air Division of the EPA explains, "The exact location outside is of course significant—standing next to a diesel bus is normally more toxic than

being at home. Also, there may be spikes in pollution, for example from a forest fire, or particularly strong winds, that make it advantageous to go inside for a period of time, although over the long run, the outdoors in any city is less polluted than indoors, because the indoor environment typically adds to outdoor pollutant loads." Natural allergens that cause some people discomfort but not disease, such as pollen, are not considered pollution. Presumably, if you reduce the toxins in your home—eliminate carpets, chlorinated water, new paint, plastic, solvents, commercial cleaners, etc.—you may create an environment that approaches the lower pollution levels of the air outside your walls. Air filters can cut the pollution level in your home, but they increase pollution outdoors when they require additional energy use.

6. Wendy Northcutt in *The Darwin Awards*, Dutton/Penguin, 2000, reported that a 1993 autopsy revealed that a man had died from a combination of a poorly ventilated room and a gassy diet, which caused an unusually high level of methane in his blood that was likely the cause of his death.

7. There are many guides to reducing the toxins in your home. The Environmental Protection Agency offers free brochures. For information about how various products inside your home affect your health, see *Home Safe Home*, by Debra Lynn Dadd, Tarcher/Putnam, 1997. For information on safer interior finish alternatives, see *Natural Remodeling for the Not-So-Green House: Bringing Your Home into Harmony with Nature*, by Carol Venolia and Kelly Lerner, Lark, 2006.

8. This is the amount the Unified Building Code recommends. However, especially if you are in a hot, humid climate, and depending on whether the windows are placed to avoid or take advantage of prevailing winds, you may want more ventilation.

9. Carolyn Roberts, author of *A House of Straw*, adapted this design to build her own house. She lives in a dusty location, near wild rodents, so she uses enclosed cabinets for storage on the porch. The sunroom is a favorite location and, similar to the ancient Roman *helocaminus*, acts as her sole source of heat in winter, and a pleasant place to be on windy days. "I have French doors between the sunroom and the main room. I shut off the sunroom in hot summer weather and on cold winter nights, but open it during the day in winter, and at night in summer." She notes that because the sun bakes the sunroom, but not the main house directly, her furniture and curtains avoid sun damage.

Designed in collaboration with Athena and Bill Steen of the Canelo Project. the working blueprints were drawn by Dan Dorsey. *A House of Straw*, Chelsea Green 2001.

10. You can contact Les Bloomberg of the Noise Pollution Clearinghouse, who wrote (in personal correspondence in 2005): "Sleeping porches for the summer are a great idea, but it doesn't mix with [your neighbor's] air conditioning. There is nothing the person who sleeps outside can do unless they have the cooperation of the noisy party. Some AC units are much quieter than others, and central air units can be shielded using a barrier of some type. But if the neighbor won't buy a quieter unit and put up a barrier, it is not going to work. Regulations are different in every community, but often are 55 or so decibels at the property line. The problem is that in a quiet neighborhood, say 25 dB, or a 55 dB AC kicking in will wake up many people." You can read a nice article about the NPC in the March 2001 issue of *Smithsonian* magazine.

11. "Biodegradable" cleaners are not necessarily healthy for your plants. Many of them are better suited for degrading in lakes and the ocean, since many municipalities treat their sewage for eventual discharge into water. Oasis laundry detergent is one "biocompatible" laundry cleaner. It degrades into nutrients that plants like, and will not salt the soil. See http://www.bio-pac.com/biopac/oasis.htm.

12. This is an example of the "hygiene hypothesis," which has been well researched. For example, see "Does Living on a Farm During Childhood Protect Against Asthma, Allergic Rhinitis, and Atopy in Childhood?" by Leynaert B. Neukirch et al., *American Journal of Repiratory & Critical Care Medicine 164*, November 15, 2001; and "Prevalence of Hay Fever and Allergic Sensitization in Farmers' Children," by Braun-Fahrlander, C. Gassner, et al., *Institute of Social and Preventative Medicine, Clinical and Experimental Allergy*, Volume 29, Number 1, January 1, 1999.

CHAPTER 6

1. These kinds of statistics can be found in many articles. There's the near classic, *Worldwatch Paper #124: A Building Revolution: How Ecology and Health Concerns Are Transforming Construction*, by David Malin Roodman and Nicholas Lenssen, March 1995. See also "The Green House Effect," by David Ireland, *Guardian Unlimited*, May 5, 2005; and "About Supplementary Cementing Materials," *Government of Canada Action Plan 2000 on Climate Change*, at http://scm.gc.ca/indexe.html.

2. Household Energy Consumption. See also Department of Energy document, "Trends in Building-Related Energy and Carbon Emissions: Actual and Alternate Scenarios," by Stephanie J. Battles and Eugene M. Burns, August 21, 2000: "Since 1990, 48 percent of the increase in U.S. carbon emissions can be attributed to increasing emissions from the building sector." And "By 1998, the residential and commercial sectors accounted for 35 percent of all U.S. energy-related carbon emissions, more than either the industrial or the transportation sectors. Most of these carbon emissions were due to energy use in buildings." See also: "Small is Beautiful," by Alex Wilson and Jessica Boehland, *Journal of Industrial Ecology*, Winter/Spring 2005: "As would be expected, total wood use in houses has increased steadily between 1950 and 1992, as houses have grown in size. But

Household Energy Consumption 1949-1997

(source Statistical Abstract, US Census, 1998)

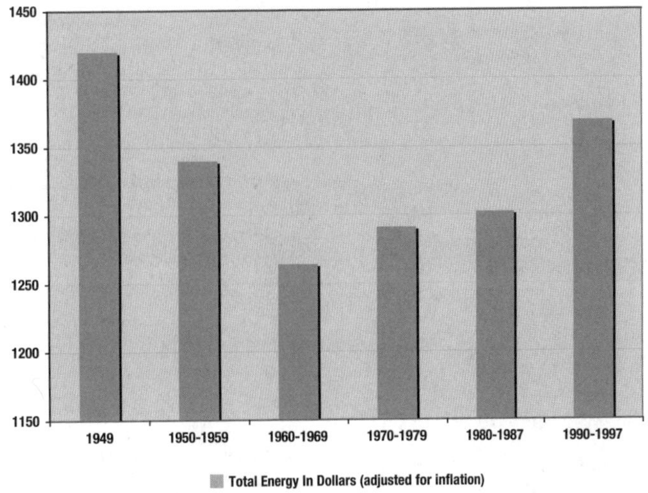

when we examine total wood use *per unit of floor area*, we find that it dropped between 1950 and 1970—perhaps due to the substitution of plywood sheathing for board sheathing and the introduction of more wood-efficient roof trusses. Then, around 1970, wood use per square foot of floor area began to increase again, and by 1992 it was up about 12% from the low point. Exactly why this is occurring is not clear; it could result from an increasing use of 2x6s instead of 2x4s for wall framing, or a shift to more complex geometries."

3. *Redesigning the American Dream*, by Dolores Hayden, Norton, 2002, p. 147.

4. *Root Shock: How Tearing up City Neighborhoods Hurts America, and What we Can Do About It*, by Mindy Thompson Fullilove, M.D., Random House, 2004.

5. Brad Lancaster wrote a detailed book about the water harvesting systems he's implemented: *Rainwater Harvesting for Drylands*, Rainsource Press, 2005.

6. See *The Arcades Project*, by Walter Benjamin, edited by Roy Tiedemann, Belknap Press, 2002.

7. See U.S. Census Bureau: *American Housing Survey for the U.S.: 2003*, issued September 2004, p. 17; and U.S. Census Bureau: *Emergency and Transitional Shelter Population 2000*, issued October 2001.

8. Information about Community Land Trusts can be found in the *Community Land Trust Handbook*, Institute for Community Economics, Rodale Press, 1982, and by contacting your local community land trust.

9. See the photo on the back cover. A story about their house appeared in *The Last Straw Journal*, Summer 2000. When we visited, it was being used for storage, not habitation, but we saw a similar structure in Missouri, made from a corn silo, that was inhabited.

10. For general information on this subject, see *Moving to a Small Town*, by Wanda Urbanska and Frank Levering, Simon and Schuster, 1996.

CHAPTER 7

1. Figures and statistics and other information about work and leisure can be found in "The Real Reasons You Are Working So Hard," *Business Week*, October 3, 2005; "Were the Good Old Days That Good? Maybe not, but the standard of living was climbing much faster," by Louis Uchitelle, *The New York Times*, Sunday, July 3, 2005; *Take Back Your Time*, by John De Graaf, editor, Berret-Koehler, 2003; *The Overworked American*, by Juliet B. Schor, Basic Books, 1992; as well as through the U.S. Census Bureau, labor statistics, and Statistics Canada, including *Perspectives on Labour and Income: Fact Sheet on Minimum Wage*, September 2005.

2. *Fertility of American Women: June 1998*, by Amara Bachu and Martin O'Connell, Current Population Reports, U.S. Census Bureau, 2000, pp. 20–526.

3. Characteristics of Children's Early Care and Education Programs: Data from the 1995 National Household Education Survey (Report No. 98-128), by S. L. Hofferth, K. A. Shauman, R. R. Henke, and J. West, U.S. Department of Education, National Center for Education Statistics.

4. I have not been able to verify this claim, although it's made routinely. "An Oregon study" is referenced, but I have never found that study. It makes sense that female homemakers are at least as exposed to chemicals as other workers since they are exposed to cleaning agents, and no government bureau regulates the occupational safety of their workplace.

5. Although all the houses are very efficient, energy savings vary significantly, depending on the habits of the homeowners.

CHAPTER 8

1. Information on household density is available through the U.S. Census. See U.S. Census Bureau, Housing and Economic Statistics Division, February 18, 2005, "Persons per bedroom." Over two-thirds of U.S. residences have more than one bedroom per inhabitant. Probably, in many cases two adults share one room and leave all other bedrooms empty. However, this number does not include nursing homes and assisted living arrangements, college and high school dormitories, prisons, and military barracks, where presumably everyone sleeps alone. Pets are not counted as "inhabitants" by the U.S. Census. Over 130 million pet cats and dogs live in the United States. They are at least twice as common in households than children. See *U.S. Pet Ownership & Demographics Sourcebook*, American Veterinary Medicine Association, 2002.

2. See *Families and Farmhouses in Nineteenth-Century America: Vernacular Design and Social Change*, by Sally McMurry, University of Tennessee Press, 1997.

3. Vicki Robin, Dolores Hayden, John de Graaf, and a variety of other writers have made related suggestions.

4. See Jane Porcino's book *Living Longer, Living Better*, Continuum Publishing, 1991. See also *Senior Cohousing*, by Charles Durrett, Habitat Press, 2005.

5. See United States Supreme Court, Lawrence v. Texas, June 2003. Although apparently about sodomy laws, this decision has been interpreted as having implications for all unmarried adults living together.

6. *Communities Directory*, updated regularly by the Fellowship of Intentional Communities, is one source of information. Also, check with your local Corporation Commission for information about local laws.

7. Information about energy use in New York can be found in the U.S. Census Bureau's American Community Survey 2002, specifically "Means of Transportation to Work for Workers 16 Years and Over," the American Housing Survey; "Green Manhattan," by David Owen, *The New Yorker*, October 18, 2004; "Ecological Footprint Assessment of New York City," by Cynthia Rosenzweig, Ph.D.; "Biodiversity, Biosphere Reserves and the Big Apple," by William D. Solecki and Cynthia Rosenzweig, *Annals of New York Academy of Science 1023*, 2004; and *Report to Mayor Michael R. Bloomberg New York City Energy Policy: An Electricity Resource Roadmap*, prepared by the New York City Energy Policy Task Force January 2004, which notes that New York City generates most of its electricity inside the city limits: "Reliability concerns require that 80% of the City's peak load be met with in-City resources under a mandate from the New York State Reliability Council and the New York Independent System Operator."

8. Clearly, Mexico City's residents, on average and per capita, use less energy than residents of Toronto or New York, and Mexico City has a more extensive subway system than Toronto. The phrase "North America," as has been noted earlier in the book, is used here to refer to the U.S. and Canada because the author could think of no better phrase.

9. *America's Families and Living Arrangements: 2003*, by Jason Fields, Current Population Reports, U.S. Census Bureau,2003, pp. 20–553. For information about men, women, and housework, see, "Is Anyone Doing the Housework? Trends in the Gender Division of Household Labor," by M. Bittman, P. England, P, L. C. Sayer, N. Folbre, N. and G. Matheson, *Social Forces*, 79, 1: 191–228, 2003; and *Understanding the Gender Gap: An Economic History of American Women*, by J. S. Gray, Oxford University Press, 1998.

CHAPTER 9

1. Part of Antarctica and a few miniscule islands or larger atolls in the Pacific may be exceptions. There are a few other areas that function as commons, because

the national governments that are believed to hold them don't police them.

2. As Erica Ritter of City Repair explains, "When good people hide indoors, leaving the public space empty and untended, it communicates to the 'bad guys' that they can act with impunity." She quotes John Campbell, of Campbell DeLong Resources, Inc., who trains landlords how to keep illegal activity off their property, as saying, "'Drug dealing is not a spectator sport," further explaining, "Criminals don't like to be watched, and many 'crimes of opportunity' are committed by people who wouldn't act criminally if they were in a friendly location that didn't suggest fear." To find research that supports this idea, see Oscar Newman and others' work on "crime prevention through environmental design," and "defensible space"; and Robert Trojanowicz's studies of "community policing." The book *It's a Sprawl World After All The Human Cost of Unplanned Growth—and Visions of a Better Future*, by Douglas E. Morris (New Society Publishers, 2005), links the increase in violence in post-WWII United States to the development of urban sprawl.

3. The Forestry Agency of Japan, the Forestry and Forest Products Research Institute (FFPRI), and Nippon Medical School jointly announced on October 13, 2005 that significant results were obtained in a study on the physiological effects of "shinrinyoku," or "forest bathing," a Japanese term referring to the therapeutic effects of forests on humans. The study shows that spending time in a forest activates natural killer (NK) cells, a type of cell known to attack cancer cells, and to increase three types of anti-cancer proteins.

4. See *Streets and the Shaping of Towns and Cities*, by Michael Southworth and Eran Ben-Joseph, Island Press, 2003; and "Why Don't We Do It In the Road," by Linda Baker, May 20, 2004, Salon.com.

5. Gideon notes that Toronto's Public Space Committee offers a "Downtown De-fence Project," which helps neighbors take down the chain-link fences that divide their properties.

6. "Residential Community Associations: Community or Disunity?" *The Responsive Communitarian*, Fall 1995, Vol., 5 No. 5. See also "Home Is Where The Rules Are," by Ronald H. Nelson, *Washington Post*, December 18, 2005.

7. For further discussion of this topic, see *Fortress America: Gated Communities in the United States*, by Edward J. Blakely and Mary Gail Snyder, Brookings Institution Press, 1997. The authors, writing about the earliest walled cities, note, "Contrary to popular belief, the walls around these settlements were seldom to protect against external invaders but rather to guard against the local villagers who might turn on the baron at any moment."

8. Gated communities, if they aren't central, are statistically more dangerous than central neighborhoods, simply because they entail more driving. Professors of Urban Planning William H. Lucy and David L. Phillips report, "Our research in 10 large metropolitan areas shows that in each area, one or more exurban counties had more deaths associated with leaving home, mainly traffic deaths, than occur in central cities from the combination of traffic deaths and homicides by strangers." *See Tomorrow's Cities, Tomorrow's Suburbs,* American Planning Association, 2006.

9. On April 24, 2005 an anonymous collective of LA art activists and designers placed bright orange elevated viewing platforms outside the entrances of three exclusive gated See www.roadsideamerica.com/pile/200505.html.

10. Jutta encourages people everywhere to tend fires in public places, and has written a handbook, which anyone can download from the Internet free of charge. See http://www.dufferinpark.ca.

11. For more ideas about common space in cities, read books by Jane Jacobs, especially *The Death and Life of Great American Cities*, Random House, 1961; and anything by Roberta Brandes Gratz. For further historical information about settlement patterns in the United States, see *The Geography of Nowhere*, by James Howard Kunstler, Simon and Schuster, 1993. For more information on Cohousing, see *Cohousing: A Contemporary Approach to Housing Ourselves*, by Kathryn McCamant and Charles Durret, Ten Speed Press, 1994; and *The Cohousing Handbook*, by Chris Hanson, Harley and Marks Publishers, 1996.

12. See *Detroit, I Do Mind Dying*, by Dan Georgakas and Martin Surkin, South End Press, 1998, for more history about Detroit.

13. The Trust for Public Land is an excellent source of information and support for people who hope to have more park land in their city or town.

CHAPTER 10

1. There's a huge body of research that contends that zoning regulations drive up costs—see "Economic Scene," by Virginia Postel, *The New York Times,* March 28, 2002; or the Cato Institute's "Zoning's Steep Price," by Edward Glaeser and Joseph Gyourko, *Regulation*, Fall 2002. There's a smaller body of research that contends that building code significantly increases housing price. An April 2004 Housing and Urban Development report of the Research Conference on Regulatory Barriers to Affordable Housing by researchers David Listokin and David Hattin reviews the literature and finds it usually contends that codes drive up housing price by under 5 percent, and that the scope of this research is limited. Listokin and Hattin suggest that, of course, more research would be needed to answer this question. On the tiny-house front, builder Scott Baxla in North Carolina notes that egress to his second floor is "my current biggest [code] infraction.... In a house that is smaller than many people's dining room, the space required for a 'legal' stairway could easily take up more than one-third of the square footage." The apparently small issue is important—wide, shallow stairs do seem to be safer, but are difficult to fit in very tiny houses.

2. See *Privatopia: Homeowner Associations and the Rise of Residential Private Government*, by Evan McKenzie, Yale University Press, 1994. In Monroe, New Jersey, a homeowner association took a married couple to court because the wife, at age forty-five, was three years younger than the association's age minimum for residency. The association won in court, and the judge ordered the sixty-year-old husband to sell, rent the unit, or live without his wife.

3. See "Checklist for gaining approval of alternative designs," *Environmental Building News*, Vol. 10, No. 9 for more thorough information about variances.

4. See "Form-based Development Codes," by David Rouse and Nancy Zobl, in *Zoning Practice*, the Journal of the American Planning Association, May 2004.

5. California AB1866, passed in 2002, strengthened legislation passed in the 1980s that already encouraged ADUs; Florida senate bill 2188, passed in 2004, and Washington State Housing Policy Act of 1993 encourages the creation of ADUs. Santa Cruz County, California, has perhaps the most ambitious program to promote ADUs, and offers floor plans and an expedited permitting process.

6. *Denver Zoning Fight Turns on Defining a Family, The New York Times*, March 26, 1989.

7. For more information about various ways that zoning and codes interfere with building small, see "Small is Beautiful: U.S. House Size, Resource Use, and the Environment," by Alex Wilson and Jessica Boehland, *Journal of Industrial Ecology,* Winter/Spring 2005, Vol. 9, Nos. 1–2.

8. For more information on the code, see *Code Check Building: A Field Guide to the Building Codes*, by Michael Casey, Redwood Kardon, and Douglas Hansen, The Taunton Press, 2003; and *Building Safety Journal*.

CHAPTER 11

1. The U.S. Consumer Product Safety Commission issued a report in 1999 that warned against "co-sleeping," saying that over 500 babies had died from the practice between 1990 and 1997. Of these deaths, 120 were attributed to smothering, i.e. people rolling over on top of the baby, and the rest were because of characteristics of adult beds—headboards and footboards provide a place for a baby to get entrapped, and waterbeds appear to be able to suffocate babies simply by being so soft. Critics of the study said it didn't control for alcohol use, and that some of the smothering deaths were probably SIDS (Sudden Infant Death Syndrome). "Adult Beds Are Unsafe Places for Children to Sleep," by Suad Nakamura, Ph.D., Marilyn Wind, Ph.D., and Mary Ann Danello, Ph.D., *The Archives of Pediatrics and Adolescent Medicine,* 1999. There has been much controversy about this study.

2. From personal correspondence with Elizabeth Pantley, author of *The No-Cry Sleep Solution*. Her own children are welcomed into their parents' bed, and also have tried a "siblings bed."

3. The British Broadcasting Corporation series is called "A Child of Our Time," and was aired in the first week of March 2005. Tom Payne filed an article about it on 03/01/2005, at mixnews.com, "Bad People Live in Small Houses."

4. I developed this exercise for a class before I discovered a similar one in the wonderful book, *House as a Mirror of Self*, by Clare Cooper Marcus, Conari Press, 1995 and recently reissued.

5. See "The New Red-Diaper Babies," by David Brooks, *The New York Times*, December 7, 2004.

CHAPTER 12

1. I confirmed this through correspondence with Susan Mudd.Similar research includes: "Run, Don't Walk: How Transportation Complicates Women's Balancing Act," by Daphne Spain; and "From Wooing Soccer Moms to Demonizing Welfare Mothers: A Legislative and Policy Context for Women's Travel," by Hank Dittmar, both from the Proceedings from the Second National Conference on Women's Travel, organized by the transportation research board. See also "High Mileage Moms"—a Report from the Surface Transportation Policy Project, available at http://www.transact.org. The average mother takes more than five car trips each day.

2. Jane Jacobs was a noted urbanist whose books include *The Death and Life of Great American Cities*, which was published in 1961 and is considered a classic text on urban planning, a field the book criticizes. Comments by Jane Jacobs in this chapter are taken from a conversation I had with her in the summer of 2001.

3. He continues, "Now hidden deep in the fastnesses of Mount Hino, I have put up eaves projecting on the south side to keep off the sun and a small bamboo veranda beneath them. On the west is the shelf for the offerings of water and flowers to Buddha, and in the middle, against the western wall is a picture of Amida Buddha so arranged that the setting sun shines from between his brows as though he were emitting his ray of light, while on the doors of his shrine are painted pictures of Fugen and Fudo. Over the sliding doors on the north side is a little shelf on which stand three or four black leather cases containing some volumes of Japanese poems and music and a book of selections from the Buddhist Sutras. Beside these stand a harp and a lute, of the kind called folding harp and jointed lute. On the eastern side is a bundle of fern fronds and a mat of straw on which I sleep at night. In the eastern wall there is a window before which stands my writing table. A fire-box beside my pillow in which I can make a fire of broken brushwood completes the furniture. To the north of my little hut I have made a tiny garden surrounded by a thin low brushwood fence so that I can grow various kinds of medicinal herbs. Such is the style of my unsubstantial cottage." *The Ten Foot Square Hut and Tales of the Heike*, by Kamo no Chomei, translated by A. L. Sadler, Angus and Robertson, Sydney, 1928.

4. See *A Hut of One's Own—Life Outside the Circle of Architecture,* by Ann Cline, MIT Press, 1997.

5. From the essay, "Where Should I Live, and What Should I Live For?" in *The Pine Island Paradox*, by Kathleen Dean Moore, Milkweed Editions, 2004.

CHAPTER 13

1. These statistics are taken from the U.S. Central Intelligence Agency website.

2. Predictions about ultimate population vary widely. At the current rate of increase, population would end up at higher than 8 billion by 2060, but at the current rate of decrease in the rise of fertility, it would not. See also *The Childless Revolution,* by Madelyn Cain, Perseus, 2002

3. The National Public Radio show *All Things Considered* had a story on May 15, 2006 about tiny houses and hurricane Katrina, including the story of Julie Martin of Mississippi, who partnered with Jay Shafer (see Chapter 10) to provide tiny houses to survivors of the 2005 Gulf Coast hurricane.

4. The Japanese placed wheels on their furniture so they could roll it out of town during fires, which clogged the street so much firefighters couldn't get through. Wheels on furniture were then banned. *Japanese Homes and Their Surroundings*, by Edward Morse, Charles E. Tuttle Company, 1887.

5. Really, no one knows how many U.S. citizens live abroad. Estimates range from 3 to 6 million (see "Finding the Uncounted," *International Herald Tribune*, February 16, 2002). The U.S. State Department estimate was 2.3 million in 1990 and 3.8 million in 2005. Over a third of U.S. expatriates live in Canada and Mexico.

6. See "Ukraine: Land of Giant Empty Houses," by Jeremy Cornah, *Offshore Real Estate Quarterly*, Winter 2001.

7. From The Blessing is Next to the Wound," interview with Diane Lefer, *The Sun,* October 2005.

8. "Effects of Household Dynamics on Resource Consumption and biodiversity," by Jianguo Liu, G. C. Daily, P. R. Ehrlich, and G. W. Luck, in *Nature* magazine, No. 421, 2003.

9. The Prison Rape Elimination Act was signed into law in 2003. Tom Cahill is part of the group "Stop Prisoner Rape."

10. Before it was changed in 1992, Article 27 of the Mexican constitution granted the government broad powers to redistribute land.

11. The Kyoto accords, an agreement to limit global warming by reducing greenhouse gases, especially CO_2 production, was signed by about 160 nations, including Canada but not the U.S. Since some countries produce less CO_2 than the accords allow, they sell their credits to other countries that cannot yet meet their limits. It's estimated that in Europe, CO_2 costs $70 to $80 per ton.

12. *Radical Simplicity*, by Jim Merkel, New Society Publishers, 2003. See also articles and books by Mathis Wackernagel and Bill Rees about the ecological footprint mode.

13. Steve Beck teaches in the Eco-dwelling program of New College, in Santa Rosa, California.

Glossary

ADU (accessory dwelling unit). A self-contained residence that has been added to a lot that already has a principal dwelling, and is either connected to or detached from the main house.

adobe. An earthen, sun-dried brick; the construction method that uses such bricks.

amortization. A schedule of payments that gradually reduces a debt; typically a schedule of house payments.

Arts and Crafts. An architectural style defined in late-nineteenth-century England and popular in early-twentieth-century California, characterized by fine craftsmanship and simple decoration.

batten. A strip of material, usually wood, nailed between two other pieces to stiffen a structure, close a crack, or to provide a place to attach a third material.

board foot. A measurement of lumber 1 foot long, 1 foot wide, and 1 inch thick, or the equivalent.

Btu (British thermal unit). A unit of measure for heat; 1 Btu is the heat required to raise 1 pound of water 1 degree Fahrenheit, approximately equal to the heat produced by burning one match.

bungalow. Possibly from the Bengali word *bangla*, a one-story house, typically with a wide porch.

CC&Rs (codes, covenants, and restrictions). Legally binding by-laws that govern the use, maintenance, and remodeling of a house and lot, usually enacted by a real estate developer, or sometimes a neighborhood committee.

cantilever. A beam or similar horizontal structure that projects past its supporting post or wall.

casement. A window that swings opens on hinges, like a door.

clapboard. A narrow board thicker on one edge, used as house siding; a house sided in such boards.

clay slip. Liquid clay used in pottery and earthen plasters.

clerestory. A small, roofed structure that rises from a roof and has a vertical window that allows sunlight to reach interior parts of a building.

cob. The Welsh name for a traditional building material, mainly composed of earth, often mixed with straw, sand, and/or manure, that forms the walls of a structure without the use of molds or formwork; normally applied by hand.

compound interest. A method, commonly used in mortgages, by which outstanding balances grow exponentially with time; in each period, the total balance grows as the sum of the remaining principal (the original loan amount), plus the interest paid on all previous periods.

cord. A measurement of wood, usually firewood, that equals 8 feet by 4 feet by 4 feet (128 cubic feet or 3.62 cubic meters).

corncrib. A cylindrical, metal mesh structure used to dry and store cobs of corn.

composting toilet. A waterless toilet that typically allows excrement to mix with sawdust or a similar high-carbon material, and over time creates soil.

Corian. An industrial product used as a countertop.

cottage. A small house, especially in the country.

daylighting. Bringing a buried stream to the surface of the earth.

double-hung. A window that has two sashes, both of which can slide open.

dumpster diving. The act of gathering discarded items from city dumpsters; any gathering of discards, for personal use or to sell or share.

earth-bermed. Buried under earth, at least on one side, typically because it is dug into a hill, or because earth has been piled on top, creating a hill.

eave. The lower, outer edge of a roof that overhangs the walls of a building.

ecological footprint. An assessment of the amount of land, and sometimes other resources, a person, group of people, or activity requires, accounting for the land used for agriculture, mining, etc., necessary to support the people or activity.

equity. The financial value of a house that exceeds the amount owed on the house.

embodied energy. The energy required to produce a material.

firewall. A thick wall of a fireproof material, typically between two dwellings that share a wall, that may rise through and at least a foot above the roof, to prevent a fire from spreading.

gable. A section of wall between two slides of a sloped roof, usually forming a triangle above a wall.

gazebo. A small, roofed, open-sided, or windowed structure, usually in a garden, and often round.

genkan. A space inside an entrance, usually with a place to take off and store shoes; from Japanese.

Georgian pile. A huge, single-family residence; recently used as the British translation of the American "McMansion."

glazed. Filled or covered with glass or another transparent material. **Glazing** usually means "glass."

golden rectangle. A rectangle where the ratio of its length to its width is (1 + ÷ 5)/2 :1, or about 1.618. The shape of a credit card is similar to a golden rectangle.

graywater. Water from sinks, showers, bathtubs, and washing machines, that instead of being wasted is used to irrigate plants near the dwelling. **Blackwater** is from toilets.

gypsum. A mined, white material currently used primarily to make sheets of wall board (a.k.a. gypboard or drywall) which form interior walls and ceilings; also used as plaster.

heat exchanger. A machine that separates heat from the air or water that contains it, sometimes to retain heat in a building while exchanging inside for outside air.

hip roof. A pitched roof that slopes on four (or more) sides.

kotastu table. A traditional Japanese low table, similar to the *mesa camilla* of Spain, that has a heating element on its underside and, ideally, is placed over a sunken area in the living room, where people put their feet. In winter a large quilt is placed under the tabletop and extends over the legs of the people sitting around the table

light clay. A traditional European building method, in which builders mix wet, high-clay-content soil with straw, and then tamp this material into wooden forms to build walls.

load-bearing. Carrying the weight of the roof.

new urbanism. A movement in urban planning begun in the late twentieth century that encourages high density, mixed-use development, scaled to allow walking as a principal means of transportation.

mezzanine. Similar to a loft; a partial floor, typically between two stories of a building, with one wall open to the building.

passive-solar. Simple, nonmechanical designs that use the sun's energy to heat or cool.

permaculture. A design pattern that incorporates indigenous knowledge and understanding of local conditions and strives to create self-sustaining systems based on nature.

photovoltaic (PV). The use of sunlight to produce electricity, typically using panels of flat, sliced crystals.

platoid. A flattened, curled form, like certain worms.

plywood. A common industrial product made by gluing thin sheets of wood into a stack, usually with each layer of wood grain placed at a right angle to the next layer, and used to build floors, roofs, cabinets, and walls.

pocket door. A door that, when open, disappears into an adjoining wall.

Queen Anne. A style of domestic architecture inspired by eighteenth-century England and characterized by unpretentious design and classic ornament, which is sometimes carved into the brick façade.

radiant heat. Heat transferred via electromagnetic waves, such as the heat emitted from a black asphalt road.

ramada. From Spanish, meaning "covered in branches"; a free-standing shade structure.

ROOO. Acronym for "room of one's own."

R-1 zoning. A zoning classification that typically allows the construction of one complete single-family residence on one lot; "R" stands for residential.

R value. A measure of insulation based on resistance ("R") to heat transfer, R-1 being the amount of resistance provided by 1 inch of wood. R-40 is considered high insulation; R-19 is standard in some areas.

saltbox. A house that has two stories at the front, and one at the back.

semi Canadian. Term for a semi-attached house, that is, two houses that share one exterior wall; known as a "duplex" in the U.S.

SIP (structural insulated panel). A sandwich of oriented-strand board with rigid insulation inside used to form walls and ceilings.

solar gain. The heat (and sometimes light) that a structure receives from the sun.

spec house. A house built with the hope (speculation) that the builder or financier will be able to sell it at a profit.

snout house. A single-family dwelling whose garage door covers a significant part of the façade.

square footage. A way to measure space inside a building, calculated by measuring either the outside walls, or each room's interior dimensions, 1 square foot (sq. ft.) being equal to an area 1 foot wide and 1 foot long: 5 feet by 4 feet equals 20 square feet; 40 feet by 20 feet equals 800 square feet.

stucco. Plaster, especially plaster that contains Portland cement, currently commonly used to cover frame buildings, making them look like masonry buildings.

stud. A vertical structural support, usually wood or steel, used especially in frame construction.

straw-bale. Construction straw (the stems of a grain left over after harvest) bundled into blocks called **bales**, stacked to form the walls of a building.

subdivision. An area of land that has been divided into house lots.

tao sabahai. A person at home (Tagalog).

thermal mass. Heat storage ability exhibited by material such as tile or concrete floors, brick walls, or a pond, that can hold heat and then release it later, thus moderating the temperature over a twenty-four-hour or 365-day period.

title. Legal ownership, or the document used as evidence of ownership; sometimes interchangeable with **deed**.

usury. The practice of lending money and charging the borrower a "user fee," i.e. interest, especially high interest.

Victorian. An architectural style inspired by nineteenth-century England and the reign of Queen Victoria, characterized by large structures, high ceilings, and elaborate decoration.

viga. Round wood, i.e. tree trunks, used as roof beams; from Spanish.

VOC (volatile organic compounds). Molecular compounds that contain carbon and evaporate easily. Commonly found in a variety of synthetic products, including paint and plastics, VOCs are pollutants and may cause cancer and other diseases.

zero lot line. A zoning term, meaning that construction is allowed or present all the way to the edge of the lot, with no "setback."

Index

Bold numbers indicate photos and illustrations. A lower case "n" indicates an endnote number.